THE AIDS BOOK

THE **AIDS** BOOK

Creating a Positive Approach

LOUISE L. HAY

HAY HOUSE
SANTA MONICA, CALIFORNIA

Hay House, Inc.
501 Santa Monica Blvd.
Santa Monica, CA 90401

First Printing, September 1988

10 9 8 7 6 5 4 3 2

The author of this book does not dispense medical advice nor prescribe the use of any technique as a form of treatment for medical problems without the advice of a physician, either directly or indirectly. The intent of the author is only to offer information of a general nature to help you cooperate with your doctor in your mutual quest for health. In the event you use any of the information in this book for yourself, you are prescribing for yourself, which is your constitutional right, but the author and the publisher assume no responsibility for your actions.

Certain names in *The AIDS Book* have been changed to protect the privacy of individuals who very kindly shared their stories in the hope of benefiting others.

ISBN 0-937611-32-8

Library of Congress Catalog Card No. 88-81685

Manufactured in the United States of America

Dedication

I lovingly dedicate this book to all of us who are searching for the inner peace that will help us go through this intense experience called AIDS—to those who have AIDS and ARC, to the parents and families of those with AIDS, to the friends and loved ones of PWAs, to the doctors and nurses and other health-care professionals, and to the "worried well."

Let us go beyond all our fears and prejudices and do everything we can on a positive level to find the answers and the cure.

With love for ourselves and for each other, we shall heal this planet of fear and dis-ease. When this experience is over, every person on this planet will have been touched, and many will have been changed in a positive way. It is time for us to all live and practice unconditional love. Love will enable the world to take a quantum leap into a new and magnificent future.

Acknowledgments

No one can approach this subject alone. It is with gratitude and thankfulness that I acknowledge all the help I have been given by these beautiful people, each contributing in their own way.

For their immense help in the editorial process, I wish to thank Christopher Riccella, Jim Neyland, and Linda Tomchin.

For doing the many interviews that were an important part of completing this work, I am grateful to Murray Salem and Christopher Duffy.

And for providing information, ideas, and invaluable assistance, I wish to express my great appreciation to Alliance, Steven Bright, Robert Brooks, M.D., Russell Carlton, Tom Caroselli, Cassandra Christenson, R.N., Rob Eichberg, Rene Espy, D.C., Sally Fisher, Nan Fuchs, Ph.D., Will Garcia, Ken Griffith, Mark Hendish, Andrew Hiatt, Michael Hollister, David Izenman, Paul Jasperson, Samuel Kirschner, Lazaris, Albert Lerner, M.D., Linda Logan, Darby Long, George Melton, Robert Morrissette, Caroline Myss, Louie Nassaney, John Oppido, Alan Peterson, Tony Petzel, Tom Proctor, David Reed, Paul Richards, Bob Rogosich, Nancy Cole Sawaya, Jimmie Schaeffer, Connie and Bill Searcy, Cristofer Shihar, David Sokolowsky, Larry Spousta, David Summers, Nadia Sutton, Ronald Tillinghast, Tom Trimm, Joseph Vattimo, Brad White, Marsha Woolf, N.D.—and all those with AIDS and ARC who have shared with me and given me so many insights.

Each chapter opens with an affirmation. Each of these is good to use when you are working on that area of your life. Keep saying and writing the affirmation that opens the chapter.

The chapters close with a treatment. This is a flow of positive ideas designed to change consciousness. Read over this treatment several times a day.

Contents

Part III
FINDING HELP, 193

Introduction

When AIDS first became popular, I thought I knew all the answers. As this dreaded dis-ease has advanced, I feel I know less and less. And yet my understanding and compassion has increased enormously. I see the issue in a more expanded light. There is far more going on with this intense experience called AIDS than we first thought. And I do not believe that we are even near to having all the answers we need to totally eradicate AIDS.

This is not an issue that touches only a few people of a special group that we can ignore. Hoping that AIDS will kill off a few people "who don't seem to matter anyway" is an attitude that does not work. We are dealing with a global phenomenon of far-reaching proportions. In fact, the very attitude of denying the first people with AIDS all the help we could muster has enabled this dis-ease to enter the mainstream of society in alarming ways.

I am sorry to think of the thousands of heterosexual people who will have to experience AIDS because society and the government and the churches did not move fast enough in the beginning stages. Every human being is worthy of love and consideration. In fact, I believe it is

1

one of the big lessons in our lifetimes to learn to give and receive unconditional love.

In the beginning stages, we thought this was mainly a dis-ease of homosexual men, because it first surfaced in the gay community in the United States. Because of this, we allowed moral issues, prejudice, and fear to cloud our response to human suffering. We are now well aware that AIDS is a human problem and not limited to any one group of people. In parts of Africa it is estimated that forty percent of the heterosexual population is affected by AIDS. Women, children, even babies can and do have AIDS. While AIDS can be transmitted sexually, it is not a sexual disease. It is a blood virus and must enter the bloodstream to find a home.

I have been working with people with AIDS (PWAs) since 1983, and in that time I have learned a lot and seen many changes take place. As a therapist, I have had a cross section of people in my practice. When AIDS first came upon the scene, people started calling me to say, "Louise, I have a friend with AIDS, what do I tell him?" I quickly realized that, if I expressed my concepts to one person and he or she tried to explain them to someone who had no knowledge of metaphysical ideas, then a lot would get lost in the translation. So I decided to create an audio tape called *AIDS: A Positive Approach*.

This tape was created primarily for gay men. One side gave my concepts of the dis-ease at that time, and the second side was a relaxation exercise with a visualization and many positive affirmations. This tape, made in August of 1983, was the first positive thing anyone had done for the AIDS situation. Slowly I began to attract AIDS clients, for they had nowhere to turn.

In January of 1985, I invited a small group of six men, PWAs, to meet in my living room. At that point, I had been working with a few of them in private sessions. One of them suggested that I form a group, so that we all could share ideas. Three of my clients agreed to meet and brought three of their friends who had also been "diagnosed." The first evening, I remember my assistant and I even cooked dinner for these six, and afterward we sat around and formulated the purpose of the group.

We did not know exactly what we were going to do, but we had to do something positive. I decided we would not play "ain't it awful." We already knew all of that. We had heard the media and its gloom and doom. We had heard the medical profession say THEY could do nothing and everyone with AIDS would be dead in one year.

We decided to take a positive approach. We gathered every bit of positive information we could and shared it. If one person was feeling better, we asked what he was doing, and everyone tried it. Eating habits were improved as we learned about nutrition. We did a lot of releasing of resentment and much forgiveness work. We did mirror work. We learned meditation and visualization. And above all, we worked on learning to love ourselves.

Fear was the biggest issue that each member was dealing with—fear of the unknown, fear of pain, and fear of death. Just coming together as a group with an emphasis on doing something positive enabled all of them to feel better. As the leader, I was able to provide strength, and they could look to me when they had questions. I did not have all the answers, yet they knew I cared and wanted to help.

At that time, I was the only person in the whole world who was offering any sort of hope at all. I did not promise any specific results. Nor did I tell them to leave their doctors. Everything we were going to do in that group was to supplement the treatment or lack of treatment they were getting from their various doctors. There were very few doctors who would even touch people with AIDS in those days. Their lack of knowledge caused them to be frightened and withdrawn rather than compassionate and caring.

As the first evening came to a close, I led a guided

visualization about being in a peaceful place where there
were many healing energies that were there to help us.
We closed with a song,"I Love Myself," by Jai Josefs. We
did not realize then that this song would become our closing song for all of our groups and would become quite
famous.

Each person felt better as he left that night. They
had released some of the worry and fear. They did not
feel that they were such helpless victims. I heard from
several the next day that they had the first good night's
sleep since their diagnoses.

The next week, these six were ready to work. We discussed and listed many other problems to work on as we
continued. More than just the dis-ease. Fear, of course.
Self-esteem, self-worth. Anger and resentment. All sorts
of guilts. The usual parental problems, plus how to tell
parents they had AIDS or even that they were gay. We
discussed sex and safe sex. How to forgive. How to feel
good about themselves when they believed they were
under a death sentence. We had no lack of subjects. We
even were willing to discuss the positive aspects of AIDS.

This group began to grow, as they brought their
friends. I bought a large urn to serve herbal teas and
wholesome cookies. In a few months, there were eighty-
five people hanging out of the windows and standing at
the door and spilling into the dining room. We moved to
larger quarters, and the next week there were 150 people
at the meeting. We still meet every Wednesday night, and
by the spring of 1988, there were over six-hundred people
at each meeting. Not everyone has AIDS. There are
friends and lovers and "the worried well." There are
women and even children. We have nurses, hospice workers, alternate therapy people, ministers, and doctors.

Doctors send people to us. We have one doctor who
works with many PWAs, and on the patient's first visit,
among other things, he or she is given a prescription to
attend our Wednesday night meeting three times. This

doctor knows it is much easier to work with someone who has a positive mental attitude.

Two and a half years later, of the original six, three have left the planet and one has left the group. The other two are still with us and doing very well. The three who died did so with a sense of peacefulness and completion of their missions on earth. The support of the group had great meaning in their lives. We accomplished what we set out to do. We improved the "quality" of their lives on a day-to-day basis. There were great healings in con- sciousness—changes in ideas and attitudes about them- selves and about life. We see this over and over again in the group.

I said goodbye to one of them recently, as he was in the process of dying. I wished him "bon voyage" on the important trip he was taking. He thanked me and told me I had been the captain of his ship for the past two years and had helped him turn what could have been a very negative experience into one of growth and peace.

I wish I could say everyone was getting better, but it is not true. We have people who have left the planet. We have people who are not doing well. We have a lot of people who have improved the quality of their lives enor- mously. We have a few, a very few, who seem to have licked the virus entirely. It is hard to get the medical community to agree, because they want to wait a few years and see. We have not found "the answer" yet. We cannot say if you do this and this and this, you will get well. We do know there are many things people can do to help themselves. Some therapies work for some people and not for others. We do our best to expose our group to all the ideas available so they can make their own choices.

We do notice that the people who are improving their nutrition and following the alternative therapies are doing the best. The medical profession is desperately try- ing to find a chemical poison that will kill the virus and not the person. So far, they have not found that. The side effects of the medications they are using are often devastating to the patients. And extremely expensive.

I personally believe that, if the government feels there is a medicine that will really work with AIDS, it is its duty to supply it free to anyone who cannot afford it. Most PWAs wind up on SSI and seldom have twenty-five cents left at the end of the month.

This Wednesday night meeting, the "Hayride," as the group calls it, is not a healing meeting. It is a support group. We get together to support each other and to network. We sing, we meditate, we share our successes and our fears, we do visualizations, and we work on loving ourselves.

In the two and a half years I have been leading this group, I have seen a lot of healing of consciousness. The steady people in this group have grown so much. People who arrived frightened and desperate are now smiling and in control of their lives. They see life in a new and different way. For many, AIDS has been an opportunity to change their lives for the better. When people are exposed to unconditional love, it brings out the best in them. Even those who have left the planet have done so in a more peaceful way.

While many children are estranged from their families everywhere, this estrangement is even more prevalent in the gay community. Gay people have all the same problems that abound in the heterosexual world, plus, they feel they must hide their sexuality in fear of ridicule or rejection.

The son or daughter is afraid to let the parents know who they really are for fear of rejection. Or the parents react out of fear or embarrassment when they learn their children are homosexual and then refuse to speak to them. We have seen many healings in the families. Families that were estranged for years are coming together in love and forgiveness.

Sexual abuse of children is a deplorable thing that happens in our society far too often. I don't think the general population is aware of how much sexual abuse many gay men had as children.

I am not a healer. I do not heal anyone. I am a very simple lady who knows and teaches the power of love; that's all I do. Sometimes, when people learn to love themselves, they create their own healing. As Dr. Bernie Siegel says in his video, *Hope and a Prayer*, "When a person changes, the new personality does not need the old disease."

I have known for a long time that the only way we are going to find an answer to this problem called AIDS is to take a positive, loving approach. There is a big lesson for all of us to learn in this crisis. I believe the very survival of the planet is involved. AIDS is part of the pollution of the planet. It is also a dis-ease of oppression and hopelessness. Or "victim-consciousness," as Caroline Myss calls it in her book, *AIDS: A Passageway to Transformation*. And it is showing us how very unloving we are. We need to address all these issues.

Many people have asked me to write down some of the things we have learned and explored in our "Hayrides," so they might be shared with others around the country and the world. Much of what we do is extremely personal or intangible because it comes from the relationships within the support group, and because it comes from love. However, in the following pages, I have endeavored to express as much as I can about what we have discovered concerning the dis-ease called AIDS. I hope it may prove of benefit.

If you are a person with AIDS, I do not guarantee you will heal yourself if you follow what I suggest. I do know, if you decide to be totally committed and consistently "do the work," you will improve the quality of your life. I share this information so that you may learn to use your own healing powers. In my workshops and support groups, I provide an atmosphere of love and acceptance where we can share the beauty of our beings, where we can change and grow. Many people find they are healing themselves.

PART I

UNDERSTANDING THE DIS-EASE OF AIDS

1

What is AIDS?

Affirmation:
This too shall pass, and we will
grow and benefit from it!

Plagues and epidemics have been with us for as long as recorded history. They are not punishments from God. They come from living under conditions that are not healthy to us as individuals or as a society. In the thirteenth century, the population in Europe was undernourished and overcrowded. Soldiers, returning from the Crusades, came home with germs and viruses that they had never been exposed to before. After several years of famine, the population was hit by the Black Death, the bubonic plague, followed by several other plagues. Within fifty years, the population was reduced by half. Because of the poor living conditions, the Plague was allowed, via fleas and rats, to quickly spread through Europe.

Our own population explosion at the beginning of this century, due to the influx of immigrants, led to conditions that allowed the influenza epidemic that broke out after World War I to spread in the same way. Again, the poor living conditions, coupled with the mixing of people during wartime, created the illness and let it spread like wildfire through the U.S. as well as Europe.

There was also the "stress" of wartime, a war unlike any the world had ever known, new weapons, much more horrible forms of death, very frightening to the soldiers fighting the wars.

I believe that we are all exposed to everything that is floating by. Like the frightened soldiers of World War I, I believe that what we pick up depends on where we are in consciousness. That is, "What do we believe about life and about ourselves?" Do we believe that "life is hard and we always get the short end of the stick" or that "life is full of war and hate" so that we are open to all illnesses, or "I'm no good anyway, so what difference does it make" or "I've always known I would die young." If our beliefs run along these lines, then our immune systems will be lowered, and we will be free to catch the "popular" dis-ease of the moment. If our immune systems are strong and healthy, then our bodies will automatically fight off whatever dis-ease may pass our way.

THE AIDS EPIDEMIC

Not everyone is affected by epidemics. Even during the days of the Black Plague, there were many who were not touched by it at all. AIDS does not strike everyone who is exposed to it. I really don't believe that morals have anything to do with this dis-ease. Codes of morality change from society to society. What is normal and natural in one society is abhorrent and rejected in another.

In America, it is normal and natural for women to show their faces and arms and legs. In Italy, women are often refused entrance to a church if their arms are bare and their heads uncovered. In the Middle East, women can be shunned by neighbors and even, in some instances, stoned to death for merely allowing their faces to be seen in public.

There are many people who claim that AIDS is

God's punishment for not being heterosexual. That is one limited way of looking at the situation. But how does that tie in with babies who have AIDS? If we really follow that line of thinking, then God's chosen people could be Lesbians, and I don't think that is what these people mean.

You see, there are homosexual men who have AIDS, there are heterosexual men who have AIDS. There are women who have AIDS. There are children and babies with AIDS. To date there are almost no recorded cases of Lesbians who have AIDS.

To view one group of people as better or worse than another is to come from a space of fear and to have a very limited view of life. Think what it would be like to have only one kind of flower on the planet. The joy of flowers is in their infinite variety, their great differences, each one beautiful in its own way. Like flowers, there are unique groups of people. Just as there are no two snowflakes alike and no two fingerprints alike, so too there are no two human beings alike.

Within the groups, there are infinite varieties. It is meant to be this way. Each face you see on this planet is another beautiful expression of God. We can learn to look at people in this way.

WHAT AIDS IS NOT

AIDS is *not* a homosexual dis-ease. It has come through the Gay community. We believe AIDS originated in a remote tribe in Africa. Some scientists believe it was transmitted to this tribe from a species of green monkey. AIDS affected many people in this African community. At some point, a group of Haitian laborers were sent to Africa to work on a project. When the laborers returned to Haiti, they brought AIDS with them. There is a portion of the Gay communities of New York and

Florida who go to Haiti to vacation and play. These gay men picked up the virus and brought the dis-ease back with them, and it began its spread throughout the Western world. It came *through* the gay community; it is *not* a gay dis-ease.

The airplane has contributed much to the swiftness of the spread of AIDS. Those few early carriers of the dis-ease unknowingly carried the virus from place to place, hastening the spread of the dis-ease. In fact, the man who researchers are calling "AIDS Patient Zero," Gaetan Dugas, was an attendant on international flights.

In St. Louis, tissue samples saved since 1969 from a fifteen-year-old boy who died mysteriously showed that he had been infected by the AIDS virus.

And the story keeps changing. I have heard that the CIA was involved with germ warfare, accidentally infecting batches of gamma globulin.

It doesn't matter how the dis-ease got here. It doesn't matter "who" brought it to us. What is important is why it is here, and how we as Divine creatures must deal with it—and to learn from the special challenges it brings.

So if you are looking for more "scare" material, you have picked up the wrong book. There is too much frightening information being passed out through the media. It is time the positive side of AIDS gets a chance to be heard.

AIDS is not an automatic death sentence. AIDS is not always a fatal dis-ease. AIDS is not the end of the world. It has been for some. It does not need to be so for everyone.

WHAT IS AIDS?

The Virus

A virus is a piece of free-floating genetic material contained within a protective protein coating called a capsid.

It is not a cell. It is not alive. It is merely a subcellular "instruction" for replication, so that is what it does—replicate.

There are basically four kinds of genetic sequences that viruses use to replicate: single-stranded RNA, single-stranded DNA, double-stranded DNA, and a peculiar RNA virus called a retrovirus.

Upon entering the body, the virus will find a host cell. It can then do one of several things: it can pierce the host cell membrane with a "spike," which is incorporated in its capsid, or it can use an enzyme to break down the cell membrane to enter it. Once inside, it will use the host cell's machinery for replication. If this does not kill the host cell, the exit of the many new viral particles will. Sometimes the virus will enter the cell and then go into dormancy. This is the case in the nerve virus herpes and in the retrovirus HIV, where subsequent infection needs a co-factor, usually stress.

After infection, the body will undergo what is called "the primary immune response." During this stage, B cells and T cells will collect at the site of the infection. The B cell will produce antibodies to the virus, while the T cells, having antibodies incorporated in their cell membranes, will "read" the invader, also called the "antigen," and render it harmless. These specialized cells are capable of doing this amazing job because of their use of the antibody.

An antibody is a piece of sub-cellular protein. Under the microscope, it looks like a "Y." It is made up of a stable region called the "heavy" chain and of a variable region called the "light" chain. It is these variable regions that read the antigen, match the invader's code, and bind to it, forming an antibody-antigen complex. This is later recognized by other cells and transported out of the body as harmless waste. This is the ideal scenario.

The HIV Virus

"HIV" stands for Human Immuno-deficiency Virus. It is one of only three retroviruses that infect humans. Because of its unique replication process, it poses an interesting challenge for us.

This virus enters the cell as a single strand of RNA. As some viruses do, it carries its own enzyme called "reverse transcriptase." When it enters the cell, it can do one of two things: lie dormant until a co-factor begins its replication process or replicate.

If replicating, it will attach itself to the DNA of the host cell. This is the chromosome, the map of life. Using its enzyme, reverse transcriptase, it will transcribe a mirror image of one strand of the DNA, forming an intermediate product called DNA/RNA complex. From this point, the virus will then "mask" itself in the genetic material stolen from the host cell and develop into a double-stranded DNA molecule—completely different from its origin. After replicating many times, this virus can "bud" through the host's cell membrane, killing it.

But because of the target cell for this virus, the HIV is a great menace: it attacks the very cells that are necessary for an immune response, the T4 lymphocytes. After budding and killing a major portion of these cells, it renders the body's immune system useless, causing the condition known as AIDS. Any subsequent attack by an opportunistic infection, such as PCP, *pneumocystis carnii pneumonia*, or Kaposi sarcoma, could be life-threatening.

HIV POSITIVE

What about those who test positive for the antibody to the virus, but do not have the condition called AIDS?

With AIDS, many people who have been exposed will never come down with the dis-ease, for their strong immune systems immediately destroy the invader.

When we discover that we have been "tested positive," it is not the end of our world. It is merely a loving message from our bodies telling us that we have gotten off track and need to make some positive changes in our way of living. Our bodies always want to be well and will do everything in their power to express optimum health. "Testing positive" is a warning symptom of an underlying cause, an attempt of your consciousness to communicate. Our job can be to find and eliminate the underlying cause. If we heed the warning, then our condition may not need to expand further into ARC or AIDS. Your healing begins when you refuse to accept that there is nothing you can do about this dis-ease.

Again, being HIV positive means you have exposed yourself to the virus. That may be all it means; it could mean much more. It is a warning signal from our own Higher Self that changes need to be made NOW! These changes can be on many levels—mental, physical, and spiritual. Knowing you have tested positive means doing everything you can to strengthen your immune system—physically, mentally, and spiritually. A strong immune system will never allow the virus to take over.

If your immune system is only slightly depressed, then your body's message is that you probably can quickly build it back up to normal ranges, if you are willing to make the necessary changes. Absolutely refuse to accept anyone's "death sentence," no matter how big an authority they are. I have heard Dr. Bernie Siegel say that:

"It is a fact substantiated by scientific research that every type of cancer known has been overcome by someone. Learning the skills of individuals who have survived cancer will significantly improve a cancer patient's chances of survival—regardless of the severity, regardless of the type of cancer, regardless of the patient's age, disposition, or economic circumstances."

Cancer is very similar to AIDS, and the same principles of healing can apply to both. Any message from our body is a personal message we are giving to ourselves, and it is up to us to heed it or to once again ignore the communication.

No one puts us at risk. We and only we put ourselves at risk. For the population at large who have not so far been exposed, I say, "Listen to the warning signals all around you." Take heed. Are you taking unnecessary risks? If so, stop it. Notice what problem areas you have in your life that could be cleansed. Do you take good loving care of your body? Are you living from your highest level? Do you express and experience unconditional love? If not, then make some changes now! It is so much easier to make the changes when you are relatively healthy than when you are dealing with fear and acute illness.

The body's immune system is very complex and strong. It is able, through the use of the variable regions on the antibodies, to create up to eighteen-billion different codes to attack invaders. So it is only reasonable that, after exposure to the HIV, it quickly reads the invader and makes an appropriate antibody to it. It is only in the body's weakened condition that it can begin to take over. It is the unique masking of the virus that enables it to attempt this. Because it used the genetic code of the T cell, which carries antibodies on its membrane, the HIV has also the capability to read the variable region of the antibodies to itself. That is, it is able to change its antigenic code, in some cases "faster" than the body can create new antibodies to defend itself.

But in most cases, the antibodies created by the body are able to keep the virus in its dormant condition, never suffering a problem, and certainly never developing ARC or AIDS.

ARC

The term ARC, to me, is a definition that is unnecessarily exclusive. Someone with ARC can be just as sick as someone with AIDS and even die from ARC, yet they are discriminated against, shut out from social security and other levels of assistance. They do not qualify for financial help or a variety of services available to people with AIDS because, although they might have severely depressed immune systems, they do not have the opportunistic infections that classify them as PWAs. They can be just as sick, just as tired—unable to go to work or support themselves—and yet they are given even less aid because they are "too well."

It is a technical discrimination and another way to show our lack of love for a suffering person. To me AIDS and ARC are almost the same, so when I use the term "AIDS," know that I am also referring to ARC.

AIDS

I see AIDS as a message from the body, the final attempt of one's own consciousness to communicate—at the point when you can't just take a pill and keep going. Now, you have to listen. We have been taught to take a pill and keep going whenever we have a cold or the flu. Listen to the ads on TV, with their reinforcement of this self-neglect.

So many people, for so many years, have treated themselves as two personas. That is to say, "This is me, and this is my body." This is the point that we begin to lose touch with ourselves. The next step for most is to say, "I can do anything to my body, and it won't hurt me." This is simply not so. There will be a point of reckoning—a point where your body will demand attention. That's when we get dis-ease. But for many of us, the deafness will continue. We'll just go to a pharmacy and buy a pill to "make us well."

To use this approach to dis-ease is to say to the body, "I don't like you, and I don't want to hear your message; shut up!" It is a lack of self-love, one of the many ways we express self-hatred.

When I talk about love, people often say, "Yes, yes, of course I love myself." All right, if you say you love yourself, then notice how do you "treat" yourself. Is it really loving? The purpose of a dis-ease is for you to get the message. With AIDS, you just can't continue until you are willing to make changes. Life does not go on the same after being diagnosed with AIDS. If you are willing to take charge and make positive changes, then your life can become better than it was before your diagnosis. If you want to play helpless victim, then you will probably fulfill the media's dire predictions.

TREATMENT

Today is another precious day on earth. We shall live it with joy. We are in the midst of an extraordinary new experience. There is no precedent for it. We are in an uncharted land, sailing uncharted waters, and yet we must know that we are divinely protected and guided.

We are not alone. As we join together in love, searching for the healing we all desire, we find the beginnings of a harmonious blending of all peoples. We now choose to go beyond our old prejudices and fears. We are aware that the soul knows no sexuality and no color. Our whole planet needs healing, for we are all one in consciousness.

Now is the time to unite and commit ourselves to transforming our world. We are one with the power that created us.

We are safe, and all is well in our world.

2

A Positive Approach

Affirmation:
With love we shall find the answers!

In this book, there are many case histories of people diagnosed with AIDS who are in the process of healing themselves. There are also case histories of people who once had AIDS and who are now in remission. By reading these often moving stories of people who have refused to accept the popular medical verdict of "terminal" illness, you too can be inspired to contribute to your own healing.

I know these stories will inspire you. The Center for Disease Control in Atlanta, Georgia, says there are no two cases of AIDS exactly alike. Each individual seems to have his or her own unique form of it. Therefore, it stands to reason that there is no one way of curing it for everyone.

If you study each person's way of healing expressed here, you may find a person or a method you can identify with and a way of exercising your healing power that appeals to you and can work for you. The people have been willing to share their own journey of this intense experience in order to help you with your healing journey.

The methods these people have used are not only

good for healing the body, mind, and spirit; they are also excellent to use as a preventive measure to maintain good health.

CASE HISTORY: GEORGE

George is a twenty-nine-year-old "head-turner." He is a six-foot, four-inch former model, with short, neatly cut brown hair and piercing blue eyes. After getting to know him, and it takes awhile because he is reserved at first, I found him to be that perfect combination of modesty and power, humility and strength.

His first symptoms of AIDS were an internal discomfort in his bones and a constant lower spine ache. It was a dull aching sensation that was hard to explain to his doctors. He then experienced night-sweats, a slight weight-loss, and enlarged lymph nodes in the groin area.

He was initially treated with an experimental drug: leukocyte dyalizate, an immune stimulator. While he noticed no negative side-effects, he doesn't think the drug did anything to improve his condition either. He bases this on the fact that physically and mentally he felt no difference on or off this drug; however, there were improvements on results of his mitigen blood-stimulation tests.

As far as his diet is concerned, George is just as matter-of-fact. While he takes a daily multivitamin, he was not that impressed with the nutritionist he consulted at U.S.C., who he felt "didn't tell me anything I didn't already know, because I've been cooking for years." He likes to cook, and he likes to eat, and he cooks whatever he likes. Somehow, one gets the feeling that George runs a very healthy natural kitchen, and it is just his modesty that prevents him from saying so.

In the beginning of his illness, his parents and his close friends were his only support. Now, however, even though his family is in northern California, they are not much support to him. He approached AIDS Project Los Angeles for support, but he didn't get what he wanted, which was a positive direction. George then tried the Shanti Foundation and was very impressed with the positive support he received there.

"Then I became involved by working in the office, and I met people who were very positive and supportive. They supported people no matter who or where they were in their condition." With some gentle prodding, George acknowledges the fact that today he sits on the board of directors of the Shanti Foundation. He also got involved with the AIDS Update about a year ago, and he knew he had found another group of positive, supportive people. He feels it was very difficult to find groups of support a year ago, "because back then people were not as open as they are now—especially people in a positive frame of mind."

Until he found these groups, he did his own work, his own form of meditation in the morning with music. "I just see myself as a very positive, healthy person." About visualizations he says, "I just use a very simple chalkboard technique, just chalk on a chalkboard, with the chalk being erased; that's my Kaposi being erased." As far as spiritual teachers, he was mesmerized by Stephen and Alexandra Levine, who conducted a very inspirational Shanti seminar. It goes without saying that George has also found inspiration in the Wednesday night Hayrides.

"Louise is important as far as showing people that they've got to commit themselves to loving themselves on a daily basis, because if they can't do that, then everything else is going to fall apart. You can't love somebody else without loving yourself. You might be fooling yourself and the other people, but it just doesn't work that way."

One of the positive aspects of AIDS for George has been the awakening of his spiritual awareness: "My spiritual path has started after all of this and has really slapped me across the face and said WAKE UP and be more aware or conscious. That is the really wonderful thing about being diagnosed. I don't really see it as that negative, other than having to deal with doctors and hospitals and the actual cancer. It's not negative at all for me."

When asked to recommend alternative therapy to others, George felt that acupuncture has been very helpful, but considers the best thing he can pass on is the advice he was given by his oncologist: "She said that the most important thing for you to do is to keep a positive attitude, and I looked at her and said, 'You've got to be kidding! How does one keep a positive attitude after dealing with something like this?' And she said, 'You've just got to, and that's all there is to it.'

"For awhile, I didn't have a positive attitude. I was just walking around in a daze, thinking, 'It's going to be a short period of time, and I won't be here anymore.' And then I kept getting up in the morning, and the sun was still shining, and I realized I had to get on with things. If you're going to live, you've got to live, and if you're going to die, then just do it. I chose to live, and I realized that, if I was going to live, I had to keep that positive outlook."

George also feels being fully involved with life and living will keep one alive. Most important to him right now is his own spiritual direction and well-being, which involves a lot of reading. George also runs every other day, not only for the exercise, but also for the escape. He meditates while he runs. He is also involved in his work at the Shanti Foundation, and he has a full-time job as a waiter. "I'll tell you what's really wonderful, and I get this all the time—that I don't look like a person with AIDS, and I know that nobody has to. It is a reinforcement that I look physically how I feel; and I feel great, so I look great. I'm not going to die from this. I'm determined to ride this out for five or six years, and in the meantime, like everyone else in California, I'll watch out for earthquakes."

I ran into George about a month after this interview and noticed that he was absolutely glowing. When asked the reason for looking even better than usual, he explained that he had just received test results that indicated his immune system was completely back to normal.

*　　*　　*

Whether you have AIDS or not, know that there is so much to be positive for. Life has provided everything for us. There is such an abundance of everything on this planet. There is so much food on this planet that everyone could be easily fed. Yes, it is true that people are starving. It isn't for lack of food. There is so much food that we destroy it to keep prices up, allowing people to starve to death out of our lack of love.

There is so much money on this planet that no one has any idea of the total amount. We have incredible wealth. Yes, it is true that many people have little or no money; it doesn't mean the money is not there.

There are billions of people in this world, all types and sizes and shapes. Yet you will hear people say they are lonely. It is not because of a lack of people. It is a fear of reaching out and fear of rejection. What keeps us deprived is our own beliefs in our lacks and limitations. To move beyond this, we need to stretch our minds—to go beyond our past and to go beyond what others told us we couldn't do.

This has been a growing experience for me in so many ways. I have been stretched in my own understanding and knowledge. My awareness of the power of love to transform is stronger now than ever. I find myself hugging people that a few years ago I would not have been able to look at. I have dropped many of my own fears as I see these beautiful young people so courageously go through their intense experiences.

This is a time of healing, for making whole—not for condemnation. We must rise out of the limitations of the past. I believe we are all Divine, Magnificent Expressions of Life. Let's claim that now!

TREATMENT

Today is another precious day on earth. We shall live it with joy. For every problem we create, there is a solution.

We are not limited by our human-mind thinking, for we are all connected with the entire universal wisdom and knowledge. We come from the loving space of the heart, knowing that love opens all doors. There is an ever-ready power that helps us meet and overcome every challenge and crisis in our lives.

I know that every illness has been healed somewhere in this world. Therefore, there is the possibility that this can happen for me. I wrap myself in a cocoon of love, and I am safe. We are one with the power that created us.

We are safe, and all is well in our world.

3

A Dis-ease of Lack of Love

Affirmation:
We are willing to open our hearts!

Why is AIDS on the planet? I think it is here to show us we are making a mess of our lives and of the planet. Our physical bodies and the physical world are in great need of healing. Our air is polluted. Fish are filled with poison and chemicals. Land is being stripped of its vegetation in many areas. We still create wars and torture each other. Our bodies are loaded with chemical foods and abused with cigarettes and alcohol and drugs of every description. We live in fear of a nuclear holocaust. These conditions are like dis-eases, and this is why I feel the whole planet has a form of AIDS.

We have not been listening to the myriad of signals both the planet and our bodies have been giving us. We are just heedlessly going ahead, pouring more junk and drugs into our bodies, pushing them beyond normal endurance. It is only natural that we treat the planet in a similar fashion, abusing it beyond belief. The AA people (Alcoholics Anonymous) know that some of us seem to need to "bottom out" before we will see the light and make some changes.

Let's know that creating AIDS is bottoming out enough, and we do not have to develop something even more awful before we listen and change our unloving and destructive ways.

It is our unwillingness to stop and listen to the warning signs our bodies give us that causes catastrophe. Because of this, the time is ripe for a disaster big enough to force us to look at what we are doing on an individual and collective level. AIDS is such a disaster. Every experience we go through is a learning lesson. This is an opportunity for us to heal ourselves and to heal the planet. The time is now.

. I ask the following questions every few months at my Wednesday night group: "Why do you think AIDS is on the planet?" and "Why do you think you got AIDS?" The answers are often: "It has given me a chance to love myself," "Now I know how loved I am," "I am finding my spiritual pathway," "I needed to change my life in every area," "I had to learn that people cared." Or as one person put it, "When I was well, I was really sick. Now that I'm sick, I feel well for the first time in my life."

One person felt so strongly about this that he wrote a letter to his AIDS, and gave me a copy. It reads:

7-22-87

Dear AIDS,

For so long now I've been angry with you for being a part of my life. I feel like you have violated my being. The strongest emotion thus far in our relationship has been anger!!

But now I choose to see you in a different light. I no longer hate you or feel angry with you. I realize now that you have become a positive force in my life. You are a messenger who has brought me a new understanding of life and myself. So for that I thank you, forgive you, and release you.

Never before has anyone given me such great opportunity. You don't know how much you have given me. You have given me the push I needed to take a look at my life, see the problems, and find the solutions. I now realize all the choices that I have in life.

Because of you I have learned to love myself, and as a result I love and am loved by others. I am now in touch with parts of my being that I never knew existed. I have grown spiritually and intellectually since your arrival. I have become a loving, honest, and caring person. So again I thank you for giving me this opportunity to have insight into my life. How could I not forgive you, when so many positive experiences have come from your visit.

But you have also led me to the realization that you have no power over me. I am the power in my world. So since I forgive you, I will now release you from my life.

I accept and love myself just as I am. I am healing, and I accept perfect health and energy as the way for me. Again I thank you, forgive you, and release you from my life.

> With love,
> Paul

From the many PWAs I have come to know, it seems clear that the lack of love—love of themselves, love of and from others—has played a large role in their acquiring the dis-ease.

AIDS to me is a dis-ease of love, the lack of love. AIDS shows us how incredibly un-loving we can be. Look at how we treat people with AIDS. They are often rejected, abandoned, isolated, and even denied the assistance they so sorely need.

We even do this to the children and babies.

Remember the shameful incident of rejection and arson in Arcadia, Florida, in 1987? Three young children with AIDS were first barred from school. As the frenzy of misinformation and panic continued, the parents were harrassed. Finally, in a conflagration of hate and fear, mobs fire-bombed their home, forcing them to leave the state, alone and destitute.

It seems to me that there is always a choice of love or fear. If we choose fear and the alienating behavior that goes with it, we go down the tubes. It is up to us. The future is ours. If we choose love and the opportunities it offers us, we will be able to heal the whole planet.

What choices do you make on a daily basis? Are your personal choices going to contribute to destroying the planet or healing the planet?

These choices are the same ones that make us love or abuse our bodies. I believe that, for many reasons, often different for each individual, a lot of people have taken to abusing their bodies. It has become commonplace in some circles to over-drink, to take drugs of various sorts, to undernourish the body, to indulge in painful, abusive sexual practices, and to indulge in mental abuse.

I believe one of the reasons so many people abuse drugs and alcohol is that we are terrified of being alone. Being alone and experiencing our feelings is very scary to many of us. We have learned to shut down our feelings. We pop pills to get rid of pains in our bodies, and we use junk-food, cigarettes, alcohol, and drugs to get rid of feelings.

Any one of these practices, let alone any combination of them, can weaken the body and lower the immune system. It is normal and natural for the body with a lowered immune system to be open to the popular dis-eases of the moment. It has nothing to do with morality. So let us dissolve the judgment and guilt. Let us dissolve the harmful practices, no matter what they may be. Let us once again take loving care of our bodies and our emotions.

It is interesting that the first people to be affected with the dis-ease AIDS are those who are oppressed or feel unable to fend for themselves—Africans, Haitians, gays, hemophiliacs, drug users, people getting blood transfusions, and the babies of people in these groups.

These are mostly people with lots of unexpressed anger and rage towards their families or towards society as a whole. These feelings may be combined with feelings of helplessness and hopelessness to make any positive changes in their lives. They are not yet aware of the power of their own minds.

Our minds are powerful instruments. It has been said many times that we only use ten percent of our brains. Have you ever wondered what the other ninety percent is for? I think we have latent abilities we cannot even dream of at this point. Some of us are capable of seeing auras, being clairvoyant and clairaudient, of channeling, and other so-called "psychic" abilities. We hear of astral travel. If I could tap into the great resource of my own brain, I believe that I could go from coast to coast without using an airplane; I could dematerialize in one spot and rematerialize in another, if I could fully realize my own potential.

I think telepathy and these other psychic abilities will be available to us all when we have the know-how. I believe there are abilities beyond our imagination within us all, and we will have the use of these abilities when we are ready for them.

They are not to be given to us now because we are not ready. We would probably use these newfound abilities to harm each other, the planet, and the universe. Look at the way we treat each other now. We need to leave pain and suffering behind. We need to really learn to love ourselves and each other, unconditionally.

UNCONDITIONAL LOVE

All of the great teachers of past and present talk about the value of unconditional love—that state of mind where we love and accept ourselves totally and therefore can love and accept others exactly as they are. We are all doing the best we can at any point in time and space. We will all make our positive changes much quicker and easier when we give ourselves and each other love that is without conditions, restrictions, and limitations. When the majority of us have learned this lesson and can practice it daily, we will be ready for the next cosmic step.

The healing lessons gays are learning through this powerful experience called AIDS are the lessons of love. We cannot be separate and distant from each other. We cannot abuse ourselves and each other. Love is the healing force, and the pathway to love is forgiveness. Many gays will share this message and move throughout the planet healing those yet to contract the dis-ease. This in turn will help to heal the rift between straights and gays.

PREJUDICE AND ANGER

When you are part of a group that receives a lot of prejudicial flak, it is easy to send back anger and hatred. After all, you believe you are justified because of the way "they" behave. The trouble with this attitude is that what you send out, you get back. What we are learning in the Wednesday group is to stand up for ourselves and to take positive action and send love to troubled spots and people. Much of this attitude has been developed by releasing fear.

When people are frightened, they behave in unloving ways. They can run from you, reject you, abandon you, try to get rid of you, quarantine you, and legislate against you. To send anger and hateful thoughts back to them only exacerbates the situation, and can lead to conflict—even wars. Revenge never works.

The buck must stop somewhere. If we are on a spiritual pathway of inner growth, then it is up to us to do the stopping.

So we take the bigots of the world, whom we see as frightened and ignorant, and we send them love. We take unrelenting family members who are unaccepting about their children, gay or straight, and we send them love. We do our best to accept these people as they are, just as we want them to accept us as we are. No person, place, or thing can harm us when we are centered in our space and love ourselves. We can only be hurt by our thoughts.

Don't scare yourself with your own thoughts. Don't react with fear. Don't give your power away. Come from a centered space where you know that life is for living.

While AIDS, in its early phase, was mostly in the gay community, we have learned that it crosses all barriers and finds a home wherever there are agreeable conditions. These conditions often are a lowered vitality and immune system and a corresponding depressed mental outlook on life that comes from a lack of self-love—the very opposite of unconditional love.

What is unconditional love? Simply put, it is the ability to love ourselves and others without rules and regulations. Unconditional love is an ideal state that the whole planet is working toward. It is the major lesson we have come to learn, and it must begin with ourselves. It is accepting ourselves and others and life without judgment of any sort. A flower is, a puppy is, a rainstorm is, and an experience is. If we say it is a beautiful flower or a cute puppy, or a bad rainstorm or a terrible experience, then we have made a judgment. Just as another could say it is an ugly flower or a destructive puppy, or a welcome rainstorm or a healing experience. They are all judgments and come from our choice of attitudes towards these events.

To say someone has red hair is a statement. To say someone has beautiful red hair or ugly red hair is a judgment. Our judgments come from our chosen perspective on any given subject or event. Have you noticed how you judge yourself? We say things like, "My nose is too long," or "My thighs are too big," or "I'm not smart enough," or "I'm not lovable as I am," or "I'm not good enough."

"My nose is too long"—for who or for what? Where did we get a standard for noses? And have you noticed that the shape of noses changes in different parts of the planet? Am I really placing my self-worth in the shape of my thighs? If I feel I am not lovable, it is because I am not loving myself. And who says I'm not good enough; where did I gather that judgment?

It is all such foolishness. My nose works, my thighs are the shape they are. Yes, I can change the shape of my nose and thighs, but it will not have anything to do with my self-worth or my self-love. I am definitely lovable if I say so, and only I can decide that I am good enough.

CASE HISTORY: BRUCE

"When I was a young boy of four or five, I was a cute little redhead with lots of freckles, and I fully expressed myself through music, art, and dance. I believed in God; I loved science; and my favorite pastime was watching cartoons on television.

"I grew up in a middle-class family, and my father was an alcoholic. As he was away from home a lot and my mother worked a part-time job in order to help support the family, I used to spend a lot of time by myself in front of my television set. In a way, my television set became a loving parent.

"My favorite program was *Popeye*. I used to watch

Popeye every day. I think he was my favorite cartoon character, because he was one of the 'good' guys, and whenever he would eat his spinach, he could beat all the odds, win all the fights, and even win the love and approval of Olive Oyl.

"When I was a little boy, I needed to believe in heroes, and I now realize how important Popeye has been to me. He was my first hero, and I thought he was what a man should be.

"Some psychologists believe that our personalities are molded by the time we are five years old. I believe this is true. I know that I created a gay sexual personality that was very much like Popeye. Instead of eating spinach, I used a lot of drugs and alcohol, and with these I could beat all the odds, win all the fights, and even win lots of hearts on Saturday nights at the baths.

"I used to hide behind leather chaps, baseball caps, and cowboy boots. With these as my disguises, and by using drugs and alcohol, I lived my life from the standpoint of a cartoon. As a result, I neglected my life, I grew more isolated and alienated from the very people that I wanted to be close to, and I felt empty and incomplete.

"Today, I realize that I am not a cartoon and that this is not a dress rehearsal. I am rather a very loving and caring man, with real needs and real feelings.

"This realization has come from my participation in two twelve-step programs, individual psychotherapy, and through my participation in an AIDS support group.

"As a participant in the Natural History of AIDS Study, conducted at the University of California Los Angeles, I was advised that my test results are indicative that my immune system may be depressed and that there are a number of men in the study with similar findings who seem to be in good health and are free of AIDS.

"Upon receipt of my test results, I went into panic; but as a result of my participation in these support groups, I was able to reach out to others and to share my feelings.

"Today, I am accepting only love in my life. I am using affirmations, and I am taking the time to hug myself and to acknowledge the cute little guy who is looking back at me when I am standing in front of the bathroom mirror.

"Today, I am participating in my life, and I am becoming my own loving parent. I am letting go of my need to be someone else. I am doing things that are foreign to me, like:

I am taking a massage class, and I am introducing vitamins into my diet. I recently took a class on the art of lovemaking, and I am learning how to be sexually responsible.

My most recent adventure in life has been my participation in a workshop at a healing center in Santa Monica.

"I am truly grateful that I decided to help myself be well, and that I am in a process of change. By letting go and releasing patterns in my life that are not helpful, I am today free to be happy and free to be me.

"I love myself, I love you, and I trust our universe."

*   *   *

We wonder how we can accept all the difficult things that are happening in our lives. But testimony like Bruce's can show us that these difficulties occur because we have practiced being unloving and judgmental to ourselves. When we as individuals treat ourselves with unconditional love, then we will not have negative experiences. We will not create them. We can learn to view and accept others without placing conditions on them, allowing them to be who they are, learning their lessons as best they can, just as we are learning ours as quickly as we can, loving them as they learn to love themselves.

If we all practice unconditional love as much as possible, I am sure that, in two generations, we could change this planet into a very loving, safe place to live.

Each of us suffers from the lack of unconditional love in one way or another. Some of us have suffered from the time of birth. If we were seldom given permission to love and respect ourselves as children, then it is most likely we will deny ourselves love now. If we are taught we are unlovable, then we often choose to treat ourselves as worthless. We can express this worthlessness in many ways. We can become IV drug users and constantly put ourselves in states where we do not have to think at all, punishing our bodies on a daily basis.

Our feelings of worthlessness might translate into becoming prostitutes, thinking, "If I'm no good anyway, what difference does it make what I do with my body!"

If we believe we are unlovable and incapable of attracting love, then we could become highly promiscuous, trying to fulfill the aching void within us. Yes, it is fun to have lots of sex, and I think that much of the promiscuity going around in recent years, with both homosexuals and heterosexuals, comes from our fear of having intimate relationships. It is easy to jump into bed; it is much harder to be open and honest and intimate with another.

Yes, the sexual revolution of a few years ago gave us all permission to be more openly sexual, and for some of us, it became a way of life and much easier than to deal with relationships. Relationships are for learning about ourselves.

TREATMENT

Today is another precious day on earth. We shall live it with joy. We accept this gift with gratitude and joy. We realize that we have no time to waste on living in the past. So we go within and, seeing with eyes of love, we seek out all the dark corners where pain and fear dwell. We no longer choose to put up with these old handicaps. We move into our heart space, and we bring the abundant light of love we carry within us. We allow this love, which sees without judgment or expectation, to flood our body, our mind, our consciousness.

This light of love shines on and dissolves all that is unlike itself. We are willing to release all old garbage. It has no life of its own; it has no truth in it. It is only an old memory that no longer exists, disappearing from our lives. We are one with the power that created us.

We are safe, and all is well in our world!

4

Making Choices

Affirmation:
We are far more than any problem;
we are the solution!

If we choose dis-ease, can we choose to cure it?
Remember our so-called "choice" of dis-ease is seldom
done on a conscious level. It comes out of our deep-
seated beliefs and our habitual ways of thinking, speaking, and acting. These belief habits create negative actions and an atmosphere where dis-ease can flourish. Let
us examine our behavior and what we can do to change
our options.

Is our only goal to heal our bodies? This would be
useless, for, if we don't change what got us into this problem in the first place, then what good would come from
just healing our bodies? We do, however, have choice.
And knowing this simple fact can make all the difference.

Too many of us think that we have no choice, that
we are just stuck where and how we are. That is not true;
we all have choices all the time. Every moment of every
day is filled with choices. The way we breathe and walk
and sit and dress and eat and react and interact are all
choices. Then there are the larger choices of lifestyles and
partners and work and even our choice of health. What
are we doing on a daily level to contribute to our vitality

and strength or to contribute to our decline into dis-ease? Our choices of thought have a lot to do with this. If we choose thoughts that make us feel good about ourselves, then our actions and reactions will probably be positive. If we choose thoughts that undermine our self-esteem, then we will be drawn to negative experiences.

What happens to us every day stems from choice. Even from the first moment we decide to once again come to this planet at a particular point in time. I believe we know in advance what various cultural and social and family experiences will be available before we enter the physical plane. How we react to these experiences is our choice. No matter what the family or society is telling us, we have choice in how we will react or whether we will accept their opinions at all. We come here at particular times so that we may experience particular circumstances that will assist us on our spiritual pathway. Our soul always knows what it is doing.

Few people consciously choose dis-ease. Subconsciously, many people do; they need the dis-ease to fulfill a need. There are many reasons for having a dis-ease:

Believing you will catch whatever is going around.
An acceptance of dis-ease as inevitable.
Ignorance of the importance of good nutrition.
To get out of or avoid something. "Oh, they can't expect me to do that if I am sick."
To have time off.
To get some rest.
To get sympathy or pity.
To find out who really loves you.
To ask for things you don't feel you deserve otherwise.
To get taken care of.
To keep someone from leaving you.
To have permission to do something you always wanted to do but wouldn't give yourself the time to do.

It's a great excuse for failure.
Self-punishment for not feeling "good enough."
Following a family reaction pattern to stress.
Or just not knowing what else to do.
We may even "need" the disfigurement that comes
with dis-ease to be loved for our inner selves.

There is an interesting occurrence that happens with
some people, both men and women, who are extraordinarily beautiful. They are usually so admired for their
beauty or their bodies that they often feel as though no
one really cares about the person who is inside. They
long to be appreciated for their minds or their abilities,
or to have their feelings respected.

These so-called "beautiful people" will sometimes
long to be ordinary or even unattractive. Sometimes they
will deliberately indulge in behaviors that will help to destroy their beauty. Or they might cultivate an illness so
that they can find out who really loves them. Beautiful
people have problems too. Unconditional love and acceptance are important to all of us.

KARMA

We hear so much about Karma; what does it really
mean to us?

Karma is simply the law of cause and effect: what we
give out comes back to us—in thoughts, in words, in actions, by our beliefs. Every effect must have a cause.
Every experience has a beginning. As the saying goes,
"What goes around comes around." The boomerang always returns to its place of origin. This concept works
both negatively and positively. All the good in our lives
is also karma that we have created in the very same way
that we created the negative.

We are never "stuck" with karma. For as we change,

we can release our old karma. Too many people use karma as a cop-out for not changing. "Oh, it's my karma; it has been with me for lifetimes. There is nothing I can do." So what! It doesn't matter how long we have had our negative pattern. What are we willing to do now to make a change? Our point of power is always in the present moment. We, and only we, can make the changes necessary to dissolve the negative karma.

What are the changes? Very simple. Stop what "we" are doing to create and re-create the problem. There is nobody out there doing things to us. There is only us creating our world. If it is our actions, then we can change the actions. Is it abuse of the body? Then let's stop it. Is it abuse of others? Then we can stop it. Do we speak harshly to others? Do we whine and express jealousy? Do we complain and blame endlessly? Are we professional victims? Then know we can change. Are our thoughts a stream of negativity? Do we believe in lack and limitation? Do we believe in suffering? Then let go of that belief. At least we can be "willing" to stop thinking that way.

When we notice ourselves in the old pattern of creating negative karma, pause. Remind ourselves we no longer want to do that. Begin to change our thinking, words, actions, beliefs, as best we can. Even a small change in our thinking helps.

Above all, we do not want to berate ourselves and do guilt numbers because of negativity from the past. The past is over and done, and whatever we need to clean up, let us do that now as swiftly and as lovingly and as joyously as we can. Let suffering be a thing of the past in our lives.

We are here to learn and to grow. Learn as much as you can. Do not limit yourself to this book. Read other books. Listen to many tapes. Take classes if you can. You will hear the same message, perhaps in different words or coming through different personalities. Immerse yourself in study; it is for your benefit. You can become an expert in improving the quality of your life. There is a reading list in the back of this book. Choose those titles that appeal to you. Go to bookstores and libraries and find others. Look for other teachers.

When we are willing to grow, teachers and classes and opportunities will pop up everywhere. Listen to what others say. Look at their lives. Find the connections between what they say and what they experience. Become your own teacher. You have the wisdom and the ability to grow far beyond your present comprehension.

WE ARE NOT STUCK
WITH NEGATIVE CHOICES

Even though most of us have made negative choices in the past, we are not stuck with these choices. We can always choose again and choose differently. We look at the choices and beliefs that do not work for us and make different choices. If we have long believed we were "not good enough" and therefore treated ourselves badly, we can make a change. We can look at where this belief came from and find it is usually from a parent or significant person early in our childhood. From our current adult viewpoint, we can decide that this opinion was the other person's hang-up and had nothing to do with us. We can now choose to love and appreciate ourselves, and automatically our thinking and our behavior will become more positive.

We may have unknowingly chosen beliefs and behaviors that led to poor health in the past and experienced those choices most uncomfortably. Yet we can now choose health, and we can learn what will contribute to creating and maintaining the best health we can experience today. Just as there are always alternative mental choices, there are also many alternative holistic pathways that can contribute to our decision to be healthy and whole.

Too often people have unknowingly been pursuing the pathway of ill-health for a long time, until there is a crisis, and then they finally become aware of different choices and begin to pursue health. They want instant results and cannot understand that it usually takes time to turn around years of self-abuse. Sometimes they become discouraged and return to the old ways, not having given themselves a real chance.

Obviously, it is always much easier to make the choice for health before dis-ease is present. For then we do not have to undo damage as well as change our patterns. I used to say to clients, "It is much easier to release our resentments before we are under the threat of the surgeon's knife, or we will have to deal with panic too." Of course, changes can take place at any time. We are in the here and now, and it is in this moment that we do our changing.

A choice for health will include letting go of our old hang-ups, as well as hang-ups from others we carried on our backs. It is these negative patterns that led to the dis-ease in the first place. Letting go of old resentments, forgiving all those who may ever have been hurtful, and a decision to love and approve of ourselves will do wonders to improve not only our health but to improve every area of our lives. The freedom we feel inside of us when we are willing to make these mental changes is part of our healing.

CASE HISTORY: WALTER

"I see myself as a warm, loving, giving person," said Walter, after being asked to describe himself. He is also very modest about his triumph over AIDS. He has been in complete remission since early 1984. He is thirty-five years old, originally from the New Jersey shore, and is a compact bundle of non-stop energy.

"Before my diagnosis, I wasn't pleased with my life. I had just gone through a number of career changes. I had been working as an executive, but I resigned and moved back to New York City after five years in California and was doing hair in theater and television. I was doing a lot of drugs, partying, and getting very little sleep. I could definitely foresee problems if I didn't slow down. I knew, if I stayed in New York, I would be dead. So I moved back to California. I wasn't happy with what I was doing, but I didn't know what I wanted to do instead."

This was in July of 1982, and it was at this time that Walter started getting severe headaches, losing weight, and experiencing night-sweats. "I went to doctors who thought I had second-stage syphilis and treated me for it with heavy doses of penicillin, and I think that was the beginning. I've blocked that period out of my memory, but in hindsight I did have lots of symptoms."

Then, in November of 1982, he first noticed that a lymph node in his groin had swelled to the size of a golf ball. He had it biopsied, and it tested positive for Kaposi sarcoma. He then went to the Boyer Clinic at U.C.L.A. and set up appointments for their testing, which included upper and lower endoscopies to see if there were any lesions internally.

Those tests confirmed his earlier diagnosis, when lesions were found in his stomach. "I decided I could either do nothing, I could do interferon, or I could do chemotherapy. I would never do chemo; I couldn't see doing nothing; so that left me with interferon. I started it when we were drawing straws, to see if we got a high dose or a low dose, and whether it would be intramuscular or intravenous. I started out with a low dosage (six-million units daily), given intramuscularly. After two months and no results, I changed to ninety-three million units a day intravenously. I would go into the hospital on Monday and stay until Friday, every other week for all of 1983; and in early 1984, I changed to outpatient for a couple of months, and then stopped treatments altogether."

His lesions had started to disappear, but he just couldn't handle any more treatments. It was too painful for Walter to continue. The treatment caused a lot of muscle aches, very high temperatures (up to 104), and severe chills. They had to give him intravenous morphine or Demerol for this.

"I was just very weak and sick and spent most of my time in bed." Soon after stopping treatment, Walter was given the news that he had gone into complete remission, and there he has stayed since early 1984.

Vitamins did not play a major part in Walter's healing. "I take one a day." As for diet, "I ate everything I could, but I did eat healthy—not health food, but healthy food. I lost weight around the time of my diagnosis, so I just kept eating, whether I felt like it or not." As a result, under his loose-flowing clothes, Walter carries 190 pounds on his five-foot, eight-inch frame.

As far as spiritual guidance was concerned, Walter relied primarily on himself and friends like Nancy Cole Sawaya. "I did go on a retreat with Stephen Levine on death and dying, but when I returned, depressed, I took an overdose of Seconal. Then about the time of my remission, I started listening to the tapes on meditations and AIDS and reading the books about the Course in Miracles." He now regularly attends the Wednesday night meetings, and not too long ago participated in the AIDS Mastery with Sally Fisher.

During his illness, Walter had very sporadic support, and his family played a very minor role. His brother wouldn't allow him to visit, and his mother was in her seventies, not well herself, and did not really understand what was going on. Most of his support came from a few friends, especially Nancy and the A.P.L.A. at that time. "I got a lot of support there and gave it too. I was scared, but I think a lot of my getting through had to do with stubbornness. There was a part of me saying that I had a disease that I couldn't live through, but there was also a part of me that believed I wasn't going to die, and that part was always stronger. I refused to die."

In giving advice to others, Walter recommends doing what is right for oneself and not doing what everyone else is saying. "Don't buy into whatever is being sold, just do what you feel in your heart is right. I think what helped me the most was being stubborn and not believing I had to die from AIDS, and that's what still helps me. I'm not buying into it. And I tried not to change everything about myself or my whole life. I didn't, all of a sudden, become a vegetarian or just eat brown rice. I didn't put my whole body and mind through total shock by trying to become this unreal person who is trying to exude only love, which I do try to do, but in a realistic sense. I really think that you have to feel that you're doing the best thing for yourself, however. I did what I needed to do for myself, whether or not other people thought it was right or wrong. If I had totally changed, it wouldn't have been a reality for me. I couldn't say, 'My life isn't working this way, so I'll become someone else.' A lot of people, by changing, are putting themselves down and making their whole life a lie."

Walter today is living the truth, following his dreams, and enjoying life to the fullest.

TREATMENT

Today is another precious day on earth. We shall live it with joy. We are willing to look beyond the problem, knowing that there has to be a solution. Within us exist the answers that we are seeking. We are one with all Intelligence that is everywhere equally present. We move beyond limited human mind thinking and align ourselves with the infinite, Divine mind, where all things are possible.

Within these possibilities are solutions beyond counting. We are secure in this knowledge, and we know that we are one with the power that created us.

We are safe, and all is well in our world!

PART II

HEALING YOURSELF

5

Our Healing Power: Change

Affirmation:
Our willingness to change
creates miracles in our lives!

Healing is to make ourselves whole. As Walter did, we all must realize it is a personal challenge. There are so many areas that need healing. Often the body needs healing, and just as often the heart could need healing. The emotions can be healed, as can our relationships; our beliefs about ourselves and even our bank accounts often need healing. Making ourselves whole is a lifetime endeavor. There is always some part of ourselves that can use a bit of healing.

I find that most of the people with AIDS who so far have followed strictly the medical route are not doing well. The medical establishment has acknowledged that it doesn't know what it is doing. Doctors don't know what to do, so they are experimenting with drugs that have lots of side-effects and can be very harmful to already weakened bodies.

The people I know with AIDS who are exploring and using alternative healing methods are doing much better than those who are following strict medical procedures that involve putting "poisons" into the body. These alternative methods can include homeopathy, acupuncture, nutrition, megadoses of vitamins, herbology, meditation, visualization, support groups, and finding a spiritual pathway that gives comfort and peace.

CHANGE

Change goes on all the time. Every breath we take is different from our last breath. Seasons change, and so do we. Yet so many of us are afraid "to change." We want the world to change, but we hold onto our old ways, fearful of letting go. We are all in the constant process of changing, and when we resist, we deny the good that is trying to enter our lives. Just as we eat food, digest it, and release the waste, so too do we attract an experience, go through it, and then release that part of it that no longer serves us. Then there are new foods to eat and new events to experience.

When we want to change, what we are really changing is our thoughts and beliefs. For as they change, so do our lives change. Now all of us have many areas of our lives that work very well. Our belief systems about these things are positive. We do not need to change what works. We look for the areas where we are uncomfortable. Just change what doesn't work or what could work better.

Again we do not have to know exactly "how" to make these changes. All we need to do is to be "willing" to change. Saying something to ourselves like, "This is not working for me, and I am willing to change. Whatever I need to do I am willing to do." Or "I now change my consciousness from illness to health, from bitterness to peace, from resentment to forgiveness."

Only you know what it is you want to change from and change to. Say so in your affirmations, clearly. We are only letting go of old beliefs.

POWER

We are powerful beings. We may not recognize it, because we may have given control of our power away to others. Still, we want to remember that we are the only thinkers in our minds. No matter what others tell us, we make the decision to accept or reject. Our power lies in our thoughts, for our thoughts are creative.

We give our power away through guilt, being unable to say "no," always wanting to please others so that we may be liked. Perhaps we are living our lives for our parents, our lovers or spouses, our doctors, our friends, our employers, or even our churches. It is another way to say "I'm not good enough," and that builds self-hatred and denial.

When we are ill, we often give our powers away to doctors and other medical authorities. As though "M.D." stood for "Medical Deities." A powerless person finds it harder to heal himself or herself. It is best when healing can be teamwork. You choose the health practitioner to help you get well. Together you make the decisions. This way, you powerfully contribute to your healing process.

We take our power back by changing our mental priorities. We realize we are important too and cannot live only for the fulfillment of others. We did not come to this planet to deny ourselves. We came to share the uniqueness that is ours. No one can live life in quite the particular way we can. We have our own talents and abilities, and we are here to use these for the good of the planet. We can use the affirmation, "I accept my power, and I now allow my own uniqueness to express itself in deeply fulfilling ways."

I do not believe it is selfish to say "I come first." I believe it is taking care of the self. You are deciding what is healing to you. You count. It is an act of loving yourself. I have noticed that women with breast cancer usually have been giving their power away for years. The breasts often represent nourishment, and these women have been nourishing everyone else and not themselves. They are great givers and forget to give to themselves. This giving is such a habit that others expect it of them. It is a big step for them to say "No." When they say "No, it is my turn now," they are taking their power back and contributing to their wellness.

Realizing your power—and using it to heal yourself, as well as contributing to the health of others—is an early step to the future health of the planet. We are all capable of contributing love and health. And through this contribution we can heal our lives.

TREATMENT

Today is another precious day on earth. We shall live it with joy. In this world of change, I choose to be flexible in all areas. I am willing to change myself and my beliefs to improve the quality of my life and my world. My body loves me in spite of how I may treat it. My body communicates with me, and I now listen to its messages.

I am willing to get the message. I pay attention and make the corrections necessary, paying attention and giving to my body what it needs on every level to bring it back to optimum health. I call upon an inner strength that is mine whenever I need it. We are one with the power that created us.

We are safe, and all is well in our world!

6

Learning to Love Yourself

Affirmation:
I am willing to love and appreciate myself!

When I talk about loving the Self, someone will often think that I mean being vain and conceited. This has nothing to do with self-love. Vanity and conceit are expressions of the lack of self-worth. Of course, we want to look well, but when we are overly preoccupied with our physical appearances, it means that we feel we are not good enough as we are. We feel insecure and are trying to make ourselves acceptable. Polishing our surface image never works, because we are putting our self-worth into our outer appearance, which is always changing. Our self-worth has nothing to do with the way we look; it is based on how much we love ourselves.

Self-love is really so simple. It is choosing to feel good about ourselves and to take care of ourselves. When we make this choice, the rest falls into place easily. Self-love is releasing all self-punishment. It is forgiving ourselves. It is letting the past go. It is making ourselves "okay." It is approving of ourselves. It is enjoying ourselves. It is loving who we are. It is being gentle with ourselves as we go through our processes.

HOW DO WE LOVE OTHERS?

How do we love others? Accept them as they are. Allow them to be themselves. Stop trying to change them. Let them take care of their own growth processes. We can't learn for another. If their behavior is detrimental to us, then we may choose not to be in their presence—and that is fine. We must love ourselves enough not to be brought down by self-destructive people. If we have many negative people in our lives, then we can look to see what pattern there is in us that attracts these people to us.

When we change, when we drop our pattern and we become different, the others will also change in the way they relate to our new personalities, or they will leave our lives so that new people who will appreciate us are then able to enter. Whichever way it happens, it is always a positive move for us when we love and accept ourselves.

Another powerful tool for healing all relationships—family, work, casual, or intimate—is "blessing with love." When someone is doing something to disrupt the harmony of your life, bless them with love. You can do it several ways. You can say, "I bless you with love, and I bring harmony to this situation," or "I bless you with love, and 'I' release you and let you go," or "I release you to your highest good."

When we do this consistently, something happens on the unseen side of life, and the situation changes for the better. I have seen this process heal relationships of every type. Bosses have become pleasant, families express love, difficult people leave, intimate relationships become honest. Those of us who have practiced this blessing with love are delighted with the results.

WHAT I BELIEVE

I believe that all events we have experienced in our lifetime up to this moment have been created by the thoughts and beliefs we have held in the past. Thoughts are powerful; thoughts are creative. Our thoughts create our reality. This is a law of nature that we are just beginning to understand and to practice. Yet we have heard the message for a long time.

My philosophy is really very simple—too simple for some people. And yet I have seen it work over and over. These are some of the main points:

1. WHAT WE GIVE OUT WE GET BACK. Always. This message has been around for a long time. Remember the Golden Rule: "Do unto others as you would have them do unto you." This rule was never created to produce guilt. It is a law of nature that also applies to our thought patterns. If we judge, if we criticize, even in thought, then we are also judged and criticized. If we love unconditionally, then we are attracting people into our lives who will give us the same unconditional acceptance and love. Thoughts of hate attract thoughts and actions of hate. Thoughts of jealousy attract lack and loss into our lives. On the other hand, thoughts of forgiveness attract healing and prosperity. Thoughts of love and joy bring not only love into our lives but incredible good, more than we can imagine—and this good is mirroring our new thoughts about what we believe we deserve.

2. WHAT WE BELIEVE ABOUT OURSELVES AND ABOUT LIFE BECOMES THE TRUTH FOR US. This is why it is important to examine what we believe. Far too often, these are

limiting beliefs of our parents or of our particular society. I often ask people to sit quietly and list some of the major areas of life and write down the beliefs they have about them. Such as, "What do you believe about the following:

Men	Lack
Women	Prosperity
Love	Aging
Sex	Work
Health	Success
Your Body	God

It is surprising how many of these beliefs were gathered around the age of five. Surely not all of those early opinions are relevant to living our lives today, and so we find periodic mental house-cleaning is most useful. As all beliefs are chosen, we can now choose only the ones that support and nourish us the most.

3. OUR THOUGHTS ARE CREATIVE. This is the most important law of nature we need to know. One idle thought does not make much difference, but thoughts are like drops of water; they accumulate. As we continue to re-think the same thoughts over a period of time, they become puddles, ponds, lakes, or oceans. If they are positive, we can float on the oceans of life. If they are negative, we can drown in a sea of negativity and despair. What is your normal attitude when you awake in the morning? Is it one of gloom and doom? Then this will be the sort of day you will find awaiting you. Is your attitude one of hope, faith, and love? Then this will be the tone of your day—an atmosphere that will bring you all that you need. Sit quietly for a few moments; notice your train of thoughts. Do you really want to have the sort of life these thoughts will produce? Begin to consciously choose thoughts that nourish and support you.

4. WE ARE WORTH LOVING. All of us. You and me. We do not have to earn love. We do not have to earn the right to breathe—we breathe because we exist. We are lovable because we exist. We have to know that and make it true for us. We are worthy of our own love as well. Do not allow your parents' negative opinions or society's popular prejudices to dim your light. The reality of your being is that you are loving and lovable. However, you have to accept this concept for it to be true in your life. Remember, your thoughts create your reality. What "they" think or say has nothing to do with your self-worth. Tell yourself right now: "I AM WORTH LOVING!"

5. SELF-APPROVAL AND SELF-ACCEPTANCE IS THE KEY TO POSITIVE CHANGES. When we are angry at ourselves, when we judge and criticize everything we do, when we abuse ourselves, we are giving out very negative vibrations, and our lives never work. It is just an old habit and has no basis in truth. How can we expect others to love and accept us if we do not love and accept ourselves? "I LOVE AND ACCEPT MYSELF EXACTLY AS I AM" is a most powerful thought and will help you to create a world of joy.

6. WE CAN RELEASE THE PAST AND FORGIVE EVERYONE. The past only exists in our minds. To hold onto old hurts is to punish ourselves today for something someone else did long ago. That doesn't make any sense at all. Too often we sit in a prison of self-righteous resentment, and that is a terrible way to live. You can free yourself. Forgiveness does not mean condoning poor behavior; it means letting go of our "stuff" on the situation—freeing ourselves so we don't recreate a similar experience. Everyone, including ourselves, is doing the best they can at

any given moment, with the understanding, awareness, and knowledge they have. To give up our resentment and replace it with understanding is to free ourselves. Forgiveness is a gift to ourselves.

7. FORGIVENESS OPENS THE DOORWAY TO LOVE. Love is the goal. Unconditional love. How do we get there? Through the door of forgiveness. Forgiveness is like the many layers of an onion. Sometimes it is best to begin with those areas that are easier to forgive, moving to the major hurts as we become more comfortable with the process. We can peel away the hurts one by one, until we come to a deep level of understanding. There we will find love waiting for us. Forgiveness and love go hand in hand.

8. LOVE IS THE MOST POWERFUL HEALING FORCE THERE IS. Love stimulates our immune system. Our love for ourselves. We cannot heal or become whole in an atmosphere of hatred. As we learn to love ourselves, we become powerful. Love moves us from being a victim to becoming a winner. Our love for ourselves attracts to us that which we need to help us on our healing pathway. People who feel good about themselves are naturally attractive to others.

9. JUST BE WILLING. We do not have to wait until we know "how" to do all these things. All we need is to be willing. Our thoughts are creative. To think "I am willing to begin to release judgment or to forgive or to love myself," is to put a thought out into the Universe. As you repeat the thought, it will put into motion the law of attraction, and you will discover new ways to help you do just that. The Universe loves you and is standing ready to help you manifest whatever you choose to think and believe. Be willing to have a good life.

When you have thought about these larger concepts, you might want to read over my ten steps to loving yourself. These have been in use since I began my work, and they have been of great use to me. They are even more simple than the concepts outlined above. Just remember, self-love is a very simple thing.

TEN STEPS TO LOVING YOURSELF

1. STOP ALL CRITICISM. Criticism never changes a thing. Refuse to criticize yourself. Accept yourself exactly as you are. Everybody changes. When you criticize yourself, your changes are negative. When you approve of yourself, your changes are always positive.
2. DON'T SCARE YOURSELF. Stop terrorizing yourself with your thoughts. It's a dreadful way to live. Find a mental image that gives you pleasure (mine is yellow roses), and immediately switch your scary thought to a pleasure thought.
3. BE GENTLE AND KIND AND PATIENT. Be gentle with yourself. Be kind to yourself. Be patient with yourself as you learn the new ways of thinking. Treat yourself as you would someone you really loved.
4. BE KIND TO YOUR MIND. Self-hatred is only hating your own thoughts. Don't hate yourself for having the thoughts. Gently change your thoughts.
5. PRAISE YOURSELF. Criticism breaks down the inner spirit. Praise builds it up. Praise yourself as much as you can. Tell yourself how well you are doing with every little thing.
6. SUPPORT YOURSELF. Find ways to support yourself. Reach out to friends and allow them to help you. It is being strong to ask for help when

you need it most.

7. BE LOVING TO YOUR NEGATIVES. Acknowledge that you created them to fulfill a need. Now you are finding new, positive ways to fulfill those needs. So lovingly release the old negative patterns.

8. TAKE CARE OF YOUR BODY. Learn about nutrition. What kind of fuel does your body need to have optimum energy and vitality? Learn about exercise. What kind of exercise can you enjoy? Cherish and revere the temple you live in.

9. MIRROR WORK. Look into your eyes often. Express this growing sense of love you have for yourself. Forgive yourself looking into the mirror. Talk to your parents looking into the mirror. Forgive them too. At least once a day say: "I love you, I really love you!"

10. DO IT NOW! Don't wait until you get well, or lose the weight, or get the new job or the new relationship. Begin now—do the best you can.

DESERVABILITY, DESERVING

Many of us refuse to put any effort into creating a good life for ourselves because we do not believe that we deserve it. Our feeling of not being deserving may have come from something as early as our toilet training or when we were told we couldn't have something on the condition that we did not eat all our food or clean up our room or put our toys away. This again is buying into someone else's concept or opinion and has nothing to do with the reality of our being.

Deserving has nothing to do with having good. It is our unwillingness to accept that gets in the way. Allow yourself to accept good, whether you think you deserve it or not.

EXERCISE ON DESERVING

Here are some questions to help you in the understanding of what deservability is—and the loving, healing power that can be gained from it. Use them as an exercise to help you in this understanding.

What do you want that you are not having?
Be clear about it and specific.

What were the laws/rules about deserving in your home?
What did they tell you? "You don't deserve." Or "You deserve a good smack." Did your parents feel they deserved? Did you always have to earn in order to deserve. Did earning work for you? Did you get what you wanted then? Were things taken away when you did something wrong?

Do you feel you deserve?
What is the image that comes up? "Later, when I earn it." "I have to work for it first." Are you good enough? Will you ever be good enough?

What "belief" is in the way of your deserving?
There is not enough money. Fear. The old message, "You'll never amount to anything." "I'm not good enough."

Do you deserve to live?
Why? Why not? Did they ever tell you, "You deserve to die?" If so, was this part of your religious upbringing?

What do you have to live for?
What is the purpose in your life? What meaning have you created? Bar-hopping and stuffing ourselves with drugs is not a meaning for life. Have you created a reason to live?

What do you deserve?
"I deserve love and joy and all good." Or do you feel deep down that you deserve shit? Why? Again, where did that message come from? Are you willing to let it go? What are you willing to put in its place? Remember, these are thoughts, and thoughts can be changed.

What are you willing to do about becoming more deserving?

Are you willing to do affirmations? Treatments? Forgiving? If so, then you will become more deserving.

It is easy to see the personal power that is stored in the way we perceive our deservability. Try this treatment. A treatment is used to establish a new thought pattern. Remember this is not the only treatment, it is an example. You may be able to create your own treatment as time goes by—and personal treatment is always best. After all, you are the expert about yourself—no one will ever know you as well as you know yourself.

DESERVABILITY TREATMENT

I am deserving. I deserve all good. Not some, not a little bit, but all good. I now move past all negative restricting thoughts. I release and let go of all the limitations of my parents. I love them, and I go beyond them. I am not their negative opinions, nor their limiting beliefs. I am not bound by any fears or prejudices of the current society I live in. I no longer identify with limitation of any kind.

In my mind, I have total freedom. I now move into a new space in consciousness, where I am willing to see myself differently. I am willing to create new thoughts about myself and about my life. My new thinking becomes new experiences.

I now know and affirm that I am one with the Prospering Power of the Universe. As such, I am now prospered in a multitude of ways. The totality of possibilities lies before me. I deserve life, a good life. I deserve love, an abundance of love. I deserve good health. I deserve to live comfortably and to prosper. I deserve joy and happiness. I deserve freedom, freedom to be all that I can be. I deserve more than that. I deserve all good.

The Universe is more than willing to manifest my new beliefs. And I accept all this abundant life with joy and pleasure and gratitude. For I am deserving. I accept it; I know it to be true.

TREATMENT

Today is another precious day on earth. We shall live it with joy. No matter how I have felt about myself in the past, today is a new day. In this new moment in time, I begin to see myself in a more compassionate way. The criticism and judgments fall away; and as they do, I become free to appreciate all that I am. I think as if my life depends on it, for I know it does.

The door opens to love, my love for myself. This is the pathway for healing. I make this the sort of day I want to remember tomorrow. Today, I begin my journey of healing. We are one with the power that created us.

We are safe, and all is well in our world!

7

Our Negative Thought Patterns

Affirmation:
I move beyond all old limitations!

In no way do I want to create guilt for anyone. Yet we must understand how the mind works in order to make changes. No one wants to be ill, and yet we seem to need every dis-ease we create, for it is our body's way of telling us that something in our consciousness is out of whack.

It isn't as though we say we want such and such illness, but we do build the mental climate where such disease can take hold and flourish. Quite often we do this unknowingly. After all, weren't most of us raised to be fearful victims or bitter and resentful about life? I have heard parents say that their children had no right to be happy and that suffering was normal. If a parent stresses repeatedly that the child is no good and will never amount to anything, the child will grow up believing it to be true.

Most parents also believe and teach their children that illness is some evil that strikes us when we are not looking. The medical profession agrees, and then tells us that only they can do something for us. Religion is also a way we tell ourselves we're not good enough. Over and over again, our powerlessness is stressed. It is no wonder we are confused and enraged when we find ourselves in trouble or in ill-health.

I'm not saying that it has to be that way. We can take charge and make positive changes.

Were we ever told as children that our thoughts create our experiences? Or that we had the power to make changes and to create a good life for ourselves? Were we told how wonderful we were and that only a joyful and loving life awaited us? Were we told that we could prosper easily and success would be ours? We could have heard these things, and our lives would be much different now.

Let's not waste time blaming our parents; they did not know any better. We are our own parents now. We can tell ourselves all the positive things we did not hear in the past.

EXERCISE ON
NEGATIVE THOUGHT PATTERNS

Try this exercise. As you read the questions, really think about the truth you have created about your parents in the past. Then, think of the new truth you can create for your future.

Write down all the things you wanted your parents to have told you. All those positive, loving messages. Then read them aloud to yourself in front of a mirror. Do this daily until the messages become true for your inner child.

EFFECTS OF
NEGATIVE THOUGHT PATTERNS

Years of practicing the negative mental thought patterns—beginning with our thoughts about our parents, have worn down our immune systems. We also wear down the ability of the body to function at its optimum level by our poor choices of foods. If we add to this feelings of being unloved, unwanted, and alone in the world, we are ripe for the passing popular dis-ease of the moment. We have created almost epidemics of cancer, PMS, candida albicans, Epstein-Barr virus, and now AIDS is also flourishing.

When are we going to get the message? We are doing something wrong somewhere. We are not bad people. We are merely off-track. Let us not berate ourselves. Let us find out what we can do to heal ourselves. No one else will do it for us. We do have the power.

When you begin to think negatively about yourself or create problems in your life, it is helpful to go over some simple questions in your mind. Try to pinpoint exactly what it is that you need out of this experience. Then imagine how you could change it positively. Here's an example.

1. What are you trying to avoid by thinking/feeling this way—or by having this problem?
2. Who are you trying to punish?
3. What righteous feelings do you want to hang on to? Why?
4. What guarantee out of life do you want?
5. How much do you like self-pity?
6. What do you get from your pain?
7. What are you afraid of losing?
8. How does all this serve you? Is it positive?

Answer these questions as honestly as you can. You will find great insights from this.

STRESS: ADDING TO OUR NEGATIVE THOUGHTS

You know, we have all had "bad" days, where everything just seemed not to go "our way."

And when we are already in a rigid negative thought pattern these sorts of days can compound the negativity one-hundred times. This is not good for us. We already carry enough extra baggage around. We must learn to release these things and let them go. Some of the everyday stresses could be:

1. Your husband/wife/lover or best friend
2. Money in general or partnership finances
3. The dog/cat or whatever
4. My favorite—meeting a schedule
5. The work situation, employees or bosses
6. The car/bus or any type of transportation

Psychologists and psychiatrists have linked every physical illness, whether it be caused or enhanced, to stressors. The things mentioned above could easily apply to this. If we could only learn to release or even manage our stress, half the battle against our dis-ease, or our "bad" day, would be won.

EXERCISE ON STRESS

Try this exercise to relieve stress. Ask yourself these questions:

1. Could I really do anything to change that person?
2. What is the smallest thing I could do now to heal my finances?
3. Do animals ever know any better? They are so loving.
4. If I get into an accident on the freeway, will it get me there any faster? Did I make an empty promise? Whose schedule am I trying to live up to?
5. Is this job the best for me? Am I able to fulfill my

creative potential at this job? Am I trying to
break away? Do I like who I work for (or who
works for me)?
6. Could I do anything to make it on time? Could
I make sure I was on time? If my vehicle is broken, can I fix it?

Then we may want to ask ourselves some general
questions:

1. Did I learn anything from this "stressful"
situation?
2. What would I do differently if it were to happen
again?
3. Was it so bad?
4. Was there any humor in it?
5. Did I meet anyone new and wonderful from this
experience?

After thinking about these questions, take some
deep breaths and release them slowly—as if you were
releasing the stressors themselves. After all, that is what
you would be doing.

HUMOR

All of this is just one form or another of positive release of negative energy. Just as rationalization, crying,
anger, and yelling could be. Laughter—humor—is another powerful tool.

In my Wednesday night meetings, I have found that
being open to humor, planned or not, releases so much
pent-up emotions. In fact, I used to have a "laugh time,"
where we all took turns telling jokes.

And laughing, just letting it all out, is not such an

easy thing for some of us. Just as it is hard for some to tell us just what they think, so it is for others to laugh— because essentially it is the same thing. Here are some questions to ask yourself when you become angry or negative:

1. Isn't the situation just so ridiculous that you would want to laugh?
2. Doesn't he/she look just like a . . . ?
3. Who or what does this situation remind you of?
4. Can't we just laugh and let it go?

Remember, the power of humor is nothing to be taken lightly. Norman Cousins, in his book, *Anatomy of an Illness*, clearly outlined his use of laughter and nutrition to completely heal his body from dis-ease.

NEGATIVE PHYSICAL CHANGES

This is such a big lesson on loving ourselves. Knowing that we are more than our physical bodies. Look at how we react to the normal and natural experience of aging. We have set up rules about aging that make all of us lose. We have made it a failure to age, something to be despised and avoided at all costs. Yet all of us who do not die young will age.

As we approach what could be some of the best years of our lives, we look at ourselves with dismay, as the wrinkles and lines appear. It used to be that the aged were revered and turned to for their wisdom. Now we scorn the elderly and push them aside to die alone or in nursing homes. We don't seem to understand how this behavior that we give out can only come back to us. I shudder to think about how those who mug and rob the elderly these days will be treated as they too grow old.

Our bodies are suits of clothing that our personalities wear. Our souls selected these particular bodies to use before we came to the planet this time. They have nothing to do with our self-worth. Our self-worth comes from how we feel about ourselves.

If we have a physical illness and there is body deterioration, how we handle that depends a lot on how we feel about ourselves. If we have self-dislike or even self-hatred, then we will use this physical experience to further these feelings. If we are at peace with ourselves, if we love ourselves, then we will accept these changes and make the best of them.

There often comes a time for most of us, sooner or later, when we must ask for help. Our natural independency makes it hard to be dependent upon others, sometimes for the most basic needs. Yet, we can do it. It is a form of accepting love. I have heard many times from very ill PWAs, "I didn't know how many people loved me." Sometimes it takes a great illness to slow us down enough to receive the love that was always there.

Sometimes the illness proceeds to the point of dying. Then many of us feel a failure, as though we have done something wrong. As with aging, we have made death a failure, something to be avoided. The medical profession will use technical methods to force the body to hold onto life far beyond the body's capacity to do so. Death, like birth, is normal and natural. It seldom comes at what we think is the right time.

With life, we always come in in the middle of the movie, and we always leave in the middle of the movie.

When death approaches, we can accept it with peace. To fight what *is* only brings pain and suffering. This becomes a time for all of us to express more love. To be with the dying person and simply say over and over, "I love you, and you are safe," is the best thing you can do for them. If you are the one in the dying process, open yourself to the love around and know that you are safe. In spite of the scary legends we have created around death, every person who has come back from a death experience talks about the peace and the incredible love that awaits as we pass through the doorway from this planet to the next life, regardless of the circumstances of their physical lives.

While it is true that we have the power to defeat every type of illness that exists on the planet, it is also true that there is a time to discard the outworn body. Let us help each other do this with peace, dignity, and even joy. Joy can be found in every phase of life, from our first breath to our last. Let us make this a loving experience. Death, like life, can be a very simple experience—peaceful, surrounded by love, a gentle slipping through the doorway.

WHERE'S THE BLAME?

I have never wanted to blame anyone for anything. For I know we are all doing the best we can at any given moment. Yes, even our parents, when they were doing their numbers on us, even they were doing their best, according to the belief systems they had been taught. We deny our own inner wisdom by accepting others' negative opinions about us. And we are all equally responsible of voicing negative opinions about others. We condition each other to be less than we can be by the way we talk.

How many of us have said that men or women, or gays, or blacks, or the elderly, or the young, or this race or that religious group, or even people who dress in a certain way are not good enough. Those demeaning thoughts go out and return to us in kind. We need to be aware of the far-reaching laws of cause and effect and how our thoughts can affect us.

TREATMENT

Today is another precious day on earth. We shall live it with joy. I now choose to throw out of my mind and my life every negative, destructive, fearful idea and thought. I no longer listen to or become part of detrimental thoughts or conversations. Today, no one can harm me because I refuse to believe in being hurt.

No matter how justified it may seem to be, I refuse to indulge in damaging emotions. I rise above anything that attempts to make me angry or afraid. Destructive thoughts have no power over me. Guilt does not change the past. I think and say only what I want to have created in my life. I am more than adequate for all I need to do. We are one with the power that created us.

We are safe, and all is well in our world!

8

Punishing Ourselves: Drug Abuse, Alcoholism, Poor Diet

Affirmation:
I bless my body with love!

DRUG ABUSE

Drug abuse is so prevalent. It has become one of the best methods of escape we have. Drugs beckon to us with great temptation. "Come play with me, and I will give you a good time and make you feel good," the drugs seem to be saying. And it is true, for awhile, the drugs do make us feel good; they alter our reality. What is not evident at first is the terrible price they will make us pay. After taking them for a period of time, our health deteriorates rapidly, and we no longer feel good. In addition, we now have an addiction, craving the drug at any price and paying almost anything to get it. We will bankrupt ourselves, rob others, ruin relationships, and destroy our self-worth.

Drugs lower our immune systems to dangerous levels. Why would we even consider taking them?

Yes, there often is peer pressure, and that may get us to try drugs once. Repeated use is another story. I have yet to meet anyone who really feels good about themselves who takes drugs steadily. We take drugs to escape. Escape ourselves. Escape our feelings. To pretend we feel good. To hide that we are in pain. To give us false endurance to further abuse ourselves.

And it all begins with not loving and appreciating who we are. We take those childhood feelings of not being good enough and try to obliterate them. This method never works, for the drugs always wear off, and we feel worse than we did before, but now we usually carry the guilt for taking them in the first place.

ALCOHOLISM

This is an old method of escape. Alcohol is also used for celebrating and for relaxing, and these reasons can get out of hand very quickly for those who have little respect for themselves. Alcohol affects the liver. Both the liver and the gall bladder have to do with anger. The gall bladder is anger and bitterness against others. The liver is anger against the self, self-hatred.

People who are alcoholic are very unforgiving with themselves. Day after day after day, they punish themselves. They conjure up excuse after excuse to over-drink because the objective is to punish and abuse themselves. Why? Because somewhere along the line as children, they bought the idea that they not only were not good enough, but that they were bad and in need of punishment.

The gay culture has such belittling rules about aging that, taken together with an early acceptance that one is not good enough, contribute to the enormous amount of alcoholism among older gay men. It is so sad to watch as drink after drink reinforces their belief that they are worthless.

POOR DIET

We all know the foods that are nourishing to us. Every time you eat fast-food or candy, doesn't an alarm go off in your head. Or don't you hear yourself saying to your lunch partner, "I never eat THIS," or "Just this once."

Everyone knows the basics of good nutrition. Yet we use the diet as another way to punish ourselves—to create obesity or health crisis in our lives.

We have become a nation of junk-food addicts. We have allowed the big food processors and their advertising to influence our eating habits. There was a time when everyone knew what good food tasted like because it was everywhere. Now we have children and young adults who have never tasted real food. They have been brought up on canned, bottled, frozen, packaged, microwaved foods and chemical concoctions that are imitations of food.

It is normal and natural for us to want to continue eating the foods that our parents fed us when we were growing up. It is an old pattern, and it is also a way the child in us still feels loved. To change our basic eating habits often feels like a rejection of our parents.

Nowhere along the line when we were growing up did we receive good nutritional information. If we received any at all, it probably came from the meat industry, the dairy industry, the packaged food industry, etc., all promoting their own products. Unless we were raised in a family who understood good nutritional practices and fed us real food, we have no concept of which foods are really good for our bodies. Doctors are not taught about nutrition. If a doctor wants to learn about food and its effect on the body, then he must take additional courses on his own. The current accepted medical viewpoint is focused on surgery and chemicals.

So nutrition for us too has become a study we must take up on our own. By trial and error, we can find the foods that give us the best energy and make us feel good. Or we can turn to a good trained nutritionist who can guide us.

CASE HISTORY: JOHN

John first noticed a small purple lesion on his leg in April of 1984, so he went to the doctor to have it checked out. The doctor told him not to worry because it was not a lesion. Then John showed it to his roommate, who said that he had a friend with something just like that, and he had died a year later. Naturally, John returned to the doctor, and this time it was diagnosed as a Kaposi sarcoma lesion. Also, John had diarrhea for about four months, and it turned out to be cryptospiridia, which is an amoeba they supposedly have no cure for. John had never been sick; he had never had night-sweats; he had never had fevers, but on August 1, 1984, he was diagnosed with AIDS.

Thus started John's "quest for health." The first place he started was his diet. He decided on a macrobiotic approach, and for three months someone would come to his house once a week to show him how to prepare macrobiotic food. He was very strict about following this diet, but then he started slipping, "because I love sweets and I love beer." Also, John only had one more lesion appear," and that was because I wanted to see a Ken Russell movie, so I had some marijuana."

Today, John considers himself a macrobiotic who cheats. "When I cook for myself, I've got rice and vegetables in the refrigerator, but if I go to Marie Callenders, I'll have a pie. I don't eat meat regularly, and I don't eat dairy products."

Also, John used a macrobiotic cure to rid himself of the cryptospiridia. For three days, "I just ate a handful of raw rice and pumpkin seeds, a handful of raw garlic and tea." He also tried some spiromycin from Canada, but he thinks it was the macrobiotic cure that worked. He has even had four negative test results to prove that something has removed this supposed incurable amoeba from his body. John is also using amino acids to build up his cells.

As a result, John still feels fine. "No night-sweats, no fevers. I exercise. I run three or four miles. I'm tired afterwards, but I'm not short of breath. I do aerobics: I swim. So, I exercise. I feel fine." When asked if he felt that he had improved, John replied, "There's nothing to improve from. I haven't been sick. But my virus has improved. I've had four cultures taken at U.S.C. and U.C.L.A., and I think I have had four negatives. It doesn't say I don't have AIDS. What I think it means is that I'm not a carrier as much as some people, because if it is not in my blood, then it's not in my saliva or my semen or whatever, but I still have a wrecked immune system, so I'm still susceptible to infectious disease."

John considers himself lucky in regard to receiving support as well. It begins with his family. "My parents are very old, and they're both very sick themselves, but they're very supportive. I told them, and my mother said, "Nothing's going to happen to you; you come from strong stock. You have a strong constitution."

Outside of his family, John feels the greatest source of support is the Wednesday night group meetings. "First I got Louise's tape and played it every night for a year, before I went to bed, I even played it in the morning. I played various tapes. I went for private consultations several times. She made four tapes for me, which I play to this day. I've met a lot of AIDS friends and a lot of positive, wonderful people from the Wednesday group. My other friends are all very supportive. I have straight friends who are very supportive, and my gay friends are supportive. Everybody's supportive."

Visualizations and affirmations are also very important to John. "I relax and hold a crystal. Crystals magnify. I have three or four affirmations. You're supposed to repeat affirmations ten times to give them time. Mine are usually about my Higher Self being in charge of my life and my body and creating perfect health in my body, and about creative work I would love to do and about relationships. I visualize the T cells as recognizing the viruses, the bacteria, and fungi that enter my body, so they carry little shields and go through my blood fighting them."

He also visualizes his blood circulating through his body and filling him with white light and Divine Love. He also visits Eetla Sorrocco and Bill Cummings. "Eetla puts her hands on me and talks and gives me nutritional tips and checks out my aura."

John has also tried a number of other alternative therapies. He has visited Charles Whitehouse for about eight months to have readings done on his aura through cyclotronics, and according to the readings, his condition or "AIDS factor" is improving. He has also visited Dr. Clifton Aldridge, an herbologist who regularly tests John and gives him different herbs, depending on what seems to be wrong. Added to that, with counseling at Tamberlain and Japanese Shiatsu therapy, John is kept rather busy with his wellness.

When asked which of the different approaches he feels has been most effective, John replies, "I think nutrition is probably one of the most important, then taking care of your mind and your subconscious and your mental immune system, which Louise and Ava do. I just do it all, and something is working, whether it's my subconscious, my mother's constitution, Louise's subconscious, the radiotronics, the herbs.

"Right now I'm seesawing. I will eat macrobiotic food and eat a piece of cake or have a drink, and yet I'll always come back and do good positive things for myself. When I do the other things that I used to hate myself for, I try to love myself while I'm doing them so they don't do a whole trip on my head. Eventually, I think I will eliminate all of the negative things, all the drinking, all the sweets, all the things that are supposedly bad for me.

"Fear is a real minimal thing with me, which is lucky. I look at AIDS as a chance to grow. I felt I made it available to myself for three reasons: my mental immune system was down the last two years; I had also had a lot of drugs and antibiotics in my body for the last twenty years for gonorrhea, amoebas, etc.; and my recreational drugs, though not a lot, were enough to keep things in a weakened state. There's nothing I can do about the drugs that were put in my body over twenty years, but my mental immune system can get stronger starting now, and I have cut way down on the recreational drugs. I just drink a little bit. So I'm not afraid.

"I have no fear, but I've been lucky. I look in the mirror, but there's really nothing to get me afraid because I'm feeling healthy and I look good. I know I have it, but I'm not afraid. I'm accepting where I'm at, and it's very good on paper, and I can say it and it's real nice, but if suddenly something starts to pop up, then I might have a lot more fear. But I'm just going to try to accept myself right where I am, right here and now, and be grateful."

There is something we all can learn from testimony such as this. AIDS is not greater than faith—faith in yourself. AIDS is not greater than God. And if you are willing to believe that the faith that you have for yourself is good and it stems from God, many positive things must happen in your life.

TREATMENT

Today is another precious day on earth. We shall live it with joy. I respect and protect my body, because my health is important to me. My body becomes more precious to me with each passing day. I love the temple, the classroom, that I live within. I am deeply appreciative of every organ, muscle, joint, and every cell in my body. I use all my senses to increase my intimate connection with my physical self.

I bless my body. I am grateful for my body. I love my body. We are one with the power that created us.

We are safe, and all is well in our world!

9

Overcoming the Negatives

Affirmation:
With love, we can overcome anything!

We have been given all the necessary feelings to help us through a variety of experiences. There is nothing lacking. There are no good feelings or bad feelings. They are just feelings, and when we allow ourselves to experience whatever feeling is there at the moment, it passes. When we run from our feelings, they are always there waiting for us. Or we go numb and we get to the point where we do not even know what we are feeling.

Feelings are only thoughts in motion in our bodies. When we realize that we create our own feelings by the thoughts we choose to think, then we will have the ability to make different choices and create different experiences.

Sometimes we create the need to feel lonely. This usually stems from childhood fear. Another reason we are afraid of being alone is that we do not accept ourselves as people. How often have you said, "I want somebody to love me?" Well, you are somebody! If you don't have love in your life, it is probably because you don't love yourself. If you can't stand to be with you, why would anyone else want to be with you?

87

When people are really sick, they have power taken away from them by the doctors, the nurses, the hospital routines. To call people "victims" is to further debase them. Let us eliminate the word "victim" right now. People with AIDS prefer to be called just that, "people with AIDS" or PWAs. Each one of us has a right to have our dignity, no matter what the circumstances.

INITIAL REACTION
TO BEING DIAGNOSED

When first diagnosed, most people go through these reactions:

1. Fear and panic
2. Denial
3. Anger and depression
4. Helplessness

When someone is first "diagnosed," the initial reaction is fear and panic. This is normal and natural. You are coming up against the unknown. You have heard many horror stories. The popular prognosis is "terminal."

Then you often go into a stage of denial. "Oh, no, not me." "It can't be." "It's not my fault." And then the anger is turned inward and becomes depression. "I'll just sit and stare at the wall."

This may turn into a feeling of helplessness and hopelessness. "It won't work." "What's the use?" "Why try?" "I may as well just write my will and give up."

Sometimes regret will set in. This is a very destructive force. We'll say to ourselves, "If only I hadn't done this, I'd be well now." This is simply untrue. The fact of the matter is that the condition that you are in is a reflection of where you were at that point in time and space.

Acceptance is the first step toward inner peace and self-love.

It is normal and natural to go through these steps. It is also normal and natural to go beyond them. Let yourself have all your feelings. Cry, rage, sulk, let your body express what is going on inside. Then ask yourself, "What can I do to make it better?" That is when you reach out for help.

ANGER

There is so much anger with AIDS. Anger at the dis-ease itself. "Why me?" And then AIDS often brings up old angers that have been buried for years. Anger at our families for demeaning and belittling us when we were growing up. Anger at them for rejecting us when we did not fulfill their dreams. And for gays, anger at the parents for the unwillingness to accept their sexuality. Anger at the abandonment that often happens when AIDS is revealed. There is anger over all the current silly rules that say a person or a group is not good enough and therefore to be prejudiced against. Anger at the government and churches for allowing so many people to die because of moral prejudice. Anger at the slowness of bureaucracy.

Then there is anger at friends and lovers who turn away in fear; there seem to be so many who don't understand. We have anger at ourselves for creating the conditions that allowed AIDS to take hold in our bodies. Anger at ourselves for not having the answers at our fingertips. For feeling helpless. For having to be dependent. Anger at seeing so many of our friends and loved ones die.

There is great anger at doctors who don't have answers and often callously hand out death sentences. Anger at the enormous monetary costs for testing and for drugs that do not cure. Anger at health-care people for not doing more. Anger, anger, anger, rage and helplessness. What can we do with all these intense feelings? How can we handle anger in positive ways? Swallowing anger and letting it settle in our bodies is not conducive to our healing. We must let these feelings out.

There are several things we can do. Sometimes we can talk to the people we are angry at and release our feelings that way. Too often we cannot. Then we turn to other methods. We can kick pillows. We can beat the bed. We can scream in our cars or into pillows. We can hit a punching bag at the gym or even run or play tennis.

We can do a meditation where we let all of our rage flow freely and then forgive both ourselves and the others. We can talk or yell at the other person using a mirror. Whenever we let out rage at another in meditation or mirror work, we want to end by forgiving them and saying that what we really want is their love and approval. If we don't, then the exercise is just a negative affirmation and is not healing to us. There is a difference between releasing and just rehashing old angers. The act of forgiving helps you to let it go.

EXERCISE ON ANGER

Here is an exercise aimed at releasing the anger we so often feel:

Look into your own eyes in the mirror. See yourself or the person you believe has done you wrong. Let yourself feel the anger come through you. Begin to tell this person exactly what you are so angry about. Show all the anger that you feel you need. You could say something like:

1. I am angry at you because...
2. I am hurt because you did...

3. I am so afraid because. . .
4. What I would really like to do to you is. . .

Just get it all out. As you finish expressing your anger to this person, then say something like:

5. Okay, that's done, finished.
6. I release you and let you go.
7. What do I believe about myself that created this?
8. What belief could I change so that I will no longer be angry?

HAYRIDE ON ANGER

Voice: "I remember my first time here, when you say, 'This is my first night.' That is an amazing experience. I wasn't going to share tonight, because I get tired of sharing all the time. But I have to tell this story, because it fits in with doctors and all.

"Two days ago, I thought doctors were just. . ., well let's just say that I grew up seeing doctors drive Cadillacs. I thought that the only reason they wanted to be doctors was to be in the country club and drive Cadillacs. It was the easiest way to make money.

"So when my doctor saw me last week for a half-hour and did nothing but stethoscope and tap my chest, and then told me I am doing fine and billed me a hundred dollars, I freaked out. I was furious. I wrote him a letter and told him so and said, 'I am really outraged.' And he sent me back a very kind and thoughtful letter, which he typed out himself, saying he couldn't run a clinical practice based on just chest tappings. He felt the time and gentleness he gives to patients is a necessary item in the healing practice. I responded in rage. I wrote that, if I need to pay for kindness, I will hire a hustler."

Louise: "Oh, you are angry."

Voice: "Anger is a major issue for me. This was one instance where it was able to come right out. I rewrote the letter three times, telling myself, 'You don't really want to hit him this hard, because he has made a sincere gesture to do something nice for you.' But I get this here, so I don't want to pay for it too.

"However, I saw where he was coming from. I wrote three different letters around midnight that week, and each one became softer and softer, but the line about the hustler was in all three of them. I decided to go to bed and sleep on it, because I was too angry. It was really hard for me to do, because I am so impulsive. I slept on it.

"The next day, my mail came, and there was a note from my doctor giving me full income-tax exemption on all of the vitamins I have been taking through a nutritionist. He saved me about three-thousand dollars on my taxes with one note. I know he is not just about money. I am really glad I didn't send that letter."

Louise: "We can all learn something from our anger."

FEAR

AIDS brings us face to face with our biggest fears. Fear of loss. Fear of rejection. Fear of being helpless and alone. Fear of pain and, of course, fear of death. It is normal and natural that we experience these fears. We acknowledge that they are there, and we want to go beyond them. Remember, the fear you have about something is always worse than the actuality. Many PWAs say after their diagnosis something like, "It's really not so bad" or "I can deal with this thing." If we insist on living in constant fear, it is very debilitating to our immune systems, and it is a terrible way to live. When people with AIDS let their fear get out of control, I ask them what they were frightened of before they had AIDS. Usually there is a long history of reacting to everything with fear.

For the person who has AIDS, the fear of loss can be immense. There is a loss of independence. For many, there is a change in their physical appearance. There can be a loss of work identity. They may be experiencing anticipated loss of every person, place, and thing they love.

This is where the support group is so helpful. Yes, talk about your fears, not to dwell on them, but to find ways to put them into perspective. Find out from others how they handle their fears. Stay away from people with negative attitudes. You need all the winners and positive people you can find to be in your life now.

As simple a thing as breathing is helpful. Letting yourself breathe deeply and fully is relaxing to the body and to the mind. Do it often during the day. You can think much clearer when you are relaxed and won't immediately jump to the worse conclusion. Meditation works for many. The affirmation, "All is well," can bring peacefulness. When we change our attitude, our experiences change too.

It is important to discuss the eventuality of death. Regardless of who we are or what dis-ease we have, it is an experience we WILL go through.

What are your feelings about death? What do you believe will happen to you when you die? Were you raised in a hell-fire and brimstone religion? Do you really believe you will burn in hell forever? If you have accepted that concept, then you will be terrified to die. Are you willing to change that belief? You are a grown-up person now; you can make new choices about everything, even your religion. Create a concept about dying that really supports you. Then you can relax and live.

GUILT

Guilt is another emotion that we want to eliminate as quickly as possible. Guilt has no purpose whatsoever, except to make us feel bad. We don't need that at all. We are in the process of loving ourselves. Unfortunately, far too many of us as children were manipulated through guilt into good behavior. Consequently, we live under a mantle of guilt about something all the time. Or we feel we can only get others to do things by making them feel guilty. That is not a healing habit.

Then there are those of us who have accepted the guilt of not being good enough, for whatever reason. Perhaps we feel guilty because of our sex or our sexuality. We may have tremendous guilt for having AIDS. Whatever our guilt feelings may be about, it is time to let them go. The past is over and done; we cannot change it. Today we can let it go. Then let us take our energy and use it to find out how we can help ourselves heal. "I love and accept myself exactly as I am" is a good affirmation for releasing this kind of guilt.

RESENTMENT

Resentment is just anger that has been buried. Instead of expressing the anger in a positive way, we swallow it or feel we don't have a right to be angry, so we become resentful and maybe even depressed. The main problem with resentment is that it lodges in the body. In time, if we accumulate enough resentment, it begins to eat away at our organs or joints. Cancer is the ultimate result for long-held resentments. It is not worth it to hang onto these old hurts. Let them go. For our health's sake, if for nothing else. How to do this? Just use good old forgiveness.

An emotion that often accompanies our resentment is grief. Learning how to deal with this powerful emotion, and using it for our greater good, will benefit our healing process and make life in general improve for us and those around us.

GRIEF

These days, we are grieving at a rate we did not know was possible. Someone was telling me the other day that 140 of his friends had died. Can you imagine the loss and grief that must be involved with seeing so many of your friends die? Lovers are losing their partners. Parents are losing children. Many of those left find it hard to talk about their experiences, because of the shame we have created around this dis-ease. When someone you love dies, it takes at least a full year to go through the grieving process. If someone is dying every few months or weeks, how do you ever get out of the grieving process? It just becomes a continuum for us.

The grieving can be intense and overwhelming. We have to dig deep into our reserve strengths to cope with these issues. There are no easy answers. Each person finds his own way. Support groups and support buddies help to ease the pain. Allowing ourselves to experience a grief-releasing meditation can be helpful. There are now groups in most cities that specialize in helping those in grief situations to cope with the intense feelings.

When we have lost someone we love, we can look at it a different way. I believe we are always connected to those we love and can communicate with them at any time. They may be gone from the physical plane, yet still the connection remains on the mental and spiritual levels. What about our memories? Don't they still exist? Are they not truly realities for us?

Having left the earth plane, they are no longer

bound by our hang-ups and fears. They have a cosmic perspective on life everlasting. Their viewpoints have so broadened that they can give us advice that is not limited by human thinking. We see part of one lifetime; they see many planes of action and the interweaving of many lifetimes. We can talk to them, complete any issues we left undone. We can ask them for help on any problem. Ask them to help you through your grief. Your loss is only on the physical level; the other connections will always be there. Do not turn away from them; stay connected.

Nutritionally, we can also deal with grief. Through my studies, I have discovered a Bach flower remedy that is helpful for easing the pain that comes with grief. It is called Star of Bethlehem and can be found at most health-food stores. It is a flower essence, totally harmless, and can be used by anyone. A few drops are taken several times a day, and it helps to ease the pain. It doesn't change the situation, but it helps relieve the acute aching void for a time.

EXERCISE ON GRIEF

My friend Samuel Kirschner has written a wonderful exercise on grief:

"Breathe; inhale and exhale. Watch your breath; get in tune with it. Watch your feelings; watch your thoughts and accept them all.

"See yourself on a pathway in a forest. It's a beautiful day; there is a light breeze, rays of sunshine coming through the trees. You come to the bank of a river. As you approach it, you see a vast, large, long river. Continue breathing. As you approach the water, you see a reflection in the water—your reflection. The water starts moving, sending little waves, and your reflection becomes blurred. As you look up, you see a little boat, and on that boat there is a presence. And you immediately identify it as your spirit guide.

"The boat comes closer and closer, and your spirit guide invites you on the boat. You embark feeling very confident. The boat moves very peacefully down the river; the current is just carrying it. You feel very supported, reassured, and safe. As the boat keeps on drifting, the light around is becoming more intense. You can barely look up there because there is so much light. The light is feeling warmer and sweeter. You feel more and more drawn into the light. The light is pulling you in; you want to go into it.

"Now as you look up, you see a little island. The light is pulling the boat. As you approach you see a crystal palace, and the color of the light is now changing into a light blue. As the boat comes to the shore of the island, you see many presences. They don't have bodies; they are made of light. These presences assist you off the boat, and you are being carried by them with your spirit guide behind you.

"Now, you begin to recognize people you have known once and who have passed on, and they are all around the crystal palace.

You are being led into the palace, into a large room made of crystals. One by one, you recognize those who were dear to you and who left the planet; and now you have a chance to speak to them, and you tell them one by one everything you had not told them before they left. They reply to you. You can ask any question you want; they answer you willingly. They all seem very happy, very peaceful.

"You let all your feelings out, for it is safe and acceptable, and welcome. You tell them how much you miss them. You tell them how much they influenced your life, and how close you felt to them, and how difficult and abrupt their departure was. They understand and accept everything you tell them, everything you express to them.

"And you tell them how it is for you without them in your world. How afraid you are for yourself. You ask for their forgiveness, and you receive it so totally you forgive yourself. And your spirit guide supports you and comforts you. And there are still some more. . . . As you continue, you tell them their life was not in vain; you tell them how much they enriched your life, how much they meant to you. You ask them to stay in touch with you, and to guide you and to stay connected.

"You keep on breathing and moving through it. If you have parents you have lost, you meet them too—family members, friends, lovers. You keep on breathing. And now, you let all the grief out; the light will absorb it. It's okay to feel what you are feeling right now.

"If you need to, turn to someone and hold them. Allow yourself to be held. Begin to feel your chest expanding. Let more air in. Breathe deeply, and let it all out. Now come slowly to the end of the line of these beautiful light beings you have connected with. They are all waving at you with so much love. They are loving you and totally understanding you.

"You know you will be with them again, and yet you have to go back now. You are still in a human body, and you still have things to accomplish and lessons to learn and work to do. As you wave to them, you now know that you are safe and that they are safe, and there is no separation. You also know that, whenever you want to connect with them, you can return to the island with the crystal palace.

"With your guide you approach the boat once again. The light still is very intense and very tempting, but you must go back. Together you embark, and you drift back on the river. As you look back, the light is still very strong. The river washes all your tears, and slowly the light becomes weaker and less intense, and your spirit guide thanks you for your willingness to be human and takes you back to the shore. And you see a clear reflection of yourself in the water, and it is bright. You're back; the grief is gone."

TREATMENT

Today is another precious day on earth. We shall live it with joy. I am open and receptive to strength, happiness, and peace. I choose to build my life upon hope, courage, and love. I now accept all good as normal and natural for me. Love is a miraculous healing power in my world. Using love, I am in charge of the rebuilding of my life.

We have the power and the strength to overcome that which seems insurmountable. We are one with the power that created us.

We are safe, and all is well in our world!

10

Forgiveness: The Way to Personal Freedom

Affirmation:
I am willing to forgive!

FORGIVENESS

Our ultimate goal is love, and the gateway to love is through forgiveness. All through this book, you will notice that I return again and again to the subject of love and forgiveness. Yes, it is simplistic. And it works! Love is the healing answer. If we are having difficulty loving ourselves, it is usually because we are stuck in the forgiveness area. We go over our justifications and get into our self-righteous mode. We may be "right," yet we are not happy. We are stuck, and we may blame everything and everyone and not look at our own unwillingness to let go.

I want to share with you parts of a letter I received from a young man who at the very end of his life decided to forgive everyone and everything and was literally reborn.

I was diagnosed four years ago with Kaposi; fortunately, for the first three years, I had no external lesions. However, in January of this year, I started getting lesions in my mouth and on my face. By October of this year, I had well over one-hundred lesions on me.

After taking a weekend workshop with you, I began going to the New York Healing Circle and working with your teacher, Samuel Kirschner. In early October, I started getting very sick. I already weighed only 122 lbs (I'm 5'11") and was in bed all the time, having no energy to even move. I was racked with fevers and chills, and finally, when I could get up, I went for a chest x-ray and was told I had PCP. The doctor could not get me a room in the hospital that day, so he gave me Bactrim to take orally.

My lover and I tried everything to make those pills go down; we even crushed them and put them into small capsules, but I would always vomit them up. I was running a high fever and totally dehydrated. A few nights later, around 11:00 p.m., after continuous vomiting, I said 'enough.' I was through with medicine and pills and hospitals. If I was to die, then I was going to do it in my own bed, in my own way.

My lover and I made our peace. He let me go. He said, if it was easier for me to die, then he would support this. I then called my mother, who had been a real support and friend. I told her I was choosing to die naturally at home, and I needed her release to let go. She said, 'I cut the cord once, and I can do it again so that you can be reborn.'

I said goodbye, and I prepared to die. Then I went through all the people in my life, forgiving them and releasing them. I also worked through all my guilt, hate, criticism, fear, and other negative areas. I spent the whole night doing this. Then I felt light, and I just waited to go. It was obvious this body was not meant to function anymore. I did everything you suggested in your book, *You Can Heal Your Life*.

The next morning, when the sun came up, I was very calm and totally at peace. Suddenly I began to feel lots of energy. I was in a really good mood and began to sing. As the day progressed, I got stronger and stronger and felt better and better. All the time with this incredible peace over me.

That evening we went out to the Healing Circle, and I shared my experience with about seventy people. I was told I was glowing with light, and it was a magical evening. Now it is several days later, and I am stronger than ever. My lesions are clearing up and fading away, right before my eyes. My father has called me for the first time in years, and our relationship is totally healed. I now know that miracles can happen if (as you say) we are willing to do the work.

I have shared this letter with many people, for it is so inspiring. The benefits of forgiving can be as small as feeling a bit lighter and freer to miracles like this one. And we do not have to know how to forgive. All we need to do is to be willing.

The "willingness" to forgive opens doors and finds the way. Sometimes the other person will even call or bring up the subject so that you may both clear the air.

EXERCISE ON FORGIVENESS

All problems in our personal relationships can be linked to a lack of forgiveness for one or the other party involved. Let's dissolve this. And remember all you can and need to do is start with yourself. Here is a simple exercise to increase your awareness of forgiveness.

1. Ask yourself what is the hardest thing to forgive. Who is the hardest person to forgive? Why?
2. If you really wanted to forgive this person or event, you know you could. What is it that you want to hold onto?
3. What would you be willing to give in return for this negativity? Could you give understanding for abandonment? Could you give compassion for the abuse and betrayal? Could you just give forgiveness?
4. Are you willing to change your old beliefs of "I am worth abusing" to "I am worth cherishing?"
5. How willing are you to give up the old ideas for a new freedom that forgiveness could bring?

CASE HISTORY: NANCY

"They always say that God never gives you more than you can handle, and sometimes I wonder just how much more I can handle, but I always seem to find the strength."

The remark is typical of Nancy, who at forty is nothing less than a live-wire. She is not your typical Beverly Hills housewife, though she does live in a spectacular hillside home. She's a happily-married petite brunette with twinkling eyes. She is the proud mother of a beautiful, recently adopted, baby daughter. She is one of the founders of the AIDS Project Los Angeles and just received a humanitarian award for her tireless work and support. She also just received her own AIDS diagnosis.

In looking back at factors that may have contributed to her diagnosis, Nancy admits, "About five years ago, I was in the fast lane, and I really like to go out and have a good time. I did, at that point, run my system down and stayed up for days on end. I always enjoyed life to what I was thinking was the fullest."

She also admits that she had never been one to consciously practice good nutrition. Then there was her work with the APLA. "I had been involved with death and dying and was denying that there was stress involved in that. I wasn't letting myself grieve, so I was storing a lot up inside me at a time when I was wearing my immunity down in other ways. I did think, though, that because of my thoughts, my involvement, and my support of others, it wouldn't happen to me. Actually, when I got involved with AIDS work, I stopped most of my bad habits and replaced them with more rewarding things."

Nancy pauses and, almost under her breath, adds, "But I still like to go out dancing once in awhile. Mostly, I think my body was taking on a lot of stress, and I wasn't finding a release for it."

Early this year, Nancy injured her leg at the gym while exercising and then bumped into a chair, causing a hematoma to form. This developed into a staph infection, which caused her to be hospitalized for an operation so the injury could drain. "I think, at that point, what immunity I had was wiped out, especially considering the massive doses of antibiotics I was given."

She came home from the hospital, and the wound itself recovered fairly quickly. Then, after walking up the stairs one night, "I went, 'Oh my God!' I just couldn't catch my breath. It took me about five minutes before I was able to breathe. Prior to that, other than occasional diarrhea, I had no symptoms at all. I was really just feeling fine and very active, so the breathing was the only problem."

Nancy went to the doctor the next day for tests, which revealed the presence of pneumocystis in her sputum. She was hospitalized for ten days on Bactrim,

"Which I supplemented with heavy doses of megadophilus to coat my stomach, so that, as soon as the antibiotics took the good bacteria off my tummy, the megadophilus put it right back. I felt fine and recommend the megadophilus to anyone going through these treatments."

She came home ten days later, felt strong, and resumed her active life again. Then, as she was returning home with her husband from making arrangements for a cruise to Alaska, "I was feeling fatigued in the car, and my husband thought I was keeping time with the radio music, but I was really having a *grand mal* seizure. I was hospitalized, but it turned out to be a non-AIDS-related, freak, one-time occurrence.

Soon after her cruise, she started the experimental drug, Compound S. "I think it is turning out to be very effective in boosting my immune system. It has practically no side-effects, and is a pill I take every four hours. The profile you have to meet is very strict, so the drug companies are not letting many people try it."

About this same time, Nancy started getting high fevers. Then, on a trip to Santa Fe, she was hospitalized for dehydration. She came home when the doctors couldn't find anything, and then her temperature shot up to 106. "I went back into the hospital, and they told me to prepare for the worst. He asked me if I had anything to say to him. 'I'm not going anywhere,' I said. 'When we need to talk about it, we'll talk about it, but for now, I'm not going anywhere.'

"I had bad dreams, and during that crisis, I had a hard time focusing on my spiritual self. I talked to God a lot, but I didn't do the inner work that I normally would be doing every day. At the time, I needed it the most. I wasn't using it, but I still knew I wasn't leaving."

They found a bacteria called emavian and gave her some experimental drugs from the CDC that she will be taking for ten months, but today, "Thank goodness, I feel wonderful."

It is no surprise then that Nancy recommends the experimental drugs that she has been given. "I have noticed a tremendous improvement since taking these drugs. The infectious disease physician was amazed at how well I was just a week after I got out of the hospital. He said he was going to start using these drugs for other people, because I was doing so well. I told him it was also because I wanted to do well."

Vitamins and nutrition are beginning to play a major role in Nancy's wellness. She sees an herbalist and she is on a vitamin program. "I do take supplements of B,C, immunoplex, amino acids, and a multivitamin. I tend not to eat a lot of junk now, but I haven't really changed my diet yet. I do take barley green, an herbal stimulant, when I want a boost of energy, instead of a cup of coffee."

Nancy has found a great deal of support around her. "I have probably found the most support within myself. Also, I am fortunate to live with people who are spiritually in tune with themselves. I've had to remove myself from a lot of my friends who are still living the fast-life, because I'm envious, and I'm not strong in that area. I know that, for me to stay home and read and do other things is a little more helpful than the things I did before.

"Many of my friends who still go out are finding themselves spiritually, and I'm happy that they have found a balance. That's what you need, a balance in your life. I don't think any one thing is going to work. It's a combination of lots of different things. Since each individual human being is different, you can't say, 'Well, this is working for that person.' It may not be your thing, so I think it is important to find what your thing is."

Nancy also recommends surrounding yourself with as much love as possible. "I can't believe how much love I've found in my life. When I was in the hospital, the Church of Religious Science prayed for me every morning in their prayer-meditations. I think it's wonderful that people are willing to take the time for others."

For many months, Nancy couldn't find it in herself to talk to her family about her condition. "I think it was the fear of rejection and a lack of forgiveness, but when the severity of my last hospital stay became apparent, I thought I had better do it. They gave me tremendous support. They flew out two days after I went into the hospital, and they stayed until they were sure I was going to do fine. Now they call me every couple of days and are just wonderful. You have to tell your family when you are ready. When the time is right, it will happen."

Meditation and metaphysical reading was a part of Nancy's life long before her diagnosis, and has helped her realize the strength of her inner mind. "I first attended the Hayrides when they were still the living room, with only about ten people. There is something about Louise that is just so calming to me. Anyway, I meditate three times a day, and do affirmations as well. Sally Fisher and the AIDS Mastery have also been an inspiration. The teachings of Ernest Holmes, who began the Church of Religious Science, have been very good. Also the Course in Miracles has been helpful to me. Right now I'm reading *I Come As A Brother*, about the spirit Bartholomew, and it makes everything very clear.

"I've never had the peace that I'm finding now. I think, when you're faced with any life-threatening disease, you are forced a little faster to look at issues you keep putting off. I think this had to happen for me to take stock of things in my life, and until I've gone through all of these things, I'm not going to be ready to go in transition and find out what's next. I believe in reincarnation, and that has a tremendous peace of mind to it. Although I still have those days when I'm scared shitless, now I'm working on my mind, letting go of the fear and being in control of what's going on. I'm using my visual imagery to remove myself from what's going on in my body."

As for giving advice to others and to other women with AIDS in particular, Nancy thinks it is the same for everyone. "I can't think of anything that is going on with me that is any different from other people. Don't read statistics, and know that your issue is your issue. You can hear what is going on with other people, but it is a very individual thing. For me, with Kaposi sarcoma in my mouth, I've decided to do chemotherapy. Some people are telling me all these horrible things, but I also hear people telling me good, successful, hopeful things. Realize you are an individual, and it is a very individual thing. People are going to die, and people are going to live, and you have to take responsibility for whether you will live or die. Right now, I'm taking responsibility to live."

TREATMENT

Today is another precious day on earth. We shall live it with joy. No one can ever take from me that which is rightfully mine. Though I may not know how to forgive, I am willing to begin the process, knowing that I will find help from every corner of my life. I choose to forgive everyone who has ever done anything negative. This is my day of forgiveness. I forgive myself for all the past hurts towards myself or others. I free myself from all burdens of guilt and shame.

I move away from the past and live with joy and acceptance in this moment. They are free, and I am free. We are one with the power that created us.

We are safe, and all is well in our world!

11

Developing a Positive Attitude

Affirmation:
I choose to enjoy my precious day!

Living with AIDS is a big lesson in "accepting what is." It may not be an experience we consciously want at all. However, AIDS is here, and we may have it. After we have gone through the initial steps of fear, denial, anger, and hopeless resignation, then we need to move into a more positive phase. AIDS is a learning time. What can we learn from this dis-ease, and how can we improve our health? We can be angry at the dis-ease and use this anger to motivate us to do everything we can to eradicate it. We do not want to be angry at ourselves. Even if we see clearly how we contributed towards our illness, we do not want to compound our problems by self-anger.

MIRROR WORK

One of the things we can do is to practice daily mirror work. Sitting in front of a mirror, looking into our eyes lovingly and saying something like: "I love you, I really love you."

Do this first thing in the morning and last thing at night. Do it often during the day if you can. If uncomfortable feelings come up, just feel them, let them pass through. These are only the old thoughts you have let limit you in the past. These negative thoughts are being eliminated by the willingness to love yourself.

You could also go to the mirror first thing in the morning and say, "I love you. What can I do for you today to make you happy?" Then listen to your inner needs. It may be a small thing for that day. As you listen to yourself, you will begin to trust yourself and will find that it is easier to trust others.

If something happens that is unpleasant for you, immediately go to the mirror and say: "It's all right, I still love you." You want to always remember that your love for yourself is more important than any event that might occur. The event will pass; your love can be a constant.

If something wonderful happens, go to the mirror and say, "Thank you." Acknowledge yourself for the good in your life. The more you appreciate yourself the more you will have to appreciate.

Look into your own eyes and say: "I forgive you, and I love you." We all have things to forgive ourselves for. We are so hard on ourselves, so judgmental and critical. We beat ourselves up for every mistake, no matter how small. We can all use forgiveness on a daily basis.

Use the mirror for talking to others. You can tell people things you would be afraid to say in person. You can clean up old issues. You can forgive them. You can ask for love and approval.

Mirror Work in Your Personal Healing

Another way we can use the mirror is in our personal healing. The mirror always tells the truth about us. And when we tell it what we want, it can only reflect those positive things. You could start by saying something like:

"I am taking good care of you. Together we will do everything we can to heal ourselves. I am willing to learn whatever I need to learn. I am willing to change and to grow. I now attract to myself everything I need on the physical level to help me in this healing process. I bless this condition called AIDS with love, and I am willing to release it and let it go. I love my immune system and do everything I can to make it strong and healthy. It is easy for me to follow my new health practices. My body gets stronger every day. I feel better, and I look better. I am at peace. All is well in my world."

Beginning the day this way will put us in a more positive frame of mind. The only way we are going to find an answer for ourselves is to take a positive approach. We cannot wait for the medical profession to find its chemical cure. We must find out what we can do for ourselves that will strengthen our immune system. Good nutrition will strengthen it. Exercise helps, as do meditation and visualizations. A positive mental attitude is a great strengthener. And, of course, love, love for ourselves and for others, is the most powerful known stimulator of the immune system.

As I have said many times, the reason so many of us have problems with the mirror is that mirrors tell us the truth. We are aware what we really think about ourselves when we look into the mirror. If we don't love who we are, we will find it painful to look into our eyes. That's when we criticize our looks. I have noticed that even the most beautiful people will criticize their looks when they do not love themselves.

On the other hand, mirrors are one of the most powerful tools when we want to make positive changes in our lives. Just looking in the mirror, telling yourself positive things, or doing "mirror work," as I call it, cuts down the time involved in changing.

I have seen numerous people change their lives by merely looking in the mirror and saying "I love you, I really love you." At first, it seems untrue or even weird. This exercise can bring up anger or sadness or even fear. Still, if we continue to do this simple affirmation every time we are in front of a mirror, our inner energy begins to shift, releasing destructive thoughts and behaviors. In time, we find that we really do love ourselves.

You can use the mirror to tell people things you are afraid to say in person. Talk to your parents, lovers, bosses, doctors, anyone you need to clear things up with. Practice "coming out" or asking for a raise or telling someone that you love them or are willing to forgive them. It is amazing how you can clear the air; and when you next see that person, something will have shifted. If you are estranged from your parents, use the mirror to open the space between you. Look in the mirror and say to that parent, "Mom, or Dad, I want you to know who I really am." Then tell them. Tell them how wonderful you are. Tell them what you want from them. Tell them how you would like it to be between you. And always end by letting them know you want their love and approval. If you do that daily for two or three weeks and then call them or go and see them, you will be amazed at the change in them.

DEALING POSITIVELY WITH NEGATIVES

If you have AIDS or an AIDS-related disease, don't just make your goal to get back to where you were before you got ill. That was not a well place to be, or you would never have been able to get this disease. With the incubation period being so long, it is as if, after you have been exposed to it, the dis-ease sits around patiently in your system waiting for you to run your immune system down so it can then take over. Lots of people are carrying the dis-ease now and will never come down with it, because their immune systems are strong and will remain strong; or if their immune systems are in a weakened condition, they will probably not get run down enough to develop an AIDS condition.

So to deal with this, you want to get your immune system so strong that not the slightest cold would dare to take hold in you. It is your responsibility. Often we give our power away in looking for a pill to make us well immediately—only to return to the actions that caused the condition in the first place.

We look for wonder cures—the "magic bullet," the quick fix. With the dis-ease cancer, people look for laetrile or other remedies to make them well. Yes, these natural and chemical remedies can be good, but they are only one aspect of healing. Body, mind, and spirit must go together. If they were to find the wonder drug to knock out the AIDS virus tomorrow, would you really be healed and made whole? Or would you just accept the cure for your body and immediately go on with your old mental and physical lifestyle, only to create something else to put in its place?

This is your life. What you do with it is up to you. None of the therapies and healers will work for you unless you want them to. If you decide to take an active part in your healing process, do it with joy and love. You have a gift of learning about your own power. Many people I have met who have overcome AIDS are now willing to teach this power of self-healing to others.

CASE HISTORY: TOM

"On Sunday, August 19, 1984, at 8:00 a.m. sharp, the gun went off for the annual San Francisco Marathon. I and several members of my running club started the run with ten-thousand other marathoners. During the race, I thought about a purple spot on my cheek that had been there two months and wasn't going away. I ran a good race and crossed the finish line, thrilled to finish the distance for the seventh time.

"Shortly after the marathon, I decided to have the spot on my cheek biopsied. The report came back positive for Kaposi sarcoma. I remember sitting stunned in the dermatologist's office, thinking, 'This must be a bad nightmare.' Strangely enough, that bad nightmare has turned into the most alive, meaningful time of my life. Oh yes, I did have my thoughts of suicide, anger, depression, shock, and 'why me?' For the next twenty-four hours after the diagnosis, I had planned out my will a dozen times and even envisioned the funeral and who might come to it!

"That evening, I was given a tape narrated by Dr. Emmett Miller, *The Healing Journey*. As I listened to it, I suddenly felt in charge of my life again in a very positive way. The next morning, I went outside and noticed the palm trees, the blue sky, the flowers, and my own personal worth and love for myself, and realized what a priceless gift it was to be alive here on earth. My life shifted at that instant to enjoying the moment, here and now, more than ever before.

"My lover gave and continues to give love and support to me. When he learned of my diagnosis, his first words were, 'That doesn't change anything between you and me. I love you, and I'll be here for you.' That made my day! He has allowed me to follow the pursuits that are important to me and others and has handled the running of our home. I love him deeply and am grateful for his efforts.

"Since I felt physically well, I decided that my having this disease was going to make a difference in the world by inspiring hope in myself and others in the face of an illness that was scaring the entire world. My first plan was to revamp an already existing AIDS seminar to make it more positive, hopeful, and spiritual. It needed much more than the shocking data that painted a grim view of AIDS. My contribution was to expand the seminar from ten people to one-hundred and to start a grass-roots campaign through the audience to not give in to AIDS, and to create a belief that, united, we could enjoy life right now, despite the disease, and eventually create the end of AIDS. I produced four of these events.

"During this time, I met Louise Hay at a Gerald Jampolsky seminar. I immediately saw the love and the magic that she possesses and vowed to buy her AIDS tape and communicate with her regularly. She helped me see on a deep level that I was not bad for being gay and that sex was not bad (Not even the baths were bad.) I started seeing how I had bought into some people's view of those things and was punishing myself for it. After starting to let go of that, my life opened up far beyond what I thought possible. I started a cleansing diet, acupuncture, imagery, and I saw Louise on a weekly basis for counseling. Now I feel wonderful.

"Then another giant opportunity arrived. The City of West Hollywood and the Shanti Foundation called and asked me to be the race director for the first annual 5 and 10-K Run, with the proceeds from the event going to AIDS organizations. I accepted and immersed myself in the planning of the event, which was a total success. There were 850 runners and 350 walkers participating. Patty Duke, among others, used her celebrity status to heighten awareness of the need for funding and education about AIDS.

"Since I was starting to become a local celebrity myself, appearing on television and radio shows and in magazines, I finally decided to tell my family about my diagnosis. When I 'came out' to them in 1979, a war zone had been created, and I was afraid it was going to reoccur. They came to Los Angeles on the day of the race, from all over the country, not supportive of my gay lifestyle, but totally in support of me, their beloved family member.

"During the emotional opening ceremonies of the party after the race, I told the audience of two-thousand what it was like for me to have my family there for me on the biggest day of my life. I then told my family that I loved them. The mayor, the city council, Patty Duke, and the entire audience stood and applauded. I was 'at one' with everyone there. It was an incredible moment! Right after that, Mayor John Heilman presented me with a proclamation that commended me for the job I did on the race, the role model I had become for people with AIDS and for the community as a whole. I was proclaimed an exemplary citizen of West Hollywood. It was truly a peak experience!

"My latest project is that I'm training for the New York Marathon. I've been approached by *People* magazine, *Esquire*, and the *London Times* for feature stories. I will tell them my life's goals are to stand for living fully, loving, hope, and determination. I work to create these goals on a daily basis and to share them with others. I am grateful for my relationships with Doug, my parents, my family, Louise Hay, and the members of the gay community. I have learned to love myself, and that has opened the way to my realizing my dreams and knowing that I make a difference in the world."

Tom has since left the planet, but there is much we can learn from his positive approach to AIDS. Is any disease worth giving up on life for? Tom lived every minute of every day. And so too can we all.

TREATMENT

Today is another precious day on earth. We shall live it with joy. Positive healing thoughts are what I choose to think about. Just as all the stars and planets are in their perfect orbit and in Divine Right Order, so am I. The heavens are in perfect alignment and so am I. I may not understand everything that is going on with my limited human mind; however, I know that, on the cosmic level, I must be in the right place, at the right time, doing the right thing.

This experience is a stepping stone to new awareness and to greater glory.

We are one with the power that created us. We are safe, and all is well in our world!

12

Getting to Know Your Immune System

Affirmation:
My immune system gets stronger every day!

Our immune systems are the guardians of our bodies. They are efficient and loyal. These systems have been working since before we were born. They destroy invaders and keep us healthy. To have and to maintain good health, we need a strong immune system. Have you ever thanked your immune system? If not, take a moment and do it now.

We are learning that love is the most powerful known stimulant of the immune system. If love boosts the immune system, then what drags it down, what depletes it? Resentment, fear, depression, rage, jealousy, despair, self-pity, rejection, regret, and self-hatred. How often and how long do you indulge in immune depleting emotions? It is normal and natural for all emotions to briefly flow through us at appropriate times. However, if you are choosing to stay in depleting emotional states, then you are not helping to heal your immune system.

How do we change our immune systems? By changing ourselves. By changing our image of ourselves. By loving who we are. By being willing to let go of the past and to forgive. Our bodies always reflect the state of our consciousness at that particular time. Remember, as we change our beliefs, we, both physically and emotionally, must also change. As we change, we often no longer need the old dis-ease. It is all part of making ourselves whole and of healing ourselves.

If we have a habitual, negative thinking pattern, now is the perfect time to change this pattern. As we release one thing, something new needs to go in its place. We could do something like this. Be willing to replace:

resentment	with	understanding
fear	with	peace
depression	with	forgiveness
rage	with	love
jealousy	with	rejoicing
despair	with	hope
self-pity	with	self-responsibility
rejection	with	acceptance
self-hatred	with	self-love

We begin the process with conscious choice. When we notice ourselves feeling resentment, we say, "No, I choose to have understanding." If we are depressed, we become willing to forgive. If we are in a state of rage or anger, we are willing for that to turn into love. If we are jealous, we are willing to rejoice for another's good fortune. If we are in despair, we are willing to be hopeful. Instead of sitting in self-pitying victimization, we become willing to take self-responsibility. Our rejection can turn into acceptance. And self-hatred can become self-love, if we are willing to let it be.

No, it won't all happen in a day. The old patterns don't go away quite so quickly. Remember, these patterns have been built up inside us for many years, so it will take time to replace them. Yet, as we continue to practice, the results become cumulative. After awhile, we find ourselves thinking differently. We notice our reactions to events are more peaceful. We don't seem to get as upset as we used to. And the events also are changing. We bring more positive experiences into our lives. All this is a positive stimulation for our immune system and for the health of our body.

CASE HISTORY: PETER

"I am an artist, and I express myself through my life with everything I do. I think everyone could express themselves and not hold things in." Peter is one of the few men around who can get away with this statement. Physically, he is a work of art. He is continually pursued by photographers who wish to use his good looks in their art. A modeling career would be an effortless pursuit for Peter, but he has different things to do. He will soon be starting on a project of a three-part giant mural at the Hollywood Bowl that will raise money for the AIDS Project Los Angeles.

Things were not always like this, however. Six years ago, Peter went through a health crisis that turned his whole life around. "I really feel that my illness was caused by my mental state and that I was playing the role of victim. Then it was too early to see if it was AIDS or ARC, because no one knew about it then. But who knows. That wasn't really the point. The point was I was at a stage in my life where I was very ill, and I was faced with the decision to live or die."

Peter had chronic mononucleosis for about six months, and the lymph glands in his neck, under his arms, and in his groin became tumorous. He got better, and then about four months later, his condition relapsed. He experienced severe weight-loss, night-sweats, dizzy blackout spells, numbness, and a sense of being continually weak. During this time, Peter was going from doctor to doctor, who could do no more than give him tests. He lost his job. He was in a destructive relationship, and his self-esteem was suffering. "I was a victim. All these things took a toll. I wasn't happy with myself, my life, or my relationship, so I got sicker. Basically, my state of being was not liking myself."

His weight dropped to 124 pounds. (He is over six feet tall.) He lost his color and started turning gray. He lost faith in his doctors, because they "didn't seem to know what was going on." It was at this point that Peter visited an iridologist, someone who reads eyes. "Eyes are the windows of the soul." He saw that Peter's body was very much off balance. The iridologist agreed to work with Peter, provided he was willing to make a commitment to his own wellness.

The treatment began with a seven-day fast of carrot juice, distilled water, and herbs. Peter's system was very compatible to the carrot juice, and it helped rejuvenate him. He got his color back. He then changed his diet by concentrating on mineral intakes through certain foods that would rebuild his body. During this time, he was also going for colonics. "When you fast, you start a process called autolysis, or self-digestion. The first thing to be digested is weak or diseased cells." At the same time, the pancreas sends enzymes to attack them as well, and there was some concern that Peter's pancreas wasn't secreting enough, so he was carefully monitored by regular visits to his nutritionist.

This whole method of treatment appealed to Peter, because it involved him directly in his wellness. "When you go to a doctor, you wait for him to tell you what is wrong, and you feel so powerless. He may give you drugs or antibiotics or nothing." In Peter's case, he was given antibiotics that did nothing to prevent severe yeast infection in his throat. This too was corrected through nutrition.

During this period, the medical doctors biopsied one of the lumps in Peter's groin, and it was found to be tumorous but benign. This marked the real turning point in Peter's illness. The doctors labeled Peter's condition as a lymphomatic disorder, or lymphoma. One of the first things he did as a result was to totally remove himself from the medical doctors' care. "There was a fork in the road, and all of a sudden there was another alternative—these nutritionists. I went to them, because they gave me hope. I was able to turn things around."

It was also during this time that Peter discovered that the path to health required a unified effort of his mind, his body, and his spirit. His nutritionist was a monk, so he was getting spiritual advice as well. "When you have an illness, it poisons your mind, and your mind is so powerful that, if you don't have that love of life, it takes a toll. When you come from that space of love, your body will respond and protect itself. I made a commitment to my mind, body, and spirit that, when I got better, nothing like this was ever going to happen to me again."

The road back to health for Peter, therefore, included work on all aspects of his life. He started learning about nutrition and taking the time to prepare the right foods for himself. He got a new job that he really loved. He started going to a gym, working out, and gaining weight. He left his lover and moved back in with his parents. "It was a time of awakening for me. I started to grow and rebuild my life again."

An important part of his commitment to himself was to heal his family and reestablish the love that was there. He had not been speaking to his parents, because they had a difficult time accepting Peter's sexuality. "In a way, my illness brought us together, because they realized it was better to have a gay son than a son who was dead. They raised me, but they don't have to live my life. We are a part of each other through love. So now I talk to them regularly, and we support and love each other. That was a big plus in my healing."

As important to Peter that others accept his sexuality was accepting it himself. "I wouldn't have my life any other way. I don't want to be straight. Part of loving myself is accepting my sexuality, accepting being gay, and being happy with it. I've been gay all my life. I was born with it. That's just the way I was, and I'm very comfortable with it. When I was a child, I was very sensitive, and because of that I was a loner. I didn't fit in with the other kids, and I was made fun of a lot. I have finally realized it wasn't me, and I stopped listening to their criticism. I stopped letting their making fun of me take a toll on my body. When I finally realized I was okay, I was able to heal myself."

When asked about spiritual teachers, Peter thinks that the strongest influence on him was his own inner voice. It is a voice that is present in everyone, and more people could learn how to open themselves to it. "It is very important, because we're entering a new age, and love is what so many of us yearn so deeply for. Yet, when it is in front of us and within our touch, people will not grasp it. There are so many people running to the various groups, trying to find the answers to life. It bewilders me, because you may look high and low, far and near, yet the answers lie within yourself."

Peter acknowledges the presence of many wonderful spiritual teachers, but thinks too few people are willing to give themselves credit for finding them or even looking for them. "I have carried my spiritual guides with me throughout my life. I have always had the voice within me. You have to make that peace within yourself; otherwise, your whole life will be in turmoil, with your mind telling you one thing and your heart another. Now I listen to both, but they listen to each other. I have always been one to go with my heart, and the more I trust in that, the more I am spared a lot of mistakes in life. It makes life more effortless."

Peter also stresses the importance of forgiveness, especially when he describes himself as someone with the curiosity of a cat. "I want to experience everything. Then you can make choices, not out of ignorance, but out of knowing. Going through life with blinders on is missing half the ride. When you're on your path and you stumble, get back up and forgive yourself. It's all a matter of choices. You choose to live in heaven or hell, and everything you do is reflected in that choice. It's not right or wrong. It's just choice. I've lived in hell, and it's just not for me anymore."

Peter's mural will be titled, "Blue Moon Trilogy." The first part he calls the "Eve of Conception," and it stands for the new awareness that health and happiness comes from the love within ourselves. "AIDS has truly given urgency to this new awareness." The second part will be called "Dawning of a New Age," and it stands for the time when the doors to self-discovery, support, and love are opened and people understand "the tremendous healing powers we all possess." The final part will be called "A Glorious Revelation," and Peter sees that happening right now.

"The more we all unite, the more quickly we will find the answers we all seek to heal the dilemma we face. We are all one, and by joining together in love, nothing will get in the way of this tremendous healing force."

TREATMENT

Today is another precious day on earth. We shall live it with joy. I know love is the most powerful known stimulant of the immune system. So I do everything I can to increase the love I have for myself and for others. I willingly release all negative thought patterns that deny or suppress this flow of love. I am completely immune to all negative ideas or experiences around me. I have no time to waste being unforgiving or resentful.

Today, I release my illness, for it is no longer of any use to me. I now affirm that every cell in my body is responding to a new strength. Every moment of this day, I am being renewed. We are one with the power that created us.

We are safe, and all is well in our world!

13

Relaxation, Meditation, Visualization, Affirmation

Affirmation:
I have the tools I need to help myself!

RELAXATION AND MEDITATION

Relaxation is essential for the healing process. It is hard to allow the healing energies to flow within us, if we are tense and frightened. It only takes a moment or two, several times a day, to allow the body to let go and relax. At any moment, you can close your eyes and take two or three deep breaths and release whatever tension you may be carrying. If you have more time, sit or lie quietly and talk your body into complete relaxation. Say silently to yourself, "My toes are relaxing, my feet are relaxing, my ankles are letting go," etc., working all the way up your body, or you may begin with your head and work down.

At the end of this simple exercise, you will be peaceful and calm for awhile. Repeating this often can create a peaceful state within you, most of the time. This is a very positive physical meditation that you can do anywhere.

As a society, we have made meditation into something mysterious and difficult to achieve. Yet meditation is one of the oldest and simplest processes we can do. Yes, we can make it complicated, with specialized breathing and ritualized mantras, and those meditations are fine for advanced students who wish to have those experiences. Still everyone can meditate now; it is easy to do.

All we have to do is to sit or lie quietly, close our eyes, and take a few deep breaths. The body will automatically relax; we don't have to do anything to force it. We can repeat the words "healing" or "peace" or "love" or anything that is meaningful to us. We could even just say, "I love myself." We can ask silently, "What is it I need to know?" Or "I am willing to learn." Then just be there quietly.

Answers may come immediately or in a day or two. Don't feel rushed; merely allow things to happen. Remember, it is the nature of the mind to think; you will never completely get rid of dashing thoughts. Allow them to flow through. You might notice, "Oh, now I am thinking fear thoughts or anger thoughts or disaster thoughts or whatever." Don't give these thoughts importance; just let them pass through like soft clouds in a summer sky.

To uncross your legs and arms and have your spine straight, if possible, is said to improve the quality of the meditation. Maybe so. Do it if you can. What is really important is to meditate on a regular basis. The practice of meditation is cumulative: the more regularly you do it, the more the body and mind responds to the benefits of relaxation, and the quicker you may get your answers.

Another easy method of meditation is to simply count your breaths as you sit quietly with your eyes closed. Count one on the inhale, two on the exhale, three on the inhale, and so on. Counting your breath from one to ten. When you exhale on ten, just begin again at one. If your mind wanders and you find yourself counting up to eighteen or thirty, merely bring yourself back to one. If you notice your mind fretting about your doctor or medications or doing a shopping list, simply bring yourself back to the count of one.

You cannot do meditation incorrectly. Any way you first attempt meditation is perfect for you. You can also find books that will teach you several methods. You may go to a class that will give you the experience of meditating with others. Begin anywhere. Allow it to become a habit, if you can.

If you are new to meditation, I would suggest you begin with only five minutes at a time. People who immediately do twenty to thirty minutes soon get bored and skip it entirely. Five minutes once or twice a day is a good beginning. If you can do it at more or less the same time of day each time, the body begins to look forward to it regularly. Meditation gives you small periods of rest that are most beneficial to the healing of your emotions and of your body.

You see, we all have tremendous wisdom within us. Inside of us are all the answers to all the questions we shall ever ask. Unfortunately, most of the time, we are so busy running around creating the soap opera and drama we call our lives that we can't even hear our own wisdom. Meditation creates the space where we can quiet down and listen to our inner selves. You have no idea how wise you are. You can take care of yourself. You do have the answers for you. Get connected. You will feel safer and more powerful.

VISUALIZATION

We do visualizations all the time; it is the same as imagining. We picture or imagine things that have happened in the past or things we wish to or fear to have happen in the future. Everyone can visualize or imagine things. If you don't believe it, close your eyes and describe your bathroom. Of course you can do this, and that is visualizing.

When we talk about "doing a visualization," we

mean to create or describe a positive mental picture of an event we wish to have happen. We can all do that, and it works.

People have written whole books about visualizations and their benefits in healing dis-ease. Dr. Carl Simonton and Shakti Gawain base most of their work on visualization methods. Go to a library and read all you can on this subject. You see, the body, which is by nature an accumulation of effect, must follow the mind, which is the causal form of such effect. As we change our mental pictures, physical changes must occur. This can be positive or negative, depending on the way we think or imagine, and these changes will happen in our experiences and in our bodies.

There are many images and visualizations we can use to connect mentally with our bodies. It is often best to use images that appeal to the child within you. It is not necessary to know technically how a particular body part looks or acts. A visual image is fine. PacMan is a favorite image for eating diseased cells. I used an image of cool, clear water flowing through my body, washing away debris, when I had cancer. Your immune system could be an army that protects you, or a cleaning crew, or gardeners pulling out weeds, or any image that appeals to you.

A positive visualization will have three parts:

1. An image of the problem or pain or dis-ease, or the dis-eased area of the body.
2. An image of a positive force eliminating this problem.
3. An image of the body being rebuilt to perfect health, then seeing the body move through life with ease and energy.

When there is a physical problem, it is best to create a visualization that has meaning to you. Then take a few minutes three times a day to sit down quietly. Relax your body with some deep breathing. Allow yourself to become peaceful. Perhaps you could play some soft music. You might have your visualization on tape, or you may just run it through your head. When you are finished, give yourself a few moments to absorb this positive experience. The cells in your body will be responding to your mental images. Repeating the visualization often reinforces the effects. Don't be concerned if you can't visualize. Just think it through. It will work anyway.

This is one I particularly like for building T-cells within the immune system. You could alter any part of it to suit your preferred mental images.

T-Cell Visualization

We know how wonderful your body is. It is a beautiful miracle. Your body is so intelligent. Your body is so smart. Your body knows how to help the healing process. Your body knows how to build T cells. Your body has been building T cells since it was first formed. Let us go to that center within you where T cells are created, the T cells building center. Let us re-employ the workers in this T cell building center. The factory may have been idle for awhile, but now it is re-opened. We are hiring many new workers, row upon row of them, all ready and willing and able to create the best T cells. These workers specialize in creating the most healthy, happy, efficient, and capable T cells. The workers are prepared. Their equipment is in tip-top shape and all is ready. The whistle blows, and it's time to go to work.

You have hundreds of workers within your inner factory now, most efficiently and swiftly creating perfect, new T cells. See each new T cell as it comes off the assembly line. Notice its perfection. Notice its health. Notice its strength. Notice how willing each T cell is to go do its own work.

All right, remember you are the owner of this factory. You are in command. See that these new T cells have the best of everything. The best atmosphere for working, good air to breathe, the best food, the finest clothing, the best equipment. Let them be surrounded with love and joy. Let them know you appreciate them. They are the best, and you treat them in the best way.

Now direct these new T cells to their post. Tell them it's time to work. See them marching off to their stations. They are happy, healthy, and strong. They have endless energy, and they love you. They want to do their best for you. They are your protectors.

The T cells are now at their stations. They are sensing the locations of the virus. The battle cry is sounded, and off they go. It is not necessary for you to go with them. These T cells are the best professionals, and they know exactly what to do. They are even now eliminating everything that does not belong in your bloodstream. You are permeated with T cells that love and care for you. They are caring for you right now. Relax and allow it to happen.

When it feels right you can come back to this room, knowing that your body is being taken care of. All is well in your world.

This is not the only visualization. The best ones come from inside you. Do not be afraid to develop your own special healing tools. Some people imagine a huge eraser, just eliminating the virus. Others envision a Pac-Man, gobbling up the virus. Do what is best for you. You will always know exactly what you need.

Remember, you have a wonderful imagination; put it to use in a positive way to contribute to your healing. Don't waste your time imagining the worst scenario, when you can use that same energy to create a positive viewpoint, which in turn can help to create miraculous changes for yourself.

AFFIRMATIONS

Affirmations, like visualizations, are something we do all the time. Affirmations are the words and sentences we think and speak all the time. We do affirmations from morning to night. What was the last thing you said to yourself just before you went to sleep last night? That was an affirmation, and it contributed to the quality of your sleep and dreams. What was the first thing you said to yourself this morning, when you first woke up? That too was an affirmation and began your day. We usually have many more negative affirmations running through our heads than the positive ones.

When we talk about "doing affirmations," we mean creating definite statements to make the positive changes we desire in our lives. Of course, affirmations are not true when you first say them. If they were already present in your life, you would not be doing an affirmation to create them. An affirmation is like a seed planted in the ground and takes time to grow into its potential. Repetition makes the affirmation grow from a seed to a flower in full bloom. Don't block your own good by saying, "Oh, I did that affirmation three times, and it didn't work." Give yourself time to create the new. Begin and practice.

Every thought we think and every word we utter is an affirmation. Far too often they are negative, and we are not aware that these words are shaping our future experiences. However, when we talk about "doing affirmations," we mean creating specific sentences to bring something new into our lives or to eliminate something we no longer want in our lives. How we do this is important. If I am working in a job I do not enjoy and want to have a new job, I cannot use the affirmation "I hate this job" and expect any good to come of it. "I hate this job" is a negative affirmation and will only keep me stuck where I say I don't want to be. "I hate this job" will not bring to me a wonderful new job.

If you leave something with anger and hatred, you will create anger and hatred in the new place, for that is what your subconscious mind will think you want. This is true for jobs and relationships and bodies. If you hate your body, it will be harder to bring a lasting healing.

The positive way to getting a good, new job would be to say something like this:

"I bless this job with love, and I now release it to someone who will be glad to have it and will do an even better job than I have. I now open myself to a wonderful new job that is creatively fulfilling. Working in a beautiful place, with compatible people, and earning a good income. There is someone out there looking for exactly what I have to offer. We are being brought together now in a most delightful way. I give thanks that this is so."

Or you could simply say, "I release this experience with love and now open myself to a wonderful new job."

Sometimes short sentence affirmations are the most helpful, for they can be repeated over and over. "I now accept a wonderful new job," said throughout the day, will tune you in to new opportunities. I like to sing them or make my affirmations into a jingle and let them play in the background of my mind. Some people write them ten, thirty, or a hundred times. Whatever method you use will work, if you let these affirmations replace your negative thinking about a subject.

"I am willing to forgive" is a great affirmation. We all have so much forgiveness work to do, and most of us don't want to forgive at all. Saying we are "willing" to forgive opens the way for us to release much of the past.

If we are fearful, we can begin to repeat, "I allow myself to be at peace." This affirmation tells your subconscious mind that you are in charge and are willing to create a new atmosphere. "I am not afraid" would not be a positive affirmation to use in this situation. You are afraid at the moment, and that affirmation is not putting anything positive in its place. An affirmation must always replace the negative with the positive. You pull out the weed and plant the new flower at the same time.

If we are resentful, we can begin to affirm, "I am willing to move beyond this experience." Or "I am will-ing to forgive." We then give our subconscious mind (or our inner self or the Universe, however you want to call it) the permission to find a new way to move beyond the old experience.

When we are working to restore good health, then we can use affirmations like these:

"I am at peace with my body."

"I accept for myself perfect health."

"I love my body and allow it to heal."

"My T-cell count goes up every day."

"I am strong and immune."

"I am fearless in the presence of all negative sit-uations."

"My spirit is perfect, whole, and complete."

"My body reflects the perfection of Spirit."

"My hair is luxurious and strong, growing from a healthy, relaxed scalp."

"The food I choose is high quality and nourishing to my body."

"I eliminate all waste products from my body with ease and with perfect regularity."

"My glands are the perfect keepers of my system."

The purpose of doing affirmations is to free ourselves and to create a better life. They are not a punishment nor a drudgery. Do your affirmations with joy and with enthusiasm; they will work faster. Above all, do them. Be conscious of your words and expressions, for they too are your affirmations.

PRAYER

The power of prayer has been used forever. For some, it is natural to turn to prayer in times of need.

I would suggest that when you pray, do it in a positive manner. Beseeching an angry old man in the sky will not provide good results. Feel your oneness with the Universe and all that is, before you begin to declare your desires. Imagine yourself in partnership with your God, and together you will work out the solution.

TREATMENT

Today is another precious day on earth. We shall live it with joy. Today I am a new person. I relax and free my thoughts of every sense of pressure. No person, place, or thing can irritate or annoy me. I am at peace. I am a free person living in a world that is a reflection of my own love and understanding.

I am not against anything. I am for everything that will improve the quality of my life. I use my words and my thoughts as tools to shape my future.

I express gratitude and thanksgiving often and look for things to be thankful for. I live a thankful life. We are one with the power that created us.

We are safe, and all is well in our world!

14

Healing the Family

Affirmation:
We are all a part of the family of love!

I believe, just as children choose their parents, so do parents choose their children. Children are great teachers and great bearers of gifts. Lifetime after lifetime, we return to further our spiritual education and growth. We interreact with the same souls over and over again. We are always working on a new aspect of our growth. When something is left unfinished in one lifetime, there will be an attempt to complete it in another.

So there are interesting questions to ask: What were the choices we made before this present incarnation? Why would someone choose to be gay in this lifetime? Why would a gay person choose his particular parents? Why would those parents choose, on a cosmic level, to have the experience of having a gay child? What is the lesson they have all come to learn? Why would a child choose to incarnate at this time, when there is such an opportunity to experience the condition called AIDS?

How do we handle the guilt of rejecting a child because it is not "just like us" or has a dis-ease we are frightened of? Why do we shut our hearts? What does this do to the ones who are rejected and to the ones who do the rejecting? What will their patterns and lessons be in the next lifetime they meet?

It is easy to reject what we are afraid of. We often run from our lessons, even though we know on a deep inner level we will meet them again down the line. We cloud this consciousness with questions like: "What will the neighbors think?" "Will they reject me if I proclaim my love for my child who is different?" "Are my values in outer appearances rather than with those I love?" "Where are my priorities? And who do I owe them to?"

There are no right or wrong answers to these questions. It is an individual pathway for all. Some of us have come here to experience rejection or pain or loneliness or dis-ease. These are all opportunities to choose love again and to advance spiritually. I do not believe we need to stay stuck in any of our negative choices. We are able to follow the message of the heart and transcend any negative experience that might result.

AIDS IS A GIFT

For parents of people with AIDS, know that this is a gift you have been given. It is an opportunity for you to experience your ability to give love. To go beyond appearances, to go beyond what you see in the body and to express the vast love you are capable of giving. Families who open their hearts and their arms to their children are experiencing great healings themselves.

The most important thing you can do for your children, with or without AIDS, no matter what age, is to love them unconditionally. To keep the lines of communication open so they may tell you anything without fearing your disapproval. Yes, they are different from you, and you are different from them. You can still love each other and support each other and grow from all your experiences.

When I hear parents complain that their children are grown up now and never call them anymore, I wonder when the parents cut the lines of communication. A child can only be told so often, "Don't say that," "Don't think that," "Don't do that," "Don't be like that," without pulling away and keeping their lives secretive and private. When we are made wrong for who we are, we stop communicating. Too many families have limited their conversations to food and the weather. Other subjects bring up disapproval. This is not experiencing love and joy.

Just as gay people have been closeted, so have their parents often been closeted about having gay children. They both share a similar pain. Shame and guilt take a terrible toll. Coming out of the closet, for both children and parents, enables the love to start flowing once again.

CASE HISTORY: ANDREW

"I was diagnosed with Burkitt's lymphoma, Kaposi sarcoma, and as a result AIDS on January 10, 1984, at which time I went into immediate treatment at Cedars-Sinai Medical Center in Los Angeles. I was first admitted for about a month and a half, then I was released for two days. Then I was back in for three weeks, and it went like that for twelve admissions, for a total of five or six months altogether in 1984.

"The only drugs that I've been on were chemotherapeutic drugs for my particular type of lymphoma. It was a rather aggressive protocol, because Burkitt's lymphoma is a very aggressive cancer; it grows very fast, and so some of those drugs were experimental. For instance, the PB16 and vincristine are used experimentally on Kaposi sarcoma, but they did not affect my lesions at all. I experienced rather uncomfortable and severe side-effects, such as nausea, hair loss, skin pigmentation, ulcerating sores in my mouth and mucous membrane areas. The most uncomfortable was the chronic nausea. The action of chemotherapy is to go after fast-growing cells, which cancer cells are, but other normal fast-growing cells, such as hair follicles, stomach lining, and skin are also affected.

"I'm obviously improved from where I was last year. I've been in complete remission from Burkitt's lymphoma since March of 1984. My blood has improved; I haven't had a T-cell count, so I don't know what that is, but my white blood count has been improving of late, and my oncologist has said on the record that, other than having the primary disease of AIDS and three Kaposi lesions, there is nothing clinically wrong with me. I'm not a sick person.

"Nutritionally, I have not done anything extraordinary at all. I am aware of what I put into my body. I try to eat good, nutritious food that will give me a full supply of my vitamin requirements. I don't take any megadoses of anything. I've chosen not to be on any heavy vitamin program, or actually any program at all. I'm just aware of what I eat. I'm not a fanatic about anything. I still eat an occasional steak, but very occasional, because I find that I don't always feel my best after red meat. But at this point, I'm just aware of what I eat and how I feel, and I try to follow good food guidelines.

"My family, from the very beginning, were very supportive of me and my illness, and the support system that I had was quite extensive. I had lots and lots of people visiting me all the time. My mom was there every day that I was hospitalized, as was my ex-lover, plus just a huge amount of other people. My father was there, my stepfather was there, and my sisters came down from northern California. I just had a tremendous amount of support. Therefore, it wasn't difficult to establish a support system, since it was there already.

"As far as what I did for myself, I read a book called

Getting Well Again, by Carl Simonton. I took it to my doctor at Cedars-Sinai, and he said if I was interested in that kind of approach, he could recommend a place in Santa Monica called the Wellness Community. It's a non-cost, non-profit organization, committed to the support of cancer patients.

"So I went and investigated and became a part of it, which was good for me and served the purpose until I finished my chemotherapy protocol in April, and I decided to move on. I felt that continuing to go to that particular group was in essence holding on to cancer.

"It was at that point that I met a good friend who introduced me to the Wednesday night Hayride group, which I began to attend. I had heard of this group probably a year before that, from a friend in San Francisco who had AIDS and gave me the *AIDS: A Positive Approach* tape. I felt very lucky to be a part of what was going on. I've learned a lot by attending the group, but it is nothing that I didn't already know. It just reinforced some basic beliefs about life and why we are here. It has also taught me how to dissolve disease by getting in total alignment with oneself—mind and body. That's an ongoing process, which I'm still doing.

"I've also been connected, for quite some time now, with Paramahansa Yogananda, who founded the Self Realization Foundation. What he teaches is pretty much what Louise teaches, just in a different manner. I was also attracted to Buddhism for the concepts of world peace and getting in touch with what they call the Buddha spirit within, or the center, or just getting in touch with oneself. It involved regimented chanting and frequent organized meetings.

"Eventually I broke away from that because I didn't feel that it was enhancing what I already knew to be the truth for myself. I felt I could accomplish the same things through meditation, which I have, and it's more effective for me. This is not to discount what those people are doing for themselves, but I think it's just as valid for them to do that as what I do for myself.

"As far as alternative therapy, I really believe that anything that anybody wants to do, that they believe in, is right and true for them.

"One thing that I have been involved in is something called Reiki. As a result of the *Newsweek* article, a man in Cedar Rapids, Iowa, contacted me, so when I went to New York, I came home through Chicago and met this person. He had set up a Reiki marathon with five people of different Reiki levels, all working on me at the same time for three hours.

Reiki is a science of energy and basically a laying on of hands, but it doesn't necessarily have to be that. It can be *in absentia* also, which I have been getting from these people. It was a very powerful experience for me. It was very relaxing while I was going through it, but a couple of hours later, I experienced a very high fever, which alarmed me a bit because I hadn't had a fever for months. But they told me that this sometimes happens when one receives the amount of energy I received that night.

"I know that there are chapters of the organization in Los Angeles and other major cities, and there are individuals everywhere who practice it. I'm not saying that Reiki is the answer. It may be the answer for some people. But I believe that it is an ongoing process to explore what's right for oneself, and anything we can do for our well-being is right and correct.

"Norman Cousins' book, *Anatomy of an Illness*, helped me in that sense and helped me on the road to realizing that positive attitude and learning to love yourself have a lot to do with recovery. I feel that getting in touch with oneself and healing from within and maintaining a positive, supporting, and loving attitude is the bottom line of what's important."

When Andrew's mother was willing to appear on the *Today* show and in *Newsweek* magazine to support her son with AIDS, it was healing for both of them. Andrew received hundreds of letters from sons and daughters and parents. Each one was touched by a mother publicly standing by her son with AIDS and saying, "I love him." Here is her story.

CASE HISTORY: HELEN CLARE

Helen Clare appears to be a typical affluent southern California housewife. She is also an example of how appearances can be deceiving. "I was director of a daycare center for forty-six years, and I took early retirement because I wanted to do other things. I'm really involved in volunteer things. I'm president of Meals for the Elderly. I'm on the library board, and I'm on the committee for day care at the local community college. And, on the side, I'm Proctor for State Examinations, which is licensing for nurses, lawyers, architects, and engineers. This is why I wanted to retire, so I would be able to do some of these other things that I was never able to do."

She is also the devoted mother of Andrew, who was diagnosed as having AIDS on January 10, 1984, and as such has appeared on the *Today* show and in an article in *Newsweek* magazine.

"I think, for some reason, Andy has never had too good of an image of himself. He was always a very sweet, gentle child, and his twin sisters, who are three and a half years older than he is, were very popular, marvelous students who achieved in every way. I think this was hard to follow. I think that having AIDS has made him get some confidence, and knowing that he can succeed like he has in this has helped his self-esteem.

"I really knew that he was gay before he told me. I thought that this was his choice, and it certainly had no negative effect as far as our relationship was concerned.

But I did feel sorry that maybe he was giving up a lot in regards to having his own family and children, but it was his choice, and we accepted it.

"At this time, I did feel that maybe his choice had something to do with me, and I went through some therapy myself to alleviate the guilt. But I don't feel that way now at all. I've been married to his stepfather now for twelve years, and when Andy 'came out,' it was to us. He is very close to his stepfather. His own father is in the picture. He has been around and is okay, but Andy doesn't have that 'close' relationship with him that he does with my husband. His real father has been very supportive of me; he knew I was taking the brunt of it, and he did visit Andy in the hospital.

"Andy had a very bad year the year before he got sick, with the airlines he was working for. They went bankrupt, and he had to leave, and he didn't know what he wanted to do, and he had had hepatitis and had been very sick with it. I really believe that all that had a lot to do with his getting AIDS. I believe that it is something within you that makes you get sick. Of course, there are germs and viruses, but your immune system drops when you are emotionally weak, which you don't realize consciously, but you can almost look back to the moment when it began to happen. I really believe that. Andy believes that even more than I do! The whole year before he got sick was so bad for him that, when he got the first pains in his stomach, he thought it was an ulcer, due to the stress he was under and anxiety at having to change his whole lifestyle—suddenly not having a job anymore.

"We already knew that Andy had AIDS before the diagnosis, as he had all the symptoms. We were all in San Francisco for a family gathering, and Andy came up on Christmas Eve. He was in terrible shape, and although he was denying it, I knew he was sick. So I suggested that he come to southern California for awhile, which he did, and he went to the doctor when he was down here; and within a few days, he was in the hospital.

"Andy was really freaked by it. He was in such terrible pain, and so out of it with all the medication that he forgot he had AIDS. He had this tumor in his abdomen and was terribly sick for about six weeks, and I said something about AIDS, and he said, 'I have AIDS?' He was so shocked I felt terrible. He started to cry. I didn't realize that he didn't know it. We hadn't talked about it for a long time, because he had been so sick, and he couldn't remember a lot that happened the first couple of months that he was sick.

"There were a couple of times when he was so sick that it was pretty tough. Andy's friends were all really good to him and were always around, and when they would leave, he would ask me to come, and then he would dump on me. I realized intellectually that I was the only person he could dump on, but it still hurt. It was hard that he was grumpy around me and always so jolly around his friends, but I knew why, and we discussed this.

"He went through so many ghastly things that he needed someone who would take the brunt of it, but all the time he was gradually getting better. When you have chemotherapy, you need a really positive reaction to it the first time, if it is going to be effective. With him, the tumor just disappeared the first time. He had this giant tumor, which had closed off one kidney and was causing him excruciating pain. Then he got sick with this fungus pneumonia, and his white blood count was so low due to the AIDS and the chemotherapy that he virtually had nothing with which to fight it.

"Before he started the chemotherapy, I asked the doctor what his chances were realistically, because I didn't want him to go through all that for nothing. He said that he thought Andy should take a shot at it, and that he deserved the chance. He said that honestly, and I trusted him, so once we had committed ourselves to that, there was no looking back, and it was a fight to the finish.

"It was terrible watching this other man in the hospital who just got worse and worse until he finally died. He was one whose family had nothing to do with him, not until the last few weeks anyway. Another guy told his mother that he had come to the hospital to die, his body had just given out, and she said to me, 'He has suffered enough; his body's just worn out; it's time for him not to suffer anymore.'

"I even thought that about Andy a couple of times in the early stages, when he was throwing up every half hour for a whole week. That was pretty tough to watch, but even then he didn't want to give up. He did say to me once, though, 'I wonder why I'm doing all of this.'

"When he got down, I was there encouraging him, but when I was down, he never knew it. I just hated to see him suffer. It has been a hard transition from being so sick and trying to get his body functioning again to getting back in the real world. But he has done it now. He hasn't had any medication now for six months—nothing. And I think Louise has been terrific for him; she is a wonderful woman.

"He went to the Wellness Community in Santa Monica, a cancer support group, but he drew out of that when he didn't have cancer anymore, and I think Louise Hay's group is a little more of what he needs right now. I think Louise's whole approach about encouraging the people with AIDS to like themselves and to raise their self-esteem is wonderful. I've had some problems with that in my own life, so I can understand.

"If anything, I think my faith has gotten better through all of this. I think I've grown, although it is a terrible way to grow—through someone else's pain. But I think I've grown in that I don't worry about little things anymore. I realize that a lot of things that used to bother me just aren't important. I feel a lot better about a lot of things. Andy and I have been together so much lately that we have spent of lot of time hashing things around, and he has helped me. He feels that you can waste so much negative energy on feelings about people and incidents and all, I just don't worry about that kind of stuff anymore. It's not worth it.

"I feel that I've been able to educate a lot of people, because of my own experiences with Andy being gay and having AIDS. Because our community really isn't exposed to this much, I don't imagine there are too many people with AIDS around here, although it is amazing what comes out. I talked to this lovely woman whom I know professionally through the community college, and she said that she had read the magazine article I was in and was inspired by it. She said that her brother died of AIDS this last November. I knew she had lost a brother, but I had no idea that was why. And another person in the Village wrote me a lovely note saying how she liked the article and that her brother was gay, and she said that, if she ever had to face anything like what we went through, she hoped she would have the courage we had. And I would probably never have known that her brother was gay. It would never have come up.

"I think that I did the very best that I knew how at the time, as a mother, and I believe that one has to accept that in oneself and not feel guilty. I heard a psychiatrist say that many mothers are feeling guilty that, at some level, they feel they are the ones killing their sons, because they are gay and have gotten AIDS. Well, I don't feel that at all.

"I feel really positive about the future, healthwise, for Andy. He's looking so good, and he is feeling so well, and in a way, he isn't like a typical AIDS patient. He has had a sore throat and a cold, and he gets over them. He doesn't land in the hospital. The last time he went to the hospital, his white blood count was up a lot. I don't think Andy is cured of AIDS, but I think he is controlling his AIDS. His immune system isn't shot now; he does have some. And I believe, with a continuing positive attitude, he can build that immune system up further."

Some final advice from Helen Clare: "You don't own your children. You're their parent, but they grow up, and they're their own person, and if you don't accept them, it's your loss. I can't understand why a parent can't accept their own child. So many of the people in the group and Andy's friends have come up to me and said, 'I wish I had a parent like you,' or 'I wish my parents would accept me the way I am.' And I feel really bad for them, because they are missing out on the truly special child or parent that they already have."

One of the hardest things for a parent to accept, and for a child to do, is to "come out." For most, it is rough at best, and at worst, can drive a wedge that can destroy a family. But it doesn't have to be this way. Like AIDS, "coming out" is a great lesson in accepting what IS. And, when we learn to accept our children for the unique, wonderful creations that they are, we can truly begin to love them.

TREATMENT

Today is another precious day on earth. We shall live it with joy. I surround myself, my friends, my family, and my home with harmony and love. I let go of every idea that hurts me in any way, even though it came from those I love. I go beyond my loved ones' limitations to a new sense of freedom for myself. I no longer impose my old limitations on others, and they are free to be themselves. I give to others what I wish to receive.

Love and acceptance flow freely between myself and everyone I know. We are one with the power that created us.

We are safe, and all is well in our world!

15

Being Gay in the Family

Affirmation:
We are blessed with a special, precious gift!

COMING OUT

For a gay person to reveal to their parents and family members their sexuality is most often quite difficult. This "coming out of the closet" takes great courage, for far too often it is received with hostility and rejection. Unconditional love gets lost and is overshadowed by false morality or "what will the neighbors think." Each person on this planet is a unique flower and is here to work on his or her own spiritual pathway. We cannot judge another without hindering our own growth. I believe, if parents have a gay child, it is something they have chosen on a soul level so they may work on their own lesson of opening their hearts. This is not to blame them for their child's gayness, but to understand and to learn what lesson comes from accepting them totally—and to love them for it.

It becomes far easier to be honest with parents when we are clear about ourselves. If we feel we are not good enough, then it is hard to convince another to accept us as we are. When we are clear about our own self-love,

153

then we come from a place of strength when we are speaking to others. In our support group, many of our members have to not only tell their parents they are gay; they must also reveal they have AIDS. This is called the "double whammy" and is painful for parents and child. Many parents choose to "stay in the closet" themselves and never want to discuss it with anyone.

Often I hear, "Oh, I can't tell my parents; they wouldn't be able to take it," or "It would hurt them too much." This is very unfair. All you are doing is trying to "live their lives for them." You are insisting you know exactly what is going to go on within them. Allow them to live their own lives and have their own reactions. How can they grow spiritually if you deny them these experiences? Telling someone who you are is not hurting them. If they choose to feel hurt, that is their own choice of reaction. There are many other feelings they could choose. Do allow your parents to live their own lives.

We suggest that the person about to reveal his gayness to the family practice in the mirror for awhile. Take the parent it is hardest to talk to and tell him or her in the mirror. The first time this is done, there may be much emotion, and that is okay, for it is being done alone in front of the mirror. The second time, it is not quite so traumatic; and as this exercise is practiced daily for a period of time, it becomes easier and easier. When the visit or the phone call is finally made, we find that somehow the vibrations between family members is much more open and receptive. If one has three weeks or so before the actual event, a lot of practicing can be done.

Begin by saying "Mom, or Dad, there is something I want you to know." Then tell them who you are. You can say, "I was afraid to tell you before because. . . ." Tell them what you want from them. Not what you *don't* want, what you *do* want. Do not say, "I don't want you to reject me." Rather say, "I want you to love and accept me and support me." Each day it will become clearer exactly what you do want to say. Send them love whenever they come into your mind. And in the meantime, work on loving yourself, for that is more important than anything else.

If, when you do tell your parents, they get angry and rejecting, remember this is their "first reaction." Let it be. Give them a little time to digest the information. As parents, they've probably suspected SOMETHING, so allow them to be who they are, just as you want them to let you be who you are. Keep sending them love, and affirm to yourself that "you have a wonderful loving, supportive relationship with your family." We have discovered this sort of "mental work" always pays off. There is always an improvement in family relationships. Sometimes a surprising turn-around. The love is there, and you can help them to find it.

If there is total rejection, then create your own family out of the people who love you. If nobody loves you, then start loving others. Find or create a support group. These support groups become substitute families. Remember, what you give out will return to you.

With parents, there are as many different reactions as there are people. Lots of gay men who have never come out of the closet to their parents, for fear of their reactions, now get the opportunity to say, "Hey Mom and Dad, I'm gay and I have AIDS, and I need your love and support." While it is true that some people have been rejected, others have found surprising reactions of incredible love.

When parents react with anger and rejection, it is because of their own fear. People who are frightened have a tendency to run away, often violently. With the media giving out so many messages of doom and gloom, it is no wonder uninformed people react the way they do. It is a natural protective instinct, a defense mechanism, if you will.

No matter how a parent reacts to you, it is in your own best interests to bless them with love. Whatever you give out returns to you. So it does not make sense to give out anger, for that is not the way to heal the situation. This is a big learning experience for everyone with AIDS—to discover the enormous healing power of love.

I am not at all suggesting you become a doormat in any way. I am saying, don't spend your precious mental moments indulging in anger and resentment. No matter how justified it seems to be, your angry, resentful thoughts will only hurt your body. It is not worth it.

Give your parents time to change their initial reactions. You keep the door open. Give them a chance to love you again.

CASE HISTORY: JEFF

Jeff, a nurse by profession, and one of our beautifuul young men from the Wednesday night group, was having a lot of difficulty sticking to his program of healing. He had had several opportunistic infections, but never a real diagnosis of AIDS. Tom was closeted, and there was a great deal of anger towards his family, especially his father, and he had never "come out" to them.

Then one day, he was diagnosed with AIDS. It was one of the best things that could ever have happened to him. It enabled him to stop being wishy-washy and make a decision to be committed to his healing program.

One of the first things Jeff did was to come out to his family. I know this was not easy for him. He called his mother and said, "I am not doing this to hurt you, but I am aware that the five percent of gay people with AIDS who are getting well have all come out to their parents, and I want to live. Mom, I want you to know I am gay and I have AIDS." His mother took it surprisingly well.

Jeff then called all twenty-eight members of his family and one by one gave them the news. When he was through, it was as if a ten-ton weight had fallen off his shoulders. He now stands taller. His face is relaxed, his eyes are much clearer. He looks much better. His commitment to his healing has become one-hundred percent. He will not eat one mouthful of food that is not on his nutrition plan. His ability to learn to love himself is growing daily. Jeff is going to make it, and it is wonderful to see.

We have had many success stories with families of group members. For those who have not come out to their families, we practice talking to mom or dad in the mirror. Looking into the mirror and saying, "Mom, there is something I want you to know. . . ." And always ending with, "What I really want is your love and approval." Love and approval is what we want from everybody. This is practiced on a daily basis for a couple of weeks or a month. Something positive happens when we do this. Somehow the other person gets the change in vibrations.

This also enables us to come from a much more centered and loving space. Then we either write a letter or make a phone call or go for a personal visit, whichever is more convenient. And guess what, the reception is much more open and loving than it was in the past. We are able to make at least some inroads to opening the loving space of the heart for each member of the family.

CASE HISTORY: LUKE

Luke is a beautiful young man who comes from a large Mormon background, where they believe that being gay is a sin. Luke's family are also elders in the church, and that made his position even more difficult. He began by sending them all love on a daily basis and forgiving them for all their and his past prejudices.

It took Luke a few months of continually doing this,

seeing his family surrounded by a loving light, picturing them welcoming him with open loving arms, etc. Then one day he received a call from his aunt and uncle, who wanted him to know that not all of his family was anti-gay and that could they please give him a birthday party. He said yes, and eight members of his family came, all staunch Mormons. He invited eight of his close friends, and I was also invited. This birthday party turned out to be an incredible mixture of love and support.

The more love we give out, the more we practice giving love, the more it comes back. It came back to Luke tenfold that night. After dinner, his uncle sang, his cousins sang, we all sang. It was a very healing evening. We even sat on the floor and did a healing circle around Luke, placing our hands on his body and sending him love and healing energy. I remember saying to his family, "If you really believed your love could heal his body, how much would you give? Please give that now."

That evening united that portion of the family in a way it had never been united before. Now we are working on the rest of the family, and it is only a matter of time before they open their hearts too.

Sometimes it is very difficult to persevere with giving out love when you are coming up against walls or you are getting anger, or you are getting rejection in return. However, if you keep doing it, it does work. More and more, people are beginning to attest to that. We are helping to open many hearts with love now.

Do you know how perfect you were when you were a tiny baby? Babies do not have to do anything to become perfect; they already are perfect, and they act as if they know it. Babies know they are the center of the universe. They are not afraid to ask for what they want. They freely express their emotions. You know when a baby is angry; in fact, the whole neighborhood knows. You also know when they are happy, for their smiles light up a room. They are so full of love.

Tiny babies will die if they do not get love. Once we are older, we learn to live without love, but babies will not stand for it. Babies also love every part of their bodies, even their own feces. They have no shame and no guilt.

You were once like that. We were all like that. Then we began to listen to adults around us who had learned to be fearful, and we began to deny our own magnificence.

You are not your parents' opinions of you. You are not what society condemns you for. You are not the medical establishment's verdict of your dis-ease. You may have felt damned by society and even your family. Don't damn yourself now because of your behavior and your attitude. It all has to do with your belief system. This is the only thing you need to change—YOUR BELIEF SYSTEM!

In my workshops now, there are always gays mixed in with some straight people, and some people who have AIDS. I talk openly about how you do and do not get AIDS, allowing people to express their fears if they have them. Within an hour or two, most of the fears are gone. People find that gays are just like anyone else, and they open their hearts to them. The ones that are the most bigoted and the most frightened, by the end of the workshop, are almost always the ones most willing to go out of their way to help the people with AIDS. Love heals. I see it happening over and over. Love heals hearts, and that is all that needs healing. Everything else takes care of itself.

OUR FAMILY BELIEF SYSTEMS

When we are very little, we learn how to feel about ourselves and about life by the reactions of the adults around us. It is the way we learn what to think about ourselves and about our world. Now if you lived with people who were very unhappy or frightened, guilty, or angry, then you learned a lot of negative things about yourself and about your world. "I never do anything right." "It's all my fault." "If I get angry, I'm a bad person." Belief like this creates a frustrating life.

When we grow up, we have a tendency to recreate the emotional environment of our early home life. This is not good or bad, right or wrong; it is just what we know inside as "home." We also tend to recreate in our personal relationships the relationships we had with our mothers or with our fathers, or that they had between them. Think how often you have had a lover or a boss who was "just like" your mother or father.

We also treat ourselves the way our parents treated us. We scold and punish ourselves in the same way. You can almost hear the words when you listen. We also love and encourage ourselves in the same way, if we were loved and encouraged as children.

"You never do anything right." "It's all your fault." "You are a bad person." How often have you said this to yourself? "You are wonderful." "I love you." How often do you tell yourself this?

Let's not blame our parents. We are all victims of victims, and they could not possibly have taught us anything they did not know. If your mother did not know how to love herself or your father did not know how to love himself, then it would be impossible for them to teach this to you. They were doing the best they could with what they had been taught as children. If they were forced to fit a certain mold to please their parents, then they would expect you to fit their mold, too. If you want to understand your parents more, get them to talk about their own childhood before the age of ten; and if you listen with compassion, you will learn where their fears and rigid patterns come from. Those people who "did all that stuff to you" were just as frightened and scared as you are. But as you increase your awareness and begin to love, they too can begin to mirror this.

TREATMENT

Today is another precious day on earth. We shall live it with joy. Not everyone has the special family that I have, nor do they have the extra opportunities to open their hearts in the way my family does. We are not limited by what the neighbors think nor society's current popular prejudices. We are far more than that. We are a family that comes from love, and we accept with pride every unique member.

We are all special, and we are all worthy of love. I love and accept each member of my wonderful family, and they in turn love and adore me. We are one with the power that created us.

We are safe, and all is well in our world!

16

Choosing Our Parents

Affirmation:
I make my choices with inner wisdom
and love!

UNDERSTANDING OUR CHOICES

I believe we choose our parents. Each one of us decides to incarnate upon this planet at particular points in time and space. We have chosen to come here to learn a particular lesson that will advance us upon our spiritual, evolutionary pathway. We choose our sex, our color, our country, and then we look around for the particular set of parents who will mirror the pattern we are bringing in to work on in this lifetime. We chose them because they were perfect for us. They are the perfect couple who are "experts" in what you have chosen to learn. The lessons we are here to learn seem perfectly matched to the "weaknesses" of our parents.

Yes, you did pick the right parents, or you wouldn't be here now. If you had really made a mistake in choosing your parents, you would have left the planet very early. I think that is what stillborn births and crib deaths are about. These are easy ways of leaving the planet. Either the entity came in too soon for its lessons or there was a mistake in choosing the parents.

We learn our belief systems as very little children, and then we move through life creating experiences to match our beliefs. Look back in your own life and notice how often you have gone through the same experience. Well, I believe you created those experiences over and over because they mirrored something you believed about yourself. It doesn't really matter how long we have had a problem or how big it is or how life has treated us. Know that any negative condition that has existed in the past can be changed now.

We come to this planet, and before we come, we choose a lesson we are going to work on. We know what we want to work on this time around. And no matter how we approach it, the subject is really love. How much can we love ourselves, despite whatever else we have created in our lives. And before we come here, I think the first thing we do after we have our lesson is to choose our sexuality. What sexuality are we going to have this time? Are we going to be a woman this time, because that is going to have a certain amount of experience, or are we going to be a male this time, because that will be different experiences. Are we going to choose to be heterosexual, which brings one set of experiences, or are we going to be homosexual, which brings a whole different set of experiences?

What do we want to experience this time? And then, I think we choose our color. What color am I going to be this time? Because again, that is going to bring different experiences. And we also decide where we are going to be born on the planet. Because that too will bring different experiences, depending on where we choose. If we are born in Africa, that is a totally different set of circumstances than if we are born in Liverpool or in Australia or Alaska or Los Angeles. These are totally different circumstances, different issues to deal with.

And after we have all of that, we look around very carefully for the perfect set of parents to mirror the stuff we came to work on. I know most of us, when we grow up, look at our parents and say, "Oh, you did it to me. It is all your fault." But I think we chose them because they are perfect for us. Just as they chose us.

I truly believe that, if parents have a homosexual child, they chose that particularly because they are giving themselves the opportunity to open their hearts on a very deep level. How much are they willing to love in spite of what the neighbors say? What the neighbors say seems to be a big issue on this planet. And it doesn't matter what society you are in: What do the neighbors say!

How much are we willing to love? How much are we willing to stay true to our natures? And to love and appreciate who we are? All the issues we have are a means for our spiritual growth. Prejudice is so ridiculous. Our experiences are not good or bad. It is the experience we have chosen with our souls.

And so often we get angry when we say we choose our parents. Who me? I wouldn't choose them for my parents. And I know, because I went through the same thing. But I think, if you had made a mistake with your parents, you would have left very early. Definitely before the end of the first year. And maybe within hours. If you have gotten here today, where you are, you have the perfect set of parents for this lifetime. And whatever stuff you need to work out with them is the stuff you will work out with them.

GOING HOME FOR THE HOLIDAYS

Holidays have always been a busy time for me in my practice. Old childhood pains come to the surface. Fear of, or resistance to, visiting the parents' home for the holidays. Fear of not having a "good" time or of being alone during the holiday season. When someone has

AIDS, these fears are magnified. The old happy holidays may now be a time of pain and loneliness. I make sure I have time to visit the hospitals on Thanksgiving and Christmas, for those can be especially difficult days for people with AIDS.

We all need love and support.

You will improve the quality of your visits home if you are willing to allow your family to be exactly who they are. Stop trying to "change them." You don't like it when they want to change you. Leave them alone. Just work on changing yourself and loving yourself. That is a full-time job. If you really want to change them, change yourself. Then they will change in the way they react to you, for you will be different.

We always want our families to forgive us and love us as we are now. Too often, we are not willing to give them the same love and forgiveness. If our childhood was painful, we find it difficult to forgive. We limit our own growth by holding onto the past. We stay stuck in the five-year-old experience, instead of living in the now. We forget that everyone is always doing the best they can with the knowledge, understanding, and awareness they have at any given moment. People who behave badly are people who were taught to be like that. They don't know how to do it any differently. Anger and self-righteous resentment will not change them. They will be as stubborn as you are. Love and forgiveness work miracles.

The affirmation, "I am willing to forgive you, and I free myself," puts the situation into perspective. For when you forgive them, YOU ARE FREE. This sort of inner mental work will heal the most stubborn family rifts. Try it, you can't lose; it may even work for you as it has for so many.

Going home for the holidays will work best if you have no expectations. Just take each moment as it comes. Love yourself in the presence of your family. This means repeating an affirmation like, "I love and approve of myself," or "I am always safe and comfortable and loved, no matter what is going on." Allow them to be. If they get too crazy at any time, love yourself enough to quietly remove yourself from their presence for awhile. Don't expect it to be just like it was when you were little. This is a different time. Take time to rest and nourish yourself. See that you get the foods your body now requires, even if you have to bring them with you. Your health is more important than their feelings. You can always say, "My doctor wants me to eat this." They will usually respect this authority figure.

Remember, every problem that you have with your family can be linked to a lack of love and forgiveness. When we dislike something that has been "done to us," we are unwilling to forgive the other for where they are coming from at this particular time. Going home for the holidays can be a joyous time for you to learn this lesson. When we forgive and love, only inner peace can exist for us.

TREATMENT

Today is another precious day on earth. We shall live it with joy. I chose these special people who are my parents a long time ago, because I knew how important they would be for my spiritual growth. I also know that they chose me for the same purpose. We are working out our lessons as best we can—loving each other as much as we are able, at any moment. We are one with the power that created us.

We are safe, and all is well in our world!

17

Our Sexuality

Affirmation:
I am at peace with my sexuality; it is
perfect for me!

When society dictates that we are "bad" or "wrong" for who we are or how we express ourselves, it is hard for us to survive. We begin to hide or to "become someone else" in order to please others. This never works and is always damaging to us.

In the gay community, we have a large group of men and women who are told they are bad or not good enough for just this kind of reasoning. And the damage is taking its toll.

As children growing up, we all develop our own Divine, unique, sexual behavior. Unfortunately, certain individuals' normal and natural sexual feelings have been scorned and belittled. Most often their parents let them know that being gay is totally unacceptable, so these children begin to hide who they are. A feeling of shame and guilt grows. Then an inevitable separation from the parents occurs, making it difficult to ever be open and honest with their families.

What most people do not realize is that, with homosexuality, we are not talking about a behavior choice. We are talking about just being. If a heterosexual were told he had to become a homosexual in order to be acceptable, he would find it impossible. Yet heterosexual society often assumes it is easy for the gay person to "just change" who they are rather than to accept themselves and heterosexuals as well.

Because of thinking like this, it has become popular to be prejudiced against gays. When will we learn that the goal of life is to have unconditional love? There is no group of people who are better or worse than others. We are all just where we are on the ladder of spiritual growth. Prejudice only holds us back in our own spiritual evolution.

Sexual orientation is just a temporary thing, chosen for this lifetime. I believe we all come back time after time and get to experience every life situation. We get to be black, white, and yellow, heterosexual and homosexual, rich and poor, intelligent and ordinary, beautiful and ugly, powerful and humble. So prejudice to me is a silly thing, because if you haven't been in a certain situation up to now, sooner or later you will be—for all situations are learning experiences.

We now have a group of mostly young men and women who in the past had to carefully hide who they were and to pretend to be who they were not. In the last few years, there has been a slight lifting of the oppression of gays, and they have been able to "come out" in certain areas of certain cities. Of course, this sudden freedom, after so much oppression, is going to be subversive and explode in rather wild behavior.

When any group of people is oppressed for a long period of time, it is a normal reaction for them to go a bit wild when the oppression lifts. So, when gay men found they could begin to come out of the closet in certain areas, to be open about who they were, they went a little crazy with the freedom. Often they found themselves participating in less than healthy activities because for so many years they were not "allowed" to act on their own instincts. When this freedom comes, they don't know what to do but party. It would be surprising if they didn't. Now it is time for the sexual pendulum to swing to a point of balance.

GUILT AND SEXUALITY

When I talk about patterns of guilt, I do not mean to imply that there is any reason to feel guilty. Especially not about our sexuality. No matter what someone else has said, no matter how high their authority seems to be, no matter how inferior "they" seem to think you are, it has nothing to do with the reality of your being.

Just for a moment, try to visualize the vastness of the universe. It is beyond our comprehension. Even our top scientists, with their latest equipment, cannot measure its size. Within this universe, there are billions of galaxies. In a far-off corner in one of these smaller galaxies, there exists a minor sun. Around this sun revolve a few pinpoints, one of which is called Planet Earth.

I find it hard to believe that the vast, incredible intelligence that created this entire universe is only an old man sitting on a cloud above the Planet Earth, watching my genitals!

Yet, so many of us were taught this concept as a child. It is vital that we release foolish, outmoded, limited ideas that do not support us and nourish us. I feel strongly that even our concept of God needs to be one that is *for* us, not *against* us. There are so many different religions to choose from. If you have one now that tells you that you are a sinner and a lowly worm, you can choose another religion. There are so many different ones to choose from. If none of the current religions suit you, begin a new one. Remember, every form of religion we know has been started by someone who was dissatisfied with the forms then available. They had their own ideas about God and the Universe and were able to gather others who were willing to agree with them and their concepts.

UNDERSTANDING SEXUALITY

It is not enough to teach children in school the mechanics of sexuality. We need on a very deep level to allow children to remember that their bodies, their genitals, and their sexuality are things to rejoice about. I truly believe people who love themselves and their bodies will not abuse themselves or others.

The sexual revolution and the women's liberation movement have brought about many changes. The sexes are coming closer together. We are finding that most of the differences are cultural and societal rules, rather than physical or mental. It is a time on the planet when more and more women are experiencing men's traditional roles and jobs. Many men also have the opportunity to experience what we have usually thought of as women's roles and jobs.

I am not advocating that everybody run around having free sex at all times. I am saying that some of our rules do not make sense, and that is why so many people break them and become hypocrites.

When we remove sexual guilt from people and teach them to love and respect themselves, then they will automatically treat themselves and others in ways that are for their highest good and greatest joy. The reason we have so many problems with our sexuality now is because so many of us have self-hatred and self-disgust, and so we treat ourselves and others badly.

In no way am I trying to create additional guilt for anyone. However, we need to look at the things that need to be changed in order for all of our lives to function with love, joy, and respect. Fifty years ago, almost all gay men were closeted, and now they have been able to create pockets in society where they can at least be relatively open. I feel it is unfortunate that much of what they have created gives so much pain to their gay brothers. While it is often deplorable the way straights treat gays, it is tragic the way many gays treat other gays.

Being too old or not pretty enough is sometimes reason for gays to ostracize each other. They will "camp" at each other to the brink of tears. This is not unity. This is a lack of respect for themselves as well as their community.

Another way gays may show a lack of respect for others and themselves is through sex. Violent, sometimes rude modes of action are taken against the partner. They may take out their personal frustrations about the world on the one they love through the exression of that love. Or promiscuous, anonymous sex could be prevalent. Sex is a physical representation of an emotional experience. Why would we want it to mirror hate, fear, and rejection?

SAFE SEX

I find the whole question of safe sex so interesting. Women have had the complete burden of safe sex for hundreds of years. If women did not practice safe sex, then they were open to the current infectious diseases, as well as getting pregnant. For the first time now, men, particularly gay men, are also beginning to understand what this frustrating experience is like. And there is great bitching and complaining. When the body is in the heat of passion, it does not want to listen to the mind giving it careful instructions on safety, saying, "Not now," or "Not this way."

One of the men brought up a question at the group

one night: "What do you say to someone who refuses to wear a condom?" He also asked the women at work the same question, knowing that they had been confronted with this problem many times. The answer will always have to do with your own level of self-esteem. If your self-love and self-esteem is high, you will refuse to have sex that is not safe. If you think little of yourself, you will probably "give in" and hope it will be all right. How much do you love yourself? How much will you allow yourself to be abused? Less and less, as your love for yourself grows.

Now, it seems to be time for men to begin to understand what women have been dealing with on the sexual level for ages. Straight men complained and screamed as the women's liberation movement began asking them to experience traditional women's roles and jobs. They were only willing to go so far.

Tantra, which has been practiced in India for generations, is a form of sex where the mind is very much involved. Sexual practices, instead of being just wild uncontrollable passion, are channeled into definite rituals. Those who practice tantric sex claim it far surpasses any other sexual experiences, and the sexual act itself can go on for many hours. Perhaps we are meant to learn a more conscious way of experiencing sex.

Is something as simple as kissing safe? Mouth kissing is not practiced by every culture. Deep French kissing is a rather recent phenonemon in our own culture. We never know if our partner has a cut in the mouth or bleeding gums. As they are not really sure if the AIDS virus can be transmitted by the mouth, it is probably best if we learn new forms of kissing. Perhaps we can turn to kissing cheeks and necks instead.

Safe sex is causing people to be creative sexually. When you cannot fuck or suck or kiss, you get to be very creative.

Men traditionally have always had more sexual partners than women; and when men get together, of course there will be a great more sex. That's all fine and good. The bathhouses fulfilled a wonderful need—unless we are using our sexuality for the wrong reasons. Some men like having lots of partners to satisfy their deep need for self-esteem, rather than for the joy of it. I do not believe there is anything wrong with having several partners, and the use of alcohol and some recreational drugs on an "occasional" basis can be all right. However, if we are getting bombed out of our heads every night, and if we "need" several partners a day just to prove our self-worth, then we are not coming from a nourishing space. We need to make some mental changes.

AGING

In heterosexual society, many women dread growing old, because of the belief systems we have created around the glory of youth. It is not so difficult for the men, for they become distingushed with a bit of gray hair. The older man often gets respect, and people may even look up to him.

Not so for most gay men, for they have created a culture that places tremendous emphasis on youth and beauty. While everyone is young to start with, only a few fit the standard of beauty. So much emphasis has been placed on the physical appearance or on the shape of the body that the feelings inside have been totally disregarded. If you are not young and beautiful, it is almost as though you don't count. The person does not count—only the body counts.

This way of thinking is a disgrace to the whole culture. It is another way of saying, "Gay is not good enough."

Because of the ways gay people often treat other gays, for many gay men the experience of getting old is something to dread. It is almost better to die than get old. And AIDS is a dis-ease that often kills.

Too often, gay men feel that, when they get older, they will be useless and unwanted. It is almost better to destroy themselves first—and many have created a destructive lifestyle. Some of the concepts and attitudes that are so a part of the gay lifestyle—the meat rack, the constant judging, the refusal to get close to another, etc.—are monstrous. And AIDS is a monstrous dis-ease.

We have set up such silly rules about aging. We have almost made it a crime to get older. We treat our elderly shamefully, not realizing that we will be treated as we are treating others. No wonder we look with fear at the first wrinkle or gray hair, seeing it as the beginning of the end of us. For awhile, some young people even decided that others were over the hill at thirty. Then those people became thirty and changed their minds. All of us are getting older every day. We are meant to experience each age. No one is better than the other; they are just different. Each age has its own special values.

In the gay culture, extreme worship of youth and beauty and the rejection of age add to the difficulties of being a gay man. If one is beautiful when he is young, he is adored and fussed over. Those not so attractive are made to feel as outsiders and never quite acceptable. No wonder there is so much "camping" in this community. And even the beautiful grow older, and the adoration ceases as they watch their old admirers turn to the newest of the young and beautiful. We have created so many ways to tell ourselves, "We are not good enough."

When we are afraid of growing older, we are in effect saying, "I am not worthwhile; only my body has importance." Bodies change; look at all the different bodies you have had since infancy. Our spirit, our essence, goes on from lifetime to lifetime. We do not have to buy into current cultural put-downs. We have the ability to know who we really are. Not what "they say we are." Only we can give meaning to our identity. We are who we accept we are. What do you accept for yourself?

To be afraid of getting older will only hasten the aging process. When we reject any part of ourselves, we create more self-hatred. We might as well just enjoy ourselves at every age. Learn what we can about how to be healthy and enjoy today. And of course, treat older people as you want to be treated when you get there.

People who get AIDS cannot escape old age either. Have you ever seen someone at the end of the AIDS experience? Their hair is sparse or gone, they are thin, their bones ache, and often they are forgetful. In my personal practice, I have often seen someone with AIDS age forty years in just a few months. Getting AIDS is not the answer to old age. To love ourselves at any age can open the door to joy.

NEGATIVE SEXUAL BEHAVIOR PATTERNS

These sorts of attitudes and behavior patterns can only create guilt on a very deep level, no matter how much we may "camp." Camping, which can be such fun, can also be extremely destructive, both to the givers and the recipients. It is another way of avoiding closeness and intimacy.

It seems to me that bondage and sado-masochistic practices have less to do with sexuality and more to do with anger against the parents, particularily the father. It is a game of "making up" and "getting even." One is saying, "Please, Daddy, don't hurt me; I promise to be good and obedient; please love me." The other is saying in effect, "You fucking bastard, I'll get even with you."

I have noticed, as people love themselves more, they move away from these practices, which are degrading to both parties. When we truly love ourselves, we cannot hurt ourselves, and we cannot hurt another person.

HAYRIDE ON SEX AND SEXUALITY

Louie Nassaney: "The concern of sex and sexuality for persons with AIDS is an important one. When I was diagnosed almost four years ago, the first thing that went through my mind was, 'Can I have sex? Was it sex that created my own illness? Or am I worthy of having sex?' I was in a relationship of three months. After a week of being diagnosed and going through all the fear and the trauma that goes along with AIDS, I decided that I was going to dump my boyfriend. What came through me at the time was that, if I was going to get well, I did not need anyone around me. If I was going to work on my KS and my AIDS, I would have to do it by myself with God. I did not want to be worried by phone calls; I did not want to be worried about having dates on the weekend. I just wanted to worry about Louie.

"It was a big decision, and there was a lot of sadness and a lot of crying, but it was a choice that I made knowingly. I did not make the decision because I was concerned over whether it was 'safe' or 'not safe.' I figured, if I needed sex, Louie could have sex with Louie. After all, sex can exist in many forms. It can be fantasy; it can be with myself; it can be with the video; it can be listening to other things; or it can be just not having sex at all.

"For about seven months, I didn't have an orgasm at all. But that had a lot to do with the treatment I was on at the time. I was on interferon; then after I decided to go off it, I spent about two months trying to decide whether I was worthy enough to go out and have sex or a relationship with anybody.

"I know what I'm saying may push a few buttons, but that's okay. If something makes us mad, maybe it also makes us learn a bit about ourselves.

"A lot of people with AIDS feel that they are not worthy of having a relationship. They don't even feel worthy of going out and trying or letting the Universe know what they need or want. They ask, 'Who wants me after I have had pneumonia and have gotten to be so skinny?' or 'Who wants me when I am covered in lesions?' Even some people who do not have AIDS are fearful of having anything today because of what they might catch.

"That may be right for them; it is a matter of choice. Celibacy is okay, if that is what you choose. Playing safely is okay, too, if you choose. But we are not even sure at this point what the phrase 'play safely' means; definitions are still changing. For awhile, it meant no oral or anal intercourse. But a study out of U.C.L.A. that has been going on for over two years now seems to be suggesting that oral intercourse is relatively safe. Out of sixteen-hundred men, the eight-hundred who said they were into oral sex only have all remained negative to the AIDS virus. But this is still only a suggestion that oral sex is safe. Time is still a big question with the development of the AIDS virus.

"After I was off interferon, I began feeling better about myself. I decided to test the field. I recall Louise telling me that it would be important for me to be honest with myself and to let my partner know what is going on with me physically before engaging in sexual activity. For a lot of us, the goal is just having someone to cuddle with. But if I found someone and that developed into a relationship, eventually I would have to tell the person I had AIDS. I might as well make the announcement up front and take the chance of having the person reject me.

"A lot of us have given up the one-night stands, because we realize that is what has gotten us into the AIDS mess in the first place. The one-night stands represent the fact that we do not love ourselves and are not loving to the person that we are with. They represent the fact that we are looking only for their sexual being; we are interested only in their genitals.

"But we have changed; we have learned. I have learned from Louise that it is safe to be honest, and that if a person rejects me, that is fine and dandy. Sooner or later someone is going to love Louie for his heart, not for his body or for his hairline.

"Then there was a wonderful article about me in *People* magazine. About seventy people contacted me, wanting to get to know me. Most were from states other than California. Only one was from the Los Angeles area. I decided to meet him, and it was wonderful to go to see someone who had just communicated with me through a letter. This person became my lover, and he has been for over two years.

"But the name of the game is 'love.' Before this, I had difficulty facing the pressures of being rejected, so I decided for awhile just to do it myself. There is nothing wrong or shameful about masturbation. It is a form of self-love. I got my foreplay, everything that I needed to make Louie happy; I got my VCR and my Al Parker videos. I turned up the music, and I foreplayed it up, and I brought out the dildo, and I enjoyed doing it to myself. It was the first time that I was actually giving myself sexual gratification. And I felt really wonderful about it.

"I didn't have to go to a bar, and I did not have to have a one-night stand. Masturbation, or making love to oneself, is something we can choose."

TREATMENT

Today is another precious day on earth. We shall live it with joy. My soul has no sexuality, and yet I have already experienced the different sexual possibilites on this earth plane many times. The sexual choice I made this lifetime is perfect for my growth. I rejoice in my sexuality, which is perfect for me. I am at peace with who I am sexually, physically, mentally, and spiritually. We are one with the power that created us.

We are safe, and all is well in our world!

18

Loving Others, Loving Ourselves

Affirmation:
I live in love and harmony with everyone!

RELATIONSHIPS

Every time I think about relationships, I keep coming back to one particular aspect of relationships; I keep coming back to that very same concept of loving yourself. If you don't love yourself, you can't enjoy a good relationship, even if you bring it into your life, because you are so nervous about it. You are so worried about what he or she is doing, and do they really love me, and do they really care? And where are they, and why didn't they call, and will they be home in time, and who are they with?

We run all sorts of numbers on ourselves when we don't love who we are. And if we have a relationship with someone who does not love himself or herself, then it is impossible to really please that person. You cannot be good enough for someone who does not love themselves. And too often, we knock ourselves out trying to be enough for a partner who doesn't know how to accept it, because they don't love who they are.

When we talk about jealousy, we are talking about

someone who doesn't love himself. And because he doesn't love who he is, he doesn't value himself; he is so insecure that he is jealous. And that is all jealousy is; it is insecurity. It is saying, "I'm not good enough, I'm not worth loving, so why would you love me, and I know you are going out and doing things." It is because we don't care who we are. If we do this in our personal relationships, it is bound to influence our workplace as well.

RELATIONSHIPS IN THE WORKPLACE

We cannot have good relationships at work if we don't care who we are, because then we get suspicious; we get jealous; or we get very self-righteous, and our little corner or little department becomes so important to us, because we are scared other people are going to take from us. We forget there is plenty for everyone.

When we love ourselves, we can stay centered and calm and secure, and our relationships at work are wonderful. If you work someplace, think about the people in your office who do not get along with others. And what is the reason? They don't care for who they are. Now, it is not that they are bad people, and if you don't love who you are, that doesn't mean you are a bad person. It means you believe some old false ideas. You accepted the idea from somewhere that you weren't good enough. And when you are not good enough, what is the thing you want most in your life? Love and approval.

And if you are not good enough, then your belief is going to be "nobody loves me," or "I'm not lovable," or "I'm not worth loving." And when you are not worth loving, that is a miserable place to live. And so you get a chip on your shoulder; you get sassy or sarcastic. You get very angry, and you exhibit behavior so that other people don't want to be around you. And then you say, "See, I knew it. Nobody loves me."

Many employers are now seeing to it that their work staffs are informed about AIDS. The Surgeon General's Report on AIDS gives clear, rational information. Yes, there are great risks if we indulge in certain behaviors; sexual contact with an infected person or sharing needles. He is also quite clear that being in a room or shaking hands or using kitchen or bathroom facilities with a person with AIDS is perfectly safe. Once we are clearly informed, there is no reason to be frightened to be working with a person with AIDS, just as we are no longer afraid to be in the office with someone with diabetes or cancer.

If you hear one of your co-workers has been tested positive or diagnosed with AIDS or ARC, please treat them as you would want to be treated if it were you. Don't play "ain't it awful" with them, but do tell them you care and you would like to help them, and ask how could you support them best. If your co-workers are fearful, see what you can do to distribute correct information on the dis-ease. Ask your boss to have a meeting where someone who is experienced can answer questions and calm fears and give out information. Most cities now have AIDS hotline groups who will be glad to come to your office and share information. Above all, dissolve any tendency to judge that person, and don't indulge in office gossip. What we give out comes back to us. Let this be a growing time for you.

A NEW RELATIONSHIP: TELLING OTHERS YOU HAVE AIDS

Who do you choose to tell you have AIDS and how? Again this is an individual answer for each of us. We all have different life situations to deal with. There is no blanket answer. However, I do know that, if you have a low self-esteem and are very critical of yourself, then the people you tell will be likely to give you a hard time. If you are strong and centered in your own self-love, then you will most likely find love and acceptance and support from those around you.

Being truthful and honest is always the best way, if you can. Of course, tell on the first date. Give the other person a chance to make his or her own decision. If he or she turns out to be an important person in your life, it will be much harder to reveal the fact later.

Tell parents immediately and ask for their love and support. Give them a chance. If there is rejection, then turn to your friends and support groups and create your own family.

It is also good to tell friends. You may lose a few of the frightened ones; let them go with love. You will find you have many strongly supportive ones.

Bosses I would tell only if necessary, unless you are sure of a supportive reaction.

There was a young man in the group who worked for one of the big utilities as an accountant. When the company discovered he had AIDS, they first tried to put him way down the hall in a small closet, while they sought to get him out of the office altogether. He came to the group one night in great agitation and having stomach pains. We explained to him the importance of blessing everyone in the firm with love, so that his own mental and physical health would remain good. At the same time, we all agreed with his idea of threatening to sue if he was forced out of a job. So he was neither a frightened doormat nor belligerent. He allowed himself to be as calm and centered as possible as he expressed his terms to the company. Yes, they did come around, and he is still working there. He also found a lot of support with most of his fellow workers.

HAYRIDE ON RELATIONSHIPS

Louise: "So we might want to talk about relationships tonight. I have a feeling there is a lot of relationship stuff in the room. You know, when you want a relationship in your life, moaning about the fact that you don't have one is not the right way to bring one in. You want to love who you are and know that you are lovable and that you are worth loving. And that everyone wants to love such a lovable person as you. And you are bringing such a lovable person now."

Ted: "Well, I created a miracle that I thought was impossible, and it is called a relationship. I wish I had heard somebody say what I am about to say when I was coming here about a year ago, but I really haven't heard this little miracle story here, and I am glad it is mine to tell actually.

"I was diagnosed about a year and a half ago. I have never had a day of sickness, a night-sweat or anything. I fly all over the world for my work. And the only evidence of my disease are the lesions that are on my body. I have gotten a lot more of them since I was diagnosed. And, as I have gotten more of them, I have been really confronted with my vanity, my sense of being a hot person, and all of those things.

"All the things I thought were important to being gay were heavily invested in being physically attractive. And just as I was getting a sense of myself being good-looking, having gone through teenage acne, and not being big enough, and all that stuff, I was really starting to get some self-confidence, and I got AIDS and Kaposi lesions. And I said, 'Goddammit.' And I was dating a man when I was diagnosed, and about ten weeks later, he left. And that was pretty shattering. But what could I expect? Who is going to hang around with somebody who has AIDS?

"And I didn't even have a lot of lesions then; he was just scared. Then I thought, well, the only ones I can date now are people with AIDS, because they are the only ones I am going to feel comfortable with. They are the only ones who are going to feel comfortable with me. And so I ended up having a few short little attractions to other men with KS. I kept trying to make each of these men work. I kept saying, 'This is one of my last chances. I don't have as many chances as I used to have. I am going to like this person, whether I like him or not.'

"It didn't work. And about six weeks ago, I was dating two men, I mean my luck hasn't been that bad, but I was very physically attracted to one and very mentally attracted to the other. It just wasn't complete with either one. I was trying to make it complete the best I could, until one of them faded into friendship, the mental one, which was nice, and the other one said, 'I just found a new boyfriend in the Mastery.'

"And I said, 'Damn the Mastery.' In fact, I always wondered why they didn't have another workshop called the 'Slavery.'

"And came Gay Pride day, and I didn't have a date. And it was such a high, wonderful day, those who were in on it with us; I mean, those who did the Louise Hay float and went to the festival. And a bunch of us were dancing our asses off till midnight, and we went to have dinner at the French Market till two, and I just didn't want that day to end. Even though walking around at the festival seeing a lot of couples was a little painful and lonely. I just didn't want it to end, because it had been the best day I had had in ages.

"So I went home, and I thought, 'I don't want to be alone tonight; I have been in so much love all day, I don't want to be alone.' And the only way I know not to be alone is to go to a bar. I don't go to bars anymore. I haven't been in bars in a long time. And I know that, if I go to a bar having AIDS and especially having lesions, which are very visible, I am not just going to meet someone casually and get a cuddle for the night. Not easily anyway.

"So I went to Cuffs, which is right around the corner from my house, and it is hardly a mirror of my self-esteem at this point. For those of you who know it, it is a pretty sleazy leather bar in Silverlake. But anyway, I walked in, and I thought there would be a lot of people celebrating, because it was Gay Pride night still, and there were four people lurking in the shadows, and one man standing in the light. And I recognized him from my gym, but I really didn't know him.

"I said a polite 'Hi,' and I didn't even want to get involved or anything, because I knew how awkward it would be. You know, I would have to say, "I have AIDS," and when he saw me with the lights on, he would go, 'Ohhh.'

"And I created all this stuff, like it is not going to work. And I just went past him and sat down and had a beer. That is something else I never do anymore. I was breaking all my rules that night. And I was slowly sinking into self-pity, which I know better than to do. He came over to me, and he sat down. And I thought, 'How can I keep the conversation on a non-sexual level,' because I don't want to get this going.

"The first thing he said was, 'I have seen you at Louise Hay. I know your story, and I want to cuddle with you tonight.'

"And I thought, 'He just hasn't seen it all yet. We'll get home, and I will take off the shirt, and he will see all the freckles, and then he will change his mind.' The next morning, when we woke up, he asked, 'What does commitment mean to you?'

"And I just went, 'Whoa, what does first date mean to me?' Anyway, the man is a rebirther. I mean, I couldn't have crossed a more spiritual path. He is heaven-sent. He is incredible. And what he is saying to me now is, 'You can run all you want to. I'm not going to.'

"And it is just blowing my mind. And I want anyone here who is maybe new with AIDS and scared that they had their last chance at love to know that you absolutely haven't. And the real miracle of this to me is that he is HIV negative."

KNOWING WHEN TO LEAVE A RELATIONSHIP

This is a beautiful testimony. But what happens when we do have a relationship and our inner selves know that it is not working out? Do we let the relationship destroy our individual spirits?

When we don't love who we are, we may allow ourselves to stay in a relationship far too long. We will take abuse in a relationship; we will be mistreated in a relationship; we will be put down. And when we do that, we are always saying, "Well, I am not worth loving, so I have to stay here and accept this behavior, because I know nobody else would want me. But where is that concept? That concept is inside of us. It is not out anywhere; it is inside of us. And when we change the belief we have about ourselves, then we are treated differently. And I can't really think of any relationship problem or area of relationships that does not relate totally to how we feel about ourselves. Always. Are we willing to love us? And the question is, if you are not, then what belief is in the way? What do you believe about yourself that is in the way of loving you? We cannot be healed and whole unless we love who we are.

TREATMENT

Today is another precious day on earth. We shall live it with joy. I am part of the symphony of life. I unite myself with harmony, my mind is centered on peace. I am in harmony with all of life. We all walk upon the same earth, we breathe the same air, and we use the same waters. The harmony I create for myself, I radiate around me to all those I come in contact with. I bring peace, love, and harmony to my ever-growing world. We are one with the power that created us.

We are safe, and all is well in our world!

PART III

FINDING HELP

19

Doctors: Helping with Our Healing Process

Affirmation:
God also works through the
medical profession!

When we have AIDS, doctors may become a dominant part of our lives. Our relationship with them is important to our healing process. Many doctors are frightened of AIDS because they know so little about it. Many have accepted that AIDS is a terminal illness and automatically give death sentences to their patients. We have to know that we are not restricted by the limitations and current dismal predictions of the medical profession. We are not statistics. We are unique individual expressions of life. We are under the law of our own consciousness, not the consciousness of medical authorities. "It may be true for you, it is not true for me" is a good affirmation to use whenever you hear any sort of dismal prediction.

It is even quite possible that you may know much more about AIDS than your doctor does. After all, you have the dis-ease—and only you know what exactly it is doing to you. So I would urge you to study everything you can find about AIDS. You need to be informed, both medically and holistically. You want to be part of a healing team with your medical advisor. Remember, that is

195

what a doctor is, a medical advisor, not the final authority and definitely not God. There must be respect on both sides. You want someone who will listen to you, who will respect your fears and questions. Who will explain various procedures and their benefits. Who will tell you of side-effects of the medications and will look for alternatives. You want your doctor to support your turning to nutrition and other alternative healing modalities. If your current doctor does not fill this picture, look for another doctor.

My friend, Dr. Bob Brooks, agrees completely with the patient working closely with the doctor. This is a brief description of his experience with working with AIDS.

"For over three years now, I have been engaged in the diagnosis and treatment of people with AIDS. Some of the people I am working with are living well beyond the projected expectations made on the basis of current statistics. These people I am referring to have an unusual sense of vitality and robustness way beyond that reported in the medical literature and popular press. When I began to encounter such individuals, I asked myself why some persons with serious illness do so well, while others fare so poorly.

"My understanding from my training in medicine and biology led me to believe that these kinds of differences were the result of genetic and constitutional factors. However, I am no longer convinced this is so. In my opinion, those persons that I see with AIDS who are doing the best are thinking about their situations differently.

"I want to share with you some of the things I have come to believe about the healing process.

"I believe that we live in many different domains simultaneously. Two distinct domains are PHYSICAL REALITY and our EXPERIENCE of our lives. Most people consider their experience of life to be a function of their circumstances. However, this notion is questionable. I believe that our experience of life is more apt to be a function of our interpretation of our circumstances.

"It is precisely because we live in a sea of language that we fail to notice the power of words. Recently, some very sophisticated research involving hypertension has demonstrated that one of the most potent stimulators of elevated blood pressure is human speech, and that one of the best ways to achieve long-term control of pathologically high blood pressure is to modify what has been called the human dialogue.

"This kind of research expands our concept of the cause of a medical illness to include another dimension of our humanity, in this instance, ourself as a languaging creature. I have seen a number of people with AIDS creating new romantic relationships after their diagnosis, some of them with people who do not have AIDS, by altering the way thy were willing to talk about themselves and what was happening to them. I'll have more to say about this in a moment.

"I am convinced that well-being resides in our experience of our lives. We can have well-being under any circumstance. Conversely, we can have any circumstance, including wealth and a strong, healthy body, and not experience any sense of well-being.

"This is a particularly difficult concept for some people to grasp, because, from this point of view, a person with AIDS can have a high level of well-being, as measured by his/her level of active participation in daily living, sense of joy, enthusiasm, or love. When their conditions are not met, there is no experience of these positive states of mind for them. However, the failure to have these powerful life experiences is not really because of a lack of a particular set of circumstances. It is more truly the result of the way that they have learned to think.

"True well-being is an individual choice. It involves a shift of position from considering oneself a victim of circumstances to a creator of experience. This shift takes a tremendous willingness to assume individual responsibility. It literally involves a willingness to experience one's SELF as being powerful enough to be the cause of one's own experience.

"This kind of talk about responsibility is very difficult, because most people hear blame when the concept 'responsibility' is used. This is the result of the way we were treated as children. When we were children and did something of which our parents did not approve, their calling us 'irresponsible' was really a placement of blame. When I see patients who refuse to acknowledge their responsibility, they are really refusing to be blamed. Of course we can refuse blame, but we cannot abdicate responsibility. We simply are responsible, regardless of whether we are too confused to acknowledge the fact of it or not.

"I believe that is why responsible persons with AIDS object so strongly to being referred to as 'victims' of AIDS. In their way of thinking, they are persons with AIDS, and they are not experiencing their lives as victims of anything. They are creating lives of love, commitment, and with high levels of well-being.

"Medicine as a discipline of physical science is powerless to create true well-being. The prevention of illness or the eradication of illness is not synonymous with well-being.

"In order to include well-being in medical treatment, we have to have an expanded context of medicine. I believe that any intervention that creates a sense of well-being can lend support to healing processes that are going on in the body. The following are components that I believe are necessary to create what I like to call a HEALING ATMOSPHERE.

"1. INTENTION: The key to any kind of healing is intention. This has been called the 'ill to live.' Without this kind of intention, ill persons will not generate the kinds of behaviors that promote survival. I have seen patients who were in the process of dying suddenly create a strong intention to live and, as a result, make miraculous recoveries. I have also seen persons who could have lived a great deal longer, given their current state of health, die prematurely simply because they didn't want to go on any longer.

"2. HUMAN CONTACT AND LOVE: The power of simple human contact and love seems to have been forgotten in this highly technological society of ours. Psychologists have documented the profound effects of lack of touch and love in infants and named this condition the 'Maternal Deprivation Syndrome.' However, to a lesser degree, I think there exists for most persons in the world today an adult deprivation syndrome. The results of this are not as obvious, yet I think they are just as serious in terms of health consequences. We all need to be loved and touched. Nowhere is this lack of human contact more apparent than in our modern hospitals, where AIDS patients are more often than not kept in a virtual prison of sensory isolation and needlessly treated as the proverbial 'lepers' of a bygone era. In general, we behave as if these basic requirements for a human existence were somehow dispensable. The truth is that no technological advance will ever replace what is basic to our human nature. I think this is beginning to dawn on most people, and underlies many peoples' anxiety about entering a modern hospital. It's as if our unconscious is creating a warning sign: 'unsafe for human being.'

"3. PURPOSE IN LIFE: The avoidance of death is not a very powerful reason to live, and reasons to live will never be generated by science and technology. A person has the best chance of surviving a serious or a catastrophic illness when he/she has SOMETHING he/she considers WORTH LIVING FOR. Reasons for living come from other domains than science, from those intensely private domains that make us uniquely human. Good physicians know this, although they may not be able to talk about it articulately. All of us in medicine have had the experience of seeing patients who had an overwhelming commitment to something or someone, and out of that commitment generated either a cure or else prolonged periods of improvement beyond what would have ever seemed reasonable under the circumstance. You cannot characterize this kind of happening in scientific terms, but you can appreciate the experience of being in the presence of an individual so committed.

"4. WILLINGNESS TO TURN WITHIN: The way we view outside authority in the West is truly astonishing. For many of us, if we read it in a book, it's true. If we experience it directly, we doubt it. We have been taught to be profoundly distrustful of our intuition and basic human experience. Yet, the wisdom of the ages has encouraged men to look inward for the answers to life's most difficult questions. I believe that the healing journey begins with a LOOK INWARD, toward ourselves, and a 'coming to know' our own truths and healing powers.

"I would like to end this short discussion with a brief statement of my position on the matter. I believe that modern medicine has contributed enormous advances to people's well-being. Of this there can be little doubt. However, a large amount of the humanity that is vital to our survival as individuals and as a species has been sadly neglected and ignored by the medical profession. I believe that we are now entering an age of synthesis and cooperation. Just as the superpowers must learn to live together, if we are to avoid final extinction in a holocaust, so must medicine learn to live with other disciplines that make a contribution to well-being. Unless physicians humble themselves and learn to respect other approaches to healing and well-being, they will continue to lose the respect of the very people they are committed to serve. This is a time for a true holism. A time to look at everything that is of value from any tradition or mode. Science alone no longer makes sense."

AFFIRMATION FOR DOCTORS

Just as doctors must begin to respect alternatives and holisms, we must be responsible for the doctors we choose to treat us. The doctors we attract reflect our own mental pictures of ourselves and of the profession. If you are looking for a doctor or thinking of changing your doctor, I suggest you do a little mental work first. Decide what you want in your relationship with this person. Then create an affirmation; you might even write it down. Something like this:

"I now have a wonderful doctor. We respect each other. We are part of a healing team. It is easy for us to communicate and understand each other. My doctor supports me and is convinced I can be healed. He is knowledgeable and supportive about holistic healing therapies. Everything we do together contributes to my healing process. I love my doctor, and my doctor loves me."

Add anything else you want to have in your relationship with this medical person. Then read this over several times a day. Also keep affirming, "I am now attracting the perfect doctor." If you have negative thoughts about doctors or have heard horror stories from your friends, just say to yourself, "That may be true for other doctors, but my doctor is not that way." Put positive mental work into creating for yourself the doctor you want. Do call your doctor by his or her first name. This will put you on an equal basis. Don't hide any part of your life from him. If he is to assist you in your healing path, he must be aware of all facets of your life. This shows you trust him. Any doctor who is offended by this is too insecure for you to be working with. A doctor is a human being, just like you, with some specialized knowledge, but not a superior being.

THE PATIENT'S BILL OF RIGHTS

My friend, Dr. Albert Lerner, has created a "Patient's Bill of Rights" to show the fact that we, as patients, are involved in creating our well-being.

"Taking charge of your existence involves all aspects of your being and all phases of your life. Your doctor/patient relationship is a pivotal one.

"1.   You have the power, with sufficient information and the physician's advice, to decide on your own course of healing.

"2.   You have the right to enter and co-create a partnership with your physician by:
   a.   Understanding the importance of your being LISTENED to attentively!
   b.   Clearly stating the purpose of your visit.
   c.   Stating clearly your needs other than the immediate problem. Example: Long-term needs such as support and advice for staying healthy.
   d.   Giving the physician an idea of your emotional make-up and the way you handle stress. Ask yourself these questions:
      —Do you hold in or express feelings of love, anger, or sadness?
      —What is going on in your personal life, interpersonal relationships, and at work? How do you deal with them?

"3. Interview the doctor. Ask questions!
   a.   What are his philosophical viewpoints on healing?
   b.   Can he carry on a dialogue?
   c.   How does he take positive criticism?
   d.   Is the physician defensive, judgmental, and hard-nosed, or open and available?
   e.   Do you feel rushed, put off, or cut off, when you go to see him?

"4. Demystify Medicine.
   a.   How was the diagnosis made?

    b.   Lab study findings and their significance.

    c.   What other findings were there?

    d.   Treatment plan. Make sure it is the least invasive.

    e.   Side reaction, if any, concerning natural or prescription medications.

"5. And finally, be willing to express your concerns. DON'T BE INTIMIDATED!!"

*   *   *

As you can see, there are many wonderful doctors out there, caring and supportive, knowledgeable and kind, really interested in your welfare, open and receptive to many forms of healing. You can find them, especially if you love yourself. There are a growing number like Dr. Bernie Siegel who realize that the patient has a lot to do with creating a dis-ease and with the healing of the dis-ease. These doctors are willing to go beyond the limitations of the standard medical practice and include the patient in the healing process. They believe in teamwork.

TREATMENT

Today is another precious day on earth. We shall live it with joy. I am a precious being and loved by the Universe. As I increase the love I have for myself, so too does the Universe mirror this, increasing love ever more abundantly. I know that the Universal Power is everywhere, in every person, place, and thing. This loving, healing power flows through the medical profession and is in every hand that touches my body.

I attract only highly evolved individuals on my healing pathway. My presence helps to bring out the spiritual, healing qualities in each practitioner. Doctors and nurses are amazed at their abilities to work as a healing team with me. We are one with the power that created us.

We are safe, and all is well in our world!

20

Dealing with Medical Institutions

Affirmation:
Every hand that touches me
has the power to heal!

HOSPITALS

In cases of cancer, it has been noticed that people who are called "bad" or "difficult" patients have the best survival rates. The patient who meekly submits to all the procedures without question is the one who often doesn't make it. If you find yourself in the hospital, do everything you can to take care of yourself. Ask for a room with a window and a view. Ask questions; insist on answers. Don't submit to procedures unless you know why. Take a tape recorder with you to record conversations with medical personnel. You are paying for these services, and you have a right to question them. Are these procedures really right for your body, or are they just what they usually do for everybody?

If you are too ill to stand up on your own behalf, take a good friend with you. Also see that you have what you need. Take tapes for your tape recorder, healing music, relaxation tapes, healing imagery tapes, etc. Use this time for studying and learning. Do visualizations of healing; write affirmations. Take some personal items to beautify your room. Bring some shirts or tops from home to wear, instead of the hospital gowns. See that someone supplies you with nourishing foods to supplement the hospital fare. Have a bowl of fresh fruit near you.

CASE HISTORY: BILL

"My name is Bill. On November 24, 1984, I was diagnosed with Hodgkin's disease. My reaction was, 'Why me?' I had quit my job three weeks before and started my own business; I had no insurance or security. My first question was, 'How long do I have to live?' I felt that, if anyone in this world was a victim, it was me.

"After the diagnosis, I went to the hospital with my lover to schedule a biopsy. On the way back home, his motorcycle was hit and nearly totaled. We were lucky not to have been seriously hurt. Shortly thereafter, his mother, who I feel is a mother to me as well, was assaulted, her throat cut. By some miracle, she lived and is now doing well. Two months before the end of my chemotherapy, my younger brother experienced carbon monoxide poisoning. I flew to Illinois to be with my family; I hadn't seen them in five years. The doctors told us that, if my brother ever came out of his coma, he would be a vegetable for the rest of his life.

"After two weeks, I flew back to San Francisco for my next treatment. On July 4, my sister called to tell me that my brother had come out of his coma and was doing fine. Two months after my treatments were finished, my grandmother passed away. I had been very close to her. I felt as if I were on a roller coaster that was never going to stop.

"My expectations of others were very high. They were going to cure me. I wanted as little involvement as possible. Chemotherapy was the only option given to me by doctors, other than to let the cancer take over and destroy me. I was skeptical of what the results would be, but decided to let them try to cure me.

"In August 1985, the treatments were over. My doctors told me I was in remission. I seemed to feel okay, so I started back at the gym. A month later, I found a lump in the left side of my groin. In just days, it became larger and more painful. My doctors told me I had a hernia. Thinking that I had started lifting weights too soon, I felt that their diagnosis made sense. After additional testing, I was informed the lump was a tumor that was growing larger each day. That really did it; I was so far down that I didn't think I would ever see light again. Still, I wasn't going to take responsibility; it was their fault that I wasn't cured.

"A few months before, a neighbor had given me a book called *You Can Heal Your Life*. I was now desperate enough to read it. I started the book near midnight and read it until six o'clock the next morning. I did affirmations and listened to the tape, *Cancer: Your Healing Power*. Exhausted, I fell asleep on the sofa. I awoke two hours later. I couldn't believe what I was experiencing; the tumor in my groin was gone. All I could feel was a lump the size of a pea, which had been the size of a walnut for the last three weeks. The strength in my legs had returned, and I was full of love and energy. I hadn't felt this good, even before I was diagnosed. It was incredible!

"From that day on, I became aware that I had to take responsibility for my life; I am responsible for what happens to me. Many good things have happened in my life since that morning. My relationship with my parents was renewed, and we are closer than we have ever been. My lover read the book and listened to the tapes and felt that he was improving himself and our relationship. I don't dwell on negative circumstances anymore. I look at the positive in everything. My cancer has been a great learning experience for me; because of it, my life has become full of joy and happiness. My life is fulfilling, as long as I remember that I love myself and trust that the Universe will take care of my needs.

"The first affirmation that I remember is from *You Can Heal Your Life*. It goes like this:

" 'I am perfectly happy to be me. I am good enough just as I am. I love and approve of myself. I am joy expressing and receiving.'

"The first time I wrote it down, I thought it was dumb and believed just the opposite. Today, it stands very true. I believe every word of it. Every morning, while I'm shaving, I smile at myself in the mirror and tell myself just how much I love me and how special I am. By the time I'm finished in the bathroom, I feel terrific.

"Presently, I am going through my second round of chemotherapy, this time taking an active part, and am having great results. My doctors tell me that my blood counts and physical appearance are better than they have been in the last year. By learning to love myself and being good to my body, I feel as if I have gone from being a one-way street to a four-lane highway."

Bill found a positive way to work with the medical community and their treatments. If you want to go this route you must remember that your willingness to participate in the action of the treatment is imperative. When you do take the drug, know that it is for your highest good. Never think on the side-effects it has caused others; only know the good it can do for you.

You can more easily accomplish this by doing an affirmation, following a daily (or weekly, etc.) ritual for taking the drug. You might say something like, "This is the perfect treatment for me and will work for my greatest good!" It is important never to be unwilling to hear the calls from the medical community and their treatments. Many chemical treatments have brought an end to many a dis-ease. In the case of AIDS, drug designers are producing new ideas every day. This is a very positive thing, for through their creative efforts in combatting

AIDS, other diseases such as leukemia, as well as many other cancers, may be cured. Therefore, in acknowledgment of the medical community, I have given you a sample list of some of the treatments available.

MEDICATIONS
Immunomodulators

These are drugs that increase the body's production of lymphocytes. Theoretically, they will boost your immune system.

1. *DDTC, Immuthiol:* In HIV positive or ARC patients, this drug seems to be the most useful. Not showing any side-effects at all, it has been able to restore normal T4 and T8 levels and ratios in some patients. Since HIV replicates in the T4 cells, some researchers believe that increasing the number of T4s in the blood could increase viral activity as well. Tests in Lyons, France, have shown that this does not happen with DDTC.

2. *IMREG-1:* This is a derivative from the body's own lymphocytes. Acting on the immune system, this drug has shown to increase T4 levels and levels of reactions to antigens such as tetanus-toxoid. It has not restored immune-response levels to normal, but since there seems to be no side-effects, it could be useful in increasing the life-expectancy of AIDS and ARC patients by reducing their risks of opportunistic infections.

3. *Inosiplex, Isoprinosine:* Although the studies on this drug are still in the early stages, feedback has shown that it increases the production of NK, natural killer lymphocytes. Also, no side-effects have been shown.

4. *Interleukin-2:* This is another natural lymphokine known also as T-Cell Growth Factor. In the body,

it has shown to proliferate all T-cell subsets. Because of this, it has the potential means of restoring the normal immune response in patients with AIDS or ARC. Since it is a natural growth factor, no known side-effects have been shown. Vitamin stores have been selling this for years, and it is widely available.

Antiviral Agents

These drugs actually work against the viral replication. They include:

1. *AL-721:* This is a harmless, high concentration lecithin/neutral lipid mixture. Ideally, it will coat the T4 cells (as well as all your cells) with an additional lipid "armor," making it difficult for the HIV to enter and replicate.
2. *Ribovirin:* Although in some patients this drug has caused some anemia, in HIV positive, asymptomatic individuals, it seems to stop the disease from progressing. It does this by inhibiting the action of the enzyme reverse transcriptase, which is essential to viral replication.
3. *Beta-interferon:* This is a derivative from the body's own cancer-sensitive cells. There has been progress in the use of this drug to treat Kaposi sarcoma, but at the expense of severe side-effects, including nausea, weight-loss, and muscular pain.
4. *Zidovudine (AZT) Retrovir:* AZT is the first FDA approved treatment for AIDS that is in wide use. This antiviral drug works against the virus by "fooling" it with an artificial form of the amino acid thymidine, which is necessary for production of viral material. In vitro, all tests show that it is

successful in inhibiting replication. In humans, although all information is not in, the drug seems to work well for one or two years, then viral replication continues. Side-effects include anemia and nausea. This was originally developed as a preventive drug, so these side-effects usually do not occur in HIV positive, asymptomatic individuals with T4 greater than or equal to 500/cc.

Some scientists think that a combination of these two variables can be the answer. Still, consult your doctor before you seek chemical treatment. Many of these are still experimental, and although you may be able to get them "over the border," you could be unnecessarily risking the limited health you have now.

Keep in mind that science is always trying to find a toxin that will kill the disease and not the patient, so look into alternative treatments. There are many holistic therapies that have been instrumental in the recoveries of people with AIDS and other dis-eases.

You can be instrumental also in the healing process of another. This can be accomplished somewhat in hospital visits. Knowing how to deal with a sick person is a gateway to personal joy and healing for all who are involved.

TREATMENT

Today is another precious day on earth. We shall live it with joy. Unknown and unexpected good is coming my way this day. I am far more than rules and regulations. Within every medical establishment there are a growing number of practitioners who are enlightened and on a spiritual pathway. I now attract these people to me wherever I am.

My mental atmosphere of love and acceptance is a magnet for small miracles every moment of the day. Where I am, there is a healing atmosphere, and it blesses and brings peace to all. We are one with the power that created us.

We are safe, and all is well in our world!

21

When Someone You Love Has AIDS

Affirmation:
My heart opens on a deeper level!

IF YOU HAVE A FRIEND WITH AIDS

If you have a friend who has AIDS, express your love in practical ways. Call daily if you can, write letters, or if you are nearby, visit often and be helpful. Sometimes the simplest tasks can be a great chore to the person with AIDS. Offer to do errands and simple household tasks. Take them to the doctor or on an outing geared to their energy levels. You could join a support group and learn how to help them and at the same time support yourself. Love unconditionally; be gentle with yourself and with them.

IF A FAMILY MEMBER HAS AIDS

If you hear a family member has AIDS, go out of your way to tell them you love them and want to support them in any way you can. They need to hear this. Love and support from you will help more than any medicine.

Do what you can to erase any guilt they may be carrying. This is an opportunity. If you have any withheld communications, any old grievances with them, now is the time to rationally talk them out and let them go. I hear over and over from people who are doing well with AIDS that their families love them and support them.

IF YOU HAVE A CHILD WITH AIDS

Now what about the children who have AIDS? I believe they have chosen parents in this lifetime who would pass this dis-ease on to them. So many of the children with AIDS have been abandoned and are alone in hospitals. Many are isolated and used for experimentation and research. That which we give out always comes back to us. If we abandon another, then we ourselves will also be abandoned, now or at some other time. If not in this lifetime, then in the next one. What goes around always comes around.

But this is not to condemn those who abandon us, or treat us ill. If we choose to behave poorly in response to this, we are not justified. Only love can heal, and we can never get even. The buck must stop at some point, so let it be with you. No matter what has happened, no matter what "they" have done to us, we need to stop the pattern and send out love. For love will attract love in return and begin the healing process.

In order to fully understand children and illness, we must learn to take a larger, more cosmic view of life. Children are under the influence of the consciousness of the adults around them. They easily pick up the thought patterns and respond to these patterns. One of the quickest ways to heal a child is to heal the consciousness, the thought patterns, of the adult. The child will quickly pick up the change in consciousness and will reflect this change in its own improved health.

This coincides with how our parents come to us. I truly do believe that we choose our parents. We choose the perfect parents who will give us the sort of experience we need for our own spiritual, evolutionary growth. New souls pick easy experiences, sort of like going to kindergarten. Old souls pick more difficult experiences for their learning lessons. Children who have catastrophic diseases, in my opinion, have chosen these experiences before they ever incarnated.

Sometimes, when we come to this planet, we do not need a long lifetime to have our lesson. We may only need a few hours or a few months or a few years, and then we are complete. We live so many times. Each lifetime is different. Each lifetime we get to experience life from a different viewpoint. If we do not handle our experience well in one lifetime, then we balance it out in the next. If one time we are the rapist, then one time we are sure to be the raped. There is so much good material written on the subject of reincarnation, do allow yourself to investigate it more.

This is not to harden our hearts to people and say, "Well you deserve it because you earned it in another life." That is not where I am coming from at all. We need to help each other transcend our old, negative patterns. I am trying to show us a larger picture of life to show us that every moment we live is important. Everything we say and do and think has meaning, and this is why we need to clean up our act NOW.

If your child has AIDS, stand by him or her. Tell all your family members and neighbors how much you love your son or daughter. Go beyond what "they" may feel or think. You will go far on your own pathway of spiritual growth. All the great teachers from the beginning of recorded history speak of unconditional love; knowing unconditional love is our biggest lesson to learn in life. We put up many obstacles to fully expressing this love, yet we can overcome them all. If we come from the loving space of the heart in all situations, we have risen above judgments, and no harm can touch us.

To treat a loved one as "damaged goods" or "sinners" or even people who "got what they deserved" will not contribute to anyone's healing. We have no time to indulge in such limiting concepts. That is the very attitude that has allowed AIDS to spread as far as it has. We are on this planet to help each other and to make this a world of love and peace and healing.

It is a new experience for us to have someone with AIDS in our lives, and we have no traditional rules on what to do and how to behave. We are all finding our way in this area. To shut ourselves off because we don't know what to do is to deny our friend or loved one support they badly need and to miss an opportunity for our own spiritual growth. I have come to believe that, when we leave this planet, the only thing we take with us is our capacity to love. AIDS gives a new chance to open our hearts on a deeper level. Accept those with AIDS exactly as they are; don't try to change them. Accept what is, and learn how to help them cope with this dis-ease on a day-to-day basis.

If you are frightened of AIDS, then ask yourself how you would react if they had diabetes or a stroke or cancer.

Someone who has recently "tested positive" can be as frightened as one who actually has AIDS or ARC, so be sensitive to this as well. In fact, the diagnosis that might follow may come as a relief, for they no longer have to "fear" having AIDS. This is where the support group can help the individual through those first scary weeks. We give them every bit of positive information we can. We suggest they embark on a nutritional health program and do everything they can to build up their immune systems. If you have a friend who has just tested HIV positive, help them through this period in the most loving way you can.

HOSPITAL VISITS

This is not an easy time for any of us. Visiting people in the hospital is becoming a more common occurrence. Some of us make almost daily visits, as friends and loved ones are dealing with intense physical experiences. It is an awkward time for everyone. We have few guidelines for behavior, and it is hard to know what to do for the patient that is really helpful.

As our knowledge of nutrition increases, we realize that it is not in the best interests of patients to bring them candy and cake. If we bring foods and beverages, it is best if we find high quality organic produce. Fresh fruits and fruit juices are far more beneficial to the body than sweets and colas. Fresh carrot juice is a good addition to hospital food.

When we visit a hospital, we need to think, "What can I do to help their healing process?" "How can I comfort them?" Perhaps they would like to be read to. You might take the patient a positive cassette tape and even an inexpensive tape recorder to play it on if they need one. Time passes slowly for people in hospitals, and one of the many uplifting tapes available can help to make that time a positive experience. It also leaves a memory of your caring even when you are not there.

Remember, it is our presence that means the most. We do not have to be clever and overly cheerful. It is enough for us just to come and to say, "I love you, and I want to give you some positive energy." And then to touch them. "Laying on of hands" has been going on since the beginning of time. It is a normal and natural gesture when someone is hurting. Even with ourselves, if we cut or bruise our bodies, we immediately put our hand over that spot to "make it feel better." This giving and receiving of energy is a blessing to both parties.

When I visit someone in the hospital, I like to massage the patient's feet. This is usually greatly appreciated. Ask permission first, and then just gently rub the person's feet. You don't have to be an expert. Just follow your own inner guidance as to what to do. You might carry a small bottle of hand lotion with you for this purpose. It is probably the nicest gift you can give someone in the hospital—loving attention and relaxing energy. The foot reflexologists claim that the feet carry energy to all parts of the body, and by massaging the feet, the whole body is benefited.

It also gives you something to do, so you don't stand around awkwardly trying to think of appropriate words. If someone has Kaposi lesions on their feet, then you could massage their hands instead. I once visited someone who had so many lesions on his body that the only place I could place my hand was a small area on his ankle.

One of my students in New York, Brad White, has a hospital visiting service for PWAs. They go in groups of three and spend about fifteen to twenty minutes with each patient and just listen, or talk, and/or massage that person. They ask what it is the person wants and do their best to fulfill that. Most of all, they give love where it is most needed.

TREATMENT

Today is another precious day on earth. We shall live it with joy. I have so much love in me that I could heal the entire planet! I now allow this love to come to the surface so that I may use it to help my loved one. I am filled with support, with hope, and with the knowledge that I can be of assistance in a myriad of ways.

I am here to love unconditionally, and I now have the opportunity to do so. We are one with the power that created us.

We are safe, and all is well in our world!

22

On Death and Dying

Affirmation:
We are at peace with
the rhythm and flow of life!

We don't know all the answers. In fact, it seems as though we know very few answers. One of the things we want to do is to make peace with ourselves, no matter where we are and what is going on, and to know that death is not a failure. It is one of the experiences that we have in life. And as I have said many times, when we go, it is our time. And I do think that we make an agreement with our souls as to when we will leave.

We have this concept that we are supposed to be here a very long time. We are here to experience our lesson for this lifetime, and then we move on to a far freer dimension, or maybe we come right back to do it again. Our death is just at the other end of the door from birth. One is coming into the planet, and one is leaving, and it is all well and natural. And I think we have been hiding from the issue of death for a very long time, not wanting to discuss it or be part of it or know anything about it. And all of a sudden, we are being confronted with the need to deal with this issue and to make it okay for ourselves whenever we go.

Also remember that death is *not* a punishment.

Death is not failure. Death is the ultimate equalizer. Death is the ultimate healer. Death is the way we leave this body, this no longer useful suit of clothing, the physical world. Just as I believe we come to this planet many times and have many different experiences, so do we leave the planet in many different ways and at many different ages. There is no right or wrong; there just is.

If you have AIDS and you decide it is best to leave the planet in the near future, do that with joy and with love also. Be peaceful about it. Share this peacefulness with those around you. Let them learn what a loving death can be. If death is frightening, do read Moody's book, *Life After Life*. It offers many examples of people who have had death experiences and returned. Each one talks about being met by such love and light. The experience changed their whole outlook on life and removed all fear of death. It is a beautiful and comforting book.

Just like you, I wish more people were getting well. I find very few really ready to make the commitment to healing themselves. It takes a willingness to commit one-hundred percent for at least six months to a year. I hear over and over, "I cheat on my diet a bit." Cheat who? Where there is a life or death situation, there is no time for cheating.

"Well, I smoke a little grass with my friends." What kind of friends are these who would encourage you to further depress your immune system? Do you need these kinds of friends now?

When I walk into hospital rooms and I see colas and chocolate cake and boxes of candy, I want to weep.

Yes, it is work, this business of getting well. Yes, it does mean changing your lifestyle. Yes, it may mean getting new friends. Are you worth it? Do you love yourself enough? Do you have a reason to live? What do you have to live for?

Some people are using this dis-ease to leave the planet. They have created a life that does not seem possible to straighten out, so they would rather leave now and work it out another time. Some people may want to leave the planet in a dramatic way that makes a statement for the gay cause or for humanity. That's okay. There is no judgment.

I know all things are possible, that every dis-ease created by us can be healed. There are always people who can go beyond the accepted opinions and create miraculous cures. What I have observed with AIDS so far is that, if we catch the dis-ease in its earlier stages and the person is willing to commit to the healing process, recoveries do take place. As long as there is some immune system working, it is possible to heal. When it has gone beyond a certain point, and that differs with each one, it is much harder to make a comeback.

There comes a time in each person's life when he or she must accept that death is now. We need to be peaceful with the timing, whenever it is. We too must learn the acceptance of death. We must also go through the experience it offers.

GRIEF

It is okay to be angry. It is normal and natural to be angry when someone you love leaves. Sometimes we feel guilty about that, especially if a person leaves the planet. We think, "Oh, I shouldn't feel anger." But we do feel it, and it is okay.

We are not used to going through the dying experience. It used to be that you were dealing with people dying when they were very old. Now we are going through a totally different cycle. We are younger, and we are dealing with our friends who are going, who are also younger. And it is an experience that we are not prepared for. We have been shunning this whole concept of death for so long, and now suddenly it is here. It is right in our

midst. And it is happening every day. It is one of the reasons I decided to have my company publish a little book
entitled *As Someone Dies*. It is filled with good, gentle suggestions about how to go through the experience. Just
suggestions and ideas. That is about all we can do—just
help each other. Reach out a hand and say, "I am here
to help."

The grieving process takes at least a full year. You
have to go through the seasons, because there are so
many things you have done with that person, and each
season will bring up some of those things. After a year,
it starts to disappear.

I have often heard people complain that so and so
is "doing all the work" and still they got sick, or so and
so "did all the work" and still they died. Their attitude
becomes "why try to change your life if you can still die."
I feel this is a very limited viewpoint of life.

Everybody dies. This is something many of us do
not want to accept. Trees, animals, birds, fishes, rivers,
and even stars all die, and so do we. And all in the perfect
time-space sequence. I believe we each come to this
planet to learn and to grow. When our particular lesson
is finished, we leave. This is an agreement with our soul.
The soul knows when it is the right time to leave.

If we look at our lives from a victim standpoint and
see death as a failure or as a punishment, then there is
indeed a feeling of hopelessness and failure. However,
this is a time of growth for us, and our goal does not need
to be limited to adding a few days or months to our lives.
What is the point of living longer if we do not improve
the quality of our lives?

IT IS OKAY TO DIE

Illness is not failure. Death is not failure. These are
experiences of life. Death is a method of being born

into the next phase of everlasting, eternal life. "Doing the work"—that is, taking better care of ourselves, learning to release resentment, forgive others and ourselves, loving ourselves unconditionally—all these enable us to go through the experience of illness or death in peaceful, more comfortable ways.

Some people say, "Well, if you 'did the work' you would not get ill at all." Yes, that is possible. We could get to a point where we never create anything uncomfortable for ourselves. I heard the Dalai Lama say, "If we had enough love, we would not need any Tibetan herbs." And yet, if we really got to that place of total unconditional love, we might no longer need to be here on this planet, where the struggle is to learn to love. The socially accepted ways of leaving this planet are illness and accidents. So we create illness and accidents in order to go.

We also seem to forget about the laws of cause and effect, and that what we give out comes back to us. Our thoughts, our words, and our actions go out from us and come back to us as experiences. A sudden bout of illness might be some old stuff coming back for us to deal with. And the lesson could be "how do we deal with it?" Do we immediately fall back into old patterns of guilt and feeling not good enough? Do we beat ourselves up because we are having an uncomfortable experience?

Every moment is a learning, growing time. If we have been learning to love ourselves, periodically we will give ourselves a test to see if it is really true, and how far we've come. How do we know if we really love ourselves until we come through a situation where in the past we would have condemned ourselves and berated ourselves and now we are being loving and gentle?

I have seen many people who came to me lonely and bitter and frightened. After a few months of work, they changed into loving, forgiving people. Not totally loving or forgiving, but much more so than they were at the beginning. Then they had another bout of illness, only this time it was much different. They were much more peaceful and even gentle with themselves. They attracted and were surrounded with many loving people to help them go through the experience. Some have to even cut down on visitors, so many want to love them and help them.

I have seen others go through the dying process so surrounded and encouraged by loving people that they were amazed. It took them to come to the dying process to learn and realize how many people really did love them. How many people were willing to take time out to care for them. It was a high price to pay for the knowledge. They could have learned this much earlier and in easier ways. We can allow the love to come in at any time. We can make our lives richer and fuller now.

Illness is not a failure. Death is not a failure. These are experiences we go through. How we experience them has to do with our own inner growth. "Doing the work" does not mean you will never have a problem. It means you will be able to go through these experiences in a different way. Instead of them being tragedies, they are something that "is." No matter how much you love yourself, you will leave the planet one day, you will die. Your mental state as you leave the planet has much to do with your willingness to clean up old issues before you go.

The sooner we clean up the old issues—forgive the family, make peace with ourselves, love who we are, allow others to love us—the sooner we can enjoy our lives now.

We are all trying to understand the larger viewpoint of life, to comprehend the metaphysical way of seeing a greater picture. We are doing our best with the understanding, knowledge, and wisdom we have at the moment. Growing and changing is not an easy task. The mind likes to stay settled. The mind will jump at any opportunity to resist the new way of thinking.

Yet you can be in control of your thoughts. Don't let your mind rule you. We don't have to jump back into the old ways of thinking, just because there is a setback. Don't let the mind find another way of resisting and becoming upset.

Let our goals be peace of mind and improving the quality of our lives today, in this moment. How can we love ourselves more? Who or what else can we forgive? I believe the main thing we take with us when we leave the planet is our capacity to love. How can we increase that capacity?

This question especially comes to mind when dealing with AIDS. When so many of our friends are dying, how can we produce this love? Is it worth it to have to love, then let go?

DEALING WITH MULTIPLE DEATHS

We have noticed that people from the group seem to go to the hospital or leave the planet in waves. Everything will be quiet, and then suddenly several will get ill, or one after another will die. This is always upsetting for the group. We rejoice when one gets better, and we are deeply saddened when once again we are confronted with our own vulnerability and mortality.

We find ourselves once again facing fear. Frustrating anger comes up and must be dealt with. It is so harmful for emotions to be stuffed inside, and that is where the support group comes in handy. We can turn to each other.

Joseph Vattimo, who works very closely with me and is of tremendous support, will sometimes get overwhelmed with emotions, as I do. Then we will fall into each other's arms and just sob helplessly. After we have let those feelings of rage and hopelessness out, we just get back to work, for there is so much to do.

Having watched so many leave in the past few years, I have noticed that often those who go with the most pain and suffering are those who have the most self-hatred and guilt. Guilt and self-hatred often go hand in hand. Guilt always seeks punishment, and punishment creates pain.

They have not been willing to let go of the pain of the past. In addition, they may have very horrendous images of what it will be like when they leave the planet.

If we were raised in a religion that stressed the burning fires of hell and we still choose to believe it, then we will most likely be terrified to die. I often suggest reading Raymond Moody's book, *Life After Life*. Those who have experienced death and have been resuscitated describe it as a beautiful experience—peaceful and very loving. They also say they will never again be afraid to die. I believe in gathering all the positive information we can about every aspect of life, including death.

Those who leave peacefully and with acceptance have often cleaned up their issues. They have looked at the old resentments and have been willing to forgive. They have often healed the rifts with their families, and they have made peace with themselves. They have learned to love and accept themselves just as they are. They have a positive concept about death, accepting that this lifetime is but one stepping-stone on their eternal journey through life.

Some people are totally rejected by their families and die in such loneliness and fear. We all want our mommies and our daddies in times of stress. We want our parents to hold us and to tell us that it will be all right and we are safe.

This is where our support group can do so much good. The group can be the surrogate family, giving love and fulfilling needs. We can be our own parents.

Our support group can also be of great help to the families themselves who are frightened and bewildered and perhaps totally ignorant of the subject. If all one knows about AIDS is what they read and hear in the media, then the experience is approached with hopelessness. There is comfort in just being with people who have gone through these issues before. Perhaps they can answer the multitude of questions. If death is approaching, then the parents can be helped through that experience too.

LIVING WILLS

There is the issue of Living Wills—making out a will, stating about how far you are willing to have the hospitals go in using mechanical or manual, heroic measures to keep your body alive. Some states accept Living Wills, some do not.

Sometimes bodies get to the point where it is not worth struggling anymore. The hospital will always have one more way they can force the body to experience a few more hours or days of life. Do you want to put up with that? This is a question that is to be looked at and decided when you are in good shape. If it is delayed too long, one may not be coherent to make the decision.

The Living Will can also state who can make the decision. Sometimes it is better to have a friend or lover who is well versed in the situation make the decision than a hysterical parent who just arrived and knows nothing.

We all die. I believe we have all died many times, just as we have been born many times. Death is not a shame, a punishment, nor a failure. We are not wrong or "not good enough" if we try to heal our bodies and still leave the planet. It is a normal and natural way to go, just as birth is the normal and natural way of coming to this plane of action. We have many chances to do it differently. The process of death is often easier than the process of birth. We struggle our way through the birth canal to arrive. We can just let go and slip away into the light when we leave.

I have seen many beautiful, peaceful deaths. These are with people who have cleared up their issues with others and with themselves, who are clear that death is a positive experience. They clearly see the light as they are ready to leave and know that so much love is waiting for them. I have also seen painful deaths, where the person is fearful and doesn't want to let go. Perhaps they believe in the Devil and everlasting hell.

If you are helping a friend or loved one go through this special time, do everything you can to make it a joy. Listen to them, allow them to share whatever they want to express. Be a comfort. Hold their hands, rub their feet. Tell them how much you love them. Let them know they will come through the light and be received with great love. There is nothing to fear. Let them know they are safe, and they will do it perfectly.

We all come in in the middle of the movie, and we leave in the middle of the movie. There is no right time or wrong time, just *our* time. All is in Divine Right Order and happening in the perfect time-space sequence. We never lose anything or anyone. We are always connected on some level.

Remember your love and your connectedness, even as you move through the grieving. Death does not end our relationship with that person. Rather, by internalizing it, we are able to deepen our lives and guide ourselves along the path of acceptance and self-love.

TREATMENT

Today is another precious day on earth. We shall live it with joy. Though we walk through the valley of the shadow of death, we are at peace. For we know that both birth and death are normal and natural experiences of life. We are surrounded by love now, and when we leave this planet we will be released by those who love us. In turn, we will be welcomed joyously by those who are waiting for us with open, loving arms.

Infinite love extends beyond the universe and beyond Death itself. Consciousness is eternal, and so are we. We are one with the power that created us.

We are safe, and all is well in our world!

23

Alternative Therapies

Affirmation:
I can nourish my system with love!

If you are determined to do everything you can to put together a program of therapies to help you in your healing process, there are several areas to explore. These have all proven beneficial for some people. Every "body" is different from every other body, so the programs will vary somewhat. Do look into these various alternatives to find the ones that work for you. Yes, you need to take charge. You need to be in touch with your body and decide which programs are best for you.

If you are a person who is still taking recreational drugs and overdoing alcohol, NOW IS THE TIME TO STOP! You must remove the toxins from your system. These toxins can include non-prescripton drugs, various chemicals, infections, parasites, and even food additives.

NUTRITION

Nutrition is a vital part of the healing process. For many of us raised on the standard American diet, it is a revelation to learn of the damaging or healing properties of various foods and beverages. Eating convenience foods, frozen and canned foods, microwaved foods, foods with chemicals and preservatives can be damaging to the body. These foods are not good for us when we are well and gradually contribute to the deterioration of the body. If we are ill, these foods hinder our body's ability to heal itself.

To improve your diet, almost all the nutritionists agree that you need to restrict sugar, all the colas and soda pops, white flour products, milk products, and red meat. And foods that contain yeast, especially if you have a yeast infection. These are either dead foods that give you little nourishment or foods that contribute to your body's problems.

Nutritionists also agree that you need to emphasize fresh foods, vegetables, fruits, whole grains (brown rice, barley, oats, rye, amaranth, wheat, buckwheat, quinoa, millet), and some fish and poultry. These fresh foods contain life-enhancing properties. The cells in your body love having them as they contain all the elements that go into repairing and renewing your organs and cells. Eat at home more. Love yourself enough to cook your own food. Make sure you get the correct nourishment you need. You will seldom find it in a restaurant. Nourish and feed yourself with love and good food. You are worth it.

There are many good books written on this subject of nutrition. I have listed several in the back of this book. One of the best in my opinion is Anna Marie Colbin's book, *Food and Healing* (Ballantine Books.) If you are serious about learning the relationships between food and your body, this is a good book to study. However, it is not the only book available.

Vitamins and minerals can be a good addition. Yet I would not recommend going to the health-food store and just picking up a few. You really need to see a good nutritionist or herbologist and have a program tailored to your particular needs. You may have no idea of what you really need, so consult someone who knows.

As Americans, our poor eating habits are not a new thing. We are now in the second generation of the Great American Diet—what I think of as non-food eating. Upon this planet is every kind of fruit and vegetable and grain to sustain life in the best possible way. We have turned away from these natural foods and become a culture of synthetic foods. Many people feel it is now normal and natural to exist on colas and cakes and packaged convenience foods that have very little nutrition in them.

The original children who began to eat this kind of non-food diet have grown up and had children, and now these children are becoming adults, and they have very little stamina; their immune systems are not as strong as immune systems were twenty-five years ago.

You may say, "Well, then why has the life-expectancy continued to increase?" This is due to the medical industry's capabilities of forcing the body to exist longer—not because of good nutrition.

Physically and psychologically, poor eating habits become another stress in our lives. How many times have you looked at a fast-food hamburger and thought to yourself, "Ugh!" Junk is junk, and we can intuitively recognize it.

The body can only handle this kind of non-supportive stress for so long. Well, "so long" has now arrived. The normal, healthy body is quite capable of taking care of itself. This is reflected in the response of our immune systems. Our immune systems were designed to throw off invaders. If we weaken our immune systems by drugs and alcohol and non-foods, then we are wide open to the popular dis-ease of the moment.

At the same time that poor nutrition became the norm, we have had the drug culture explode upon our society. I have never been able to understand why the authorities allowed drugs to take hold. It would have been so easy to squelch it at the beginning. Now, we have thousands of drug addicts who must have their fixes and will do anything to get them, including stealing, mugging, and murder. To lessen this to a degree, the government even finances treatment of heroin with a less addictive drug, methadone. In many areas, the streets are unsafe because of it. Drugs and alcohol have become a way of life for many people.

So we now have this group of young people who have all the problems of other people and have been taught by their parents and by society that they are not good enough and not acceptable as they are. Many gays have parents who will not even speak to them. It is not surprising that lots of gay people jumped on the drug- and alcohol-abuse bandwagon. "I've been told I'm no good, so it doesn't matter; let's party!" And party they have—morning, noon, and night, when possible.

CASE HISTORY: ALBERT

"I was feeling rather ill, not myself, when I went to the doctor's office that fall day. It was November of 1984, to be exact. My whole body seemed a bit sluggish, and there was a persistent dryness in my throat and a white coating on the back of my tongue. I knew what thrush was. I had seen it enough times on people with AIDS.

"My doctor was reluctant to do a culture on my throat, as he thought it was a waste of my time and money, but I pressed for it. It came back positive, to his and my surprise. At this time, I also had a battery of tests done, including a T-cell test. My T-cell ratio was .96—not too terribly dangerous, but nonetheless low. I wanted it going no lower.

"My doctor also gave me a prescription of Mycelex torch throat lozenges, which cleared up the thrush, but after a few weeks, the fungus was back.

"Over the next nine months, I made some changes in my life that have brought on some significant changes in my health and well-being.

"I started with nutrition and cut out all sugar, honey, and corn sweeteners. Overdoing it on sweets has always been easy for me, so this was a good start. Absence of sugar gives me more energy. I haven't consumed any alcohol or drugs in three years, so that wasn't a problem, but had I still been using or drinking, I am sure my health recovery wouldn't have been as rapid. Mostly, I ate whole foods, lots of vegetables, fruits, meat, poultry, and grains. Dried fruit is good too, especially raisins, which are wonderful for the blood and also a wonderful source of iron.

"I went to my local health-food store and bought lots of vitamin C, 1500 mil., and took one with each meal, and in the morning I would take a teaspoon of acidophilus, mixed in a cup of water or juice.

"Isoprinosine was making a name for itself in Mexico. I was told that it somehow stimulated the immune system, so off I went to Tijuana. The amount I took for the first half of the dosage was six a day, two with each meal, but after five or six months I started feeling "bouncy," a bit dizzy, so I laid off for a month. Then, for the second half, I changed the dosage to three a day, one with each meal. This agreed with me more, and I finished the isoprinosine up.

"A friend told me about the Wednesday night 'Hayrides' and invited me along to sit in and learn a bit more about the Louise Hay approach to good health and positive thinking.

"I owned many of the tapes and played them often. I found in them a wonderful sense of peace and contentment when listening—a voice in me wanting more of this new way of dealing with life and health.

"Yes, eating good foods, vitamins, and other medications were definitely agreeing with me, but more important, I had to start to get honest and centered within myself. I had to begin the process of making the mental changes that were to bring about a profound alteration in my attitude regarding my life and health. The Hay group and the book, *You Can Heal Your Life*, have taught me about making positive affirmations in all areas of my life, not only just my health. Also, mirror work and meditations have played a big part in my continuing good health.

"In August of 1985, I went back to my doctor for the same tests. I no longer have thrush; my T-cell ratio is 1.9; and I even had the HTLV-3 test done (against the doctor's wishes), which came back negative.

"I thank God for many things in my life today—a wonderful, supportive family, who approve of who I am and what I do, good friends, work, a happy future in a line of business that I feel creative in and enjoy on a daily basis. Most of all, I love and approve of myself, and for the first time in my life. From that seemingly simple statement, I have affirmed a wonderful life and continued good health for today and the future."

HERBOLOGY

I have noticed that, for every illness that human beings can create, there is an answer in nature. It is just a question of finding it. If we can create a dis-ease, then we can find the cure. Herbal remedies are as old as the planet itself. In modern times, we have moved away from them to find the instant symptom reliever in the chemicals of the drug companies. However, the chemical drugs often have side-effects that can be almost worse than the original disease. Herbal remedies take a little longer to take effect. They are not just symptom suppressors. When they do their work, the body is brought back into balance and health.

Dis-ease means the body is out of balance. Chemical drugs suppress symptoms; they take care of the immediate problem; they do little to bring the body into balance. It is the imbalance that created the problem in the first place. Herbal remedies go directly to the cause of the disease; and as this is what is corrected, the symptoms gradually disappear.

I believe we will find an herbal remedy to help eliminate AIDS. Remember, the medical profession is still spending billions of dollars a year to find the cure for cancer. The herbal practitioners have been curing cancer for years. So we know that there are herbal combinations that contribute to the cure of cancer. I believe that one or two herbs added to the herbs already used for cancer will create the combination that will be the natural healing agent for AIDS. There are a group of monks in Tibet who are working on finding an herbal formula now.

Herbs can be used to detoxify the body, improve circulation, tone organs, and perform many other healing actions. Herbs are slower than our fast-working western medicines; however, there are fewer side-effects, and herbs do get to the cause of the problem. There are many good herbologists around. It is worth looking into this alternative healing therapy. Chinese herbology is becoming more widely known, and many people are getting good results from it. Garlic and Pau d'Arco tea are some of the popularly used herbs these days.

VITAMIN C

Vitamin C therapy—that is, taking massive doses of Vitamin C to eliminate allergic reactions to drugs and to build the body's defense system—could also prove beneficial. Linus Pauling, in his book *Vitamin C and the Common Cold*, in 1970, was the first to suggest taking massive doses to fight and prevent dis-ease. Robert Cathcart, M.D., of Los Altos, California, and Keith Barton, M.D., of Berkeley, California, have both been working successfully with AIDS patients for some time, using large doses of Vitamin C. You must work with a professional if you take any of these therapies.

HOMEOPATHY

Homeopathy has been around since the late eighteenth century. In the early part of this century, it was widely used in this country, but fell out of favor with the rise of modern allopathic medicine. The British royal family still uses homeopathic medicine exclusively. It is a system of using natural substances to alleviate symptoms.

"Homo-" and "homeo-" are the Greek root for "same" or "like." So homeopathy is in fact the treatment of ailments with like substances. One dis-ease would have a specific substance to extract it—one that would "act" or is "like" the dis-ease itself.

A consultation with an experienced homeopath is best. If you cannot find one, then you might read Dana Ullman's book, *Everybody's Guide to Homeopathic Medicine* (Tarcher, 1984), to give you some basic knowledge.

EXERCISE

Exercise is another positive habit you may want to develop. It is a personal thing, so create an exercise program that is perfect for you. Exercise also stimulates the energy of your body. If not overdone, it can make you feel better. A workout at the gym three times a week is great. A half-hour walk each morning or evening is also good for your body. Get out and get moving, if you can. At home you can still do simple exercises and imagine yourself doing a more strenuous routine. Over a period of time you will find yourself doing these more strenuous activities.

Remember, the mind always has effect over the body, and a mental exercise routine will tide you over until you can get going again on the physical level.

ACUPUNCTURE

Look into acupuncture, which is a five-thousand-year-old Chinese system, based on the energy flow in the body. When we are ill, often our energy gets stuck. There are many meridian points used that can strengthen the body's defensive energy. Acupuncture activates your own healing energy system. I use it periodically for general well-being. The positive effects of acupuncture can include increased energy or well-being, improved respiratory status, decreased size of nodes, relief of night-sweats and diarrhea, and discontinued drug or alcohol abuse.

BODY WORK
Massage Therapy

And, of course, do explore massage therapy. Many of us, and particularily PWAs, carry a lot of fear and tension. Massage brings an enormous amount of relaxation to our bodies and to our minds. In San Francisco, there is a beautiful woman named Irene Smith, who has devoted herself in the last few years to massaging only PWAs, and at this point has probably massaged more people with AIDS than anyone else. Irene has now become a teacher of others willing to work with seriously ill people. Make massage a regular part of your life. If you can't find or afford a professional masseur or masseuse, then exchange with a friend. Or create a small massage group of three or four friends who take turns massaging each other.

Reiki

Reiki is a channeling of Divine healing energy through people. Simply put, Reiki is the laying of hands. Our hands are powerful tools in the healing process. Everything we touch will feel our own personal energy. And when we concentrate this energy on healing, it can be done. During my Wednesday night group meetings, I always have the Reiki tables out. Some of the therapists are professional, and some are just people who want to help. Nevertheless, the healing energy still works the same.

Trager

Another useful body therapy is Trager. Developed by Milton Trager, it is a simple procedure involving only one body part at a time. For example if, say, resentment is stored in the arm, the therapist would take the arm in his hands and rock and rock and rock. As this happens, the patient begins to release his hold and his resentment. This continues until all of the negativities are released. It is a good lesson in letting go.

Rolfing

Rolfing is more specific and concentrated than Trager. There are specific charts that show where pent-up emotions, resentment, hatred, etc., are stored. Then through a concentrated massage of the area, pinpointing the storage site to usually a very small place, it is gradually worked out. This method was developed by Ida Rolf, who feels that a more intensified and concentrated effort is necessary.

MENTAL WORK
Crystal Healing

The power of crystals has been known and been in use for thousands of years. From the ancient Egyptians to the scholars of Greece and Rome, crystals have been known to have special properties that could help in our spiritual and physical healing. Crystals basically store and magnify thoughts, light, any type of energy.

There is even a method of crystal healing, with charts specifically directing the correct crystal to the part of the body in need. Again, here all that is needed is a thought, a positive thought, of health or safety—anything you need from the Universe. It is believed that your crystal will store this thought, then magnify it into the Universe. The Universe will, in time, mirror this thought into your personal healing.

Many books are available about the complex and diverse aspects of crystal usage.

Mental Attitude

As we have talked about repeatedly in this book, your mental attitude will have much to do with your emotional well-being, which in turn will affect the health of your body. Your program will want to include study and practice of what Gerald Jampolsky calls "attitudinal healing," changing the way you choose to look at situations. Look into studies like the Course in Miracles, or take classes in Silva Mind Control or self-hypnosis. Expand your spirituality and your grasp on the larger side of life.

You may want to find a counselor who is experienced in dealing with the many issues involved with having AIDS. You need to get the negative feelings up to your conscious level and express them. Your local AIDS group usually has someone trained in handling these special aspects of your new life. If you can't find a counselor, then use a friend or your support group. If there is no one available, then use your mirror for release. Talk to your mirror, tell it everything; let your hurts and fears out and also your love and joy. Sometimes we have to be our own counselors.

Do find someone else you can help. Come out of yourself. Helping another is beneficial for both of you. It might be someone in your support group; it might be someone who has no one at all. No matter what your condition, you can do something for another. Just a daily caring phone call can mean a great difference to another soul in pain.

TREATMENT

Today is another precious day on earth. We shall live it with joy. The spiritual food required by my mind and body is a constant flow of love. I show love to myself in a panorama of ways. I see this love expressed in the choices I make for myself. I feel it in the love I surround myself with. I love myself enough to feed myself only nourishing foods and beverages. I love myself enough to have a diet of positive thoughts and actions. I bring to myself loving help for every area of my life. We are one with the power that created us.

We are safe, and all is well in our world!

24

Support Systems

As the epidemic of AIDS has continued, I have watched the gay community come together in a united way to help their brothers and sisters in this time of need. It is clear what love can do. Shanti, APLA, Aid for AIDS, and the local AIDS project centers around the country are working unbelievably hard and opening their hearts to fill in the gaps missed by the government and churches. Gay people are discovering how deeply they are capable of loving and giving. We humans often seem to need a tragedy or a war to unite us and bring out the best in us. This is truly a time of war—against our greatest fear, that of the unknown.

Support groups are one of the most important things we can have, especially when we have a problem. We all need love and support at all times; however, when there seems to be an insurmountable problem, then the support group is vital. A support group can be as simple as three friends getting together in a positive way or as large as my West Hollywood group of over six-hundred people. Whether the group is large or small, the principles are the same. I wasn't an expert when I began my group. But through the years I have learned some simple pointers you might want to keep in mind if you are thinking of starting a group of your own.

HOW TO START A SUPPORT GROUP

How do you start one? Just gather two or three friends and follow these guidelines. If you do it with love in your heart, your group will grow. People will be attracted to you like a magnet. Don't worry about where you will meet if you get bigger; the Universe will find a way. Write to my office. We will give you an outline on how to hold your group. Be there for each other.

1. If the group is small enough, have everyone introduce themselves at the beginning and state why they are there.
2. Don't waste time just playing "ain't it awful." You have already listened to far too much of that nonsense.
3. Gather positive information about the dis-ease. Photocopy informative material to pass among the group.
4. Listen to each other. Give each person time to share, if they wish. Give positive feedback.
5. When someone has a problem, pool your resources to help them find a positive answer.
6. Practice affirmations. Create them for specific situations. For instance, at one meeting you could all create an affirmation for raising the T-Cell count. This would bring your minds together in constructive, positive ways.
7. Do a visualization each time. Let different people lead them. The visualization can be spontaneous or read, or you can even play a tape. Be sure to relax the body as you begin.

THE HAYRIDES

In my own support group, we begin with a welcome. Then we have about ten minutes for announcements. Next, we turn the lights down and sing or do a chant for about five minutes, followed with a short meditation.

After the meditation, the healing tables are opened. We have several folding tables and some massage tables. People who want to receive healing energy lie on the tables, and others who want to give love and energy surround the tables, placing their hands on the person lying down. We have several Reiki practitioners who always willingly offer their healing hands. These healing tables are ready throughout the meeting, and those lying down can still hear all that goes on.

Open Discussion

I will then talk for awhile on the subject for the evening. Then we open the room for sharing. People can either comment on what was being discussed or share their own experiences in that area. They can ask a question or tell us of their problem. The discussion can go in any direction. I think it is this flexibility that makes the evening turn out to be exactly what we need. Many nights, we have great guest speakers.

We concentrate on the principles I teach, approaching life from the standpoint that we have the power to make positive changes in our lives. How to do that is what the meeting is about. We do a lot of work on dissolving resentment, on forgiving, and of course on how to love ourselves more. We have decided not to pay attention to the negative news reports on AIDS. We read as little as possible about it, and when we do see an AIDS story with its fatalistic attitude, we remember to say to ourselves, "It is not true that everyone is dying. I know of people who are living and healing themselves." We cannot give in to those who are determined to see AIDS as a dis-ease that kills everyone. We do not have to agree with them. Bless the media with love, and know it has no power over us. We make the decision of what to believe. We believe in life, in love, and in healing.

Towards the end of the meeting, we do some healing work. We move all the chairs to the side of the room. Then we either sit in a large circle on the floor holding hands and doing a visualization or we do what we call "healing triads."

Healing Triads

Healing triads consist of three people sitting down together and removing their shoes. Then one person will lie down, with one person sitting at their head and the other person sitting at their feet. Do your best to make the person lying down as comfortable as possible, perhaps putting a small pillow or jacket under their head or even putting their head on your lap. If you have a crystal with you, place it in the heart area, with the point up; it gives a little extra energy. We lower the lights and play the same music each time. I use "Bamboo Flute," for it has certain qualities I associate with healing. We center ourselves by breathing a few times, and then we chant three "oms," that ancient healing sound.

The two people sitting up rub their hands together until they feel warmth and tingling in their fingers. Then they place their hands on the person lying down and just send love and healing energy. Everybody does it perfectly, because our inner intelligence guides our hands. We stay in that position for about five to ten minutes, during which I give a meditation or visualization. I use the phrase "and so it is" to close each one; it lets us know that meditation is over. We then change positions so each person will get to experience each position, which is quite different. At the end of the third meditation, we once again chant three "oms" to close the circle.

Then we sit up, hold hands, and sing our song, the one we have been closing the meeting with since we first began. It is called, "I love myself." Jai Josefs wrote this song years ago for the Ken Keyes group. The words are so perfect for the work we do that it has become a signature tune.

CREATING A HEALING CIRCLE

My friend in New York City, Samuel Kirschner, has another group called the Healing Circle. I find this very useful in creating the intimacy that is needed for healing power. Here are some excerpts from his handout on creating a Healing Circle.

"The engine that drives a healing circle—what makes each and every person walk through the door and choose to become open and vulnerable in a group of mostly total strangers—is the yearning for growth, and the search for empowerment and enlightenment to grow more. It is the search for a safe and fertile space.

"Space has a lot to do with a Healing Circle. A circle is such a powerful geometric form, flexible and yet inviolable, continuous and yet inclusive, capable of infinite expansion and yet steady and strong and reliable. A circle doesn't force people into line or put them in a box or threaten them with a lot of sharp edges. A circle is a nurturing shape, like the womb where we all began to grow and learned our first lessons about love.

"After attending Louise Hay's workshop three years ago, several of us realized we needed an ongoing way, like her workshop, to maintain and continue loving ourselves. At the beginning, all it took was inspiration and the willingness to hold the space for each other. I cannot conceive of life being the same without this group of people. Some have become my loved ones, others my friends. Each week, I feel myself growing eager for the circle to form so that we can be together again, and I can get another shot of healing energy.

"One of the most gratifying things about our circle is that it has begun to throw off seeds. Not only have we succeeded weekly at holding the space for each other, but we are now exploring holding the space for other groups to form in other boroughs and counties around the metropolitan area.

"If a circle is powerful enough to reach across a city to seed other circles, then perhaps there is no limit to the seeding that can be done. We can take the energies generated by the group and project them throughout the city. Healing Circles can be extended into prisons, can be used to visit old Healing Circle members too sick to attend, and can even give support to health-care professionals in danger of 'burnout.'

"*Getting Started:* What are the most basic elements? How do you create a space that supports people in a feeling of wholeness? What is a Healing Circle, and how does it work to encourage self-empowerment while serving as a forum for the exchange of information and ideas? It focuses the ultimate goal on inspiring and challenging the participants to accept responsibility for their healing and for their lives. It focuses on the ultimate tool: creating a positive and loving atmosphere that breaks down barriers, where anything can be said and where isolation comes to an end.

"*Companions:* Communication is the very first step in forming circle. That is, finding the courage to pick up the telephone or host an exploratory dinner party or stand up in another social group and say, 'I need support from my friends, and I would like to give support in return.' This is the way the ball gets rolling. It is about taking that step, finding that courage in the love of friends and colleagues, and trusting the Universe that no harm will come from following intuition. Newsletters written for PWAs, drug hotlines, and other organized support groups such as AA and health-care professionals all help to get out the word.

"*Atmosphere:* Finding a space, at the beginning, is as easy as finding someone with a living room large and comfortable enough to accommodate your circle companions. Exploring lighting and the warmth of light, sound, and how to control it while sitting in a circle, the optimum shape and height of a room, ventilation, plants, surface treatments, and what a room ought to feel like, and the personality that the room can bring to the circle. Space can be the greatest expense for a healing circle. Promoting space or financing it can be done without deterring those unable to pay for attending the group.

"*Completing the Circle:* Holding the space starts with holding hands and breathing together. This unifies the circle's energy.

"*What is Appropriate for How Many:* Having a sense of what might work for two people, for twenty—even more.

"*Proposing a Theme:* In large groups, topics can help unify the flow of energy and attention, and they can stimulate comments from people who have been afraid to share their fears.

"*Visualizations:* Geared toward entering deeper personal spaces of healing, visualizations work with forgiveness, gratitude, the inner child, joy, and finding the Higher Self. There can be a surprising amount of hidden talent in a group, eager to lead visualizations. Visualizations are recommended at least once every evening.

"*Personal Stories/Sharing:* What's going on in the lives of the people who have walked through the door? Why are they here? What do they hope to get out of their experience? Have they learned something about healing in the last week?

"*Music:* Music opens the heart, affects breathing, and unifies the group's energy. It can have an immediate healing effect. Choice can vary, but any music that is serene by nature can be helpful as background for a process, and simple catchy songs can be wonderful for group join-ins. Louise Hay's *Songs of Affirmation* are particularly recommended.

"*Movement:* At the middle point of the evening, people get tired, and there is a need for energy to be expressed physically. At that point, everyone is asked to stand, and exuberant, danceable music is chosen. Everyone is encouraged to move in whatever way they feel like. This is usually a highlight of the evening.

"*Modalities of Healing:* Here we emphasize herbal treatments, homeopathy, acupuncture, body work, nutrition, attitudinal healing, rebirthing, etheric healing, and more. The circle is a forum for the exchange of information about ways each member has explored healing himself. It is also a place to introduce remarkable doctors and a place to support health practitioners in their work.

"*Philosophy:* The underlying philosophy of the Healing Circle is a self-created reality: that we are responsible for our lives, and thus everything in life is an opportunity for growth and transformation. For everyone, but especially for those with AIDS, we share a message of hope and healing. It is our privilege to share time and space with people who have chosen such a brave path. We respect and honor this particular path, and support them and ourselves in rising above the fear and panic being spread by the media. We are beings of love and light— limitless in our ability to heal our lives."

HUGS

Last but not least at the Hayrides, we have "hug time." I suggest we hug as many people as we can. This also gives us time to talk to each other. Perhaps someone has shared a problem during the meeting; at hug time, several others will come up to share solutions. It also gives people time to come and talk to me privately and to share a hug with me.

We want to have people leave the support group feeling better than when they walked in. They get a positive lift. This feeling can last for days. They also have met others they can call and connect with. Sometimes, two or three sentences on the phone can make an enormous difference in our day. So the group is a take-off point to building the support you need on a daily basis. At this group, you can ask for what you want, and if possible we supply it.

We have hospital visiting teams that visit our members who need comfort and laughter. We collect food for the APLA food distribution program, for those with AIDS and ARC who cannot pay for the basic necessities of life. Some are interested in the political issues and bring information on that. Talented members often offer their services, and it can be anything from offering to clean a house to a free haircut to singing for the group. The possibilities are endless.

NETWORKING

If you don't want to attend a large group or begin a group of your own, you might want to network. Networking is simply sharing what we know with each other—positive information and services. Spread the good news.

TEDDY BEARS

When we are very little, teddy bears are often our first friends. We can tell them all our secrets, and they never snitch on us. They give us unconditional love and are always there for us and help to soothe our troubles. When we grow up and have problems, it is the little child in us that gets scared, and the teddy bear speaks to that part of us. Adults can still find teddy bears very comforting. I would like to see every hospital bed have a teddy bear for patients to hold in the dark of the night when we are scared.

There is a doctor in New York who complained that I taught grown men infantile behavior by suggesting they have teddy bears. I have a feeling that he was never allowed a teddy bear. In fact, the medical community is beginning to acknowledge this useful "medicine." Patients at St. John's in New York who undergo bypass surgery each get a teddy bear. It serves a dual purpose. When the patient feels a cough come on, he is instructed to squeeze the teddy bear to keep the stitches in his chest from bursting. I'm sure a secondary result is a feeling of love and security.

TREATMENT

Today is another precious day on earth. We shall live it with joy. I know that I am not alone on this planet. Every person, place, and thing is interconnected. What harms one harms us all. Therefore what heals one helps to heal us all. As we are willing to love and support each other, we help to heal the whole planet. We are love, we share love, and we are healed with love.

This day holds only pleasant experiences for us. We are one with the power that created us.

We are safe, and all is well in our world!

25

Healing the Planet

Affirmation:
We envision our complete healing!

The planet has come to a space where there is a great division among the ways people are viewing life.

On the one hand, there are those who choose to create darkness around them. They live in fear and hatred and look for the worst in life. There is widespread drug abuse and war and torture and oppression and famine. There are those doomsday predictors who look forward to the nuclear end of life here on earth.

On the other hand, there are now many consciousness-raising groups. All over the planet, people are gathering together to learn the processes of the mind and how thoughts work. There is a great yearning to learn more and to love more—to improve the quality of all our lives and to save and heal the planet.

Those of you who have chosen to incarnate this time as homosexuals have also chosen on a deep level to be a part of the healing process of the planet.

*   *   *

Each person on this planet has self-worth and is worthy of his or her own love. It is our own self-rejection and our own self-hatred that causes all problems on this planet. The microcosm always works and reflects its positiveness or negativity on the macrocosm. We have always had groups of people telling other groups of people that they are unacceptable or not good enough. Who is the object of prejudice depends on where you live on the planet. People who are frightened and do not feel good about themselves seem to need another group to denounce. This is never healthy for us or the planet.

As I have said many times, when we really love ourselves, we cannot hurt ourselves, and we cannot hurt another person. And that to me is the answer to world peace. Unconditional love is the goal we are all here for. It begins with self-acceptance and self-love.

Now what about the people who have AIDS who are not gay? What kind of abuse have they experienced? How do they work in the grand scheme of healing the planet?

These people are often malnourished and underprivileged, so that their bodies are in a weakened condition. They may be heavy drug and alcohol users. One thing I feel sure of, with all the people who have contracted this disease, there is a lot of self-hatred, a lot of resentment, and a lack of self-love. Again, this contributes to the condition of the planet.

It is the lack of self-love that creates the atmosphere where we are open to abusing ourselves. If we believe we are no good and are filled with guilt, then we must find a way to punish ourselves. What better way than to abuse our bodies?

People don't say, "I want to have AIDS." They do unknowingly create conditions within and around themselves that are receptive to disease. AIDS is the popular disease of the moment.

AIDS came from nowhere, and it will go back to nowhere when we no longer have need for it. All plagues, all epidemics pass in time and are learning lessons on an individual as well as planetary level.

* * *

As I have said before, I do not have all the answers about AIDS. This is a multi-faceted condition that involves the entire planet. I am sharing my beliefs at this moment, with the knowledge I have.

In our support groups, we have decided not to pay attention to the news reports on AIDS. We read as little as possible, and when we do see an AIDS story with its fatalistic attitude, we remember to say to ourselves, "It is not true that everyone is dying. I know of people who are living and healing themselves." We cannot give in to those who are determined to see AIDS as a dis-ease that kills everyone. We do not have to agree with them. Bless the media with love, and know it has no power over us. We make the decision of what to believe. We believe in life, in love, and in healing.

And so you see, I do not have the ultimate answer to healing all cases of AIDS. I wish I did. I can only help you improve the quality of your life if you choose to have it so. All healing is ultimately self-healing. The doctor, the therapist, the technician, the nurse, the healer, and the many alternate holistic practitioners, all have different methods and different approaches to healing your body. You are the one who decides if the methods will work or not.

If your deep inner decision is to stay on the planet and get well, then give your healing one-hundred percent. Be totally committed. It will be an interesting experience to be totally for yourself in every way, to give yourself total support. You may even like this way of living, after you get used to it. If you really want to live well, you will never go completely back to the old ways of abusing yourself.

Perhaps on a deep level, you have already made the decision to leave the planet; perhaps your lesson is finished, and you do not want any of the methods to work. Whatever decision you make, it is the perfect decision for you. You are not here to please other people and to live your life their way. You are on your own pathway and working at your own level. You are here to learn and grow in understanding and compassion and love. When you have completed your lesson for this lifetime, you will leave. It may be soon, it may be a long time from now. Whenever it is, let it be peaceful.

Continue to learn to love yourself more. Let that love include other people. Give to them the unconditional love you want to find for yourself. Do everything you can to be happy, and bring that joy into every area of your life.

As Jerry Florence from Alliance says in his song, "Life begins again, Hallelujah!"

TREATMENT

Today is another precious day on earth. We shall live it with joy. Wholeness is my goal. I will accept nothing less. I am one with every person, place, and thing on this planet. I choose to contribute to making this a world where it is safe for us to love each other. Where we are loved and accepted as we are and encouraged and supported to become all that we can be. I see the best in everyone and help them to bring out their most joyous qualities. This love and acceptance I give out, I find wherever I turn.

I see this world with abundant lands, clear, fresh waters, clean air, with everyone well-fed. I see peaceful, secure, healthy, productive, free people in every land. We are all whole and complete.

I am at peace with myself and the world I envision. We are one with the power that created us.

We are safe, and all is well in our world!

I love you!

Resources

BOOKS

Bartholomew, *I Come As A Brother* (Taos, NM: High Mesa Press, 1986).

Colbin, Anne Marie, *Food & Healing* (New York: Ballantine Books, 1986).

Cousins, Norman, *Anatomy of An Illness, As Perceived by the Patient* (New York: Bantam Books, 1981).

Cummings, Stephen, and Dana Ullman, *Everybody's Guide to Homeopathic Medicine* (Los Angeles: J.P. Tarcher, Inc., 1984).

Fuchs, Nan Kathryn, Ph.D., *The Nutrition Detective* (Los Angeles: J.P. Tarcher, Inc., 1985).

Gawain, Shakti, *Creative Visualization* (San Rafael, CA: Whatever Publishing, 1978).

Hay, Louise L., *You Can Heal Your Life* (Santa Monica, CA: Hay House, Inc., 1984).

Johnson, Elizabeth A., *As Someone Dies* (Santa Monica, CA: Hay House, Inc., 1987).

Levine, Stephen, *Who Dies? An Investigation of Conscious Living and Dying* (New York: Doubleday & Co., 1982).

Levine, Stephen, *Meetings at the Edge: Conversations with the Grieving and Dying, the Healing and the Healed* (New York: Doubleday & Co., 1984).

MacLaine, Shirley, *Out on a Limb* (New York: Bantam Books, 1983).

Moody, Raymond, *Life after Life* (New York: Walker & Co., 1987).

Myss, Caroline, *AIDS: Passageway to Transformation* (Walpole, NH: Stillpoint Publishing, 1987).

Pauling, Linus, M.D., *Vitamin C, the Common Cold and the Flu* (New York: W.H. Freeman, 1976).

Siegel, Bernie S., M.D., *Love, Medicine and Miracles* (New York: Harper and Row, 1986).

Simonton, Carl, M.D., *Getting Well Again* (New York: Bantam Books, 1980).

AUDIO TAPES

Christiansen, Cassandra, RN, *A Guidance Through Death* (Santa Monica, CA: Hay House, Inc., 1988).

Fisher, Sally, *AIDS and Anger* (Los Angeles: Northern Lights Alternatives, 1986).

Fisher, Sally, *Living Powerfully with AIDS* (Los Angeles: Northern Lights Alternatives, 1986).

Hay, Louise L., *AIDS: A Positive Approach* (Santa Monica, CA: Hay House, Inc., 1983).

Hay, Louise L., *Cancer: Discovering Your Healing Power* (Santa Monica, CA: Hay House, Inc., 1983).

Long, Darby, *AIDS, The Next Step* (Santa Monica, CA: Creative Imagery, 1987).

Long, Darby, *Deciding to Get Well* (Santa Monica, CA: Creative Imagery, 1987).

Siegel, Bernie S., M.D., *Love, Medicine and Miracles* (New York: Caedmon, 1988).

VIDEO TAPES

Hay, Louise L., *Doors Opening: A Positive Approach to AIDS* (Santa Monica, CA: Hay House, Inc., 1985).

Hay, Louise L., *You Can Heal Your Life Study Course* (Santa Monica, CA: Hay House, Inc., 1988).

Siegel, Bernie S., M.D., *Hope and a Prayer* (Santa Fe, NM: Realidad Productions, 1986).

SUPPORT GROUPS

AIDS Mastery Seminars, Sally Fisher, Northern Lights Alternatives, 13530 Moorpark Avenue #4, Sherman Oaks, CA 91423, 78 West 85th Street, New York, NY 10024.

AIDS Project Los Angeles, 7362 Santa Monica Blvd., West Hollywood, CA 90046.

Alcoholics Anonymous and other 12-Step Programs, in cities throughout the world.

Boston Healing Circle, c/o Santa Fe, 528 Tremont Street, Boston, MA 02116.

On Death and Dying Seminars, Stephen Levine, Box 100, Chamisal, NM 87521.

Hayride, Louise L. Hay, West Hollywood Park, West Hollywood, CA.

Healing AIDS Newsletter, 3835 20th Street, San Francisco, CA 94114.

L.A. Center for the Living, 1600 N. Sierra Bonita, Los Angeles, CA 90046.

Lerner Medical Center AIDS Support Group, 1750 14th Street, Suite A, Santa Monica, CA 90404.

Los Angeles Shanti Foundation, 9060 Santa Monica Blvd., West Hollywood, CA 90069.

Love Heals, c/o Dennis Lee Rezba, P.O. Box 130254, Houston, TX 77219-0254.

Metaphysical Alliance, 2261 Market Street #465, San Francisco, CA 94114.

The New York Healing Network, c/o Samuel Kirschner, 148 East 28th Street, New York, NY 10016.

People with AIDS Coalition, Inc., 263A West 19th Street, New York, NY 10011.

Religious Science International (headquarters), 3130 Fifth Avenue, San Diego, CA 92103.

San Francisco Shanti Project, 525 Howard Street, San Francisco, CA 94105.

Index

Louise L. Hay, author of the New York Times bestseller, YOU CAN HEAL YOUR LIFE, is a metaphysical counselor, teacher and lecturer. She has assisted thousands of people in discovering and using the full potential of their own creative powers for self-healing and personal growth.

If you would like to receive a catalog of products and information about future workshops, lectures and events sponsored by the Louise L. Hay Educational Institute which assists people in loving themselves, please detach and mail the postcard below.

I would like to be placed on the Hay House, Inc. mailing list.

NAME_____

ADDRESS_____

_____

Book in which this card was attached:

_____

To: HAY HOUSE, INC.
   P. O. Box 2212
   Santa Monica, CA 90406

WHITE NIGHTS

A THRILLER

Ann Cleeves

Minotaur Books ◪ New York

A THOMAS DUNNE BOOK FOR MINOTAUR BOOKS.
An imprint of St. Martin's Publishing Group.

WHITE NIGHTS. Copyright © 2008 by Ann Cleeves. All rights reserved. Printed in the United States of America. For information, address St. Martin's Press, 175 Fifth Avenue, New York, N.Y. 10010.

www.thomasdunnebooks.com
www.minotaurbooks.com

The Library of Congress has catalogued the hardcover edition as follows:

Cleeves, Ann.
   White nights / Ann Cleeves.—1st U.S. ed.
      p. cm. — (The Shetland Island quartet ; bk. 2)
   ISBN-13: 978-0-312-38433-3

    1. Murder—Investigation—Scotland—Shetland—Fiction. 2. Shetland (Scotland)—Fiction. I. Title.

PR6053.L45 W48 2008
823'.914—dc22

2008020630

ISBN-13: 978-0-312-38442-5 (pbk.)

First published in Great Britain by Macmillan,
an imprint of Pan Macmillan Ltd

D 10 9 8 7

For Ingirid Eunson,

with thanks for great times at Gunglesund

Acknowledgements

Thanks to everyone who has helped with this book. Helen again explained crime scene investigation so even I could understand. Sara and Moses brought fresh and expert eyes to the first draft. Sarah Turner provided valuable encouragement when the Shetland quartet was first conceived. And Julie made the editorial process a pleasure.

Prologue

The passengers streamed ashore from the cruise ship. They wore light jackets and sunglasses and jerseys tied around their shoulders. They had been told that the weather was unpredictable this far north. The ship was so big that from this perspective, looking up at it from Morrison's Dock, the town beyond was dwarfed. Row after row of windows, each with its own balcony, a floating city. It was midday in Lerwick. The sun was bouncing off the still water and the great white hull was so bright that you had to squint to look at it. In the car park, a fleet of buses waited; the tourists would be taken to the archaeological sites in the south, to see the seabird cliffs to photograph the puffins, and for a guided tour of the silverworks. At some point there would be a stop for a Shetland high tea.

Waiting at the foot of the gangplank was a performer. A moving piece of art or street theatre. A slender man, dressed like a Pierrot. A clown mask on his face. He didn't speak, but he acted out a pantomime for the visiting travellers. He made a lavish bow, one hand held across his stomach, the other sweeping towards the floor. The tourists smiled. They were willing to be entertained. To be accosted in a city was one thing – a city housed beggars and disturbed people and it was safest to turn away, not to catch the eye – but this was Shetland. There could be nowhere more safe. And they wanted to meet the local people. How else would they have stories to take back home?

The clown carried a bag made of red velvet and sewn with sequins. It glittered as he moved. He wore it slung across his body, the way elderly women, worried about street theft, carry their handbags. From his bag he took a handful of printed flyers which he began to distribute to the crowd.

Then they understood. This was an advertising stunt. Perhaps this place wasn't so different from London, New York or Chicago after all. But they kept their good humour. They were on holiday. And they took the brightly coloured paper and read it. They had a free evening in Lerwick. Perhaps there was a show they might take in. There was something about this guy that had appealed to them. He made them smile, despite the sinister mask on his face.

As they climbed into the buses, they watched him disappear down a narrow lane into the town. He was still handing out his leaflets to passers-by.

Chapter One

Jimmy Perez glimpsed the back of the street performer as he drove through the town, but it didn't
register. He had other things on his mind.

He'd just landed at the airstrip in Tingwall after a
short break in Fair Isle, staying on his parents' croft.
Three days of being spoiled by his mother and listening to his father complain about the price of sheep. As
always after a trip home, he wondered why he found
it so difficult to get on with his father. There were
never arguments, no real antagonism, but he always
left feeling an edgy mixture of guilt and inadequacy.

Then there was work. The pile of paper he knew
would be waiting on his desk. Sandy Wilson's expense
forms, a day's labour in themselves. A report to complete for the Procurator Fiscal about a serious assault
in a bar in Lerwick.

And Fran. He'd arranged to pick her up at
Ravenswick at seven-thirty. He'd need to get back to
his house to grab a shower before then. This was a
date, wasn't it? The first real date. They'd been knocking around together for six months, friends, but now
he felt giddy as a teenager.

He arrived at her house dead on time, his hair still
wet, uncomfortable in a new shirt which had a

starchy, stiff feel to it, faint creases down the front where it had been folded in the packet. He was always nervous around clothes. What did you wear to a party to celebrate the opening of an art exhibition? When the woman who haunted your dreams and distracted your days was one of the artists? When you hoped, that night, to take her to bed?

She was nervous too. He could tell that as soon as she climbed into the car. She was dressed up in something slinky and black, looking so sophisticated that he couldn't believe he'd have a chance with her. Then she gave that quirky grin that always flipped his stomach, made him feel he'd just spent three hours in *The Good Shepherd* in a westerly gale. He squeezed her hand. He wanted to tell her how stunning she looked, but because he couldn't think how without seeming crass or patronizing, they drove all the way to Biddista in silence.

The gallery was called the Herring House: once they had dried fish here. It was at the end of a low valley, right on the water, on the west coast. Further along the beach there was a small stone pier where the fishing boats had pulled up to unload their catch; a couple of men still kept boats on the beach. Walk out of the door and there'd be the smell of seaweed and salt. Bella Sinclair said that when she'd first taken over the place there was still a whiff of the herring in the walls.

Bella was the other artist exhibiting. Perez knew her, as almost everyone in Shetland knew her. To chat to at parties, but mostly second-hand, through the stories that were passed around about her. She was a Shetlander, Biddista-born and -bred. Wild in her youth, they said, but now rather unapproachable, intimidating. And rich.

He still felt flustered after the rush from the plane and by the sense that this was his one chance with Fran. He was so clumsy with people's feelings. What if he got it wrong? When he held out his hand to shake Bella's he saw that it was trembling. Perhaps too he'd picked up Fran's anxiety about how her paintings would be received. When they began to circulate among the guests, to look at the work displayed on the bare walls, he felt the tension building even more. He could hardly take in what was happening around him. He talked to Fran, nodded to acquaintances, but there was no real engagement. He felt the pressure build against his forehead. It was like waiting for a thunderstorm on a warm, heavy day. It was only when Roddy Sinclair was brought on to play for them that he could begin to relax for the first time. As if the rain had finally come.

Roddy stood framed by light in the middle of the space. It was nine in the evening, but still sunshine came through the windows cut into the tall, sloping roof. It was reflected from the polished wooden floor and the whitewashed walls and lit his face. He stood still for a moment, grinning, waiting until the guests started to look at him, absolutely sure he would get their attention. Conversation faltered and the room grew quiet. He looked at his aunt, who gave him a smile which was at once indulgent and grateful. He lifted his fiddle, gripped it under his chin and waited again. There was a moment of silence and he began to play.

They had known what to expect and he didn't

disappoint them. He played like a madman. It was what he was known for. The show. That, and the music. Shetland fiddle music, which had somehow caught the popular imagination, was played on national radio, raved about by television chat-show hosts. Impossible to believe – a Shetland boy in the tabloids for drinking champagne and dating teenage actresses. He'd hit the big time suddenly. A rock star had named him as his favourite performer and then he was everywhere, in newspapers and on the television and in glossy celebrity magazines.

He hopped and jigged, and the respectable middle-aged people, the art critic from the south, the few great and good who'd driven north from Lerwick, set down their glasses and began to clap to the rhythm. He fell to his knees, lay back slowly so that he was flat on the floor and continued playing without missing a beat, then sprang to his feet and still the music continued. In one corner of the gallery an elderly couple were dancing, surprisingly light-footed, arms linked.

The playing was so furious that the watchers' eyes couldn't follow his fingers. Then suddenly the music stopped. The boy bowed. The people cheered. Perez had seen him play many times before, but was still moved by the performance, felt a jingoistic pride in it, which made him uncomfortable. He looked at Fran. Perhaps this was too sentimental for her. But she was cheering along with the rest.

Bella walked from the shadow into the light to join Roddy. She held out an arm, a self-consciously dramatic gesture to acknowledge the performance.

'Roddy Sinclair,' she said. 'My nephew.' She looked around her. 'I'm just sorry that there weren't more people here to see him.' And in fact the room only contained a scattering of people. Her comment made it suddenly obvious. She must have realized that because she frowned again. Clearly she wished she hadn't mentioned it.

The boy bowed again, grinned, raised his fiddle in one hand and his bow in another.

'Just buy the paintings,' he said. 'That's why you're here. I'm only the warm-up act. The pictures are the main attraction.'

He turned away from them and took a glass of wine from a long trestle laid out against the one bare wall in the room.

Chapter Two

Fran had already drunk several glasses of wine. She was more nervous than she'd expected to be. When she'd worked on a London magazine she'd attended dozens of these events: first nights, openings, exhibitions. She'd circulated, chatted, remembered names and faces, hidden her boredom. But this was different. Some of the paintings on these walls were hers. She felt raw and exposed. If people rejected or dismissed her work, it would be as if they were dismissing her. She wanted to shout to the people who were catching up on island gossip, who stood with their back to the art: *Look properly at the images on the walls. Take them seriously. I don't care if you hate them, but please take them seriously.*

And there were fewer people here than she'd expected there to be. Bella's openings were always well attended, but even some of the people Fran had invited – people she'd considered friends – had failed to show. Perhaps they had only been polite when she'd mentioned the exhibition. They'd seen her art and didn't care for it. At least not enough to turn out on a beautiful evening, when there were other things to do. This was the time of year for barbecues and being on the water. Fran took the poor turnout personally.

Perez came up behind her. She sensed the movement and turned. The first thought, as it always was when he caught her in an unguarded moment, was that she wanted to sketch him. Her fingers itched to be holding charcoal. It would be a fluid drawing, no hard edges. Very dark. Perez was a Shetlander. His family had lived in the islands since the sixteenth century, but there was no Viking blood in him. An ancestor had been washed ashore after the wreck of a ship from the Armada. At least that was the story he told. She wondered if he'd just bought into the myth because it was a way of explaining his difference. The strange name. There were a few people in the islands with his dark hair and olive skin – black Shetlanders, the locals called them – but in this gathering he stuck out, looked exotic and foreign.

'It seems to be going well,' he said. Tentative. He seemed in a strange mood tonight. Nerves, perhaps. He knew how much this meant to her. Her first exhibition. And anyway, they were feeling their way in the relationship. She was keeping her distance, her independence. If she got tied up with Perez, she wouldn't only be taking him on. It would be his family, the whole Fair Isle thing. And he'd be taking on a single mother. A five-year-old child. Too much to contemplate, she thought. Only she *was* contemplating it. In these long summer nights, when it never seemed to get dark, she thought of him. Pictures of him rattled around in her head, like old-fashioned slides dropping into a projector. Occasionally she got up and sat outside her house, watching the sun which never quite

9

set over the grey water, and thought about how she would draw him. His long body turned away from her. The bones under his skin. The hard spine and the curve of buttock. And it was all in her imagination. He had kissed her cheek, touched her arm, but there had been no other physical contact. Perhaps there was some other woman in his life. Someone he dreamed of when he too was kept awake by the light. Perhaps he was waiting for a decision from her.

Soon after they'd first met she'd gone south for a month. She'd told herself it was for her daughter's sake. Cassie had been through the sort of drama that would traumatize an adult and Fran had thought time away from Shetland would help her recover. When Fran had returned Perez had contacted her, asking how things were with her and the girl. Professional interest, Fran had thought, hoping however that perhaps there'd been more to it. An easy friendship had developed. She hadn't pushed it; she was still an outsider here and she wasn't sure exactly what was expected. The failure of her marriage had shattered her confidence. She couldn't face another rejection.

'It's not going well at all,' she said now. 'There's hardly anyone here.' She knew she sounded ungracious, but couldn't help herself. 'You'd think people would come, if only for the free wine and the chance to see Roddy Sinclair.'

'But the people who are here are interested,' he said. 'Look.'

She turned away from him and back into the room. Perez was right. People had turned their attention from the wine and the music and had begun to promenade around the gallery, looking at the paintings, stopping occasionally to concentrate on something specific. The space was evenly divided between her work and Bella's. The exhibition had been designed as a Bella Sinclair retrospective. She was showing thirty years' worth of art; pictures and drawings had been pulled in from collections all over the country. The invitation for Fran to show with her had come out of the blue.

'You should be proud,' Perez said. She wasn't quite sure how to react. She hoped that he would say something flattering about her work. Tonight, jittery and exposed, she could use the flattery.

But his attention was turned to the visitors. 'There's someone who seems very keen.' She followed his gaze to a middle-aged man, who was smart in an arty, unbuttoned sort of way. Slim, almost girlish figure. Black linen jacket over a black T-shirt, loose black trousers. He'd been standing in front of an early self-portrait of Bella. It was Bella at her most outrageous. She was dressed in red with a scarlet gash of lipstick as a mouth, her hair blown away from her face, at once disturbing and erotic. It was an oil, the paint thick and textured, the strokes very free.

Then he moved on to stand next to Roddy Sinclair and to stare at a work of Fran's, a drawing of Cassie on the beach at Ravenswick. Something about the intensity of his looking made her uncomfortable, though it wasn't the sort of picture that would allow him to recognize Cassie in the street. He looked horrified, she thought, not keen. As if he'd just witnessed an atrocity. Or seen a ghost.

'He's not local,' Perez said. Fran agreed. It wasn't just that she didn't recognize him. It was the man's

11

style, which marked him out as a soothmoother. The clothes; the way he held himself and looked at the picture.

'Who do you think he is?' She looked over her glass, tried not to seem too obvious, but still he was staring at the drawing, lost, so she didn't think he'd notice even if he turned round.

'Some rich collector,' Perez said, smiling at her. 'He's going to buy everything here and make you famous.'

She giggled. A brief release of tension. 'Or the arts reporter for one of the Sundays. I'll feature in an article about the next new talent.'

'Seriously,' he said. 'Why not?'

She turned to look at him, assumed that he was joking again, but he was frowning slightly.

'Really,' he smiled again. 'You are very good.'

She wasn't sure what to say, was groping for something witty and self-deprecating, when she saw the man turn round. He fell to his knees, much as Roddy had done when he was playing the violin. Then he put his hands over his face and began to weep.

Chapter Three

Perez thought that at this time of year everyone went a bit crazy. It was the light, intense during the day and still there at night. The sun never quite slipping behind the horizon, so you could read outside at midnight. The winters were so bleak and black that in the summer folk were overtaken with a kind of frenzy, constant activity. There was the feeling that you had to make the most of it, be outside, enjoy it before the dark days came again. Here in Shetland they called it the 'simmer dim'. And this year was even worse. Usually the weather was unpredictable, changing by the hour, rain and wind and brief spells of bright sunshine, but this year it had been fine for nearly a fortnight. The lack of darkness hit people from the south too. Occasionally their reaction was even more extreme than the locals'. They weren't used to it: the birds still singing late into the evening, the dusk which lasted all night, nature slipping from its accustomed pattern, all that disturbed them.

Watching as the man dressed in black knelt in the pool of sunshine and burst into tears, Perez thought it was a case of midsummer madness and hoped someone else would deal with it. It was a theatrical gesture. The man wouldn't have come here on his own initiative. He would have been invited by Bella Sinclair, or been brought by a regular visitor. The Herring House wasn't easy to get to from the south, even once you reached Lerwick. So it would be about a woman, Perez thought. Or he would be another artist, wanting to draw attention to himself. In his experience, people who were really depressed, who felt like crying all the time, those people didn't seek out the limelight. They hid away in corners and made themselves invisible.

But nobody went to the man's assistance. The people stopped talking and watched in a fascinated, embarrassed way as he continued to sob, his face turned up now to the light, his hands at his sides.

Perez could sense Fran's disapproval beside him. She would expect him to do something. The fact that he wasn't on duty meant nothing. He should know what to do. And it wasn't only that. She took advantage of the fact that he was devoted to her. Everything had to be at her pace. How long had he waited for this date? He was so desperate to please her that he would fit in with her plans. Always. He hadn't realized before how subject he was to her will and the knowledge hit him suddenly. Then, immediately after the rush of frustration, he thought how churlish he was being. She'd nearly lost her daughter. Didn't she deserve time to recover after that? And surely she was worth waiting for. He walked up to the weeping man and squatted beside him, helped him to his feet and led him away from the public's view.

They sat in the kitchen where the young chef, Martin Williamson, was filling trays of canapés. Perez knew him, could have given his life history, told you the first names of his grandparents after a few seconds' thought. The Herring House had its own restaurant and he ran that. Tonight, herring featured of course. Small slices curled on circles of soda bread. It had been pickled and there was a clean scent of vinegar and lemon. There were local oysters and Shetland smoked salmon. Perez hadn't eaten since lunchtime and his mouth watered. Martin looked up as they came in.

'You don't mind if we just sit here for a while?'

'You'll have to stay well away from the food. Health and safety.' But he grinned. He'd been happy as a child, Perez remembered. Perez had seen him at weddings and parties, had an image of him always laughing, in the middle of the mischief.

Now he went back to his work and took no notice of them. The sound of fiddle music came from the gallery. Roddy had been brought back to fill the awkward silence and get the people in the mood again for spending. Still the stranger was sobbing. Perez felt a moment of sympathy, thought how heartless he was to have been distracted by the food. He couldn't imagine making a show of his grief, thought that something dreadful must have happened for the man to be crying in public. Or that he was ill. That must be it.

'Hey,' he said. 'It can't be that bad, can it?' He pulled up a chair for him, settled him into it.

The man stared at him as if he was realizing for the first time Perez was in the room.

He wiped his eyes with the back of his hand. It was a childish, unsophisticated gesture which made Perez warm to him for the first time. He dug in his pocket for a handkerchief and handed it over.

'I don't know what I'm doing here,' the man said.

He was English, but not southern English, Perez thought. He thought of Roy Taylor, a colleague who worked out of Inverness. He came originally from Liverpool. Was this man's voice like Roy's? Not quite, he decided.

'We all feel like that sometimes.'

'Who are you?'

'Jimmy Perez. I'm a detective. But that's not why I'm in the Herring House. My friend's one of the artists.'

'Herring House?'

'This place. The gallery. That's what it's called.'

The man didn't respond. It was as if he'd shut down, was lost again in his own grief, as if he'd stopped listening.

'What's your name?' Perez asked.

Again there was no response. A blank stare.

'Surely there's no harm in telling me your name.' He was starting to lose patience. He'd thought this was the night when he could sort things out with Fran. He'd imagined staying at her house. There'd been fantasies which would have shocked the people who knew him, which had shocked him. Cassie would be sleeping at her father's. Fran had told him this, and that was a good sign, wasn't it? Usually he found it too easy to be swept up in other people's emotions. Today he had an incentive to resist this weeping stranger.

The Englishman looked up at him.

'I don't know my name,' he said flatly. No drama now. 'I can't remember it. I don't know my name and I don't remember why I'm here.'

'How did you get here? To the Herring House? To Shetland?'

16

'I don't know.' Now there was an edge of panic in the man's voice. 'I can't remember anything before the painting. That painting of the woman in red hanging on the wall out there. It was as if I was born staring at that painting. As if that's all I know.'

Perez was starting to wonder if this was some sort of practical joke. It was the kind of prank Sandy would think was funny. Sandy, who came from Whalsay and worked with Perez, had a juvenile sense of humour. The whole team would know the boss was here tonight with the English lady artist and he wouldn't put it past them to try to wreck his evening. They would think it a great joke.

The man had no sign of a head injury. He looked so sleek, so well-groomed it was hard to think he might have had an accident. But if it was an act, he was convincing. The tears, the shaking. Surely that would be hard to fake. And how would Sandy know him? How would he persuade this man to set up the stunt?

'Why don't you empty out your pockets?' Perez said. 'There'll be a driving licence, credit cards. We can give you a name at least, track down some relatives, some explanation of what might have happened.'

The Englishman stood up, reached into the inside pocket of his jacket. 'It's not there,' he said. 'That's where I always keep my wallet.'

'You remember that, then?'

The man faltered. 'I thought I did. How can I be sure of anything?' He began in a slow, meticulous way to search the other pockets. There was nothing. He took his jacket off and handed it to Perez. 'You check.'

Perez did, knowing as he did that there would be nothing to find. 'What about your trousers?'

17

The man pulled out the pocket linings, stood there looking terrified and faintly ridiculous, the white cloth hanging against the black trousers.

'You had nothing with you?' Perez asked. 'A bag? A briefcase?' He realized he was sounding desperate. His fantasy of a night spent with Fran was fast disappearing.

'How would I know?' It came out almost as a scream.

'I'll go and look.'

'No,' the man said. 'Don't leave me.'

'Has someone hurt you? What are you frightened of?'

He thought for a moment. Had some trace of memory returned? 'I'm not sure.'

'Come with me if you like.'

'No. I can't face those people.'

'You remember seeing them?'

'I told you. I remember everything after the painting.'

'Was there something specific about the picture to disturb you?'

'Perhaps. I'm not sure.'

Perez stood up. Now they faced each other across the table. The chef had left the kitchen and Roddy Sinclair had stopped playing. From the gallery came the quiet murmur of voices. 'I'm going to find out if you had a bag with you,' Perez said. 'And if anyone knows you, saw you arrive. You'll be safe here.'

'Yes,' he said. But his voice was uncertain. He sounded like a child trying to convince himself that he wasn't afraid of the dark.

In the gallery Fran was deep in conversation with

a large woman wearing a flowered tent. Fran was a
little flushed. As he walked past he gathered from the
conversation that the woman had bought one of
the paintings and they were discussing how to ship it
south. A tourist, he thought. It was that time of year.
Obviously a wealthy tourist. She was saying how
much she admired Fran's work and asking if perhaps
they could discuss a commission. He felt suddenly
very proud of Fran.   •

Bella came up to him, having walked straight past
an elderly man who was trying to catch her attention.
With her grey hair cropped very short, long silver earrings and a grey silk shirt, Perez thought she looked
like a large silvery fish. Something about her mouth,
too, the wide pale eyes. But she was attractive still.
She'd been known as a beauty when she was younger,
a legend, and something about her still demanded
attention. 'Thank you for dealing with that poor man,
Jimmy. What was wrong with him?' She fixed him
with her grey, unblinking eyes.

'I'm not sure.' Perez never gave away any information unless it was necessary. It was a habit learned
from childhood. There was so little privacy in the
small community where he'd grown up that he'd cher-
ished every scrap. And now, at work, information was
valuable currency, which could be leaked out too
easily. In other, more anonymous places, it didn't
matter if a policeman was a little indiscreet. A word to
a spouse over dinner, a funny story in a bar. Nobody
ever knew. Here, the stories had a way of coming back
to haunt the teller. 'Do you know him, Bella? Is he a
dealer? A journalist? He's English.'

'No. I thought perhaps Fran had invited him.'

'He seemed very taken with your self-portrait.'

She shrugged, implying that interest in her work was only natural. .

'Did you see him come in?'

'He walked in just before Roddy started playing. I've seen him perform dozens of times so my attention wasn't as fixed as everyone else's.'

'Was the chap on his own?'

'I'm sure he was.'

'You didn't notice if he had a bag with him when he came in?'

She shut her eyes briefly, trying to visualize the scene. Her memory would be reliable. She was a painter.

'No,' she said. 'No bag. His hands were in his pockets. He seemed quite relaxed at that point. He stood at the back of the crowd, just watching until Roddy stopped playing. Then he walked over to my painting, before moving on to the drawing of Cassie. He seemed very moved by it, didn't you think?' She stood waiting for a response.

'He seems a bit confused,' Perez said at last. 'I don't know. A breakdown perhaps. I might try to get him to a doctor.'

But by then Bella seemed to have stopped listening. She was looking around her, trying to gauge the interest in the art.

'That's Peter Wilding talking to Fran,' she said. 'I hope she's being nice to him. He's a buyer.'

The woman in the flowery dress had left Fran and her place had been taken by an intense middle-aged man in a white shirt, with very dark hair. Fran was talking and he was bending towards her, head slightly on one side, as if he couldn't bear to miss a word.

Bella gave a little laugh and walked away. Deliberately Perez walked past the couple on his way into the kitchen. Wilding was talking now. His voice was low and Perez could tell he was gushing about the work, even though the individual words merged into the background noise. Fran didn't even notice Perez.

At the kitchen door he stopped. Martin Williamson had his back to him; he was rinsing out pans at the sink. The mystery man had gone.

Chapter Four

Kenny Thomson looked down at the Herring House. He kept a boat on the beach beyond. It had been pulled up above the tideline, and the weather was so still that it was fine where it was. Later in the year, he'd get it on to a trolley and tow it up on to the grass, covered with a tarpaulin, so the high tides and the storms wouldn't drag it back into the sea. But for now it was easier to leave it on the beach. He was thinking that it might be a good night to go out and try for some piltock, but knew he probably wouldn't go. He enjoyed the fishing but not so much as when he'd been a boy and a young man. Willy, one of the old Biddista folk, had taken him and his brother out in his boat when they were children. And when they'd grown up the two of them still liked fishing together. A fine night and he'd be on the phone to Lawrence: 'Do you fancy a couple of hours on the water?' But now Lawrence had left Shetland for good and it wasn't quite the same. There were other men who could make up a party and would be keen enough to be asked. But Kenny knew he would have to make an effort to be pleasant to them. He would have to pretend to be interested in their lives – their work, their wives. With Lawrence there had been no pretence at all.

He was aware of the party going on at the Herring House. He hadn't been invited, but he knew just the same. At one time Bella had always invited him. She'd drive up the track in that smart four-wheel-drive – although why she needed a car like that when she only went these days to Lerwick or to Sumburgh to get the plane south, he couldn't say – and come into his house, not waiting to be asked.

'You will come, Kenny, won't you? You and Edith. I'd like you to be there. We wouldn't have the Herring House if it hadn't been for all the hard work you and Lawrence put in.'

And that was true too. Once she'd taken it into her head to buy the place and do it up, they'd been there most nights after he'd finished with the sheep or in the fields, working on the building. Most of the labouring work had been theirs. A labour of love, Lawrence had called it. And it was true they'd been paid very little. But it had been hard to make any sort of living from crofting then and with the children growing up the extra money had been useful. Bella had probably thought she was doing them a favour. Those days all the men could turn their hands to anything.

After they'd finished working Kenny would go home to Edith, leaving Lawrence to talk to Bella. Sometimes it would be so late when Kenny walked up the track to the house that he'd be sure Edith would already be asleep. But she was always awake, waiting for him. She'd never been one for an early night. In the winter she'd be sitting by the fire knitting. He'd known it was late because the house was tidy – the only time it was ever tidy, with the two children there during the day. This time of year she'd be outside working in the garden, even in the small hours of the morning. She'd spit out one of her sharp comments about Bella taking advantage of him before going with him into the house. It might even have been before Eric had started school, and that was hard to imagine. Now they were both grown up. Ingirid was about to have a child of her own. She was a midwife close to Aberdeen and Eric was farming in Orkney.

Now Bella didn't ask any more. She knew Kenny wouldn't go. Edith might have been glad of a chance to dress up at one time. To go to the fancy party and drink the wine and listen to the talk about art and books. One way of getting their money's worth out of Bella, at least. But Kenny had always put his foot down. Usually his wife was the one who laid down the law, but when it came to Bella Sinclair he was firm. 'Lawrence might still be here if it wasn't for her.' Once he had almost added, *That woman broke his heart.* But Edith would have mocked him for being so sentimental. She'd always had a wicked tongue in her head, even as a child. She still did. He smiled. More than thirty years married and he was still scared of her.

He looked at his watch. It was nine-thirty, later than he'd thought. At this time of year it was easy to lose track. He came up on to the hill every night unless the weather was so bad that there was no point to it. To check the sheep, he said, though that was an excuse. It was an escape from Edith tapping away on the computer, a time for himself. When Edith was working, he felt that the house was just an extension of her office and he never felt comfortable there. In the winter he'd sometimes drive over the hill with a shotgun and a torch, after rabbits. The rabbits got caught in the glare of the spotlight and then they were easy enough to take. He had a silencer on the gun so he didn't make a noise getting the first one; he wouldn't want to frighten the others away. He didn't much like the taste of rabbit, the flesh was too sweet and slimy, but hidden in a pie with plenty of onion and chunks of bacon he'd eat it occasionally. Usually though he ended up throwing most of the carcases away.

A waste, Edith said. There had been no spare money when she was a child and she still imagined the return of the bad times, even though she had a good job and he took on a bit of building work beside the croft. She resented money ill spent. But they had savings now. They wouldn't starve in their old age or be dependent on their children.

He called to Vaila, his dog, and turned back towards his house. He could see it on a slight rise in the land just in from the water, with the Herring House much taller beyond. Further along the shore was the graveyard. In the old days before the roads were built they'd carried the corpses for burial by boat. That was why in Shetland the graveyards were always close to the water. He thought he'd quite like his body to be carried to its grave in his own boat, but he supposed there'd be some reason why it couldn't happen like that now.

His attention was caught by movement on the road. His eyes weren't as good as they had been, but he thought he saw someone leaving the gallery. He watched. He pretended not to be interested in Bella's doings but he couldn't help being curious. Usually her parties didn't finish this soon and this guest didn't get into a car and drive back down the length of the voe to the big road towards Lerwick. Instead the person turned up the road the other way, past the post office and the three houses on the shore towards the jetty. After that it only led to the old manse where Bella lived, and to Kenny and Edith's house. Beyond Skoles the track petered away into a footpath across the hill to the next valley. The only people to use that were Kenny, when he was checking on his sheep, and holidaymakers walking.

Kenny stood and watched the figure until it disappeared out of sight where the road fell into a dip. He was running, a strange loping run, leaning forward so it looked as if he was going to tip over. Kenny thought that was typical of the people Bella knocked around with. Artists. They couldn't even run like other folk. She'd always attracted strange people to her. The summers when they were all younger the Manse had been full of outsiders, drifting in and out with their odd clothes, weird music coming through the open windows, and always the sound of their talking. Yet now she was quite alone, apart from that nephew of hers. She should have stayed with Lawrence.

He carried on up to the hill, making a rough count of the sheep in his head. Later in the week he'd have to round them up and bring them down for clipping. There were a couple of chaps from Unst who were coming to help him, and Martin Williamson had said that he'd give a hand too.

When he got to the house it was gone eleven o'clock, but Edith was still in the garden. She was hoeing between a row of beans, pushing away the weeds with short aggressive jabs. She must have been stuck on the computer for most of the evening though, because she hadn't done so much. When she heard him coming she looked up. He thought she looked very tired. She'd had a meeting in Lerwick all day and that always wore her out.

'Come away inside,' he said. 'The mosquitoes will bite us both to death.'

'Just let me finish this row.' He stood watching her bending over the work and he thought how stubborn she was and how strong.

'Did you see that man?' he asked, when she straightened at last and rested the hoe against the wall of the house.

'What man?' She looked up, pushed a stray hair from her face. He thought she was prettier now than she had been when she was young. When she'd been young her face had been a bit pinched and there'd been no flesh at all on her. What he'd felt for her then, it hadn't been love. Not the sort of love they showed on films, at least. The sort of love Lawrence had felt for Bella. It hadn't been that way for him or for Edith. But they'd got on and he'd known it would work out. They wouldn't irritate each other unduly. Now that she'd reached fifty, sometimes he looked at her with wonder. Her face was hardly lined, her eyes so blue. There was a passion between them that they'd never had the energy for when the children had been young.

'What man?' she repeated. Not annoyed that she'd had to repeat herself, but half smiling as if she could tell what he was thinking.

'A man running away from the Herring House. He must have come past here.'

'I didn't see,' she said.

She stood up, linked her arm into his and led him inside.

Edith got up early every morning. Even when they were on holiday or away visiting the children she was usually up before him. He heard her in the kitchen, moving the kettle on to the hot plate, then the door opening. He knew what she would be doing – pulling on her boots over her pyjamas to go outside and let out the hens. She didn't start work until nine and they'd have breakfast together before she set out. He didn't find it so easy to leave his bed, but at this time of year Edith had trouble sleeping at all. Often when he woke in the night to go to the bathroom he could tell she was awake, lying very still beside him. She'd put thick curtains at the window, but something about the white nights threw her body clock out. It took some people that way. When he didn't sleep he became tense and frazzled and the thoughts raced around his head. Edith became pale, though she never complained of being tired and she never missed work. Once, he'd persuaded her to go to the doctor to get some sleeping tablets, but she'd said they made her feel slow and heavy all the next day so she didn't feel on top of things at the centre. He was glad when the days got shorter and she returned to her old self.

Kenny liked the half-hour they had together over breakfast before she left. By the time he was washed and dressed, she had the tea made and there was the smell of toasted bread. Edith was in the shower; he could hear the water tank refilling.

She was the manager of a care centre for old and

disabled people. He still found that hard to believe –
his Edith, in charge of staff and a budget, going to
meetings in Lerwick, smartly dressed with her hair
tied up. She trained all the care staff in Shetland in
manual handling, showing them how to move the
people in their care safely. He marvelled at her
strength and determination. Taxis and a bus brought
old folks from all over this part of Shetland to the
centre. Sometimes she talked about her clients by
name and it shocked him to realize the men and
women he'd known in childhood as strong, rather
frightening characters were now frail, confused,
incontinent. He thought, Will I come to that? Will I
end my days playing bingo in the day centre? Once he
had mentioned something of the sort to Edith and
she'd answered tartly, 'You will if you're lucky! With
the oil revenue fallen to nothing and the cutbacks, the
centre might not be there when we need it.' He never
mentioned his fears again. His only comfort was that
he expected to die before her. Women always lived
longer than men. He couldn't imagine what it must be
like to live alone.

He poured tea and put butter on the toast and she
came in, dressed, her hair still wet but tied into a knot.

'What are your plans for today?' she asked.

'Singling neeps,' he said.

She pulled a face in sympathy, understanding
what boring, back-breaking work that was, hoeing out
the unwanted seedlings to leave space for the turnips
to grow.

'Oh well,' she said. 'It's a nice day for it.'

But since yesterday evening he'd been thinking
that he might get out in the boat today after all. He

didn't say anything to Edith. She worked so hard and he felt like a boy considering playing truant from school.

She finished the toast on her plate, then she was away into the little bedroom, which had once been Ingirid's room and which Edith now used as an office, to gather up her papers into her bag. He walked outside with her and kissed her before watching her drive off.

He'd intended to do a couple of hours with the neeps before getting out the boat, but found himself making the short walk down to the beach, to the hut where he kept the outboard and his lines and pots. There was a little breeze. Easterly. He wondered for a moment if he wanted company after all, and started thinking who might be free to go out with him. Martin Williamson was a pleasant young man, but most days he put in an hour in the shop before he started working in the café at the Herring House. He stopped for a moment and in the silence heard the puffins on the headland beyond the pier. There were fewer than there'd been when he was a boy, but still enough for him to hear them chattering as he approached.

He walked across the shingle that separated the sand from the road. It was a bit of a short-cut, but he made sure he watched his feet as he went. Once he'd ricked his ankle here and it had been painful for days. He stopped when the Herring House threw its shadow on to his path, just to see if anyone was about, but it looked empty. The gallery café opened for coffee, but not until later, and there were no cars parked outside.

The hut stood by the side of the road, just where it joined the jetty, a couple of hundred yards further on. He and Lawrence had put it up and it was solid enough, though some of the corrugated-iron panels on the roof would need replacing in the next year or so. They never bothered locking it – it was used by all the Biddista men who kept a boat – and nobody much else strayed to the jetty. Once everything people needed was delivered here by ship – coal and corn and animal feed. Now a few holidaymakers in yachts put up for the night, but he hadn't even seen many of them yet this year. There was a heavy bolt on the door, so they could fasten it from the outside to stop it blowing in the wind. Today the bolt was unfastened and the door was a little ajar. Kenny tried to think who might have been in the hut last, who might have been so careless. It would only take a sharp squall to have the door off its hinges. Roddy Sinclair, he thought. It would be just like him. That boy had no consideration. Once he'd held a sort of party in here and Kenny had come in the next day to a pile of red tins, an empty whisky bottle and a strange lad in a sleeping bag. Kenny pulled the door open and took in the familiar smell of engine oil and fish.

Because he'd been thinking about Roddy Sinclair, he assumed at first that the figure swinging from the ceiling was one of the boy's pranks. Roddy had got drunk at Bella's party and thought he'd cause mischief. Kenny knew when he got closer it would turn out to be a fertilizer sack filled with straw, dressed up in a black jacket and trousers. The head was smooth, gleamed a little. Realistic, Kenny thought. He pushed the figure. It was surprisingly heavy, not made of straw at all. Its shadow swung backwards and forwards on the back wall of the hut and it twisted on its rope so for the first time Kenny saw the face. It was made up by a clown's mask, shiny white plastic reflecting the morning sunshine coming through the gap in the door, with a grinning red mouth and blank staring eyes. Then he saw that the figure had real hands. Skin. Bony knuckles. Fingernails, smooth and round like a woman's. But this wasn't a woman. It was a man, with a bald head. A dead man hanging from one of the roof joists, his toes only inches from the ground. Beside him, on its side, was a big plastic bucket. Kenny thought he must have turned it upside-down to use it as a step, then kicked it away. He felt the hysteria rise in his stomach. He wanted to lift away the mask; it looked indecent on a dead person. But he couldn't bring himself to do it. Instead, he put his hands on the man's arms to hold him steady. He couldn't bear the thought of him swinging there, a scarecrow on a gibbet.

His first thought was to call Edith on his mobile phone. But what could she do? So, feeling a little foolish and faint, he went back outside, sat on the shingle and dialled 999.

Chapter Five

Perez heard the news on his mobile as he was on his way in to work from Fran's house. Before that, light-headed through lack of sleep, he was so absorbed in recalling the events of the night before that he was driving automatically, unaware of his surroundings. In his head was the music Fran had put on her CD player when they first got in – a woman singing, something lilting and Celtic he hadn't recognized. He wondered if he was reading too much into what had happened with Fran. That was his way. He brooded. His first wife, Sarah, had said he expected too much from her, that he made emotional demands. I should be tougher, more resilient, he thought. More of a man. I care too much what women think of me.

Then he got the phone call and he forced himself to concentrate. Work was a constant, something he did well. And Sandy, who had never been the most articulate person, always got incoherent at times of stress or excitement. It took Perez's full attention to deal with him.

'We've got a suicide,' Sandy said. 'Kenny Thomson found him hanging in that hut where the Biddista lads keep the stuff for the fishing.'

'Who is it?' Perez asked.

The voice on the end of the phone interrupted. 'Kenny Thomson. You'll know him. He's lived out at Biddista all his life. They croft that land that runs away up the hill from the voe . . .'

'No, Sandy. I didn't mean who found him. Who's the suicide?'

'I don't know. Kenny didn't recognize him. At least he said he couldn't tell. I'm just on my way.'

'Don't touch anything,' Perez said. 'Just in case.' He knew Sandy shouldn't need telling and knew anyway that he'd forget about the warning as soon as he got there, but it made him feel better to say it.

It was only as he drove down the road he'd taken the night before that he remembered the man who'd broken down in tears in the Herring House. Perez hadn't made much of an effort to find him. He'd gone out of the kitchen door and looked on to the beach and up at the road, past the graveyard, but there'd been no sign. If he'd felt anything at all, it had been relief. The man must have been in a car after all – how else could he disappear so quickly? So he had recovered, if indeed he'd been ill. It had occurred to Perez briefly as he stood for a moment before going back to the gallery that he should let someone know. But who? And what would he say? *Keep a look out for a chap who cries a lot. He might have amnesia.* Listening to the suck of the tide on the shingle, he'd decided not to bother. Some tourist, he'd thought, disturbed or drunk or drugged. This time of year the islands seemed to attract them. They came looking for paradise or peace and found the white nights made them even more disturbed.

Instead of wondering about the nameless stranger,

he'd been thinking of Fran, of the shape of her under the lacy black dress she was wearing and what it would be like to touch her.

He'd walked back to the gallery. From the road he saw the party continuing through the long windows, but had the sense that things were already winding up. Roddy was looking out at the sea, still holding the fiddle loosely under his chin, as if it was another limb, a part of his body. Inside again, Perez could see that the artists were disappointed. They had made some sales, but they'd expected a bigger crowd, more of a buzz. Fran took his hand and whispered that she'd like to go home. Despite the flattery from the intense man with the black hair, she needed cheering up. Part of him was glad she was a little bit sad. It gave him an excuse to comfort her.

Now he thought the suicide was too much of a coincidence. The mystery southerner had been clearly distraught, unbalanced even. The dead man had been found only a few hundred yards from the Herring House, where the stranger had last been seen. Perez hadn't considered the possibility that he would take his own life. He felt guilty that he'd been so care-less, responsible for a stranger he'd only once met. Then he tried to form in his head the words he'd use to explain the situation to Fran. Would she blame him for the man's suicide? And hoping against the odds that, when he reached the hut by the Biddista pier, he would find that someone altogether different had killed himself.

He took the road north and west through White-ness. Here twisted fingers of land ran into the sea and it was hard to tell where the line of the coast lay. There were lochs and inlets, so the land beyond looked like islands. In the low meadows flowers everywhere – buttercups, campion, orchids which his mother would have been able to name. In this light, at this time of the year, on impulse visitors bought up the old houses for second homes.

The road narrowed, became single-track with occasional passing places, then turned a bend in the hill, so Perez could see Biddista laid out in front of him. The cemetery, then the Herring House, close to the beach, the hut on the jetty, and beyond that, three terraced single-storey houses. The largest held the post office and shop. Then the track wound on past the Manse where Bella Sinclair lived until it came to Kenny Thomson's croft. Once the community had been bigger. There were traces of ruined houses in a number of Kenny's fields. He'd bought up the land steadily as folk moved out, either too old to carry on crofting or because they could get a better wage working for the council in Lerwick. Now the houses would be tarted up and sold for a fortune, but when he'd started expanding the croft there was no demand for them and he'd got the land dirt-cheap. The kirk had been pulled down years before when the population declined, the stone carried away for use throughout the island. Now this was all there was to Biddista, a community isolated from the rest of the island by the hill on one side and the sea on the other.

Sandy's car was pulled in to the side of the road. He was sitting on the harbour wall smoking a cigarette. Perez, who had worked for a time in Aberdeen and dealt with more real crime in a month there than Sandy had in his entire career, wondered what he would do with the butt when he was finished. Throw it on to the ground and contaminate a possible crime scene? Instead, seeing Perez approach, Sandy stood up, pinched out the cigarette and hurled it into the tide. A different sort of pollution.

'Where were you?' Sandy asked. 'I tried to phone you at home.'

Perez ignored the question and Sandy didn't follow it up. He was used to being ignored.

'I let Kenny get on back to his place,' he said. 'No point him staying around here and we'll know where to find him. He was in a bit of a state. It hasn't bothered me so much. It doesn't look real, does it? With that thing over his face.'

'What do you mean?'

'Didn't I tell you? You'll see.'

Perez walked to the shed, stood in the doorway and looked in. The body hung from a thick noose tied to a rafter close to the apex of the pitched roof. The face was turned away from them, but Perez recognized the clothes. Black trousers, black linen jacket. Only when he went a few steps further forward did he see the mask, grinning. He felt suddenly sick, but forced himself to look into the hut again. He took in the scene, the overturned bucket. On the face of it this was certainly suicide.

Sandy had come up behind him. 'The doctor will come as soon as he can,' he said. 'But he might be a while. There's an emergency call-out. I said that was all right. Our man isn't going anywhere.' Sandy had an anxious-to-please, peerie-boy air about him still. It made Perez want to reassure him that he was doing OK, even when he got things wrong.

'Good. Who did you get hold of?'

'That new man who's just moved in at Whiteness.' Sandy paused. 'What do you think's going on there, with the mask?'

'I don't know.' Perez had found it so disturbing that he'd turned his back on the hanging man. It was the bare shininess of it, the manic grin. After the gloom in the shed, the sunlight, reflected from the water, hurt his eyes for a moment.

'He must be a tourist,' Sandy said, with absolute certainty. 'Not anyone from Biddista at least. Not according to Kenny. He could tell that without seeing the face. And a place this small, he'd know. I haven't checked his belongings for identity. You said not to touch.'

'Good,' Perez said again, distracted. He was remembering the man the night before, standing with the linings of his pockets pulled out. There would be nothing to identify him in his clothes. He began to run through the process he'd follow to trace him. Phone calls to hotels and guesthouses. Check with NorthLink and British Airways. They might have to wait until the man failed to turn up for his return trip south before they got a name for him. This time of year there were more visitors than locals on the islands. Despite himself he was interested. What had led first to the loss of memory and then for the man to become so desperate that he took his own life?

'What do *you* think the mask is about?' Sometimes he asked Sandy questions, not expecting much of an answer, but because he wanted to make him think, hoping that it might become a habit.

'I don't know. Making some sort of statement, maybe?'

What sort of statement? That his life had been a joke? He hadn't been laughing much the night before.

'I'm sure I saw the man last night,' Perez said. 'He was one of the guests at the Herring House party.' Then, as the thought suddenly occurred to him, 'I wonder where he got hold of the mask? He certainly didn't have it on him then.'

This time Sandy didn't answer. I shouldn't have left the man alone, Perez thought. He was frightened of being left alone.

'Do you mind waiting here for the doctor? I'll go and chat to Kenny Thomson. He might have some idea who the dead man might be, where he was staying. If someone in Biddista has been taking paying guests, Kenny will know.'

Sandy shrugged. 'It seems a weird sort of place for a visitor to want to stay. What would you do all day here?'

'Look at it, man. The peace. Nothing to do. This is what they come for.'

Sandy looked out across the water. 'It's more likely he came up from Lerwick specially, chose the loneliest sort of spot he could find to do away with himself.'

But Perez thought he hadn't just come here to kill himself. He'd been at the party for a reason.

Chapter Six

Perez walked up the track to Kenny Thomson's house. He was very tired now and his brain felt sluggish. He thought the exercise might make him more alert. Skoles, the Thomson place, was more like a farm than a croft. Since he'd bought up the land all around him Kenny had more sheep than he needed for his own use and there were cows in one of the low parks near the house. But everything was still done in the old way. Perez liked that. A field of tatties just coming up, the lines straight and true, and a field of neeps. In lots of places crofters were selling sites for new housing, but it seemed Kenny hadn't been tempted to go down that route.

Perez tried to remember when he'd talked to Kenny last, but couldn't think. He might have nodded to him in town, bumped into him at Sumburgh or in the bar on the ferry. But Kenny was more than a casual acquaintance. The year of Perez's sixteenth birthday, Kenny had spent the whole of one summer in Fair Isle and they'd worked together. It was the time they did the major work on the harbour in the North Haven. Kenny had been brought in to oversee the building work and Perez had been one of the labourers, his first proper job over the school holidays. He

still remembered the blisters, the aching back and the
ease with which Kenny, twenty years his senior, slender and dark then, could lift a Calor cylinder under
each arm when he helped the islanders unload the
boat, the way he could work all day at the same pace
without seeming to get tired.

Kenny had started off lodging in the hostel at the
Observatory, but after a couple of weeks had moved
down the island to stay at Springfield with the Perez
family. It was further away from the site, but he felt
awkward in front of all the birdwatchers, he said, and
it would be a bit more money for them if they took
him on as a lodger. In the evening he would shower
and then join the family for dinner. 'Kenny's no bother
at all.' That was what Perez's mother had said, and it
had been true. He had been unobtrusive, considerate,
setting the table and helping her with the washing-up
afterwards. A perfect guest.

Now, Perez tried to remember what the two of
them had talked about as they were digging out drains
and mixing cement. Kenny hadn't given very much of
himself away. He'd listened to Perez talking about his
plans for college and how much he hated life at school,
but he had hardly talked about himself at all. Occasionally he'd let something slip about his life in
Biddista and the other folks who lived there, but very
rarely. And would I have been interested anyway?
Perez thought. Kenny just seemed middle-aged and
boring. A stickler for doing things right. He was
already married to Edith, who had been left behind.
She'd been staying at Skoles, taking care of Kenny's
father, who was still alive. Kenny had mentioned
Edith, but not with great affection. It couldn't have

been easy for her, Perez thought, looking after an old man who wasn't even a relative. Kenny should have been more grateful.

Then suddenly he remembered a party that had taken place in the Fair Isle hall. A return wedding: an island boy who'd gone away to marry a southerner in her own town, then brought her back to celebrate properly on the Isle, the lass wearing the long white wedding dress and carrying flowers just as she would have done in the English church. There'd been a meal in the hall, all the island invited, and afterwards a dance. Perez remembered Kenny dancing an eight-some reel with his mother, swinging and lifting her until she laughed out loud. His father, watching from the side, had seemed slightly put out. Perhaps Kenny had been a little drunk that night. Perez himself had been drinking too, so perhaps his memory was at fault. Soon after the party Kenny had returned to the Observatory to stay. When Perez had asked why, he'd been as unforthcoming as ever: 'It suits me better just now.'

When he came to the house, Perez knocked at the kitchen door. He stood for a moment. There was no answer and he was wondering if he should let himself in when Kenny came up behind him, a scruffy dog completely silent beside him.

'I was looking out for you,' Kenny said. 'Sandy said he'd called you. But I thought I might as well get on with some work. We're planning on clipping the sheep at the end of the week.'

'Do you want to carry on? We can talk just the same.'

'No, I was about ready for a coffee. You'll join me?'
The kitchen was tidier than most croft houses

Perez had been in. Kenny stood at the door and unlaced his boots before walking inside with stockinged feet. Perez checked that his shoes were clean before following. The room was square with a table in the middle, a couple of easy chairs close to the Rayburn. The fitted cupboards and the fancy appliances all Kenny's work, Perez thought, but chosen by Edith. A jug of campion stood on the windowsill, its deep pink matching a motif in the wall tiles. Everything planned and ordered. The breakfast things, still unwashed on the draining board, were the only items out of place.

Kenny must have seen Perez looking at them. 'I'll have those done before Edith gets in,' he said. 'It only seems right when she's been at work all day. Are you all right with instant? Edith likes the real stuff – Ingirid bought her a fancy machine for Christmas – but I've always thought it kind of bitter.'

'Of course,' Perez said. 'Whatever you're having.' He could have done with a strong espresso, but knew it wouldn't be right to ask.

. He waited until Kenny joined him at the kitchen table before starting the questions.

'What time did you find him?'

Kenny considered. Everything he did would be slow and deliberate. Except dancing, thought Perez, remembering the scene in the Fair Isle hall. He was a wild dancer.

'It would have been about ten-past nine this morning. Edith had left for work around half-past eight and I was thinking about starting on the neeps; there aren't many days like this, even in the summer.' He smiled. 'I was tempted by the fishing. Thought we might have

43

a bit of a barbecue tonight if I got lucky and brought back some piltock or mackerel.'

Perez nodded. 'I know you didn't see his face, but do you have any idea who the dead man might be? We need to identify him.'

Another pause. 'No. I'd never met him.'

'But you might have some idea?'

'Bella had one of her parties last night. The place was full of strangers.'

Not so full.

'You weren't there yourself, Kenny. I thought she always asked Biddista folk to her openings. I thought you were the inspiration for her work.'

Kenny's face was brown and lined. It cracked into a brief mischievous smile. 'That's what she tells the media. Did you see that TV documentary about her and Roddy? I'll never believe anything I see on the TV again. They came to film in Biddista, you know, followed me around one day and you'd think from the programme I was some great landowner, almost a laird.' The kettle came to a boil. 'Don't be taken in by the stories, Jimmy. Bella Sinclair always thought she was better than us. Even when we were at school and she was living in a council house down at the shore. It was true that she could always draw, mind, even as a scrap of a girl. She seemed to see things differently from the rest of us.'

'Do you know if she had any people staying at the Manse with her last night?'

He shook his head. 'I've told you, Jimmy, we don't mix with Bella these days. We wouldn't know. I don't think she has such big parties staying in the house as she did before. The old days, the Manse was always full of strangers. Even then it was as if Biddista folk weren't good enough for her. Maybe she's finally growing up and she doesn't need people telling her how wonderful she is all the time.'

'Roddy was at the Herring House.'

'Then he'll be staying with her at the Manse. Slumming it until he gets a better offer.'

'You don't like the boy?'

Kenny shrugged. 'He's been spoiled rotten. Not his fault.'

'He was at the St Magnus Festival in Kirkwall and Bella persuaded him north to play for her.'

'He's a fine musician,' Kenny said. 'Just as she's a fine artist. I'm not sure that excuses the way they treat folk, though. Roddy used to tag along after my children when he came to stay with Bella. He was younger than them but he still used to boss them about. And later he took my Ingirid out a few times. Thendumped her. She cried for a week. I told her she was well out of it.'

'I just know what I read in the press.'

'Well,' Kenny said. 'That's only the half of it. Even when he was at school he was a wild one. Drinking. Drugs too, according to my kids.'

Perez found himself eager to hear the stories about Roddy's exploits. It probably had no relevance to the death of a strange Englishman, but everyone in Shetland was fascinated by Roddy Sinclair. He'd brought glamour to the islands.

'I did see someone leave the party,' Kenny said. 'I was just on the hill there behind the house. Someone dressed in black. I wondered if it might be yon man in the hut.'

'What time was it?'

The pause again. The deliberation. 'Nine-thirty? Maybe a little later.'

Perez thought that would fit in with the disappearance of the Englishman.

'Did he get into a car?'

'No, he didn't go towards the car park. He came this way, up towards the Manse. But he was a good way off. I couldn't swear it was him. He was running. The man I saw. Running as if the devil was after him.'

Not the devil, Perez thought. Me. I'd assumed he'd gone towards the big road south and if I'd spent more time looking I'd have found him. Why would he come this way? If he had run away from the beach towards the Manse and Skoles, how did he find his way back to the jetty with a noose round his neck? Then he thought how frightened the man had been about being left alone. Perhaps someone else was chasing him too.

Perez could tell that Kenny wanted to be away outside, and besides, he could think of nothing else to ask. He knew that there would be other questions, later. He'd wake up to them in the middle of the night. He stood in the garden waiting while Kenny stooped to put on his boots.

'Would Edith have seen the man?' It had come to him suddenly that from the house she might have had a better view.

Kenny squinted up from where he was crouching. 'She didn't see him at all. I asked her.'

'Will you both be in this evening, if I need to speak to you again?'

Kenny straightened. 'We'll be around here somewhere. But there'll be nothing more to tell you.'

*

As Perez walked back towards the shore, the sound of the kittiwakes on the cliffs beyond the beach got louder. He didn't care much for heights. While the other kids clambered down the geos at home, he'd stayed well away from the edge. But he liked to see the cliffs from the bottom, especially at this time of year when the birds had young, the busyness of them all jostling for a place on the ledges. The tide must be full now. The water had almost reached the boats pulled up on the beach. As he approached Sandy, a Range-Rover drove down the coast road, past the Herring House.

The doctor, Sullivan, was a Glaswegian. Young, bright. He'd fallen for a Shetland woman and loved her so much that he'd followed her north when she was homesick in the city. They said he could have been a great consultant, but had given it up to be a country GP. How romantic was that! *They said.* More stories, Perez thought. We all grow up with them, but how can we tell which of them are true?

Sullivan obviously hadn't found the shift too great a sacrifice, because he was whistling when he got out of the car and grinned at them.

'Sorry to keep you, gentlemen. A lady in Whiteness was further into labour than she'd realized and we delivered her baby at home. A very bonny little girl!'

Perez wondered if he'd be so cheerful in the winter. There were incomers from the south who couldn't face the endless nights and the wind. These light nights would soon give way to the storms of the autumn equinox. Perez loved the dramatic change in the seasons but it didn't suit everyone.

Sullivan took a quick look at the body from the door, then returned to his car. When he came back he was carrying a heavy torch. He shone it into the corners of the hut, lifted a small wooden stepladder that had been hooked on to nails in the wall.

'I need a closer look. That's OK?'

Perez nodded. If this turned out to be a crime scene, they'd be lucky if the CSI from Inverness got there that day. Best he got all the information he could now. 'Just try not to touch anything else.'

The doctor had set up the stepladder so he was level with the hanging man. He shone the torch at the neck.

'Problems?'

'Maybe. Not sure yet. It looks like he died of strangulation, but that's not unusual with hanging. They don't often go with a quick break of the neck, especially with such a short drop.' He came down a couple of steps. 'If I had to place a bet, I'd say he was strangled and already dead before he was strung up. Look: this rope is very thick, but there's another mark on the neck here and the angle's rather different. The mark from the thick rope doesn't quite hide the thin one.' Now he was standing back beside them. 'I'd like a second opinion before I call this in as murder, inspector. I'm new here. I don't want to make a fool of myself.'

'But you're pretty sure he didn't kill himself.'

'Like I said, inspector, if I was a betting man, I'd say he was already dead before he was hanged. And if I was on my home territory I'd have no hesitation. But it's not my place and you'll not get me to commit myself until someone with a bit more experience has taken a look.'

Perez looked at his watch. If this was a murder investigation he'd need to get the team from Inverness in on the last plane of the day. There was still time, but not much. 'How soon can you get your second opinion?'

'Give me an hour.'

Perez nodded. He knew he wanted it to be murder. Because of the excitement, because this thrill was what he'd joined the service for, and in Shetland there weren't so many cases to provide it. And because if the man hadn't killed himself Perez wasn't responsible, couldn't have foreseen it.

Chapter Seven

Lying on her bed, watching the sunlight on the ceiling, Fran tried not to get seduced by the sense of well-being. She had felt equally euphoric after her first night with Duncan and look what had happened there! He'd been sleeping with a woman old enough to be his mother all the time they were married and had made a complete fool of Fran. Thinking about it still made her squirm inside. A breeze from the open window blew the curtain and she had a glimpse of a fat black ewe, chewing, only feet from the house. The curtain fell back into place and Fran pushed images of Perez from her mind.

When she had left Duncan, the temptation had been to run back to live in London, to her gang of friends, the anonymous city streets where nobody knew of her humiliation. But there'd been Cassie to think about. Cassie was nearly six now, had more freedom here than she'd ever have had in London. She had a right to know her father. And Fran had come to love Shetland, despite its bleakness, so she'd moved into a small house in Ravenswick, rented it over the winter to give herself time to make up her mind about where she wanted to be. Three months ago she'd bought it. She'd committed to Shetland. She wasn't sure, though, whether she could commit yet to Jimmy Perez. It was all too much to deal with at once.

Safer to concentrate on the failure of the party at the Herring House. She wasn't sure what she'd expected of the exhibition opening, but she'd certainly hoped it would be more of an event. Even with Roddy Sinclair trying valiantly to bring a sense of occasion, the evening had been an anticlimax. The room half empty. Very few of her friends had been there to share the celebration. She had dreamed of having the chance to show her work for so long that she felt cheated. And what would people remember? Not the art at all, but a strange man having hysterics.

Yet the residual disappointment, the childish 'It wasn't fair' couldn't prevent her thoughts drifting back to Perez. To the first, slightly clumsy, coffee-tasting kiss. To the line of his back, just as she'd imagined it, the knots of his spine against her fingers.

The phone rang.

She assumed it would be Perez and got quickly out of bed, walked naked into the living room which was also her kitchen, thinking she would tell him she had no clothes on. That would excite him. Wouldn't it? She had so much to learn about him. The dress she'd worn to the opening was lying in a heap on the floor. On the table the dregs of coffee in a jug, two glasses.

She picked up the phone. 'Hello.' Keeping her voice low and inviting.

'Frances, are you all right? You sound as if you've got a cold.' It was Bella Sinclair.

She'll blame me, Fran thought, for the disappointing turnout last night. If Bella had been the only person exhibiting, they'd have come. 'I'm fine,' she said. 'A bit tired.'

'Look, I need to talk to you. Can you come here? What time is it now? Eleven-thirty. Come for lunch then, as soon as you can.'

What does she want? Fran knew it was ridiculous but she was starting to panic. Bella had the ability to intimidate. Perhaps she wants money from me, she thought. Compensation for the expenses involved with setting up the party and the lack of sales. And she had no money. But of course she would obey Bella's summons.

'Shall we meet in the Herring House café at twelve-thirty?' she suggested tentatively. It would take her at least that long to dress and drive north.

'No, no.' Bella was impatient. 'Not the Herring House. Here, at the Manse. As quick as you can.'

Driving to Biddista, Fran thought she should have put up more of a fight, arranged to come another day. Just because she admired Bella's work didn't mean she didn't have a mind of her own. Once she'd been known as strong-willed, assertive. But that had been in the old days when she had a proper job and a bunch of friends and she lived in London. Now she was struggling as an artist and to find her place in the community. As she drove past the Herring House she was wondering what the girls from the magazine would have made of Perez, so she didn't register the cars parked at the jetty or the small group of men standing outside the corrugated-iron hut. They were part of the landscape. Men planning to get out fishing. My friends would say he wasn't my type, she thought.

Not strong enough to take me on. They'd say the relationship would never last.

The Manse was a square, stone building, imposing, on a slight rise, looking down to the sea. Fran had seen it from outside but never been in. All her previous meetings with Bella had been in the Herring House café, with Martin Williamson dancing attendance with coffee or tall glasses of wine. Bella must have heard the car on the gravel because she had the door open before Fran had climbed out. She was wearing jeans and a loose linen shirt. Even at home she had style.

'Come in.'

Once there had been a kirk standing between the house and the beach, and the architecture of the Manse reflected the religious connection. Inside, the staircase was lit by a tall thin window, two storeys high, a church window but with clear glass which let the sunlight in. Fran stood just inside the door and took it all in. 'What a wonderful house!' She saw at once that was the right thing to say. Bella knew it was a wonderful house, but she liked to be told. She relaxed a little, became less imperious.

'Come into the kitchen. It's last night's leftovers, I'm afraid, but there are plenty of those.'

'I'm *so* sorry so few of the people I invited came. I had asked them.'

'Don't blame yourself,' Bella said. 'Oh no, you mustn't blame yourself.'

Fran expected some explanation then, but Bella was moving on and talking about Biddista and the house, not about the party.

'I grew up in Biddista, you know. Not here in the Manse, but in one of the council houses down on

53

the shore. They *were* council houses then. They've all sold now. None of the people I grew up with could afford them. Willy was the last of them to live there and even he wasn't a council tenant in the end.'

Fran was a little flattered that Bella assumed she knew who she was talking about, was treating her as a Shetlander. She hadn't a clue of course, but she let Bella continue.

'There was still a minister living in the Manse in those days. An Englishman who'd been a missionary in the Far East and treated us as natives who needed educating. The kirk had already gone by then and he held services in the dining room. Sometimes in the middle of a dinner party, I think I can hear the hymns.'

The kitchen, at the back of the house, seemed a little dark after the sunlight in the hall. It too still had something of the church about it. A dark wood bench under the window which could have been a pew, a high ceiling. All the ceilings seemed very high to Fran. She was used to being able to reach up and touch hers. Bella lifted plates covered with cling-film from the fridge and Fran recognized the buffet food from the night before.

'I need wine,' Bella said. 'Let's see if Roddy has left any. He was still up when I went to bed last night, but I doubt if even he could have drunk his way through everything that was left. There are cases still in the Herring House.' She returned to the fridge and came back with a bottle. 'Would you like a glass? This one's rather good.'

Fran shook her head. 'Will Roddy be joining us?' Despite herself she was attracted by the celebrity of Roddy Sinclair. Being a Shetlander was his trademark and his unique selling point, but for her he represented life away from the islands, her old life of wine bars and serious shopping and tabloid gossip. She told herself that world was shabby and vulgar, but she missed it. She found it alluring, caught herself reading *Hello!* magazine when no one was looking.

Bella looked at the clock. 'I don't think Roddy's been out of his bed before mid-afternoon since he left school. Unless he had a plane to catch.' She set plates and cutlery on the table, lifted cling wrap from the trays of food.

Fran still didn't understand the reason for the urgent summons. Was it just Bella reminding herself that she had the power to make things happen? 'You said you wanted to talk to me. It sounded important.'

'Perhaps I overreacted.'

'I'm a busy woman, Bella. Will you tell me what this is about?' Something of her old confidence reasserting itself.

Her tone seemed to shock Bella because there was a moment of silence. She is *such* a drama queen, Fran thought. She doesn't move a muscle without calculating the impression she'll make. Bella got to her feet, reached into her bag and pulled out a folded sheet of paper.

'This is what it's about. Andy from Visit Shetland dropped it in this morning. He couldn't understand it, of course. He had a day off yesterday and came straight to the party from his home.' She put the paper on the table, unfolded it and slid it towards Fran. 'I don't suppose you know anything about it?'

It was a computer-generated flyer, printed in red and black on white. Not professionally printed, but not badly designed. Fran noticed that before reading the words.

EXHIBITION OPENING CANCELLED
Because of a death in the family.
SHORELINES
An exhibition of original art by
Bella Sinclair and Fran Hunter in
The Herring House, Biddista
has been cancelled.

The family requests privacy at this time.

Fran looked at it, confused. She could see that Bella expected a reaction, but felt foolish because she couldn't understand what lay behind the scrap of paper. 'What is this? Why would I know anything about it?'

'They were all over Lerwick yesterday. Posted in the window of the tourist office, on the noticeboard in the library and handed out to visitors coming off the cruise ships. Scalloway too. It's hardly surprising there wasn't much of a turnout at the party.'

'Of course I don't know anything about it,' Fran said. 'I mean, nobody in my family's died.'

'Nor mine. So what is this about?' Bella was in dramatic mode again. 'A mistake? A tasteless prank? An act of sabotage?'

'Why would anyone want to sabotage an art exhibition?'

Bella shrugged. 'Jealousy. Spite. I don't think I've upset anyone enough for them to bother with something like this. Not recently at least. What about you?

A first exhibition's a big deal. Anyone out there who'd want to spoil it for you?'

'That's a horrible idea. No. Absolutely not.'

'It couldn't be your ex playing games?'

'Duncan and I are being civilized at the moment, for Cassie's sake. Besides, it's not his style. He has a temper but this is petty and unpleasant. Anonymous too. Duncan would want everyone to know it was him.' She nodded towards the flyer. 'He'd think that beneath his dignity.'

'A prank then.' Bella's voice was quiet. 'A joke that got out of hand.'

The doorbell rang. There was an old-fashioned pull which rang a bell in the hall. Perhaps the bell was cracked because the sound was tinny, grating. Bella seemed relieved by the interruption, jumped to her feet and hurried away. She returned followed by Perez. He nodded to Fran, gave an embarrassed little smile.

'I saw your car in the drive.'

'Were you looking for me?' Fran felt confused, as if the day was spinning out of control. It's the lack of sleep, she thought. She longed suddenly for dark nights, thunderclouds, rain.

'No. I need to talk to Bella. It's work.'

'I should go then.' She was relieved to have an excuse to leave. She didn't want an inquest into the fiasco of the launch. The flyers were obviously part of some stupid game played by Roddy and his friends. It was the sort of imbecility he was famous for. Bella had been the target and she, Fran, had been caught in the crossfire. Later she'd be angry. Now she just felt

57

embarrassed. It was like being caught eavesdropping on a very personal row between a married couple.

'No,' Perez said. 'I need to talk to you too.'

She had a sudden panic. 'What's the matter?'

'Not Cassie,' he said. 'Nothing like that.'

Bella went to the fridge and absent-mindedly poured more wine. 'If it's about the flyers cancelling the party last night,' she said, 'we know about them. Hardly a police matter, I'd have thought, even here. We don't want to press charges.'

I might, Fran thought. Don't speak for me.

'This *is* why you're here, Jimmy?' Bella picked up the paper between her thumb and index finger as if she could hardly bear to touch it, then dropped it on the table in front of him.

Perez frowned as he read it. Fran decided the information was new to him. 'That's why so few people turned up last night,' she said. 'These were all over Lerwick, apparently, and because of the final line, nobody liked to phone.' She wanted him to know she *did* have friends, and that they would all have been there to support her if it hadn't been for this.

'I'll have to take the flyer with me.'

'I've told you,' Bella said sharply, 'I don't want to press charges.'

'Do you think that little scene last night could be related to this?' he asked. 'The hysterical Englishman who claimed to have no memory?'

'Another attempt to disrupt the party? I suppose it could. Certainly after that drama people started to leave. He made them uncomfortable.' Bella looked at him over her wineglass.

'There's a body in the hut on the jetty,' Perez said.

'We're pretty sure it was the man who caused the scene last night.'

'Really!' For a moment Bella seemed to take an unsophisticated pleasure in the news. It was a story, gossip to pass on. 'How did he die?'

'We're not sure yet. The circumstances seem a little unclear.'

What are you hiding? Fran thought.

'My God,' Bella said. 'Don't you think that's a bit spooky? The flyer, I mean. "A death in the family". Do you think he was predicting his own death?'

'But he wasn't family, was he?'

'Don't be silly, Jimmy. Of course not. I don't have any immediate family left. Only Roddy and he's still alive, thank God.'

'We want to inform the man's relatives and he has no ID. Are you sure you didn't recognize him, either of you?'

'Quite sure,' Fran said.

'I didn't know him last night.' Bella was twisting the stem of her glass. 'But that doesn't mean he wasn't an acquaintance. Someone from my past. I've met so many people and my memory isn't what it was. I'm an old woman now, Jimmy.'

She smiled, waiting to be contradicted.

It seemed to take him a moment to understand the rules of the game. Fran found that she was holding her breath. This was such a blatant cue for a compliment. Would he really have the nerve to ignore it?

At last he smiled. 'I'm sure you'll never seem old, Bella.'

In the silence that followed, Fran saw the scene as a painting. A gloomy Dutch interior, all dark wood and shadow. Bella's face in profile had an anxious, almost haunted look, and the lines of stress round her eyes made Perez's words seem cruel, mocking.

'I wonder if I might talk to Roddy.' He leaned forward. Fran could smell the soap, her soap, on his skin.

Bella seemed about to refuse, but there were footsteps on the wooden floor outside and the kitchen door opened. Roddy Sinclair stood, backlit by the sunshine flooding through the long window in the hall. He yawned and stretched, aware that they were all looking at him.

'A party,' he said. 'Oh good. I do love a party.'

Fran pulled up by the side of the road opposite the Herring House. She didn't want to park too close to the jetty, to be thought the sort of rubberneck who's excited by road accidents and blood. But the beach was so beautiful here and she needed to clear her head. She sat on the wall, looking out over the water.

She saw a figure walking towards her along the road, followed his progress. It was the dark-haired man who'd talked to her about her painting the night before. He'd spoken with such passion about her work that she'd been flattered and hoped that he would buy a piece. She'd thought he was a dealer because he'd talked with knowledge and authority and was surprised to see him still in Biddista. She struggled to remember his name. He'd introduced himself the night before. Peter Wilding. It had seemed familiar to her then and again she thought it should have some meaning to her.

'Ms Hunter. I hope you don't mind . . .'

'No,' she said. 'Of course not.'

He sat beside her. 'I wanted to tell you again how much I enjoyed your work.' There was an element of self-mockery in his voice. *I know this is unsophisticated. To be so obvious in one's admiration.*

'You're very kind, Mr Wilding.'

'Peter, please.'

Then she remembered how she knew the name. She'd read an article about him in the *Observer*. Something about contemporary genre fiction. 'A writer of fantasy for intellectuals', hadn't that been how Wilding had been described? 'You're a writer.'

'Yes.' He was clearly delighted that she'd recognized him at last.

'Are you staying in Biddista?'

'Yes, I'm renting a house here. Just temporary. But I love Shetland. I'm hoping to make a more permanent arrangement. I've vague ideas of writing a fantasy series based around Viking mythology. It might work, don't you think? And it would be wonderful to have the landscape to set it in.'

She was pleased that he seemed to value her opinion. He waited for her to answer, as if it really mattered to him.

'It would be fascinating,' she said. There were times when she missed the old London life. The talk of books and theatre and film. She thought he would be an interesting person to have around, entertaining, full of new ideas.

'I wonder if you'd agree to have a meal with me sometime,' he said. 'I don't have much scope for cooking where I am, but perhaps we could go out.'

The invitation shocked her. After Perez's diffidence,

there was something daring about the way Wilding simply asked for what he wanted. And she couldn't help being flattered. It sounded like an invitation to a date, but she could hardly say she was unavailable for romance. Perhaps he just wanted to discuss her art, to commission a work from her.

'Yes,' she found herself saying. 'Yes, I'd like that.'

He gave a quick nod. 'Good. Are you in the phone book? Then I'll give you a ring.' He turned and walked quickly the way he'd come. Later it seemed strange to her that neither of them had mentioned the dead man who was still hanging in the hut on the jetty, the police officers and the cars. Because she was sure Wilding would have known what had happened there. He was the sort of man who would know.

Chapter Eight

Perez took Roddy outside. 'Shall we just take a bit of a walk? I could do with the fresh air.' He didn't want a conversation in front of the two women. Roddy revelled in an audience. He would make things up to provide a decent story, feel an obligation to entertain them. Roddy pulled a face, as if fresh air was the last thing he needed, but followed Perez out anyway. It was in his nature to please, even if there was no immediate payback. He made a good living because he was charming.

As they left the house, Perez heard Fran tell Bella that she would leave too. He supposed she had to pick Cassie up from school, imagined her waiting at the school gate and swinging Cassie into her arms as the girl ran to her out of the yard. He loved watching the two of them together.

Roddy walked ahead of him out of the garden between the big stone gateposts. He had a long, bouncing stride and Perez had to step out to keep up. 'What were you doing in the Herring House last night?' he said. 'I thought you only played fancy gigs these days.'

'Bella asked. I was in Orkney anyway for the St Magnus Festival. It didn't seem such a big deal to come

63

on up.' He paused. 'My aunt doesn't really take no for an answer.'

'How long are you planning to stay?'

'A few days. Then there's a tour of Australia. I'm looking forward to it. I've never done Oz before.'

'Do you always stay with Bella while you're in Shetland?'

'Usually. She's the only family I have here now.' He didn't need to explain. This was another myth and he would assume that Perez would know. How his dad had died when he was a boy and his mother had fallen for an American oilman, gone back to Houston with him. How Roddy had refused to leave. Aged thirteen he'd stood up to them all, said he couldn't leave the islands. He was a Shetlander. It was the story that had appeared on CD covers and had been told to chat-show hosts. 'I'm a Shetlander.' And didn't the islands love him for it! Bella had provided a home for him. Spoiled him rotten, according to Kenny Thomson. Turned him into a performer. Encouraged his ambition. Funded the first CD. Designed the cover and sent it off to all her arty friends in the south. That story didn't appear so much in the papers. The official version had it that he was discovered by a producer who happened to be in Lerwick on holiday and heard Roddy play at the Lounge, the bar in town. In that version Roddy was an overnight success.

'You don't mind her wheeling you out to support her openings?'

'Why should I? I owe her. Besides, her events are always a bit of a laugh.' He was walking beside Perez along a path which led over Skoles land. It climbed steeply. Eventually they would end up at the top of the cliff, next to the great hole that was known as the Pit o' Biddista. Perez planned to have the conversation finished by then. The boy stopped abruptly and turned to Perez. 'What's this about? They were looking so serious in there. Is it my mother? Is she ill?'

'No,' Perez said. 'Nothing like that.'

There was a moment's silence and Perez wondered if Roddy was going over in his mind other possible explanations for the police to be calling. The cannabis or cocaine which Perez was pretty sure they'd find in his room if they looked. A hotel prepared to press charges after a particularly rowdy party.

'Did you think there were fewer people at the opening last night than Bella was expecting?'

'Yeah, I was surprised. She usually gets a good turnout.'

'Someone was spreading these all over Lerwick and Scalloway yesterday.'

Perez had slipped the flyer into a transparent plastic bag and he gave it to Roddy to read. Roddy stopped, leaning against an outcrop of rock in the hill.

'You don't think I had anything to do with this?'

'It might have been someone's idea of a joke.'

'But not mine. I told you. Bella took me in when I wanted to carry on living here. If it wasn't for her I'd be speaking with a Texas accent and playing country and western. I owe her.'

'Any idea who might have thought it funny?'

'No. There doesn't seem much to laugh about. That bit about a death in the family, it's just sick.'

'There has been a death,' Perez said. 'That's what I'm doing here.'

'Who?'

'There was a stranger at the party last night. He made a scene just after you finished playing. Got on to his knees and starting crying.'

'Guy in black. Shaved head?'

'Yes.'

They'd started walking again and Perez could smell the bird shit and the salt in the air. The grass was cropped short here. There were patches of thrift and tiny blue dots of spring squill. They'd almost reached the top of the cliff. He slowed his pace.

'Had you ever seen him before?' Perez asked. 'Before he lost it the man seemed really interested in the paintings. I don't know, not just idle curiosity. As if he knew something about art. You don't remember coming across him at one of Bella's other events?'

'What does Bella say?'

'She was reluctant to commit herself either way. He could have been an acquaintance, but she couldn't be sure. Her memory's not as good as it was.'

'Bollocks.' Roddy still had breath to give a choking laugh. Perez was starting to pant. 'Bella's as sharp as she always was. Sharper, if it comes to business. If your guy was a dealer or critic she'd have recognized him the minute he came into the room.'

'And you? Did you know him?'

'Sorry. Never seen him before in my life.'

Although they were some way from the edge of the cliff they could see the water now, glittering and fizzing against an offshore craig. Perez sat on the grass. A gannet was hovering in the thermals. 'Sorry,' he said. 'I'm not as fit as I should be. It's all desk work these days.' He hoped Roddy would sit with him, but the boy walked on. He stood with his back to Perez, looking out, arms slightly away from his body. The late-morning sun was right above him, his own spotlight. From where he was sitting Perez thought he would disappear. One more step and he would tumble into space. It looked as if all Roddy had to do was reach out his hand and then he would touch the tip of the gannet's wing. An illusion, Perez knew. A trick of the light and the way the land dipped towards the cliff-edge. But it made him feel sick. He could feel sweat on his forehead, hoped it wasn't showing.

'You haven't asked how the Englishman died.' He hoped that would be enough to catch the boy's attention and Roddy did turn towards Perez, walk a few steps closer.

'What was it? An accident?' And that was the most probable scenario for unexpected death in the islands. Too much to drink. Narrow and precarious roads. Especially for a stranger.

'Kenny Thomson found him hanging in the hut by the jetty.'

'Suicide then?'

'Most likely.' The official version until the GP from Whiteness got his second opinion.

'Poor sod,' Roddy said, and then he did come and flop on the grass beside Perez. But the words came easily, without any thought behind them. He was young and lucky and couldn't imagine how desperate you would have to be to take your own life.

'Or murder.' The words sounded fierce to Perez and he knew he shouldn't have spoken. Not until it was all official. But he wanted Roddy to take the matter seriously. At the moment it was a game to him. Besides, Perez trusted the young Glaswegian doctor, and by the time the team arrived from Inverness the whole of Shetland would know what was going on.

'Murder!' Still the boy's mouth had a twist at the corner as if this was also a joke, too incredible to be true.

'It's a possibility,' Perez said. 'You do see why I have to find out who he was.'

'Really, I'd never met him before.'

'Did you speak to him at all during the evening?'

'He was standing in front of a painting by Fran Hunter. That silhouette of the child on the beach. I thought it was bloody brilliant. I mean I love Bella's work and I don't want to be disloyal but I thought that painting the best piece in the exhibition. I can't get it out of my head; if it hasn't sold yet, I think I'll buy it. Save it for when I have a home to move into. I was next to him, looking at it too. And he spoke to me. "Good, isn't it?" That was all he said.'

'Accent?' Perez asked. 'I couldn't place it, and you've travelled more than me.' How old was Roddy Sinclair? Twenty-one? Twenty-two? And already he'd played his fiddle all over the world. Except Australia, and soon he'd have been there too.

'North of England,' Roddy said. 'Yorkshire? But it was only three words. I can't be certain.'

'How did he seem?'

'Like someone admiring a painting. I mean calm. Ordinary. I walked away and five minutes later he was causing all that fuss, on his knees and bawling. It seemed really bizarre.'

So what had happened in those five minutes? Perez thought. A sudden blankness which had scared the stranger so much that he'd fallen apart? Or had the amnesia been an act, turned on for the audience? To disrupt the event further, like the flyers of cancellation scattered all over the town.

'What did you do after you'd finished playing?' Perez asked.

'I got pissed. It wasn't much of a party, but I thought I should enter into the spirit of the event.'

'Who were you drinking with?'

'Whoever was around, but everyone drifted off very early. In the end it was just me and Martin. He was clearing up. I don't supposed I helped much, but at least I could keep him company, keep his glass topped up.'

'You two old friends?'

'Well, he's a bit older than me. But in the scale of things in Biddista, we're both children. If I'm staying with Bella we usually get together for an evening. If Dawn will let him out to play.'

'What time did you leave the Herring House?'

'Can't remember, I'm afraid, and it's hard to tell, isn't it, at this time of year? I mean, all night it looks as if it's just dusk. Martin might know. He was marginally more sober than me.'

'You left together?'

'Aye. I remember standing outside waiting for him to lock up. I had a bottle of wine in each hand. I'd invited him back to the Manse to carry on the party. You know how it seems a good idea at the time?'

'Anyone else about?'

'No. It was all quiet. I do remember thinking that. Most places in the world there's something. Traffic noise. Music. A siren in the distance. Here it was just the birds. The water on the shingle. Then I started singing and Martin told me to shut up or I'd wake his daughter.'

'Martin walked up to the Manse with you?'

'No, in the end he went all sensible on me. Said Dawn would kill him if he didn't get back at a decent time and he'd promised to help in the shop in the morning. I walked with him as far as his house, then carried on by myself.'

'Still no one else about?'

'I didn't see anyone.'

'Was Bella up when you got home?'

'No. The place was empty. Quiet as the grave.'

Back on the jetty, the GP's car had gone. Sandy was still sitting by himself. He never seemed troubled by boredom. Perez wondered what he could be thinking about, sitting so still and nothing to occupy him. Some woman, perhaps. Sandy was given to brief and violent infatuations. The relationships never lasted and each time he was left disappointed and confused.

Perez thought his own record was hardly any better. Now he was infatuated too. Perhaps he was making as big a fool of himself as Sandy always did. He felt himself grinning and decided he didn't care, looked at his watch to cover up the daft smirk. It was nearly one o'clock. Sandy was troubled by hunger and would soon be pressing for a lunch break. When he saw Perez approaching he jumped off the harbour wall.

'I've just tried to phone you.'

'No signal on the hill,' Perez said. There were black holes for mobiles all over the islands.

'The doctors have just gone.'

'And?'

'They're agreed. Murder.'

Chapter Nine

So now it was official. They couldn't just call out the paramedics, cut down the stranger in black and hand his body over to the health authority. Perez looked at his watch. The squad from Inverness wouldn't get to Aberdeen in time for the ferry, but they should just make the last plane of the evening in. He was already dialling to let his team in Lerwick know what was happening, get things moving.

'Are you OK to stay here, Sandy? Mark it out as a crime scene and keep folks well away. I'll get them to send someone to relieve you as soon as we can.'

He supposed he should go back to town. There was all the bureaucracy that came with a suspicious death. His first priority should be to identify the dead man. He should speak to the Fiscal, start the legal process of the investigation. But really he wanted to stay in Biddista. There were other people here to talk to and he thought he'd get more out of them than would the incomers.

'Hey, I'm starving. Let me just go over to the shop to get some chocolate, huh?' Sandy could whine like a two-year-old. Perez thought sometimes he had the brains of a two-year-old; then he'd surprise them all with his technical competence – he was better at IT than anyone else in the office. Perez couldn't help liking him.

'You stay here. I'll get you something.' Before Sandy could object he was halfway across the road. He could hear the Whalsay man shouting after him. 'A Mars Bar then. And crisps. Salt and vinegar. And a can of Coke. Not the bloody Diet shite.'

The shop had been built on to the last house in the terrace and was hardly bigger than an English suburban garage. There were shelves all round the walls for self-service and a refrigerated counter with a lump of Orkney cheddar and a couple of pounds of vacuum-packed streaky bacon. In one corner, the post office: a rack of official forms and some scales for weighing parcels. A young man stood behind the food counter. Perez recognized Martin Williamson, the chef who'd prepared the food for the exhibition the night before. Williamson's father had run a hotel in Scalloway until he'd drunk all the profits and the family had sold up and moved into Lerwick. The father had died soon after. He'd fallen into the water at the ferry terminal, full of drink. Rumour had it that he'd jumped, but nobody had seen him fall, so how could they know?

Yet Martin had a reputation for good humour. Even at the old man's funeral, he'd been heard cracking a joke with one of his friends. There were people who'd disapproved of that; others thought he was putting on a brave face. The story would be linked to him for ever. It defined him: Martin Williamson, the man who laughed at his father's funeral. 'He's always been a bit of a clown,' his mother was quoted as saying when the complaints got back to her. Apparently, the comment had been made quite without judgement.

ANN CLEEVES

Aggie Williamson had her name over the shop door and lived in the house attached. The same rumour-mongers who gossiped about old man Williamson's drowning explained her sudden affluence, the ability to buy the business, as the result of the payout from the insurance company after her husband's death. She'd grown up in Biddista and had always wanted to return there. She'd never settled in Scalloway or in the hotel. She was a quiet and withdrawn woman and the noise of the hotel's public bar, the stress of facing strangers who came to holiday there, had unsettled her. She could scarcely make much of a living from the Biddista business, but the Royal Mail paid her a little, and anyway she preferred it when the shop was empty. Then she sat on the high stool next to the post office and read romantic novels set in the past.

Martin lived in the house set in the middle of the terrace with his wife Dawn and his young daughter. He helped his mother out when he wasn't working in the Herring House. He had ambitions to open his own restaurant.

All this Perez knew, although his dealings with the family had been limited. He wondered occasionally how it must be to live in a community where the back stories to people's lives remained untold. Exhilarating, he thought. It could be possible to reinvent yourself with every encounter. But it might be flat and a little cold too. Biddista had even fewer people than Fair Isle, where he grew up. He thought the folk here would make sure they had some secrets to keep to them-selves. Nobody liked to think their neighbours knew everything about them.

He realized that he must look very odd, just standing there, deep in thought, and roused himself. The shop was gloomy. The only light came from the open door. In the shadow he saw a small child playing on the floor, a box of toys beside her. In her arms she held a knitted toy, a strange animal with elongated limbs and a snout. She held it round the middle and bounced it along the floor as if it was dancing. Martin looked at him over the counter, saw him staring at the toy and laughed.

'Don't ask what it is. Alice took a fancy to it at a sale of work and now we can't get it off her, even to wash it.' He grinned. 'Twice in two days: what brings you to Biddista again so soon?'

Perez ignored the question. 'I thought you ran the café in the Herring House. Aren't you there today?'

'The gallery's not open on a Tuesday. I give my mother a bit of a break by standing in here.'

Perez walked around the shelves, pulling off chocolate bars and crisps. No salt and vinegar. Would cheese and onion do? Sandy could be picky about his food. I can't believe that I'm really worrying about this, Perez thought, that I'm just about to start a murder investigation and I'm bothered by Sandy's choice of a snack lunch. He landed up at the counter, took his wallet out of his back pocket. 'That man who was at the gallery last night,' he said. 'You saw he was a bit upset. Did you recognize him?'

Martin shook his head. 'He looked like a visitor to me.' He began to ring up Perez's purchases on the till.

'I left him in the kitchen with you. What made him run off suddenly like that?'

Martin looked up, a packet of crisps still in his hand. 'Hey, it was nothing to do with me. I was still working on the buffet. Waste of time in the end, half of it was uneaten. They didn't get as many people as they were expecting. Bella was furious.'

'So what happened? Did he just get up and walk out without a word?'

'I don't know what happened. I carried a tray of food out to set on the trestle at the back of the gallery. When I got back to the kitchen he'd gone. Maybe he just sorted himself out and went home.'

'No,' Perez said. He saw that the girl was engrossed in her game, but still lowered his voice. 'He didn't do that. He's still there in Kenny Thomson's hut. He's dead. Hanging from one of the rafters.'

Martin's mouth stretched into the beginning of an embarrassed laugh.

'You're joking?'

'No,' Perez said. 'Why would I joke about something like that? Kenny found him. He hasn't said anything to you?' He found it hard to believe that this was news to Martin. A place like Biddista, information escaped, seeped into general knowledge without any effort. 'Didn't you wonder what Sandy and the doctors were doing out there?'

'I've been in here since the shop opened. Nursing a bit of a hangover.'

'Why would you think I was joking?' How tasteless would that be? he thought. Like claiming a death in the family had caused an art exhibition to cancel its opening.

'Well, I mean, it's a shock. Did he kill himself?' Suddenly Martin lifted his daughter into his arms. He looked out of the doorway, down to the hut and Sandy,

who was still sitting on the harbour wall. 'Why would
he go into Kenny's hut to kill himself?'

'Was Kenny the only person to use it?'

'No, we just call it that because he built it. Everyone living in Biddista can leave their gear there.
Kenny, me, the new chap who's moved into the house
at the end of the row, Bella, Roddy.'

'Who's the new chap?'

'He's from England. A writer. Peter Wilding. Here
to finish a book, he said. Willy, who used to live in that
house, moved into sheltered housing last year and
Wilding moved in. I'd never heard of him but he obviously does all right at it if he can afford to take the
summer out. He doesn't seem to do much writing.
Mostly he's sitting at his upstairs window, staring out
over the water. Maybe waiting for inspiration, huh?'

The girl struggled to be released from his grip and
ran back to her toys.

'Does Wilding have a boat?' Perez asked.

'No. I asked him out when I was going with Kenny
once, just to be friendly. But a bit of a breeze blew up
and it made him kind of nervous. I think he felt ill. I
don't think he'd go out again.'

'Why does he need to get into the hut then?'

'He asked if he could leave a couple of boxes of his
things there. Willy's house is very small.'

'If he's from England maybe there's a connection
with the dead man.'

'They can't have been friends though. A strange
kind of friendship at least, to see someone you know
upset and do nothing to help him.'

'What do you mean?'

'Wilding was at the party at the Herring House last

night. Bella invited him. She likes famous people. He was there when the stranger had that turn. If he'd known him he surely would have said so then.' Then Perez remembered Bella mentioning the man, only she'd described him as a collector.

'You can't think of anyone else round here who might have been putting up the dead man? We can't find a car.'

'No one around Biddista takes in paying guests.'

'What time did you leave the Herring House?'

'It was probably about eleven before I'd finished clearing up.'

'I understand Roddy Sinclair kept you company.'

'We had a few drinks. There were plenty of bottles open. It would have been a waste not to finish a couple of them.' Martin grinned. Is he really like some care-free child? Perez thought. Is it true that he wasn't even moved by his father's death?

'He invited you back to the Manse to carry on with the party?'

'He said he'd promised Bella he'd stop drinking on his own. I think she worries about him. He gets a bit wild sometimes. Last time he was home she suggested he go somewhere to dry out.'

'Did he?'

'Of course not. He's young. He drinks a lot. He's only different from any other Shetland boy his age because he has more money. He'll grow out of it.'

'You didn't go with Roddy to the Manse?'

'No, I knew I'd be there all night. He started to make a bit of a noise as we left the gallery. Dawn has to be up early for work and I knew she'd not appreciate the racket. That brought me to my senses.'

'Was anyone around?'

'Nobody.'

'Any lights in the houses?'

'I'm not sure. This time of the year when it's not so dark out, you don't really notice.' He paused. 'I think Wilding was back sitting at his upstairs window looking out.'

'Can you remember when he left the party?'

'Sorry. I was in and out of the kitchen all evening. People seemed to disappear quite quickly after the chap caused the scene. Roddy played a couple of numbers then everyone drifted off. I guess Wilding went then.'

'Do you know anything about this?' Perez slipped the flyer cancelling the exhibition on to the counter.

Martin read it, frowning. 'I don't understand,' he said. 'Who died? Bella didn't say anything about cancelling to me.'

'Nobody died,' Perez said. *Only an Englishman dressed in black.* 'It seems to have been some sort of practical joke. Or someone wanting to wreck the opening. These were all over Lerwick yesterday.' ·

'It's pathetic.' For the first time in the conversation Martin seemed serious. Intense.

'What is?'

'People being so jealous of Bella. Because she's good at what she does and makes money from it.'

'Do you have anyone specific in mind?'

Before Martin could answer, the child turned back from the toybox to face them.

'Look at me!' She was wearing a clown's mask. Her hair, caught in the elastic, stuck up around it. The mask was identical to the one the stranger was still

79

wearing as he hung in the jetty hut waiting for the crime-scene investigator from Inverness. Perez felt his stomach flip as it had earlier that day. With a flight of fancy he thought the mask stopped the child looking human. It was as if someone had stolen her soul.

But Martin only laughed. 'Hey, Alice,' he said. 'Where did you get that? It's really freaky.'

The girl giggled and ran out of the shop into the sunshine without answering.

Chapter Ten

The child ran into her grandmother's house, leaving the door ajar after her. Her mother wouldn't be at home. Perez knew that, as he knew all the other things about the family, the information gathered without any effort on his part, over the years. Dawn Williamson was a teacher at Middleton, the nearest primary school. Martin and Aggie looked after the girl between them while she was at work. Dawn was an incomer, so his understanding of her background was a little sketchy. She'd already moved to Shetland, was already teaching in the school when she took up with Martin.

Perez took the carrier bag of food back to Sandy, left it on the harbour wall beside him and crossed the road again before the man discovered his requests hadn't been exactly met. He stood on the pavement outside Aggie's house and knocked at the door. He liked Aggie. He'd returned to Shetland just in time to be involved with her husband's accident. He'd taken a statement from her, had respected her calm, the way she refused to speak badly of the dead man.

Aggie let him in. She recognized him at once.

'Jimmy Perez, what are you doing in Biddista?' There was a trace of nervousness in her voice.

Wherever you were in the world, a policeman on your doorstep meant trouble. When he didn't answer, she went on, 'Well, come away in. You'll tell me in your own good time.'

He couldn't think that he'd seen Aggie since her husband's funeral, but she'd not changed – a trim, slight woman now in her early sixties. Standing at the square table, covered in patterned oilcloth, she was preparing for baking. In front of her stood a set of scales, a china bowl, a bag of flour and another of sugar, three eggs loose on a saucer, a wooden spoon. He could have been in his mother's kitchen in Fair Isle. She had a mixing bowl of exactly the same pale yellow. Aggie had been greasing a baking tray with a margarine wrapper. Alice had run ahead of him and was sitting on a tall stool drinking juice from a plastic beaker. The clown's mask had been pushed back from her face but still rested on top of her head.

Aggie wiped her hands on a dishcloth. 'Now,' she said, 'you'll take a cup of tea while you're here.' She pushed the kettle on to the hotplate of the Rayburn. The first trace of surprise at seeing him on the doorstep had disappeared. But then nothing seemed to shock her. She hadn't been shocked when her husband walked off the dock into the water.

He looked over to the granddaughter and she realized he didn't want to talk in front of the child.

'Come away, Alice,' she said. 'A lovely day like this, you don't want to be stuck indoors. There'll be time enough for that when you start school. Outside with you.' She opened the kitchen door and chivvied her into a long, narrow garden. They watched her climb on to a wooden swing, still holding the woollen toy in

one hand so she had to grasp one of its limbs and the
rope together. The rope looked like something you
might see on a ship. Like the rope forming the noose
around the Englishman's neck..

'There's a dead man in Kenny's hut,' Perez said.
Again he didn't think this could be news to her. She'd
have seen Sandy sitting on the wall all morning.
Surely she'd have gone out to ask him what he was
doing there. But if it was old information, she wasn't
letting on.

She'd already started beating the sugar and margarine and looked up sharply.

'Not Kenny? No, of course, it can't be Kenny. He
walked past the house a little while ago. Fast, as if he
didn't want to speak. Who then?'

'An Englishman,' Perez said. 'A stranger. He was at
Bella Sinclair's party last night, but nobody seemed to
know him.'

'How did he die?' she asked.

'We don't have all the details yet. He's hanging
from one of the rafters.' He paused. 'You weren't there,
at Bella's party.'

Not a question, and she picked up on that. 'But you
were? I'd heard you'd become friendly with Duncan
Hunter's wife.'

'She's not his wife any more, Aggie.' Why had he
felt the need to say that? He was annoyed that he'd
reacted to the comment. Perhaps it was because she
made him think of his mother, and he'd always needed
to justify himself to *her*.

'Aye well, none of my business anyway.' She hesitated. 'Bella asked me to go along, but you ken,
Jimmy, it's not my thing. All sorts of folk I don't know.'

'Not my kind of thing either, really.'

'And I find Bella kind of scary. Even after all these years.'

He smiled. He understood what she meant. He found Bella scary too. 'You must have grown up together. Here in Biddista.'

'Aye,' she said. 'We all lived in these houses. Willy was in the end one. He never married and his mother had died by the time we were old enough to notice. The Sinclairs were in the middle house. And I lived in here with my mother and father.'

'So you're back where you started.'

'I never really wanted to move away.'

'Bella just had the one brother?'

'Alec, Roddy's father.'

'What was he like?

'Oh, he was a quiet man. Not at all like his son. He had cancer, you know. So sad for such a young man. He got very thin in the end. It must have been terrible for Roddy. Maybe that explains why he turned out so wild.'

Perez thought he could see a faint flush on her face and wondered if she had felt something special for Alec Sinclair, but perhaps that was just the heat of the kitchen. 'Kenny Thomson was at Skoles then too,' she went on, eager, it seemed, to change the subject. 'Him and his parents and his brother Lawrence. So nothing much has changed at all. Lawrence moved into Lerwick and then he left Shetland all together.'

'You haven't heard of any strangers around? Maybe one of the houses on the way to Middleton has started taking paying guests?'

She shook her head. 'Not that I've heard.' She

cracked one of the eggs against the bowl and used both thumbs to pull the shell apart. 'It couldn't have been Peter Wilding? He's the man who's taken over Willy's house. He's an Englishman.'

'Martin would have recognized him. He met my stranger last night.'

'Then I can't help you.'

'Have you had any visitors into the shop in the last few days?'

'A few. A group of young Australians at the beginning of the week wanting cold drinks. And there was a tour bus yesterday. It stopped at the Herring House so folk could have coffee. Most of them walked down here afterwards to stretch their legs, buy postcards and sweeties. But they were all elderly people. How old is your man?'

'Not that old. Forty. Forty-five.'

'Not old at all then.' Another egg went into the bowl. She sifted a spoonful of flour on top, folded it in carefully.

Perez waited until she'd finished before asking, 'Where did Alice get the clown's mask?'

'Why do you need to know, Jimmy? Do you want to get one for Fran Hunter's lass?' A faint mischievous smile, hoping to make him react again.

'No, not that.' He paused, then thought there was no harm in telling her. Word would get out soon enough.

'The dead man was wearing something like it.'

She stood quite still, the bowl under one arm, the spoon in her other hand. Perhaps she had the picture in her head of a man she didn't know, the kiddies' mask around his head. 'I didn't buy that thing for Alice.'

'Neither did Martin.'

'It must have been Dawn then. If you like I'll talk to the child. See if she remembers. If you think it's important . . .'

He shrugged. 'It might help us identify him. There's not much else to go on.'

He was thinking that he might ask Dawn about the mask. She'd know more about it than Alice. He was intrigued by the coincidence and was tempted to drive to Middleton to talk to her. But he couldn't justify the time. He wanted an incident room ready and waiting when the Inverness boys got in. He didn't want them thinking the Shetland team couldn't handle a serious crime. Last time they were here the thing had dragged on too long. Besides, he didn't want to make such a big deal of the man and the mask. If he turned up at the school and pulled Dawn out of her class, he'd have rumours spreading throughout the islands. He remembered the last murder they'd had in Shetland, the fear that seemed to freeze the community and change it into a quite different place. This was different. This was a stranger. But he didn't want that icy panic to take over again.

'If Alice can't help, maybe you could mention it to Dawn,' he said.

'I will.'

'And I don't want news of this getting out just yet. I'd like to inform the relatives first.' *If we can ever find them.*

'Don't worry, I'll not tell anyone and I'll ask Dawn to keep it to herself.' She spoke with a quiet assumption that her request would be honoured. Perez couldn't imagine Fran being as compliant with his mother's wishes. She'd had a successful career before she moved to Shetland. Her confidence had taken a bit of a knock recently, but she still knew her own mind. Fran and my mother, he thought. How will that work?

Aggie set down the mixing bowl and walked with him to the door. He realized for the first time that she was anxious for him to be gone.

'I'm sorry,' he said. 'Perhaps this is difficult for you. The way Andrew died . . . I should have realized.'

She gave him a long, hard stare. 'My husband's death was an accident. Not like this at all.'

'Of course.' He could feel his face become red, turned away quickly and walked out.

Back in the street he heard the distant sound of a foghorn. Here the sun was still shining and he thought at first they were testing it. Sometimes they did that and it always shocked him, hearing the great booming noise in full sunlight. Then out to sea he saw the thick bank of mist. It was just below the horizon but it was rolling closer. Further south it must already have hit the land.

Sandy had strung the tape around the hut. Blue and white. POLICE. DO NOT ENTER. There was a police car parked, blocking off any vehicular access to the jetty. Now Perez could send Sandy back to Lerwick. It was just a matter of saving the scene from any further contamination before the CSI arrived. He wondered if Sandy had thought to tell the doctors that the CSI would need their shoes, and maybe their clothes for comparison. It was his fault; he should have reminded him.

He was halfway along the road when his phone rang. Morag, one of his team. He'd set her to book places on the last plane for the Inverness team.

'What's it like there with you?'

'Sorry?' Was she being polite? Passing the time of day? Did she have no sense of urgency?

'I've just had Sumburgh on the phone. They've got thick fog.'

'Any chance of it lifting this afternoon?'

'I've just been on to Dave Wheeler.' Dave was the met. man who lived in Fair Isle. He took all the weather readings for the shipping forecast. 'Highly unlikely, he says. And the airport say they're not expecting any more planes in or out today.'

Perez switched off his phone and stood for a moment. The sun was already covered in a milky haze. So the team from Inverness wouldn't be in today. If the fog stayed down and they had to get the ferry tomorrow evening they wouldn't arrive until seven o'clock the following morning. He was in charge. It was his investigation. He'd thought it was what he always wanted.

His phone rang again. 'Jimmy. It's Roy Taylor here. From Inverness.'

So, not his case at all.

'This is how I want you to play it until we arrive.'

Chapter Eleven

Singling neeps was the sort of job you could only do if your mind was somewhere else. It hurt your back, and thinning out the tiny turnip plants took no concentration or thought. It was mindless. The worst thing was when you looked up, thinking that by now you must have nearly finished, done half the field at least, you'd see you'd hardly started and there were rows and rows still left ahead of you.

When they'd been boys, Kenny and Lawrence had played games to make it less boring. Had races, working down the rows next to each other. Lawrence always won. He was faster at most things than Kenny. But not so thorough. Kenny's rows were always tidier, the plants evenly spaced, so he hadn't minded Lawrence winning. Though it would have been nice to be first once in a while.

Today, while he was working in the field, Kenny found himself thinking quite a lot about when they were children. The games they'd all played together. Perhaps that was to take his mind off the sight of the body swinging from the roof of his hut, the hut he'd built with Lawrence. He wondered if he'd think of the dead man every time he went in there to get his boat ready.

He'd begun with the neeps as soon as Perez had gone and now it was time to stop for lunch, but he had that compulsion to carry on, at least until he'd come to the end of the row. So he pushed the hoe backwards and forwards down the line and remembered what it had been like here nearly fifty years ago. When he'd been a peerie boy, all scabbed knees and snotty nose, blushing like a girl whenever anyone spoke to him.

Today there was only one child in Biddista, Aggie Williamson's granddaughter, Alice. When he'd been growing up there'd been five – him and Lawrence, Bella and Alec Sinclair, and Aggie, who hadn't been a Williamson then. He struggled for a moment to remember her maiden name. Watt. She'd been Aggie Watt. A timid little thing. Looking at her now when he went into the post office, seeing her with her nose in a book, he thought she'd hardly changed in fifty years. She'd looked like an old woman when she was a child. Small and peaky and delicate.

Lawrence and Bella had been just like each other even then. Headstrong and determined to get their own way. And bright. Fighting to be top of the class in Middleton School, laughing at jokes nobody else could understand, annoying the teachers with their cheek and their quick, slick answers. In competition, but attracted to each other just the same. Kenny had only wanted not to be noticed.

Now there were three of them left in Biddista. Bella had turned into a grand artist. She'd been away to college, studied in Barcelona and New York, but she'd been living in the Manse for more than twenty years. Aggie was back staying next door to the house where she'd grown up. And he was in exactly the same place, doing much the same things as he had as a child. It occurred to him that fifty years ago to the day he could have been in this field helping his father to single turnips. Only two of us escaped, he thought. Alec died while he was still young and handsome. And Lawrence ran away when Bella broke his heart.

He reached the end of the row and straightened his back, felt the muscles pull in his shoulders. If Edith was here she would rub them for me, he thought, pull the tension out of them. And he thought how much more skilled Edith was at touching him now than when they'd first got together. There was a lot to be said for getting older.

Edith's family hadn't come from Biddista. He hadn't met her until he started at the big school. She was a few years younger than him. They'd gone in on the bus together, but he'd hardly noticed her until he was fifteen. She'd had freckles then and curly hair. Mousy brown with a touch of red in it. He'd been too nervous to ask her out and the first approach had come from her. She'd always known what she wanted. Later he brought her to Biddista, and she'd met the others – Lawrence and Bella, Alec and Aggie. She'd never quite fitted in. They'd been kind enough to her, even Bella, but Edith had always kept herself a little bit aloof.

As he straightened he saw that the sun had gone in, covered by a bank of mist which had slid in from the sea. Further inland it was still clear. Standing still after the work he felt the cold air dry the sweat on his forehead and his neck.

In the kitchen he put the kettle on and looked in

the fridge for food. At one time Edith always made him lunch. When he was doing building work and it was too far from home she'd pack him up sandwiches, a thick piece of date slice or that chocolate biscuit cake they all called peat. If he was out on the croft, there'd be something hot on the table for him when he came in. Soup usually. Then she got the job in the care centre and even before she was made manager and started at college things had changed.

'We're both working now. You'll have to look after yourself. It's only fair,' she'd told him.

Kenny could see the justice in that. It was the sort of thing Bella might say. Bella had never married because she wanted to keep her independence. 'I like being a single woman. I celebrate being alone.' Kenny had read that in one of the Sunday papers. An interview with Bella after an exhibition in Edinburgh. Edith had brought back the paper one of the days she was at college and shown him.

There was some cold lamb in the fridge left over from the roast they'd had on Sunday. He sliced it up and made a sandwich with it. By the time he'd finished doing that the kettle had boiled and he made tea. Now the fog was so thick that he couldn't see anything out of the kitchen window. Not even the wall which marked the end of the garden or his truck standing outside the door. He was glad now he hadn't taken the boat out. He didn't have any of that fancy GPS equipment. He'd have been left to find his way back to the jetty using a compass and chart, and he was a bit rusty these days. He hoped Edith would take care driving back from the centre. It would be easy to leave the road in this weather, or to hit something coming in the other direction. Since seeing the man in black hanging in his hut, he'd had death at the back of his mind.

He sat in the easy chair with his plate on his knee and the mug of tea within reach on the Rayburn, listening to the news on Radio Shetland. There was nothing about the dead man. But Jimmy Perez wouldn't be able to keep it quiet for very much longer. Then he switched the radio to long wave for the shipping forecast. That was habit. When he finished eating he felt himself doze. Half asleep, he found himself remembering the summer he'd met Jimmy in Fair Isle, working in the South Lighthouse. It seemed even longer ago than when he'd been a boy, singling neeps.

Kenny came to with a start and realized that someone had opened the door. He knew where he was at once. It had been one of those afternoon naps that are more like daydreaming than sleep. His first thought was that it must be Edith, home early for some reason, and he decided they might go to bed. He liked sex during the day more than anything. It seemed stolen time to him, illicit. But when he turned, his arms slightly open to hold her, he saw that it wasn't Edith at all. It was Aggie Williamson. The mist was caught in her hair. Millions of tiny drops of water trapped in the thin, wispy tangle. Silver on grey.

'Aggie,' he said. 'Is anything wrong?' They had known each other for all that time, but still she had never come into his house uninvited. Even as a child, when she'd wanted to play with them, she'd hung around outside waiting for them to join her. She'd never knocked on the door. Bella and Alec would just have burst in, sat at the table, assumed that the milk and biscuits were for them too.

'That policeman came by,' Aggie said. 'Perez. He told me there was a body in the hut.'

'I know. I found the man.' He preferred to think of him as a man rather than a body. Had she just come to gossip? It seemed unlike her. Usually in places like Biddista the shop was the place for gossip, but Aggie never encouraged it. She sat behind the counter. Her book would be face down, but you could tell she was waiting to get back to it. She still seemed preoccupied by the story, indifferent to the rumours being spread.

'Do you have no idea who he is?' she asked.

'I couldn't see his face,' Kenny said. 'It was covered with a mask. A clown's mask.'

'Jimmy Perez said that too.' She paused, fixed him with her eyes. 'It couldn't have been Lawrence?'

She waited for Kenny to consider the possibility, watched for a reaction, and when none came she went on. 'Martin described him to me. He saw him alive. Might have been the last person to see him alive. I just couldn't help thinking . . .'

'The dead man is English,' Kenny said. 'He spoke with an English accent. Perez told me.'

'Lawrence has been away for a long time. He might speak differently now.'

'You're talking as if you want it to be Lawrence,' he said.

'No!'

'I would have recognized him,' Kenny said stubbornly. 'Even without seeing his face.'

'Would you? Really? How long is it since he's been

here? Years. Certainly he left before Alice was born and I can't mind any visits.'

Kenny tried to fix a picture of his brother in his mind. To see his height, the proportions of his body. He thought of the man he'd seen the night before loping down the track. Could that have been Lawrence?

'When's the last time you heard from him?' Aggie asked.

Kenny knew exactly, but he wasn't going to tell Aggie. He wasn't going to admit that Lawrence cared so little for him that there'd been nothing but a second-hand message left with Bella. 'Lawrence says he's going away again. He told me to tell you.' Kenny hadn't even been there to say goodbye when his brother left. Perhaps Lawrence had chosen the moment especially. He'd known that Kenny would persuade him to stay.

'The man in the hut isn't Lawrence,' he said.

He thought she would say more to convince him that it might be, but she suddenly gave up the fight.

'Of course,' she said. 'You're right. I'm being foolish. I don't know what's been wrong with me to day. My head's full of all kinds of fancies. You would know your own brother.' She paused. 'After the policeman left I even wondered for a moment if it might be Andrew. They didn't find his body until weeks after he fell. The tide was so strong, the coastguard said he must have been taken out to open water. I thought maybe he survived after all. For all those weeks I kept hoping. There was some chance he'd survived, swum ashore somewhere, taken himself away to sober up.

95

Even when the body was washed up, it could have been anyone.'

'Andrew's dead,' Kenny said.

'I know. It's my imagination. I think, What if . . . and then I'm carried along by the possibility. The story.' She gave a little smile. 'I'm sorry, I shouldn't have come.'

'Have some tea while you're here.' Now, he felt sorry for her, living all on her own. She had no one to take her to bed on stolen afternoons.

'No,' she said. 'I just shut up the post office and ran up here. I need to get back. I might have customers waiting.'

'It's the time of year,' he said. 'The light nights. It makes us all go a little bit mad.'

Chapter Twelve

Roy Taylor was head of the Inverness team. He'd be the senior investigating officer once he arrived. Perez had worked with him before and they'd become friends of a sort. Not close friends. Perez knew nothing about his private life, didn't even know if he was married. But they'd come to an understanding about the case they were working on.

Now, listening to Taylor's impatience, Perez was irritated. He didn't need telling that the priority was to get an ID on the victim. He'd only officially *been* a victim for half an hour, for Christ's sake. Sandy should have arrived in Lerwick now. He'd be on the phone, chatting to the lasses in the NorthLink office at Holmsgarth, checking with Loganair on the BA bookings. It was the sort of work Sandy liked and was good at, routine and not too demanding. Perez was confident they'd have a name by the end of the day. At this point there was little else they could do. He knew that Taylor's impatience had little to do with his handling of the case. He'd be frustrated because he was still in Inverness, because he hadn't set out for Aberdeen the minute he got the call. If the weather had changed just a little earlier, if they hadn't banked on getting the last plane into Sumburgh, they'd have been able to reach the ferry before it sailed and at least they'd be in Lerwick at seven the next morning. Taylor was a man who liked to be in control. Perez could imagine him, angry with himself and taking it out on the rest of the team.

Perez was hungry now too. Fran had woken when he got up, made mumbled offers of toast and fruit, but he was already late for work by then. He was tempted to head back for town, thought of bacon sandwiches, fish and chips. Something warm and greasy and filling. But for completeness' sake he thought he should talk to Peter Wilding, the Englishman who had taken on Willy Jamieson's house. He could tell Taylor that he'd spoken to everyone who lived in Biddista then. Taylor wouldn't be able to pull him up on that.

Wilding was sitting in the upstairs window, looking out, just as Martin had described. The fog had made the day so gloomy that he'd switched on a light in the room. Perez could only see him when he reached the end of the terrace and even then the view wasn't so good. He thought the man had been watching him all along, from the moment he'd pulled up in his car. He'd have watched Perez go to Skoles and to the Manse, seen him in the shop and in Aggie's house. It seemed odd to him that a man should take so much interest in the trivia of everyday life. In Perez's experience, women were the nosy ones. Why would this Englishman care what the people of Biddista got up to? But Wilding's curiosity might be useful. There was a real possibility that he'd seen the stranger.

The writer must just have seen Perez as a silhouette coming out of the mist. Why is he still sitting there, Perez thought, when there's nothing to see? As soon as he knocked on the door, Wilding left his place at the window. Perez heard footsteps on wooden floor-boards, a key turning in the lock. The door must have warped because it stuck against the frame. Did the locked door mean the man hadn't been out yet that day? Or that security was a habit brought up from the south?

He recognized Wilding as soon as he came to the door as the dark man who'd been talking to Fran at the gallery. He was tall, rather good-looking, Perez saw now. He was wearing a striped collarless cotton shirt and jeans, canvas shoes. The writer smiled. He didn't speak but waited for his visitor to explain himself. Perez found the silence disconcerting.

Perez supposed he should show his warrant card, but couldn't quite remember what he'd done with it and introduced himself instead. 'I wonder if I could ask you a few questions.'

'Oh, please do. Any excuse to stop staring at a blank laptop screen.' It was a rich voice, as if he was constantly amused by a private joke. Perez had imag-ined a writer with a deadline to meet as brooding, self-absorbed, but now there was no hint of that. The man stood aside. 'I noticed that there's been some activity on the jetty. Is it about that, I wonder?' Perez remained silent. 'Oh well,' Wilding went on. 'No doubt you'll tell me when you're ready.' His eyes were so blue that Perez wondered if he was wearing coloured contact lenses. It pleased him to think of Wilding as vain.

Willy Jamieson had been born in this house and lived in it until he'd moved into sheltered housing. He'd scratched a living from fishing and, when he was younger, from odd bits of work for the council. Perez could remember seeing him by the side of the road sometimes, helping the contractors lay new tarmac. He'd never married, and when he'd moved out the house was in much the same state as the day his parents had moved in. Perez supposed that he'd bought it from the council. Wilding must be the owner now, or be renting it privately. He was hardly a normal council tenant.

Inside the house, Perez could see across a passageway into a small kitchen which held a deep sink with one tap and a Calor gas stove. The table, folded against one wall, looked as if it had been left behind by Willy. There were no fitted cupboards, no washing machine. The only additions were a small fridge, balanced on the workbench, and a coffee grinder. The place had an air of impermanence. A squat. It was as if Wilding were camping out here.

Wilding seemed untroubled that Perez could see the primitive nature of his domestic arrangements and gave another of his smiles. 'Let's go upstairs. It's more civilized there. Can I make you tea? I'm sure Aggie will have offered you tea earlier, but I expect you could use another by now. Or coffee perhaps? Coffee is one of my few luxuries here. I grind the beans every time.' He spoke slowly and Perez had the sense that he was considering the effect of every word. But perhaps it was just that he'd spent too long on his own in his upstairs room and conversation no longer came easily.

Perez was tempted by the coffee. It would be a long day and he would need something to keep awake and alert.

'Coffee would be fine.' He paused. 'One of my luxuries too.'

'Ah! Another addict! I can recognize the signs. Splendid. Go in and make yourself at home. The room at the front. I'll not keep you waiting long.'

He had followed Perez halfway up the stairs, but now he turned and went back to the kitchen, moving very lightly for such a tall man. All his movements were easy and unhurried. It was as if he'd expected a visitor and had planned in advance the words he would use and the way he would move.

As Wilding had said, the workroom was more civilized. The bare, unvarnished floorboards were hidden by a woven rug in the middle of the room. The desk was old, leather-topped and obviously his own. He'd made some makeshift shelves from bricks and planks and they were crammed with books. There was a CD player and a rack of discs. A large unframed canvas hung on one wall. It was of a field of hay, which had been cut and piled into untidy heaps, under a fierce yellow light. Perez thought it might be by Bella Sinclair and felt ridiculously pleased with himself when he approached and saw the signature. He would tell Fran later. He was still staring at it when Wilding came in, pushing the door open with his foot. He was carrying a cafetiere and two mugs on a tray, a box of shop-bought cakes. He had learned the convention of island entertaining. It was considered impossibly rude not to offer a guest something sweet to eat.

'I don't have any milk,' he said, in no way apologetic. 'But I could run to the shop if you're desperate.'

'I drink it black.'

'Splendid!' A favourite word. 'You have the chair,

inspector. I'm quite happy on the floor.' And he lounged, legs outstretched, still managing to dominate the room.

Perez would have liked a cake, but it seemed they were just there for show. He couldn't ask for one without seeming greedy. 'Martin says you're a writer.' Perez was interested in the man, his profession. Every witness statement and confession was part fiction, but he couldn't imagine conjuring a whole story from thin air, couldn't see where you would start. 'Do you write under your own name?'

Wilding laughed. 'Oh yes, inspector, but don't worry if you've never heard of me. Few people have. I write fantasy, an acquired taste.' He seemed rather pleased that he was unknown. 'Fortunately I do quite well in the States and Japan.'

Perez thought some comment of congratulation was expected, but wasn't sure what to say. Instead he sipped his coffee, took a moment to enjoy it.

'Have you had any visitors recently, Mr Wilding? Friends from the south, perhaps?'

'No, inspector. I moved here to escape distractions. The last thing I need is people under my feet.'

'There was an Englishman in Biddista yesterday. You might have seen him.'

'Nobody came to the house and I was in all day.'

'But not in the evening. Then you were at the exhibition at the Herring House. As was the Englishman.'

'And so were you! Of course, I recognize you now. You were there with the attractive young artist. Ms Hunter. A great new talent. Art, I must confess, is another of my luxuries. I love Bella's work. It was she who inspired my first visit to Shetland. And so I was delighted to receive an invitation to the opening. There were fewer people than I was expecting. I suppose I'd thought it was going to be more of a local event.'

'People are very busy in the summer.' Perez wondered why he felt so defensive. It wasn't the time to explain that the event had been the subject of a practical joke, but he didn't want the man thinking there was no interest in Shetland in Fran's work. 'Do you remember the man who became a little emotional?'

'The guy in black? Of course.' Wilding paused, for the first time dropped the light, affected tone. 'I felt sorry for him. I've suffered from mental-health problems too. I understood his desperation.'

'You thought his distress was genuine?'

'Oh I think so, don't you? It seemed real enough to me.'

Perez didn't answer.

'What happened to the man?' Perez thought Wilding seemed unnaturally concerned about a stranger. 'Has he been admitted to hospital? Sometimes, for a short while, it's the only solution with depression.'

'I'm afraid he's dead,' Perez said.

Wilding turned his head away. When he looked back, he'd regained some control, but his voice was still unsteady. 'The poor man.'

'Are you sure you didn't know him, Mr Wilding?'

'Quite sure, inspector. But it seems a terrible waste. Suicide. The worst sort of tragedy.'

'We don't think the man killed himself. We believe he was murdered.'

There was a silence. 'When I moved here,' Wilding said at last, 'I thought I'd escaped mindless violence.'

Oh, we can do mindless violence, Perez thought. Scraps in bars, fuelled by drink and frustration. But this death wasn't like that at all.

'What time did you leave the Herring House?' he asked.

'Soon after you. The heart seemed to go out of the party when the man made that scene.'

'Did you come straight back here?'

'I walked along the beach for a while. It was such a lovely evening. Just as far as the rocks and back. Then I came inside.'

'What did you do then?'

'I made coffee, brought it here to the window.'

'Did you see anyone? You have a good view of the jetty from here.'

'No. It was surprisingly quiet. I think the last people must have left the Herring House when I was walking. I didn't notice anything when I was on the beach. I was thinking about my book. There's this sticky patch with the plot. It's been troubling me for a few days. I was concentrating on that.'

'But you were here, with your coffee, by eleven o'clock?'

'I can't remember looking at my watch. But yes, I must have been. I hadn't been out so long.'

'Roddy Sinclair and Martin Williamson left the gallery at about eleven. Did you notice them?'

'No,' Wilding said. 'But that doesn't mean they weren't there.'

'Apparently Roddy became rather rowdy.'

'All the same I didn't notice them. My mind was still elsewhere, inspector.'

'On your book?'

'Yes, the book. Of course.'

Standing in the road outside the house, Perez tried to decide what he made of Wilding. What had really brought him here? He couldn't see Shetland as a natural home for the man. Did he have no friends or family to keep him in the south? There was something unsettling about the intensity of his gaze and the voyeuristic pleasure he took in watching his neighbours.

Chapter Thirteen

In her office at the top of the converted textile mill in Denby Dale, West Yorkshire, Martha Tyler was putting together the rehearsal schedule for the week. This show was about bullying. The next would be around racism. Schools didn't seem interested in hiring the Interact theatre-in-education group to entertain their pupils; there always had to be a message. The young actors with their new degrees in performance rolled their eyes when they saw the scripts, clunky with politically correct jargon, but it was work. They might dream of the Royal Shakespeare Company or a lucrative television ad, but Interact work counted towards their Equity card and the pay kept them in beer.

The company shared the mill with other small businesses – there was a decent wine merchant in the basement, a middle-aged woman who made silver jewellery, and an acupuncturist – but Interact had the whole of the top floor. One big space for rehearsals, a couple of offices and a small room with a microwave and a kettle where they took their breaks. This wasn't one of the smart conversions that had taken place in other parts of Kirklees. The mill was a rackety jumble of stairways and levels. The floors were uneven and the windows leaked.

Two of the actors had already arrived. Martha could hear them in the tea room, sharing stories of a nightmare tour of Hull which had become apocryphal – the teacher who'd had a breakdown in the middle of a performance, kids pulling knives, a pregnant fourteen-year-old who claimed to have gone into labour. All exaggeration. That was the trouble with people in the theatre business. They began to believe their own fictions. You could never tell where the acting stopped. That made her think of Jeremy. If you believed all his stories, he'd travelled the world, acted with Olivier and made love to at least half a dozen minor Hollywood film stars. She didn't believe a word, of course. Why would anyone like that end up running a crummy theatre-in-education company in West Yorkshire?

Martha checked her mobile phone. Still no call from him. What had started out as mild irritation had changed to anger and now to concern. Jeremy was an arrogant prat and a congenital liar, but he made his living from Interact and he cared about its reputation. Martha was at the company as part of a higher apprenticeship in arts management. After taking a good degree in drama from Bristol, the apprenticeship seemed a better option than an MA. There was a modest bursary and the chance for hands-on experience. Jeremy was taking the piss, of course. Her placement at Interact wasn't supposed to provide him with an unpaid skivvy, yet it wasn't unusual for him to disappear for a couple of days, leaving her in charge.

'It's great practice, love. Think how it'll look on your CV.'

But he'd been away for four days now and she hadn't heard anything. She'd tried his mobile, but it seemed to be switched off.

She tried to remember exactly what he'd said this time. They'd been in the pub the week before, the end of a debrief on the drugs-awareness tour of the Midlands. For once he'd been almost generous, had bought a couple of rounds for the actors. There'd been a suppressed excitement about him. She'd come in from Huddersfield on the train, so she'd been drinking too. Somehow she'd found herself sitting at a small table next to him. The rest of the group had been drinking all afternoon and were singing some dreadful song from the show. She'd had a struggle to make out what Jeremy had been saying.

'Something's come up, love. A great chance. You can cope on your own for a bit, can't you? A girl with your talents. I'll pay you, make it worth your while.'

She'd thought perhaps it was an audition. She'd worked around actors enough to recognize the excitement that came out of the possibility of a part, the part that would change a career. Even actors as old as Jeremy fell under the magic, lost all their reason. She couldn't understand it herself. She'd never been bitten by the acting bug. Jeremy told everyone that performance was his first love. He'd set up Interact to pay the bills and because the rent on the mill was subsidized for the first year, but made it clear that if the right offer came his way he'd wind up the company like a shot. There were always deals in the offing. A friend who worked for Granada was planning a soap which had a part just right for him. He'd bumped into a script editor who thought he was perfect for the lead

108

in a ninety-minute drama. None of these possibilities ever came to anything.

Martha had never seen Jeremy act, but she had watched him lead rehearsals. She thought he probably was a bit better than the average jobbing actor. He held her attention, and anyone who could bring those dreadful lines to life must have some skill. But theatre was all about luck and if it hadn't happened for Jeremy by now, she thought it was hardly likely to. If he'd been to an audition, even in London, he should have been home days ago. If he'd set his heart on a part, failed to get it and been drowning his sorrows, he should be back by now. If by some remote chance he'd been given the part, he'd want to tell them all. So where was he?

There were footsteps on the bare wooden stairs. She looked out through the open office door, hoping to see Jeremy leaping up, two steps at a time. For someone who drank so much he was remarkably fit. But it was Ellie, another of the actors. Martha looked at her watch. Ten more minutes and she'd have to start the rehearsal without him.

By late afternoon she knew she wouldn't get any more out of the team. She'd always wanted to direct. A natural bossiness, her friends said. But even in university, working on small student productions, direction had been more rewarding than this. Only one of the actors had done more than glance at the script. There was little scope for characterization. At least by now she'd blocked in the moves and helped them put some meaning into the words. There wasn't much else she could do until they'd learned the lines.

She sent them home with threats and bribes. In the office she checked her mobile again. Still no message.

She wasn't sure what she could do, who she should tell about Jeremy's disappearance. He lived alone. She had an idea that he might have been married once, but he didn't talk about children. He lived in Denby Dale in a little terraced house close to the mill. Everyone in the village knew him, but she didn't think he had any close friends. The regulars in the Fleece chatted to him most evenings, but she doubted they had any more idea about his private life or background than she did.

It didn't occur to her to go to the police. Jeremy wouldn't want anyone prying into the business. She thought he probably sailed very close to the wind when it came to VAT and health and safety. She knew he paid some of the actors cash in hand. Besides, it was ridiculous. He'd said he'd be away for a few days. He hadn't yet been gone for a week. All the same she hated the feeling of helplessness. She wished he would phone her.

The actors had gone back to the digs in the village where they stayed when they were rehearsing. None of them was local. Jeremy employed different actors for each tour. Martha locked up the office and on the keyring saw the spare key to Jeremy's house. He'd given it to her when he'd asked her to stay there one morning to let in the plumber – the sort of work experience not set out in the apprenticeship job description. She'd offered it back to him, but he'd told her to hang on to it.

She thought it wouldn't do any harm to go in and look. It would set her mind at rest. Perhaps he'd returned from wherever he'd been and been taken ill.

The house was a traditional weaver's cottage, part of a terrace close to the viaduct, backing on to the River Dearne. The first floor had a row of windows to let in the light to make working the loom easier for the textile workers. It was very narrow. A kitchen and small living room on the ground floor, two bedrooms and a bathroom upstairs. She'd had a quick snoop round while she'd been waiting for the plumber.

She unlocked the front door, which led straight from the pavement, struggling for a moment with the unfamiliar key. The door stuck when she pushed it. There was a pile of mail inside. She picked it up and put it on the table.

'Jeremy!' Not shouting. She didn't really think he was there. Jeremy wasn't the sort to get ill – at least not without an audience. It seemed very hot and air-less, as if the cottage had been shut up for a long time. Now she felt foolish, imagined neighbours watching her. But she couldn't just leave without checking upstairs. She closed the door behind her and opened a window. A train rattled over the viaduct and she imagined she could feel the vibration of it under her feet.

In the tiny kitchen there was a sweet, unpleasant smell. The gas cooker was covered in grease and there was a layer of white fat on the bottom of the grill pan, but she didn't think the smell came from that. Even if it did, she wasn't going to clean up for him. She wanted a good report on her placement but there were some things she wouldn't do to get one. She wondered what would happen to her if Jeremy never came back. Would they pass her work experience anyway?

111

On impulse she opened the fridge and the smell got a lot worse. There was half a packet of sausages which must have been well past their sell-by date before he left and were now revolting. She lifted them into a carrier bag, opened the back door into the yard and dumped them in the bin, thinking that Jeremy owed her bigtime.

In the main bedroom there were signs that he'd left very quickly. One of the drawers was open and clothes spilled out. The bed was unmade, though she thought that didn't mean much. She'd never yet met a man who made a bed when he got up. It was hard to judge how much he'd packed. She looked in the wardrobe. His favourite black linen jacket, the one he thought made him look cool, even when it was crumpled and grubby, was missing. The small suitcase he used when he went for overnight trips to check on a performance was there, propped against the wall in a corner. She didn't see a bigger bag. Did that mean he'd been planning to be away for longer all the time? That he hadn't told her because he thought she'd refuse to take charge while he was swanning off on holiday? Too right, she thought. What sort of mug do you think I am?

Perhaps she should phone the Arts Council officer who was supervising her placement. Drop Jeremy Booth right in the shit. But she knew she wouldn't do it. She'd developed an affection for the man. He made her laugh. But when he finally got home, he'd owe her. She'd stand over him in his office and dictate the report she wanted, wait until he'd signed it and post it off herself.

The small bedroom was at the back of the cottage. It had a view of the yard and the dustbin, then to the river and the bigger houses beyond, their trees and gardens. It was set up like an office with a desk and PC, a filing cabinet and bookcase. On the wall was a cork pin-board. It had notes about rehearsals, things-to-do lists, scraps of reviews cut from small regional newspapers, a few faded photos which looked as if they'd travelled with him.

One was of a youngish man. She thought it must be of Jeremy, though it was hard to tell. The man in the photograph had hair and a beard. He was wearing a jersey and jeans. She couldn't imagine Jeremy look-ing so casual. But the features were the same, the long straight nose, the fine cheekbones. He was sitting on an upturned boat on a beach. The second photograph was of an older man, wearing navy overalls. He had crinkly grey hair and he was beaming into the camera. He stood between a small boy and a pretty young woman with a serious face. Then the same woman with a man a little older, who stood with his arm around her shoulder.

On the way downstairs, Martha was shocked by the sound of the phone ringing. She found it on the living-room wall, picked it up before the answerphone cut in.

'Hello. Jeremy Booth's phone.'

There was a silence.

'Hello?'

'Is Jeremy there?' A young woman's voice.

'No, I'm sorry, he's away at the moment.'

The phone went dead.

Chapter Fourteen

When Jimmy Perez woke the next morning it was still to thick fog. His house was in Lerwick, close to the pier. It backed on to the sea and the outside walls were green to the high-tide mark. The fog made the light different. There was no reflection from the water; it was like waking in winter. His first thought was of Fran and the second was of the investigation.

He'd wanted to visit Fran the night before, but it had been late by the time he'd finished work. He'd phoned to explain, had been too eager in his apologies, he realized now, had assumed too much. Perhaps she'd had no expectations of a visit. She was from the south, sophisticated. There, they would do things differently. He looked at the clock by the bed. Seven: she would be awake now. Her daughter was an early riser. Fran had laughed about that, said she had fond memories of life before motherhood, long lie-ins with the Sunday papers, coffee and croissants which left crumbs in the bed. The memories of his youth had been very different. His parents had always found work for him on the Fair Isle croft. He thought it would be good to lie in with Fran on the Sunday mornings when Cassie was with her father. He would like to take her breakfast in bed.

He put the kettle on for coffee and went into the shower. Back in the kitchen, which was as narrow as a ship's galley, he switched on the radio. A blast of music from SIBC, then a five-minute news slot and the first report of the stranger's death.

'A tourist was found dead in suspicious circumstances yesterday in Biddista. The police are anxious to identify him.' Then a brief description and a request that anyone who might recognize the dead man should phone the incident room.

It struck him that the tone would be very different if the dead man were a Shetlander. The fact that he was described immediately as a tourist took any sense of panic from the news. It was as if the reporter was describing an incident that had occurred elsewhere. A visitor's death was almost a source of entertainment.

While he made coffee and stuck two slices of bread into the toaster he listened for the weather forecast. The fog should clear around midday. Perhaps Taylor and his team from Inverness would get in after all today on the plane. Taylor would be pleased. Thirteen hours on the ferry would be purgatory to him. He would be like a tiger caged for transport. Perez imagined him, lying straight and stiff on the bunk in the dark cabin, trying to relax and to sleep. When they'd worked together previously he'd thought Taylor the most restless man he'd ever met.

As he left home, he saw that the cruise ship was still moored at the dock. Usually the huge liners spent very little time in Lerwick. The passengers disembarked, caught the complimentary bus to the town centre, had a trip round the tourist and information centre, the *Shetland Times* bookshop and the gift shops, then went back to the luxury of the ship. Sometimes he would bump into a group of them in Commercial Street. Most were from the United States. They stared around them at the tiny shops, the passing people. He felt like an animal in a zoo.

In his office he phoned the harbourmaster. When was the *Island Belle* due to sail? Could Patrick arrange a visit for him before she left?

'You'll have to be quick. She's scheduled to leave on the midday tide.'

'I'll go now,' Perez said. 'As soon as you can fix it.'

He drove down to Morrison's Dock, parked facing the water and was distracted for a moment by a seal lifting its soft face out of the water. When he was a boy he'd used the Fair Isle seals for target practice with his father's shotgun until his mother had found out.

'What harm did they ever do to you?'

'William says they take fish and that's why the catch is so poor now.' William was an older lad, at that time the fount of all wisdom and knowledge.

'Nonsense. The catch is so poor because we've been over-fishing the North Sea for years.' His mother, who had been a member of Greenpeace when she was a student, still had theories about the environment that his father found dangerous and extreme.

To be honest, Jimmy had been glad of an excuse not to shoot the seals any more. He'd hated the slick of blood which floated on the water when he'd hit the target. Sometimes he'd tried to miss, but William's ridicule had been hard to face too.

Patrick must have warned the cruise ship that he was coming because it seemed they were expecting him. He was shown at once into the purser's office.

After *The Good Shepherd*, the mail boat which ran from Grutness to Fair Isle, the NorthLink ferries had seemed enormous. But this was monstrous, a towering white skyscraper of a ship, taller than any of the buildings in Lerwick. The purser was a lowland Scot. It seemed Shetland wasn't his favourite stop on the tour.

'You'll have heard that a tourist was killed yesterday in Biddista?' Perez asked him.

'No.' Implying, *Why would I care?*

'Have any of your passengers explored the island that far west?'

'Look, inspector, we don't usually spend this long in Lerwick. It's a bit of a dead loss. They come expecting something scenic and it's not exactly pretty, is it? Grey little houses. We do the seabird tour and the silverworks then everyone heaves a sigh of relief and we're off to Orkney. St Magnus' Cathedral – now that is a building worth taking a photo of. And the Highland Park distillery.' The thought of malt whisky seemed to cheer him immediately.

Perez had an urge to defend Shetland, to say it had a beauty of its own, that there were visitors who loved the low horizons and big skies, the huge bare hills, but he could tell that the purser would never be a convert. 'Why are you here so long this trip?'

'A problem with one of the engines. It's fixed now, thank the Lord, and we can be on our way.'

'You're not missing any of your passengers then?'

'No one's reported one missing. Have you any evidence to suggest your dead man is one of ours?'

'There was nothing to identify him at all.'

The purser seemed relieved. He stood up.

'They could leave the ship if they wanted to?' Perez said. 'I mean you don't lock them in?'

'Of course not. But most of our passengers are elderly. They prefer to stick to the organized trips.' He sat down again. 'Look, if they wanted adventure they wouldn't choose a cruise with a bunch of geriatrics.'

'Where did you take your passengers the day before yesterday?'

'They had a free morning to look round the town and in the afternoon we took them on a bus trip, down to the RSPB reserve at Sumburgh Head for puffins. Tea in Scalloway.'

'I'm surprised the exhibition at the Herring House wasn't on the schedule. Bella Sinclair's a big name. I'd have thought some of your customers would have enjoyed meeting the artist.'

'A couple of them mentioned it. When we had to stay the extra night I considered fixing up transport for them to go, but in the end it was cancelled, wasn't it?' He gave the impression he was pleased he'd avoided the bother.

'Who told you it was cancelled?'

'Nobody told me. Not the people organizing the exhibition, at least. But there was a guy handing out flyers at the gangplank when they went down for the trip into town.'

'Did you see him?' Perez demanded.

'No, I wasn't on duty just then.'

'Could I get to talk to someone who did?'

The purser looked at his watch and sighed.

Perez sat where he was and said nothing.

The purser stood up and gestured for Perez to follow him. An elderly couple leaned against the rail on the upper deck looking out at the town. The mist was already starting to clear, so at least there was something to look at. They were thin and brown and they were holding hands.

'Honeymooners,' the purser said as they approached. 'You'd think at their age they'd have more sense.' His tone changed when they were within earshot. 'Come and meet Dr and Mrs Halliday, inspector. I think they might be able to help you.' For the first time since Perez had entered his office he smiled.

Perez found the sudden transformation in his attitude and body language disturbing. But this was the man doing his job. It was all about playing a role.

The Hallidays were from Phoenix, Arizona. They were collectors of contemporary art. They even owned a small Bella Sinclair. 'We were so disappointed that the exhibition opening was cancelled, inspector. George here had fixed up a taxi to take us and bring us back.'

'Can you describe the man who gave you the flyer?'

The couple looked at each other. 'It would be helpful,' Perez said. He wondered why they hesitated.

'I guess it's hard to say,' the man said, 'because of the fancy dress. That was all I noticed.'

'Fancy dress?'

'Well, yes. He was dressed like a clown. Not the sort with a red nose and bright clothes. This one was all in black and white. Classy, you know. Like something from the *commedia dell'arte.*'

'Was he wearing a mask?'

'That's right. A mask. I remember because our kids always used to find them kind of scary.'

*

By the time Perez reached the police station, the sun was shining. Taylor had been on the telephone to say that they were already at the airport at Dyce and scheduled on the first available flight out. 'You'll meet me and take me straight to the scene.' No question.

In his office Perez looked at his watch. He only had half an hour before he'd have to set off for Sumburgh. He wandered into the incident room. Sandy was on the phone and didn't notice him. It was clear that this was a personal conversation with one of Sandy's Whalsay friends. There were arrangements to meet for drinks, gossip about some woman. Perez reached over and cut the connection. Sandy began to splutter indignantly, then stopped.

'Not enough work, Sandy? That's fine then, because there's something I'd like you to do for me. A guy dressed as a clown was handing out flyers at Morrison's Dock the day before yesterday to all the passengers coming off the cruise ship. Someone else must have seen him. Go and talk to anyone who was working there. Did anyone chat to him? Find out who he was and where he was staying.'

'You think he's our victim?'

'Two strange men dressed as clowns in Shetland on the same day? A bit of a coincidence, wouldn't you think?'

Sandy looked sheepish and grinned. 'Someone phoned for you,' he said. 'Kenny Thomson.'

'What did he want?'

'I don't know. He wouldn't speak to me. Nothing that won't wait. He said it wasn't urgent.'

So Perez left without phoning Kenny back, allowing more time than he needed for the drive south, thinking he could make the call from his mobile while he was hanging round at the airport. He had to drive right past Fran's house on the way to Sumburgh. He saw her silhouette in the window of the bedroom she used as a studio. She was working. He imagined her standing in front of her easel, frowning, oblivious of everything going on around her. She said her work was all about concentration. Sometimes she spent all day on a piece, not even stopping to eat. He admired her passion, but he didn't quite understand it. He couldn't concentrate for more than twenty minutes at a time without wanting coffee, contact, the feedback of other people.

He speeded up and carried on down the road. Sumburgh was crowded with people who'd been trapped in Shetland by the fog. There was competition for places on the first plane south and some of the passengers were irritable. There was an English family: a man and a woman, a toddler in a buggy, a baby in a sling. 'What sort of place is this?' the woman said. Her voice was too loud, she needed other people to hear her. 'A bit of mist and everything grinds to a stop. If this is your idea of an adventurous holiday, Charles, you can keep it. Next year we're going back to Tuscany.'

As she set down a piece of charcoal, Fran caught a glimpse of Perez's car driving past. She paused for a moment, half expecting him to stop, but he drove on. She watched with relief as he continued down the hill. The thought of him had been at the back of her mind all morning, but she didn't want to dwell on it now.

She had so little time to work. The school day was short and there were only a few more hours before she would need to collect Cassie from class. She turned back to the sketch, an idea for a larger piece, her head full of colour and shape. Perez was forgotten.

Chapter Fifteen

Edith had taken a day off work. Kenny was delighted. He liked nothing better than having her at home all day. This was how things had been arranged when his parents had been living here – his mother had never gone out to work. And it had been like this when his own children were young. Even when he was working outside it made him happy to know that she was in the house.

Because Edith wasn't in a rush to get off to work, they had breakfast a little later than normal. Edith made the coffee she liked, spooning the grounds into the cafetiere, which she put on the Rayburn to keep warm, and pouring in the water from the kettle slowly and carefully. Kenny thought that later in the afternoon, when he'd finished the neeps and they'd walked on the hill together to look at the sheep, they would make love.

Looking at her standing with her back to him, reaching into the cupboard to fetch down her mug, he thought he would like to take her back to bed with him now. Her hair was still pinned up from her shower, so her neck was bare. She wore jeans which fitted well around her backside. He liked her in jeans so much better than in the smart work clothes. Even in middle age her body was firm.

He went up to her and stroked her neck with fingers which he knew were rough. She turned round and smiled at him, knowing just what he was thinking.

'Not now,' she said. 'You'll have to wait.'

And of course he would have to wait, because in these things women always got their way. They held all the cards. You couldn't force them. He supposed that was how it should be but sometimes he thought it a little unfair.

At the table he watched her eat toast. Wholemeal now, always. She bought the bread from a bakery in Scalloway. She put lots of butter on and it had melted. Some had dripped on to her fingers and she licked them. At first she had been quite unselfconscious, then she saw him watching her. She smiled again and licked the fingers on her other hand very slowly. A game. Now he was quite content to wait until later before he took her to bed. She would play the game for him all day and the anticipation would be better than getting what he wanted straight away. The thought of that made him feel a little faint and he didn't catch immediately what she was saying.

'It seems wrong keeping that dead man in the hut for a whole day.'

'The fog kept the police from Inverness from getting in.' The evening before, he'd gone to the bar in Middleton and everyone was talking about it. He'd only stayed for one pint. The pleasure the people took in having a dead body close by seemed unnatural to him. If it was someone they knew they'd have behaved differently, but some people were even telling jokes.

'I thought it was suicide. It seems a lot of fuss about a suicide.'

Kenny didn't know what to say. He thought of the body swinging from the rafter. When he'd told Edith about the dead man she'd been so kind to him and had understood immediately what a shock it had been.

'Oh my dear, you shouldn't have had to see that.'

People died occasionally at the care centre. She said she'd never got used to it, but it seemed to him she took everything in her stride.

'Aggie Watt came here yesterday,' he said now. 'She asked if the body could be Lawrence.'

'It couldn't be,' Edith said. Then, 'Or could it? Surely you'd have recognized your own brother.'

'I'm pretty sure it's not Lawrence, but I'd like to see the man again without the mask. I've been thinking about it.' He'd lain awake a long time in the night, worrying about how Lawrence might have changed over the years, whether he might have made a terrible mistake. He'd thought Edith was awake, but he hadn't told her about his fears, hadn't felt able to tell her before about Aggie's visit. He'd needed to sort out in his own mind what he thought before discussing it with her. 'I wondered if I should ask that Fair Isle man, Jimmy Perez. Would they let me look at him again?'

She thought about it for a moment. 'Yes,' she said. 'I think you should ask him. I don't think for a moment it is Lawrence, but it might set your mind at rest.'

Kenny thought he would phone Perez. He wouldn't wait until the policeman was back at the jetty. He

125

didn't want to see the dead man again there. Lying out in a mortuary somewhere, the mask taken from his face, that would be different. More dignified.

All morning while he was working in the field he caught glimpses of Edith. She'd done a pile of washing and once the fog lifted she came to hang it out on the line behind the house. He stopped for a moment and watched her, so deft, lifting the sheets from the basket, folding and stretching them and pinning them on the line. He waited for her to turn and wave to him, but she didn't seem to notice he was there. When he went down for his coffee, she had just finished washing the kitchen floor. She was on her hands and knees on a folded towel, wiping the last corner with a cloth. He stood in the porch in his stockinged feet. Again she must have heard him come in, but she didn't acknowledge his presence until she'd finished. Then she turned and smiled at him.

'Just wait for a minute until it dries.' She was still kneeling at his feet and had to tilt her head to look up at him.

'Why don't we walk down to the Herring House?' he said. 'Get one of Martin's posh coffees there. He'll surely be open now.'

'I can't go looking like this.' But he could tell she was pleased by the suggestion.

'Why not? You look lovely. You always look lovely.'

They walked down the track together, hand in hand. Kenny felt as if he was on holiday too. He took a quick look towards the jetty. There was a police car there and tape stretched right across the entrance, but nothing much seemed to be happening. He guessed that the police from Inverness hadn't arrived yet.

126

The café at the Herring House let in all the light whatever time of day it was. Extra windows had been built into the wall facing the water.

There were more people there than you'd usually get on a weekday morning, and Kenny recognized some of them. A couple of elderly ladies from Middleton who'd taken a trip out in case there was anything to see. They turned out for any reported accident or disaster. A journalist from the *Shetland Times*. It occurred to Kenny that the plane bringing in the Inverness police would also be carrying reporters from the national press. Now he was here he felt awkward. He supposed he and Edith were just like the others; they'd come to the Herring House in hope of news.

Martin Williamson came out from the kitchen to take their order. He had a light, almost dancing, way of walking that made Kenny think of a racehorse just before it went into the stalls. Kenny nodded at the other customers. 'At least it's good for business, then, having a dead body next door.'

Martin grinned. 'Aye. I'll not be sorry when they take it away though. It seems kind of weird, leaving it there all night. Mother's in a right state about it. I don't think she slept.'

'I know she's upset. She came to see me yesterday.'

'You can't blame her,' Edith said. 'When you think what happened to your father. It must bring it all back.'

'Have you heard when the police from Inverness will get here?' Kenny asked. He was thinking that Perez hadn't phoned him back. When the dead man was taken away he'd have a chance to see him, then he'd know for certain that it couldn't be Lawrence.

The more he struggled to conjure his brother's features in his head, the more they became blurred and slid away from him.

'First plane out of Aberdeen,' Martin said. 'They'll be in any time.'

Kenny asked for a cappuccino for Edith and a latte for himself. They always had the same when they came here. Because it seemed like a holiday he added a couple of pieces of cake to the order and Martin danced away.

They'd almost finished when Roddy Sinclair made an entrance. He stood at the door and heads turned. Everyone recognized him and there was a brief moment of silence before the conversation continued. He looked as if he'd just got out of his bed. His hair was tousled and he still seemed half asleep. Or maybe, Kenny thought, he'd been up all night. He didn't find a table and wait for Martin to take his order, but walked towards the kitchen, leaned on the doorframe and shouted in.

'Double espresso. Strong as you like.' There were other people at the tables waiting to order, but nobody seemed to mind him jumping the queue. Typical Sinclair, Kenny thought. They're arrogant, the lot of them. Across the tables, one of the Middleton old ladies smiled at the boy and gave him a little wave. Kenny thought that was typical too. Women would let the Sinclair boy get away with anything.

Roddy tilted his body away from the doorframe so he was standing upright.

'Fantastic view from here,' he said. 'It always surprises me.' He sauntered towards them. 'Do you mind if I join you?'

'We'll be going soon,' Kenny said, but the boy seemed not to hear and sat down anyway. Outside now there was strong sunshine. A sailing boat was on the water halfway to the horizon. Kenny tried to work out who might own it and decided it didn't belong to anyone local.

Roddy leaned forward across the table. 'I understand you were the one to find the body.' His accent was just as strong as when he'd been a boy. Kenny wondered if he practised at night in his Glasgow flat, in the hotel rooms in exotic cities. It was his trademark. He nodded.

Martin carried across the coffee. Roddy nodded his thanks, but continued to look at Kenny, and waited till Martin had moved away before continuing the conversation.

'You're sure he was a stranger?' he asked. 'You'd never seen him before?'

Kenny allowed himself to be distracted a moment by the smell of the espresso. If it tasted as good as it smelled he could be converted too. He didn't want to make a scene here in front of Edith, but he wanted to tell Roddy Sinclair to mind his own business. What right did he have to interrupt them here? Spoil the time he had with his wife?

'I didn't recognize the man,' Kenny said.

'He was here at Bella's launch,' Roddy said. 'But I didn't take much notice of him then.'

'You saw him alive?'

Kenny almost asked Roddy if the man could have been Lawrence, but what would Roddy know? Lawrence had left when Roddy was still a small boy. He was living in Lerwick with his parents and only came to Biddista to visit Bella. He had been an annoying boy even then, spoiled, running wild about the place.

'Yes. I wish I'd talked to him. If we knew who he was and where he'd come from, we could just get back to normal.'

What would you know about normal? Kenny thought. It seemed a strange thing for the boy to say. Normal was the last thing Roddy had ever wanted. He wanted drama, a different woman every night. Surely he'd be enjoying this small excitement.

Roddy turned to Edith. 'What do you make of all this?'

'Nothing,' she said. 'It sounds very callous, but I can't get excited by the death of a man I didn't know.'

Roddy was about to answer, but he was interrupted by the sound of a car driving down the road outside. Two cars. Everyone's attention was turned to the window. The old ladies from Middleton stood up so they could get a better view. Quite shameless. Despite himself, Kenny swivelled round in his chair so he could see too.

Jimmy Perez got out of one of the cars. With him was a tall, heavily built man with a bald dome of a head. You could tell even from this distance that he was the boss. There were two other men and a woman, and a couple of police officers Kenny recognized: Sandy from Whalsay and young Morag. Suddenly he didn't want to be here any more, staring down at the spectacle like children at the circus. He stood up and waited for Edith to follow him home.

Chapter Sixteen

Roy Taylor wasn't sure what he felt about being back in Shetland. Certainly he was pleased to have finally arrived; all that waiting in Aberdeen had made him feel he was about to explode. And at least they'd got in on the plane. He hadn't liked to tell the rest of the team – he didn't believe leaders should admit to weakness, all that sharing, caring stuff wasn't for him – but he felt queasy on the Mersey ferry. An overnight crossing on the boat and he knew he'd have thrown up.

Now, standing at the front of the queue waiting to get off the plane, that memory of the Mersey ferry suddenly made him homesick. A series of images played in sentimental succession in his head. The view of the Liverpool skyline from the river, Scouse voices in busy pubs, singing his heart and soul out in the Kop on a Saturday afternoon. It made him wonder if it wasn't finally time to go back. His father was dead and couldn't hurt him now. He dwelled briefly on the possibility of returning, then pushed it from his mind. He had other things to think about.

He'd headed for Inverness because it was the farthest place from home he could find. There'd been a masochistic pleasure in landing in a town so alien, so unlike anywhere he would otherwise have chosen to live. As if he'd wanted to punish himself as well as the family he'd left behind. And now he was back in Shetland, which was even more remote and more strange.

The plane door opened. He took the steps at a trot and strode across the tarmac to the little door in the terminal building. He'd given instructions that his team should only bring carry-on luggage. They'd wasted enough time and he didn't want them hanging around again for the stuff from the hold to appear.

Jimmy Perez was waiting for them. They'd worked well together on a previous investigation and had got on, perhaps because they had such different styles. If Perez had been a full-time member of his team, Taylor would have found the unconventional attitude, the long hair and the lack of urgency irritating. Here in Shetland, the quiet approach seemed to work. Perhaps too well. Taylor had always been competitive, and mixed with the affection was a residual resentment because Perez had been credited with solving the Catherine Ross case.

All the same he greeted Perez with warmth, taking his hand and clapping him on the back.

'How're things, Jimmy?'

The rest of the group should know that there would be no territorial rivalry on the case. Besides, it couldn't be easy for Perez to have a senior officer fly in to take over the most interesting cases. Taylor himself wouldn't be able to bear it.

They drove north and west, missing Lerwick, the only place in the islands where Taylor had felt anything like at home. At least in Lerwick there were shops and bars, chip shops and curry houses. If he thought of the space all around him, he felt giddy and nauseous. It was the sleepless night in the Holiday Inn in Aberdeen, he thought. Once he got stuck into the investigation he'd feel on top of his game once more.

To pull himself back he began to fire questions at Perez, who was driving.

'Are you telling me that in a place as small as this no one can put a name to him?' He knew Perez would resent the tone, but couldn't help himself.

Perez paused for a moment before answering. 'We get fifty thousand visitors a year. Many of them have little contact with local people. It's not that surprising it's taking a while to trace him.'

'All the same, someone must have missed him by now. A guesthouse. Hotel.'

Perez didn't answer. He had this knack of keeping quiet if he had nothing to say. Taylor had never been able to master it.

The cars slowed down and they pulled up next to a small jetty. It looked to Taylor that they were in the middle of nowhere. You couldn't call it a village. A couple of houses built along the road and that was it. On the way they'd passed the gallery, which was built almost on the beach. It seemed an odd set-up to Taylor. Who would come all this way to look at a few pictures? Perez had roused himself from his silence to explain that that was the last place the victim had been seen alive.

'I was there,' he said. 'At a party to celebrate the opening of the exhibition.' Taylor thought he had more to say but was waiting for another time, when there was nobody else listening. He reminded himself to ask him about it when they were alone.

He got out of the car to the shrieking seabirds and the smell of seaweed and bird shit. Behind the row of low houses the hill rose steeply. He thought, Why would anyone want to live here? He recognized it from a documentary there'd been about the folk musician Roddy Sinclair. Quite a long sequence had been taken in Biddista; the camera followed him round the place, showed him talking to the crofters, visiting the shop, drinking with his mates. Then it had been back to London and Glasgow, the music and the groupies.

Taylor didn't go into the hut. From what Perez had said there'd been enough contamination of the scene already. Now they could let the CSI get on with her work. He'd just wanted to get a feel of the place before they started. And he was glad he'd come. He had this sense that everyone in Biddista was staring at him. He could feel the eyes. He didn't look at the houses to check if there were people staring from the windows; he didn't have to. He wouldn't have understood what that was like just from chatting to Perez. This was a place where it was impossible to keep secrets. He couldn't believe that nobody knew who had killed the man. Perhaps they all knew. Perhaps it was all one huge conspiracy.

He turned back to Perez. 'Why don't we leave them to it? Let's get into Lerwick, just the two of us, and you can fill me in on the details.' He phrased it as a suggestion, but he knew Perez would have no choice but to agree.

In the car he was aware of the sea to the right of him, but all his concentration was on Perez. 'You say you were one of the last people to see the victim alive. What was he doing?'

There was one of those pauses. Perez pulled into a passing place to let a woman in a clapped-out van squeeze by.

'He was weeping.'

Taylor wasn't sure what he'd been expecting. Not that.

'What do you mean, weeping? What had upset him?'

Another beat of silence. 'He didn't know. Or so he claimed.' And then Perez told his story. About the stranger who caused a scene at some arty-farty do by bursting into tears and then claiming not to know who he was or how he'd got there. Taylor knew better than to interrupt. He was full of questions, but he had to let Perez tell it in his own way.

'You see why I believed it could be suicide,' Perez said. 'Yet I was never quite convinced.'

'Were you convinced that the guy had really lost his memory?'

Perez considered. Taylor waited. He wanted to shout, *It's a simple question, man. How long does it take to come up with an answer?* He could feel the tension of waiting constricting his breathing.

'No,' Perez said at last. 'I never really was.' And that was good enough for Taylor. Perez might irritate the shit out of him, but he was the best judge of character Taylor knew. He watched men like David Attenborough watched animals.

'Why pretend?'

This time the answer came more quickly. 'I don't know. I've been thinking about it since I found the body. Maybe he wanted to spoil the opening of the exhibition. But why would a stranger from England

135

want to do that? What could he have against Bella Sinclair or Fran Hunter?'

Taylor recognized the name. 'Isn't that the same woman who found Catherine Ross?'

'Aye.' There was a small flutter of the eyelids. 'That's why I was there. She's become a sort of friend.'

Anyone else and Taylor would have taken the piss. *What sort of friend would that be, then? The sort you sleep with?* But he didn't want to offend Perez. No way could he work here without the man on his side.

Perez changed the subject. 'It's possible that the victim tried to stop the opening from happening at all. Someone went round Lerwick giving out flyers which said it had been cancelled. He was wearing a mask like a clown.'

'But neither of the artists recognized him?'

A silence. 'So they say.' Another pause. 'The flyer said the opening had been cancelled because of a death in the family. Almost as if he'd been predicting his own murder.'

Lerwick wasn't as grey as Taylor had remembered, but the last time he'd been here had been midwinter. Today the sun was shining and the people weren't huddled into heavy coats. The light was reflected from the water. Moored in the harbour was a boat kitted out like a theatre. It had a red tarpaulin banner slung over the side advertising the most recent production.

He nodded towards it. 'That's new.'

'No,' Perez said. 'It's been coming for as long as I can remember, but it's only here in the summer. It travels around the islands. The visitors like it.'

'God,' Taylor said. 'I'm starving.' He'd had a horrible bun on the plane and it seemed ages ago.

They bought fish and chips and ate from greasy paper looking over the water. Taylor recalled it wasn't far from here to where Perez lived.

'You still in the same place?'

Perez nodded.

'You haven't moved in with the gorgeous Ms Hunter yet then?' He knew it was none of his business but he couldn't help himself. Curiosity, a vital character trait for a cop. He knew he was a tiny bit jealous too.

Perez finished the last of his chips. 'It's not like that.'

Taylor was going to ask what it *was* like, but the business of the dead stranger was more important.

'Who do you think killed the victim? Someone local?'

'There are people in Biddista who have things to hide,' Perez said at last. 'But it doesn't have to be murder.'

Taylor nodded. He understood that. The police turn up at the door and there's always something to feel guilty about. Speeding. Defrauding the taxman. Having it off with the wife's best friend. The detective picks up the guilt. It's easy to believe that it's to do with the current case.

Perez shook out the chip paper and a couple of herring gulls came squawking at his feet. 'I need to make a call,' he said. 'Meant to do it earlier. Kenny Thomson, the guy who found the body, left a message for me.'

He walked a few feet away from Taylor and stood

to his back to him, so he couldn't hear the conversation. He wasn't sure he'd have understood it anyway. When Perez lapsed into dialect he could have been talking another bloody language. He remembered how he'd felt when his mother had left them and moved to north Wales. There'd been an access order which his father had kicked off about. The arrangement hadn't lasted long but for nearly a year Taylor had been sent to spend a weekend with her every month. Walking into a shop, everyone staring, everyone speaking a language he couldn't understand. He knew they'd been talking about him. And about his mother setting up home with the respectable chapel man. Leading him astray. *Hussey*. A word stolen from the English.

Perez had switched off the phone and was waiting for Taylor to ask about the call.

'Well?' Taylor asked.

'He wants another look at the body. Imagination going into overdrive if you ask me. He thinks it could be his brother.' Perez paused, corrected himself. He always liked to get things right. 'No, he doesn't think it could be him. Wants to check that it isn't.'

'Wouldn't he know his own brother?'

'He left to go travelling. Hasn't been back in years. And Kenny didn't get a brilliant view. Only side on, and then there was the mask covering the face. Like I said, it's just a matter of ruling him out. It's obviously been bothering him.'

'I thought you said the victim was English.'

Perez shrugged. 'People's voices change. They put on an act.'

'What did you tell him?'

'That he can come and have a look this afternoon,

before the body goes south on the ferry for the post-mortem.'

Taylor felt a thrill of excitement. This was his first chance to engage with the case. He'd never been a hands-off manager.

'I'll be there too,' he said. 'You don't mind?'

Perez didn't answer. He knew it wasn't really a question.

Chapter Seventeen

Kenny Thomson arrived at the undertakers' before they were ready to let him see the body. There were two men to greet him: Jimmy Perez, who always reminded him of that summer he'd spent on Fair Isle, and the big Englishman he'd seen get out of the car at the jetty.

They sat in a dark little waiting room. In one corner there was a bowl of silk flowers. There was a heavy, kind of floral smell in the air. It couldn't come from the silk, of course, and he wondered what was making it.

He was thinking about that when Perez introduced the English detective, so he still wasn't sure of his name and what his rank was.

'What's all this about then, Kenny?' Perez said. He had a quiet, hesitant way of talking, thoughtful, as if he was weighing every word before he spoke.

'It's probably nothing,' Kenny said. 'But I thought, Better to check. Better than lying awake at night wondering.'

'Tell us a bit about Lawrence,' Perez said. 'Just while we're waiting.'

And Kenny found himself talking about Lawrence, the older brother who was bigger and stronger than him, who left Kenny in his shadow. 'He was the sort of man who'd walk into a room and everyone would start smiling,' he said. 'When he went I missed him. Everyone in Biddista missed him.'

'Why did he go? Was it for work?'

Then Kenny saw that they didn't want to know that Lawrence lit up the room when he walked in. What they wanted was facts and dates. But he had more than that to tell them.

'He had work here,' he said. 'Plenty of work. He wasn't so interested in the croft. He didn't really have the patience for it. He was more one for quick results. He was a fine builder. He started off working for Jerry Stout and learned the trade from him, then when Jerry died he took over the business. He and Jerry put a new roof on the Manse when Bella moved in. Then Lawrence converted the Herring House. Eve Eunson drew up the plans, but he did all the work on it. More of a labour of love. That's what he called it. He was down there more than twelve hours a day, getting it ready for the opening. I did some labouring for him when I could. Bella didn't pay him what he was due. Once the gallery was finished he had offers of work from all over Scotland. He didn't need to live away. He could have stayed in Shetland and just travelled for the work.'

'Why did he go?'

Kenny wasn't sure how much to say. 'I don't know. I wasn't there when it happened. He was besotted with Bella. Whatever she asked he did. He always had plans to marry her. That's what I think. It was always a dream at the back of his head. No one else would live up to her. He saw other women from time to time, but you could tell he wasn't serious about them. Bella kept him hanging on a string all the time the Herring House was being built, then once it was finished, I think she made it clear he had no chance with her. She was too selfish to settle down. She'd got what she wanted from him.' Kenny knew he sounded bitter but he didn't care. Whenever he thought about it, he was angry.

'When was this, Kenny?'

'It was that summer I was in Fair Isle working on the harbour. They'd asked Lawrence to do it, but he was tied up with the last finish on the Herring House and he put the work my way. He knew I was looking to expand the croft and the money would be useful. I never had the chance to say goodbye to him.'

'He didn't ask your advice about leaving?'

Kenny smiled to himself. When had Lawrence ever asked anyone's advice? 'That wasn't his style,' he said. 'He was kind of impulsive. It wasn't the first time he'd gone off without telling anyone. When he was nineteen he disappeared; he just left a note for my parents. That time it was backpacking round Australia.'

'What did he intend to do this time?'

'I think maybe the Merchant Navy. He was always talking about that. The way to travel and get paid for it. He was always easy in a boat. You know the kids in Biddista, they're out in a dinghy almost as soon as they can walk. It was natural for him.' Kenny stopped speaking for a moment. He was thinking of one of those still summer evenings. Him and Lawrence out after mackerel. The boat at anchor, moving with the swell. Lawrence on his feet, balanced, and laughing at some joke Kenny had made.

Perez looked at him, waiting for him to continue.

'Besides,' Kenny went on. 'It was a great romantic gesture, wasn't it, running away to sea? Lawrence would be one for the big romantic gesture.'

'When did you last hear from him?'

'I never have. He left a message with Bella to say he was leaving and he was never in touch with us again.' He turned to Perez. 'He could have phoned me at the hostel, couldn't he? To say goodbye. We didn't have mobiles then, but he could have tracked me down somewhere. Maybe he was frightened I'd persuade him to stay.'

'Will you recognize him, do you think?' Perez asked.

'I've been thinking about that. I got out some photos.' There'd been one of him, Lawrence, Edith and Bella standing on the jetty grinning into the camera. He couldn't remember who'd taken it. Aggie maybe. Though surely she'd have been married by then. She wouldn't still be living at home. But she'd come back to Biddista whenever she could. She'd never been able to stay away.

'All the same, it's been a long time. And people look different when they're dead.'

'He had a birthmark on his right shoulder,' Kenny said. 'However he's changed, I'll know him by that.'

'We could check that for you. If you don't want to look at the body again.'

But Kenny shook his head. If this did happen to be Lawrence, he wanted to identify him for himself. This was his brother.

143

Then, it seemed, it was time to look at the body. Kenny couldn't tell why suddenly they decided the time was right. Nobody came in to tell them. He thought the delay had probably just been an excuse to get him talking.

The body was lying on a steel table. There was no one else in the room. Perez stood by the table and prepared to lift back a sheet so Kenny could see the face. The English policeman still hadn't said anything, except for a few words of greeting when Perez had introduced him, but he'd followed them in and now stood at Kenny's shoulder. Kenny wished he'd move back a bit to give him some space. Perez turned and Kenny nodded to show he was ready.

As soon as he saw the face he knew it wasn't Lawrence. There was no likeness. He wondered how he could ever have doubted his first impression. He should never have listened to Aggie Williamson. He should never have got caught up in her panic. Lawrence had a full, deep forehead and a mouth which was wide, even when he wasn't laughing. This man had delicate features, thin lips. It could have been a woman's face, if it hadn't been for the slight stubble on the chin, the hairy eyebrows. Kenny had a terrible desire to giggle. He pictured the corpse suddenly as one of those drag queens who appeared sometimes on the television, with a false bosom and a blond wig. He supposed it was the release of tension, the relief.

He realized he should say something.

'No,' he said. 'That's not Lawrence. Definitely not.'

'We'll just look for the birthmark, shall we? Just to make sure. You know how the mind plays tricks.' And Perez folded the sheet back again, very neatly, like a

144

nurse or a soldier preparing a bed for inspection. Now
the shoulders and the top of the body were exposed.
They must have taken off his clothes. The man's chest
was covered in fine grey hair. Kenny thought he'd
been a self-conscious man. He'd shaved his head when
his hair turned grey. Lawrence could be vain, right
enough, but there was no birthmark on the shoulder.
This wasn't him.

'No,' he said. 'I've not seen this man before in my
life.'

'Are you sure?' Perez was poised, holding the sheet
in both his hands. He was leaning across the body.
'This couldn't have been the man you saw running
away from the Herring House the night of the party?'

Kenny thought about that. 'Aye,' he said. 'It could
have been. If he was dressed in black. He seems the
right sort of height and build. But I couldn't swear to
it. He was a long way off.'

Then Perez replaced the sheet and they returned
to the small room with the dusty silk flowers. Kenny
had thought the meeting would be over now. It would
be all right to go. He imagined Edith waiting for him
at home. He'd wasted most of the afternoon, driving
here and then sitting in this room, waiting.

But it seemed the Englishman had other ideas.
'You don't mind if I just follow up a couple of points?'
Kenny wasn't sure if he was asking Jimmy Perez or
him.

'Will it take long?'

'Not long at all.'

'Could we go out then?' He wanted to escape that
strange, sweet smell. He needed some fresh air.

'Of course we can go out. Let's get you a drink

145

somewhere. I expect you could do with one. I could use one myself. You'd think you'd get used to dead bodies in this business, but I never have.'

So Kenny found himself in the Lerwick Hotel, tucked in a corner in the bar. A couple of men were sitting at a table in the restaurant, drinking coffee after a late lunch. Businessmen of some kind, Kenny thought. Something to do with oil or tourism. They weren't local. Otherwise the place was deserted.

Taylor came back from the bar with three whiskies and a jug of water. Kenny couldn't remember ordering a drink, but perhaps he had. He was more shaken than he'd realized. Probably it was good not to go back to Edith straight away in this state. Taylor waited until his glass was nearly empty before he put his question.

'Someone killed that man,' he said. 'They strangled him and then stuck a noose round his neck and hoisted him up on to the rafter. Do you know anyone who would have been capable of that?'

'It wouldn't have taken such a deal of strength.' Kenny thought for the first time of the practicalities. 'He was a slight man. Not a lot of weight to him. The rope to make the noose was there in the hut. Anyone could have done it.'

Taylor smiled. His head was like a skull just covered in skin. When he smiled all his teeth were suddenly visible. 'I wasn't thinking of that. Though you're right of course. But I wasn't thinking about who might be capable physically. I meant mentally. Who do you know who could do that? Follow the man, or lure him into the hut, kill him, set out the body so it looked like suicide. Who would be calm enough to do that? Who would have the nerve?'

Kenny felt sick. It had never occurred to him that the murder had been planned. There was violent crime in Shetland, but it was never premeditated. It was men fighting in bars when they were steaming drunk, falling out over some woman or some imagined insult.

'I don't know,' he said.

'Really?' Taylor leaned forward, so Kenny could smell the whisky on his breath. 'The way I understand it, you grew up with most of the people who live in that community. You know them better than anyone. Who could commit murder then lie about it the next day?'

'I don't know,' Kenny said again. 'If you live that close to people you don't pry. You don't try to get under their skin. You have to live alongside each other and everyone needs some space. Do you understand what I'm saying?'

'Yeah,' Taylor said. 'I think I do.'

That was when he said he didn't have any other questions. He thanked Kenny for his help and said he could go.

It wasn't until Kenny was driving down the hill towards Biddista and he saw the light on the water that he realized what he intended to do. This evening, after he'd shared a meal with Edith, he was going to take his boat out and try to get some fish. It was a perfect evening for it. Then he was going to track down Lawrence.

He'd accepted his brother's going too easily. He'd got into the habit of doing just what Lawrence told him. He'd left a message with Bella for Kenny.

'Tell him I'm going away again.'

But things were different now. Bella was almost an old woman. Why shouldn't he come home? And these days it was easier to find people. There was the internet. Edith knew all about the internet and she would help him. Driving up to the house, he felt excited at the prospect of seeing Lawrence again. He imagined meeting him from the boat. Lawrence would walk down the stairs in the terminal. He'd see Kenny there to meet him and he'd throw back his head and laugh.

Chapter Eighteen

Cassie was already in bed when Perez turned up at Fran's house. He'd phoned earlier to ask if he could call. 'It might be late. If you'd rather not be disturbed . . .' She'd been surprised by the effect his voice had on her. A sensation that the floor had disappeared beneath her feet.

'No,' she'd said quickly. 'It doesn't matter how late you are. I never get to bed before eleven and this time of year it's impossible to sleep anyway.'

She was sitting on a white wooden bench by the side of her front door looking out over Raven Head when he arrived. She'd had one glass of wine and was thinking she might help herself to another when she heard the car on the road. He pulled in to the verge and walked up the short path, then sat beside her. He looked very tired.

'I'll fetch you a drink,' she said. 'Beer? Wine? Whisky?'

'Could I have some coffee?' She thought then that he wouldn't be staying. She supposed it would be less complicated. There was Cassie to think about. The night of the exhibition, Cassie had been staying with her father. She didn't want Cassie to wake up and find Jimmy in her mother's bed. Not yet, not until she'd

149

had a chance to explain to Cassie what was going on. But all the same Fran was disappointed.

She left him sitting outside and put on the kettle. When she carried out the mug he was still sitting in the same position, his hands on his knees, his head slightly bent. It was as if he was too exhausted to move.

'It must be that sleepless night catching up on me,' he said. 'Strange. I didn't feel so bad yesterday.'

'Sorry.' She was still standing and stooped to put the mug on the bench beside him.

'Oh no,' he said. 'Don't be sorry. I wouldn't have missed it. Not for the world.' Then he lifted his head so she saw the shadows under his eyes, and a couple of grey strands that she'd never noticed before in the hair which always seemed to need cutting.

'Nor me.' She tried to form the words to tell him what the night had meant to her, but he cut in on her thoughts.

'I have to ask some questions. Work. I'm so sorry it has to intrude.'

'It always will, won't it?' she said.

'Perhaps. Sarah could never cope with it.' Sarah was his ex-wife, married now to a doctor, living happily in the borders with children and dogs.

'I don't *think* it'll be a problem,' she said. 'I could never understand someone who wasn't passionate about their work.'

'Am I passionate?'

'Oh yes,' she said. 'I can testify to that.'

He laughed, and she felt some of the tension go from the situation.

'Ask away,' she said. 'But I'll get some more wine

first!' She was glad she still felt easy with him; really nothing between them had changed. When she returned she sat beside him again.

'It's about the exhibition,' he said. 'Why would anyone want to spoil it for you?'

'I don't know,' she said. 'Unless it was some warped idea of a joke. And then I don't think I would be the target.'

'You're thinking of Roddy Sinclair?'

'Perhaps. He's the only person I can think of who might go to those lengths. He has a theatrical sense of humour.'

'According to the tabloids,' Perez said.

'You're right, of course.' She looked at him across her glass. 'We can't assume that anything they say is true. I've met him a couple of times through Bella, but I don't really feel I know him at all.'

'We think the murder victim distributed the flyers cancelling the show. In Lerwick at least. He was seen handing them out to passengers coming off a cruise ship.'

'But he was a stranger. Why would he want to spoil things for us?'

'He was a stranger to you. Are you sure Bella didn't know him?'

'If she did, she didn't let on.'

'Has she made any enemies? People in the business maybe?'

'Come off it, Jimmy. That sounds a bit melodramatic. Are you saying some artist she might have offended went to all that bother just to spite her?'

'Is she in the habit of offending people?'

Fran chose her words carefully. 'She's never been particularly diplomatic about expressing her opinions.'

'Meaning?'

'If she hates a piece of work she'll say so. To whoever will listen. Big style.'

'Has she upset anyone in particular?'

'Not recently as far as I know. Not a professional at least.'

'Who then?'

When she didn't answer immediately, he took her hand. 'Look, you know I'll find out. It's impossible to keep that sort of thing secret here.'

She almost said that her ex-husband Duncan had kept his affair secret, but that wasn't true. She hadn't known about it, but the rest of the islanders had. Of course that had made the whole separation much more humiliating.

'Look,' he said. 'This is murder. Loyalty to a friend doesn't come into it.'

'I've never thought of Bella as a friend. That seems a dreadful impertinence. Like saying Albert Einstein was a best mate! She's a superstar.'

'She'd love to hear you saying that.'

Fran thought he understood Bella better than she did. She'd known all along she'd tell him and she began the story. 'You know I teach an adult-education art class. I've been running it since Christmas and some of the group are really very good. And they all enjoy it. We decided to have a midsummer show. Just a bit of fun, I thought. A chance for family and friends to see what the group had been up to. We took over the hall in Sandwick and had a meal together afterwards to celebrate. I invited Bella along to give some feedback. It was a mistake. She wasn't as tactful as she might have been.'

'What happened?'

'She took the pieces one by one and gave a critique of each. I thought she was unnecessarily harsh in her criticism. I'd expected her to give some pointers for improvement, to be encouraging. I didn't think she'd lay into my students. I felt terrible afterwards.'

'Did she have a go at anyone in particular?'

'There was one piece. A watercolour. It wasn't the sort of thing I'd do myself, but I actually rather liked it. It was a landscape. Delicate and detailed. For some reason Bella took against it. She said it was bland. "Sickly and disgusting". The artist should just give up. She had no sense of artistic vision. No courage. It was quite an outburst. Terribly embarrassing.'

'Who was the artist?'

'A teacher from Middleton. Dawn Williamson.' Fran saw Perez give a small flicker of interest. He paused for a moment. She thought he was wondering how much to say to her.

'You know Dawn's husband is Martin Williamson?' he said at last.

'The chef at the Herring House?'

'Aye, they live in Biddista. Maybe a bit of a coincidence. Bella is Martin's boss. Do you think there was something personal in her attack on the painting?'

'There couldn't have been. The paintings were unnamed. How would she know?' But again Fran thought this was a place where people did know things. Word got out in a way that was almost like magic.

'How did Dawn react to the criticism?'

'She was obviously upset. Who wouldn't have been in such humiliating circumstances? But she was very dignified. I mean she didn't shout or threaten revenge. She went very red and thanked Bella for taking the time to look at the piece.'

'So at that point Bella knew who'd painted it?'

'Yes. Dawn made a point of standing up and saying it was her work.'

'Did Bella seem surprised? Embarrassed because she'd been slagging off a neighbour, the wife of an employee?'

'No. I couldn't tell what she was thinking. You know what Bella's like. Suddenly she came over all grand-artist. She had another appointment. Her agent was coming up from London. She had to rush off. Perhaps that was to cover her awkwardness.'

'When did this happen?'

'About ten days ago.'

'Have you had a class since?'

'No, I put off this week's because of the exhibition.' Fran drank the wine slowly. Now they were sitting in shadow. She saw everything in soft focus. Like some cheesy photo for a women's magazine, she thought. No hard edges here. Perhaps it was the drink. 'I think Dawn's quite fond of me,' she said. 'I mean, she knew how much the exhibition meant to me. More than it did to Bella. All my class did. I don't think she would have ruined it for me, even if she'd wanted to get back at Bella.'

He didn't respond and she wondered if he'd fallen asleep, sitting upright just where he was. Then he said abruptly, 'Shall we go inside?'

'I'm sorry. Are you cold?'

154

'No. But we're a bit public here. A night like this everyone will be out.'

'They all know we're friends.'

'I thought,' he said, 'we were rather more than that.'

He took her glass from her hand and led her into the house.

He was very quiet and almost painfully restrained. It was quite different from the last time. Then they'd had the house to themselves and they'd both acted like irresponsible teenagers. Every now and then he would ask, 'Is this all right? Are you sure you're OK with this?' They stayed in the kitchen, and she drew the curtains, although this time of year nobody drew curtains in a living room. Anyone driving past would see Perez's car and know just what they were up to. She knew he was thinking about Cassie, but wished he wasn't quite so thoughtful. He should have been thinking about her, be so caught up in the delight of her that rational thought was impossible. Besides, the sheepskins she threw on to the floor from the sofa and the back of the rocking chair weren't as soft as they looked. The bed would have been so much more comfortable.

Yet afterwards she thought this was as good as she'd known. How strange that is, she thought. How we play tricks with our minds.

She poured herself more wine and watched him dress. She wanted to tell him what she was feeling but sensed he wouldn't be one for post-match analysis. Perhaps he was suddenly aware of her looking at him because he stopped, one leg in his trousers, stooped and gave her a grin.

She wished she had a camera, but knew that the image would stay with her for ever.

It was eleven o'clock. She pulled back the curtains. There was still enough light to see colour and she could make out the line of the horizon and the shape of Raven Head. A huge container ship on its way south. She made more coffee, though her mind was already more alert than it had been all day. She felt as if she'd just woken up.

'Do you think Dawn hired someone to spoil the exhibition for us? It seems so elaborate. Not like her at all. She's a down-to-earth Yorkshirewoman.'

'I don't know.' Now he seemed reluctant to talk about work.

'And even if she did, what has that to do with the murder? Are you saying Bella found out what was going on, strangled the man and strung him up to teach him a lesson? It's ridiculous.'

He said nothing.

'Of course it could have been me,' she teased. 'If I'd found out what he'd done. This was my first major exhibition. I had more to lose than Bella did.'

There was a pause. She didn't think he was going to reply.

'Of course I know it wasn't,' he said lightly. 'You're the one person it couldn't have been – I was with you all night.' He went up to her and put his hands on her shoulders, pulled her towards him and kissed her forehead. 'I'll always remember that evening. Not for the murder – that was work and in time it'll be an interesting case, nothing more – but because it was the first night I spent with you.'

He rinsed out his mug under the tap and set it

carefully on the draining board. She stood at the door and watched him walk to his car. Soppy git, she thought. Then, So he *is* serious about me, after all. That she found a little scary. She stared out over Raven Head, lost in thought, until he drove away.

Chapter Nineteen

Perez arrived at the school in Middleton at eight-fifteen. He reckoned Dawn should already be there by then, but the kids wouldn't have arrived. He didn't want to talk to her in Biddista with Martin in attendance, though he wasn't sure why. Perhaps because Martin would try to lighten the conversation, would shy away from any serious discussion. Perez knew the teacher by sight but he'd never spoken to her. She hadn't been a part of the family when Martin's father drowned.

The school was a low modern building, with a football pitch to one side and a playground to the other. It looked over a narrow inland loch. A bit of a breeze had blown up and the water was whipped into small waves. The children came from the houses scattered over the surrounding hill and from settlements as far as the coast. Like all the Shetland schools Middleton was well maintained and well equipped. The oil had brought problems to some communities but it had its benefits too. Shetland Islands Council had negotiated a good deal with the companies to bring the oil ashore and the income had been channelled into community projects.

There was already a line of cars parked in the yard

and the main door was unlocked. No one was in the office and he wandered through to one of the classrooms. A young bearded man was writing on the board.

'I'm looking for Mrs Williamson.' Perez hovered at the door. Even this school was much bigger than the room in Fair Isle where he'd sat to do his lessons, but the smell was familiar.

'Are you one of the dads?' The man was polite enough, but hardly friendly. Perez wondered what it was about schools that made him uneasy. Maybe all adults felt exactly the same way. Too big and clumsy for a place built for children. He supposed a stranger walking into his working environment would be intimidated too. Then he thought he would love to be a dad. It was something he'd always wanted. He wouldn't mind then the effort of coming into school, of attending parents' evenings and nativity plays.

The man had turned from the board and was waiting for him to reply.

'No,' Perez said. 'No, I'm not.' He was thinking how to explain his presence without causing Dawn problems when he heard footsteps on the corridor behind him and he saw her walking towards them, a mug of what smelled like herbal tea in one hand. She was a little older than Martin, he thought. Early thirties, curly red hair, a wide mouth.

'Mrs Williamson,' Perez said. 'Could I have a word? It'll not take long.' He couldn't tell if she recognized him. Perhaps she thought he was a parent too.

She took him into a classroom and he sat on one of the children's desks, feeling a moment of

159

wickedness because when he'd been a boy sitting on the desks wasn't allowed.

'I'm Jimmy Perez,' he said. 'I'm looking into the death of that man in the Biddista hut.'

She nodded as if to say she knew who he was. 'Is it about that mask that Alice was wearing? Aggie said you were interested in it. Maybe I should have got in touch with you before, save you dragging all the way out here, but I don't think I'll be of much help. Is it important?'

He couldn't think of any reason not to explain. 'We're treating the death as suspicious. He was wearing a mask just like the one Alice was wearing. It might help us trace him.'

He saw that he'd shocked her. She seemed suddenly very pale.

'Can you remember where Alice got the mask?'

'It was the Middleton Sunday teas,' she said. 'I bought it for her there.'

The Sunday teas had become a Shetland institution, almost a tradition, though Perez couldn't remember anything like that happening when he was a boy. Then, Sunday had just been a time for the kirk and the family. Now local ladies would provide tea and home-bakes in the nearest community hall on Sunday afternoons in the summer. There were always plants for sale and a bring-and-buy stall. It was a place to meet friends and catch up on gossip, and funds would be raised for a good cause.

'Do you remember who was selling it?'

'Some lass I didn't recognize. She must have got them cheap when she was south, because she had a whole load of them. Animals mostly, then there were the clowns. I tried to persuade Alice to go for a cat but she wasn't having any of it.'

'Was anyone else from Biddista there that afternoon?'

'No, we were on our own. Aggie usually comes with us, but she wasn't feeling well. Martin was working in the Herring House. It was quite nice to spend some time with Alice, just the two of us.'

'It can't be easy living so close to your mother-in-law.' Perez was thinking of his ex-wife Sarah's mother, a formidably competent woman who ran the Women's Institute and won prizes for the spaniels she bred. And again he was distracted by thoughts of how Fran would get on with his own mother. Sarah had found her unconventional, rather intimidating. He thought Fran might like her.

Dawn gave a little smile. 'I should be grateful. I wouldn't have been able to come back to work full-time if she hadn't offered to mind Alice. But families are never easy, are they? Aggie thinks I'm bossy and I should be a better wife to her son. She never quite says it, but I know that's what she's thinking. Martin laughs it off. He doesn't see it as a problem. I don't usually, but it was good for Alice and me to run away to Middleton together.'

'Was anyone else you recognized there?'

'Some of the families from school. As I said, nobody else from Biddista. That doesn't mean they weren't there later, though. We went in early, just as it opened, and we didn't stay long.'

Some of the children had arrived in the yard. Through the window Perez watched two boys chasing each other, grabbing hold of each other's jerseys, rolling over on the ground. Did boys always end up fighting?

'How did you land up here in Shetland?' Probably it had nothing to do with the case, but he was always intrigued by the different routes incomers took to the islands.

'I did my education degree in a college in West Yorkshire. So close to home that I could take my washing back at the weekends. I wanted to see a bit more of the country. When I saw this job advertised, I thought, Why not go for it? I only expected to be here for a couple of years. Now I know I'll never live anywhere else.'

'That'll be down to Martin.'

'Oh,' she laughed, 'I fell for the islands before I fell for him. I'd rented a place in Scalloway when I first moved here. Aggie and Andrew ran the hotel there then and Martin worked in the bar. He made me laugh. We started going out . . . Before I knew it, I was married with a child on the way.'

'You look well on it.'

'I love it all. Teaching in a place like this still has its challenges, but if I think of some of the schools where I did my teaching practice, there's no comparison. And Martin is pretty much in charge of the café and restaurant at the Herring House. Bella doesn't interfere too much.'

'How do you get on with her?' he asked.

Dawn shrugged. 'We don't usually mix in the same circles. She likes to give the impression that she's rooted in the community, but she's away a lot of the time. She and Aggie grew up with each other; now she talks to Aggie as if she was some sort of servant when she comes into the post office. Or she's so patronizing she makes me want to throw up.'

'I understand tact isn't really her thing.'

Something in his voice made her realize what he was on about. He saw she was a very bright woman. Nothing would need spelling out. The kids would get away with nothing in her lessons.

'You've heard about her putting me down at the art class then.'

He hoped she wasn't going to ask who'd told him. 'All sorts of things come up during the course of an investigation.'

'She just made herself look a bit daft,' Dawn said. She turned her back on him and continued talking as she wrote on the whiteboard. He wished he could see her face, judge her reaction to what she was saying. 'It was an amateur show. A bit of fun. Why did she take the thing so seriously?'

'Why do *you* think she did?'

'God knows. Maybe she's not as confident as she makes out and she needed to come across as the grand artist by showing us up. Pointless. We all know we're not in her league.'

'Do you think she recognized it as your painting?'

She put down the marker pen and turned back to face him. 'I'm sure she did. I was doing the sketch for it out on the hill one evening after Alice had gone to bed. Suddenly I found she'd come up behind me and was looking over my shoulder.'

'Did she comment on it then?'

'Not really. I think she made another put-down comment, like it was nice for me to have a hobby, a break from the family.' Dawn paused. 'I know it

163

sounds stupid, but sometimes I wonder if she's jealous of me. I *do* have a family. I even usually get on with my mother-in-law. Aggie's a love, despite what I said just now. Bella must be lonely most of the time, rattling around the Manse on her own.' She hesitated. 'I haven't told anyone here yet, but I found out a couple of weeks ago that I'm pregnant again. I'm thrilled to bits. We'd been trying for a while. So I couldn't really get worked up about Bella behaving like a spiteful six-year-old in front of my painting.'

'Congratulations.' Sarah had been pregnant once. Perez too had been thrilled to bits. Then she'd had a late miscarriage and it had seemed like the end of their world. It *had* marked the beginning of the end of their marriage.

'Thanks.' He saw that she couldn't help bursting out in a huge grin.

'Do you think Roddy is a substitute child for Bella?' he asked.

'Perhaps. But he's not much to be proud of, is he?'

'Lots of people would think so.'

'He's a grand musician,' she said. 'And he can hold an audience. When you listen to him play it's easy enough to be taken in by him.'

'Has he done anything specific to upset you?'

'Nothing serious. Apart from getting my husband bladdered every time he comes home. The last time was Alice's birthday, and Martin missed the party.'

Perez wanted to ask if that wasn't Martin's responsibility – Roddy Sinclair had hardly tied the man up and poured the drink down his throat – but he found himself a little in awe of Dawn Williamson. It was the pregnancy, he thought, and the fact that she was so untroubled by Bella's outburst. Besides, what did it have to do with this investigation? A bell rang. The children jostled into the school and formed a chattering queue outside the classroom door.

'I'm sorry,' she said. 'I don't think I've helped much.'

'I'm sorry to have disturbed you at work.'

She must have given a sign to the children because they began to file in, blocking the door. He had to wait for a moment until they were all at their desks. He shook hands with the teacher and began to leave.

'Give my best wishes to Fran,' she said. 'She's a brilliant teacher. I loved the exhibition.'

He wondered how much she knew about their friendship. What had Fran told her?

'Were you there at the opening?' He couldn't remember seeing her.

'I had a look before most of the people arrived.'

'Did you see the man who died?'

'How would I know?' The children were getting restless. They were expecting the register and assembly. Perhaps that was why Dawn's answer seemed a little curt. She wanted him gone so she could give her full attention to her work.

'He was the one who caused the scene by crying.'

'I must have left before then.' She reached into the drawer of her desk and brought out the long thin register, opened it, held a pen in her hand. 'I didn't see that.'

'If you were outside and on your way home you might have seen him arrive. Slight, shaved head, dressed in black.' He was standing at the door to let her know that he was about to go and his words were gabbled to show he was hurrying. It would only take a moment for her to answer this last point.

She stood poised, torn between calling the names of the children and considering his question.

'I think I did see him. He was getting out of a car.'

'Was he driving?'

'No. Someone dropped him off.'

'Anyone you recognized?'

'No. It was a young man. The car was pretty old and battered. And no, I didn't see the number and I don't know what kind it was. It was white, I think. But mucky.'

She saw he wanted to ask her more, but cut him off. 'I'm sorry. There's really nothing else I can tell you. And I have to get on with my work.'

From the corridor he watched her. She smiled at each child as she called out his or her name. Further down the hall other classes were already gathering for assembly. The bearded man was playing the piano. By the time he reached his car the children had begun to sing the first song.

Perez drove back to Biddista. The evening before, Taylor had arranged for a sketch of the murdered man's face to be released to the national press. Until they had identification, he said, they couldn't move forward. Perez had taken the comment as a statement of his own incompetence. He should have focused on tracing the victim, not spent two days drinking tea in croft kitchens. Yet now, Taylor was keen to get to know the people in the community too.

Driving west, the sun was behind him and made the driving easy. At least he had something to offer Taylor. A battered white car, which had dropped the victim off. He'd get Sandy on to finding that. If he didn't know already who it belonged to he would by the end of the day.

The land tilted slightly and Perez had a view down towards the main road from the south and Biddista beyond. He could see all the houses. The three small ones at the jetty, the Manse and Skoles. Already he knew more about these people than he did about his own neighbours. He realized then that he hadn't yet talked to Kenny's wife, Edith. She'd been at work when the body had been found and would probably be at work today. It would be something else for Taylor to pull him up about.

Chapter Twenty

Martha lived in a flat over a launderette in a leafy suburb of Huddersfield not far from the Royal Infirmary. She'd lived alone since leaving university, and enjoyed it, but now she wished there was someone at home to share her worries with. Someone to tell her not to be foolish, or to sit with her while she phoned police stations and hospitals. It was Thursday and there was still no word from Jeremy. Tomorrow would be the last day of rehearsals. Tomorrow night – or afternoon if they got their way – the cast would go home for a weekend's break and on Monday the tour would begin.

There had never been a production that had had no input from Jeremy. He always supervised the last run-through and gave notes. Even the actors had begun to comment about his absence. There was a middle-aged woman, Liz, who was a regular. She did the Interact gigs for fun and pin money. Her kids had left for university and it seemed that her husband bored her to tears. Martha thought the work made her feel young and irresponsible again. Liz was already starting to ask questions.

'Where on earth has he disappeared to, darling? We are all going to get paid, aren't we?'

Money was another problem. Jeremy had left a couple of hundred pounds cash in the office as a float, but with diesel for the van to buy and subsistence while the troupe was on the road, that wouldn't go far.

Martha took the Penistone line train from Huddersfield to Denby Dale. She owned a car, but she tried not to use it if she was going to the office: there was always a possibility that it would break down on the way home. The train went through a wooded valley. The small stations were strewn with hanging baskets full of garish flowers. Liz was already in the Mill, waiting outside the Interact door. She followed Martha into the office.

'Is there anything you're not telling us, darling? Jeremy's not done a bunk, has he? I don't think it would be the first time.'

'What do you mean?'

'As I understand it he had a perfectly respectable life until he was in his mid-twenties. Marriage, a kid. Then he left them one morning to try his hand in the theatre. Vanished without a word. He'd joined an amateur dramatic society and got bitten by the bug, apparently. I always said those am-dram groups should come with a health warning.'

'When was this?' Martha was thinking that there was no sign of the family in Jeremy's house. No photos that could relate to them. Unless he'd ended up marrying the woman on the beach. Surely he'd have kept a picture of his own child? Bloody actors, she thought. This will be one of Liz's stories. They're all liars and self-dramatists.

'Oh, yonks ago,' Liz said airily. It was obvious that her knowledge was sketchy. 'And you wouldn't know

169

now. He never sees them. Not even the child – who must be quite grown-up. Jeremy could even be a grandfather. Now there's a scary thought.'

'He never mentioned any of this to me.'

'He never mentions it to anyone unless he's maudlin drunk, and then it all comes out. Or most of it. Even then I think there's stuff he's not telling.' Liz had been leaning against the door. 'So what do you think? Has the stress been too much for him again? Has he pissed off to start a new life somewhere else?'

'Of course not. He owns that house. It's a major asset. And he wouldn't go away and leave all his stuff.'

'I wouldn't be surprised if the house isn't mortgaged to the rafters,' Liz said.

'Nonsense.' But Martha wasn't as sure as she sounded. She'd seen the books, seen what schools were prepared to pay a theatre group in order to tick a few boxes for the Ofsted inspectors, but actors and premises and the minibus didn't come cheap. 'This is a profitable business. And Jeremy likes money. I'm sure he'll be back.'

Late in the afternoon when they'd all gone, Martha sat in the office alone. She'd fended off the actors' questions all day, even giving the impression that she'd heard from Jeremy, that he was out pitching for work and he'd be back early next week with plans for a new project. She could see that Liz hadn't believed a word, but she'd not said anything and the others had been taken in.

Now the strain of putting on a brave face was too much for her. She picked up the phone – strictly work calls only, according to Jeremy's instructions, but where was fucking Jeremy now? – and talked to her best mate Kate.

'Do you fancy a drink in town? Early before it gets busy. Straight after work?'

Kate was a trainee reporter on the *Huddersfield Examiner*. She liked gossip. No one else might be interested in the disappearance of a middle-aged actor, but Kate would surely listen to her concerns. There'd be a relief just in talking it through.

'Have you seen the papers today?' Kate had ambitions beyond a local daily in West Yorkshire. She took the qualities and read them every day.

'No.' I've been too busy, Martha thought, suddenly sorry for herself. Keeping this bloody show on the road.

'There's some guy they're trying to identify. They found the body up north somewhere. "*Suspicious circumstances*". That means murder. There's a drawing of him. It looks just like your boss.'

There was a giggle in her voice. Like she was saying, *Weird coincidence, huh?*, but not believing that it really could be Jeremy. Martha couldn't speak, found she could hardly breathe.

Kate must have sensed something was wrong. 'Martha, what is it?'

'My boss, Jeremy. He seems to have disappeared.'

'My God! Don't move. I'm coming to get you now.' Martha knew this wasn't just about Kate coming to support a friend. It was Kate smelling a story a mile off and wanting to be on it before anyone else found out.

Chapter Twenty-one

It was the apparent lack of urgency around the investigation that got under Roy Taylor's skin, made him fidget and itch. There was so much to do and these local guys seemed to think there was all the time in the world. In his own patch he'd have shouted and ranted and soon got his staff moving. And he'd have felt better for letting off steam. Here he knew he had to contain his temper, and that added to the tension and the impatience.

He arrived at Biddista a quarter of an hour before he'd arranged to meet Perez, but still he felt irritated because the man wasn't there. At the jetty the scene tape had been removed and any of the locals could get in now to fetch out their gear for fishing. Waiting for Perez to arrive, Taylor thought fishing would be like torture to him. Being on the sea in a small boat. Not being able to move. Having to remain quiet. Wanting to throw up as soon as they left dry land. He knew he wouldn't be able to bear it. He'd end up diving into the water to escape, just to be moving. Then he realized that Perez's car had pulled up beside him. Five minutes early. He had a moment of disappointment; he would have liked an excuse to criticize, even inside his head. He had to be so pleasant to Perez that it hurt.

They sat for a moment on the low wall that bordered the road.

'Got anything for me?' Again, as Taylor asked the question he hoped, in a perverse way, that there was nothing. Every relationship for him was a sort of competition and he liked winning, even here when it was part of the job to be cooperative. The last Shetland case had ended with Perez as a local hero. Taylor would never let it show, but it still rankled. That wasn't how events should have played out. He should have been the one to make the difference, to reach the conclusion. The stranger coming in to clean up town, like in all those cowboy films he watched on the telly when he was a lad. He knew it was pathetic and childish, but he couldn't help it. The fact that his work had been recognized more widely within the force helped, but each case was a challenge. He needed to succeed every time.

'A couple of things,' Perez said.

'Great,' Taylor said, shaking his head up and down to prove how pleased he was. 'Great.'

'I've found a witness who thinks she might have seen the victim being dropped off here. I've got Sandy tracing the driver. And the same woman says that the plastic mask over the victim's face could have been bought at the Middleton Sunday teas last week.'

'Sunday teas?'

Perez considered. 'I suppose the English equivalent would be a village fête.'

'We didn't have many of those in Liverpool.' Taylor wasn't sure where he'd feel more alien – here, miles from anywhere, surrounded by sea, or in an English village with a vicarage, spinsters on bicycles, duck ponds. He thought he didn't really feel at home anywhere. Perhaps he should go back to Merseyside. Just for a long weekend. See how it felt. He still wasn't sure he could contemplate a permanent move.

'How do you want to play it today?' he said. He had to ask. Whatever he felt about being the boss, this was always going to be Perez's show. His patch. Besides, by now Taylor didn't really care who they saw first, he just wanted to make something happen.

Perez hesitated and Taylor made the decision for him, couldn't help himself.

'Let's go and see the artist. Bella Sinclair.' From everything he'd heard, Taylor saw her right at the centre of the case, a fat spider in her web. The victim had been at her party just before he'd died. He'd been involved in some sort of campaign to persuade people not to turn up. Taylor couldn't believe the dead man was really a stranger to her.

He looked at Perez, wanting some sort of response. Maybe his approval. That's what he expected from his own team. *Great idea, boss.* But again, he thought, you could never really tell what Perez was thinking. In the end the Shetlander looked at his watch and smiled. 'Why not?' he said. 'She should just about be out of her bed by now. Another hour or so and you might be able to speak to the boy too.'

If he'd been on his own Taylor would have taken the car, just to get there faster, but Perez started walking up the road and he followed. Perez gave a slow running commentary as they moved.

'This is the post office and shop. Run by Aggie Williamson. She was a Watt before she was married, grew up in Biddista. Her son Martin was working at the Herring House the night of the party. It was his wife Dawn who thinks she might have seen the victim climb out of a car.'

Taylor listened intently, tried to fix the details in his head. This was the stuff he had to digest if he was to have any chance of getting on top of what was going on here. He'd make notes later, but the concentration needed to memorize them made the players in this game seem more real to him. He needed to know these people better than he knew his own friends and family. They had to become a part of his life. Perez had the advantage of understanding them already.

The commentary continued. 'The end house has been rented by an English writer called Wilding. Peter Wilding. He was at the party too. I spoke to him. He claims not to have seen or heard anything, though he seems to spend most of his life staring out of the window.'

Perez paused.

'You don't believe him?' Taylor asked.

'I don't know. There was something weird about him. Maybe I just didn't take to the man. He's sort of intense.'

'What sort of stuff does he write?'

'Fantasy, he says.'

'Stories, then. Made-up stuff.' Taylor had never seen the point of stories. When he read, it was history or biography. He liked to feel he was learning. It wasn't just time wasted. As he walked past he turned his head up to the window and saw the upper body and face of a man. The man, dark and good-looking if you were into thin and moody, was sitting at the desk which faced the view, but he wasn't looking out. He

175

seemed lost in concentration. Taylor realized that he hadn't noticed them. Hardly an ideal witness, then. He wondered if the same point had occurred to Perez and turned his head surreptitiously to check. But Perez was looking the other way, out to the sea.

'That's Kenny Thomson's boat,' he said. 'You'll not be able to talk to him until later.'

Taylor was impressed by Bella Sinclair's house. He tried not to let himself be affected by shows of wealth and comfort, told himself he despised them, but deep down he was jealous. He would have loved this space, this view. Sometimes he even caught himself watching those shows about houses on the television. Not the embarrassing ones, the makeovers, all tacky décor and quick fixes, the home-made furniture you could tell would fall apart within days. He liked the programmes about grand building projects, the chateaux in France brought lovingly back to life, the mills and warehouses turned into breathtaking apartments. If ever he went back to Liverpool, he'd like one of those terraced houses near the cathedrals. One time the streets had been the scene of the Toxteth riots, but even then he'd been impressed by their elegance.

Perez rang the bell and they stood for a moment to be let in. Perez had his hands in his pockets, a bit of a slouch. Taylor consciously straightened his back. He wouldn't have been surprised to be greeted by some kind of servant, but he saw as soon as the door was opened that this must be the house's owner. She had the style to carry it off.

'Jimmy,' she said. 'What do you want now? I was

176

just about to start work.' She was wearing jeans and a loose blue smock, which was spattered with paint. She had a thick silver band around her neck and matching earrings.

Perez didn't answer directly. Taylor sensed that Perez didn't like her, but couldn't work out how he could tell the antipathy was there. Certainly Perez was perfectly polite.

'This is Roy Taylor from Inverness,' he said. 'He's in charge of the investigation.'

She looked at Taylor, held him in her gaze. She stared at him as children stare at very fat people, or at people with a deformity, with a look that was at once frank and curious.

'Come up to the studio. We can talk while I get on with the prep.'

It was one of the corner bedrooms, not a huge, clear space as Taylor had imagined, but rather cluttered. There were two windows, one looking north on to the hill and the other west over the sea. There was a tall Victorian chest of drawers which reached almost to the ceiling. One of the lower drawers was half open and revealed a pile of white paper. An easel leaned unused against one wall; on another was a stainless-steel sink which looked as if it had been installed recently. Although she made a show of preparing to work, Taylor thought her heart wasn't in it. She wanted to impress them, to let them know how valuable was her time, but really she was desperate to know what they were there for.

'Is there any news?' she asked. 'Do we know yet who that poor man was?'

The only place to sit in the room was a Shetland

chair, made of driftwood, a rough drawer built under the seat. On it was curled a black and white cat. They all remained standing and it made the conversation seem awkward, hurried, as if they'd just met on the street and were about to move on in opposite directions.

'We think he was involved in spreading the word that your exhibition had been cancelled,' Taylor said. 'Seems a weird thing for a stranger to do.'

Bella looked at him with the same curious gaze.

'I've already explained to Jimmy that I didn't know who he was.'

'So why would he do it?' Taylor was persistent. 'Sounds to me like someone with a grudge.'

'If he had a grudge, I don't think it was against me.'

'What do you mean?'

'It wasn't only my exhibition. It was a shared project. I was working with a new artist – Fran Hunter.' Taylor noticed that she didn't look at Perez during this conversation. He was meant to notice.

Bella continued. 'Fran's English. It seems the stranger was English. More likely, surely, that she knew him than I did.'

At that point Perez interrupted. 'Did Fran give any indication that she recognized the man?'

'I'm not sure she noticed him. She was too busy talking to Peter Wilding.'

There was a silence. Taylor couldn't understand what might have caused the awkwardness. What was Perez keeping from him?

'Is Roddy around?' Perez asked. 'I think DCI Taylor would like to talk to him too.'

'Roddy's leaving today,' she said. 'This was only

going to be a flying visit. He's off to Australia next week.'

'You'll miss him.' Taylor couldn't tell if Perez meant the words. It sounded almost as if he was mocking her. But Bella answered without question.

'I will. And I'm not sure when he'll be back. Each time he comes he seems less at home here. Maybe it's easier for him to be a Shetlander when he's away from the islands.'

'Where will we find him?' Perez asked.

'He *was* packing, but I think I heard him go out.' She paused. 'You might find him in the graveyard. He goes there sometimes, usually just before he leaves, to say goodbye to his father.'

Chapter Twenty-two

Roddy Sinclair was just where Bella had said he'd be. The graveyard was a bleak sort of place and Taylor thought he wouldn't want to end his days here, right next to the sea, drowned with salt spray during the gales and picked over by seabirds. Most of the head-stones were very old and misshapen, looking, Taylor thought, like a mouthful of crooked teeth. Roddy had moved away from the graves and was standing by the low drystone wall, looking out over the water. He wore a bright yellow sweatshirt with a design on the back which could have come from an album cover. Taylor recognized him immediately; the floppy fair hair and the grin. What must it be like to have people know you wherever you went?

On the beach to the north a young man was playing with a child, holding both her hands and swinging her around. It was a long way off but they could hear her laughter. Perez muttered under his breath that the man was Martin Williamson, the chef at the Herring House, and for a moment Taylor's atten-tion was distracted. Another suspect. Another life to explore. Roddy didn't seem to hear anything of the conversation. He was lost in his memories. He only turned to look at them when Taylor spoke.

'Sorry to disturb you.' Taylor thought it was best to be conciliatory. He'd first seen Roddy Sinclair on a television chat show. He'd been flicking through the channels, looking for football, and had been about to move on when something about the conversation held his attention. The boy had a confiding way of speaking which made the audience feel he was giving away secrets. A couple of months later he'd been on the TV again. The documentary. Taylor would have liked to be a celebrity. He found the idea of such attention, the small courtesies and luxuries, immensely appealing. And despite himself he was attracted by famous people, a little over-awed by them.

'This is DCI Taylor,' Perez said. 'He's in charge of the investigation into the man who was killed at the jetty. We shouldn't take up too much of your time.'

'No problem.' The young man smiled. He looked to Taylor like a boy, much younger than his actual age. A schoolboy, too young to drink, too young to drive. Perhaps that was part of his appeal for the people who bought his music. 'I come here sometimes to talk to my dad. Daft, huh?'

'Were you very close?'

'We were. I was an only child. Maybe that had something to do with it. And then he was ill for quite a long time. He couldn't get out to work so much, so he was in the house more than my mother was. He read to me a lot. We played music together.'

'What work did he do?'

'He was an engineer. He worked for one of the oil companies. He'd travelled a bit before he came back to Shetland. Mostly in the Middle East. They think maybe that was where he got the skin cancer. He was

181

very fair-skinned. By the time he was diagnosed it had spread. For a while he seemed well, just as he always was, and it was like one great long holiday. Then he got very weak and thin. But we still managed to play together almost to the end.'

Taylor wished he could think of his own father in those terms, with fondness and the memory of shared activities. He looked again at the couple on the beach. It was low tide and the sand was flat and smooth. The man had fixed together a red box kite and was getting it into the air. They watched as he passed the string to the girl, then stood behind her, helping her to control it.

'Martin's a fantastic father,' Roddy said. 'I hope I can do as well when the time comes.'

Taylor had a sudden image of a leggy actress from a soap. Hadn't there been a story that Roddy was dating her, of a proposal even? There'd been a picture in a tabloid paper that he'd picked up in Aberdeen Airport while he was waiting for the fog to clear. Both obviously drunk, stumbling out of a nightclub. It was hard to imagine them in Shetland, playing happy families on a windswept beach.

Perhaps Roddy had followed his line of thinking. 'Not that I'm planning on settling down any time soon. My dad died when he was young. If I'm taken early I want to have had a great life before I go.' He paused. 'I'm glad my father's buried here. Biddista always seemed more like home to me than the house in Lerwick.'

'You spent a lot of time here even before you came to live with Bella?' Perez asked the question in that hesitant way he had, as if he didn't want to intrude, but he was so interested that he'd overcome his scruples. Taylor felt a mild irritation at the interruption. He was leading this interview.

'Yeah. I was never an easy sort of kid. Hyperactive. I never slept much. It can't have been great for my mother, with Dad to look after. So I came here to stay with Bella most weekends and holidays. I loved it. There was always something going on. People staying. Artists. Musicians. Maybe that's when I got addicted to partying. And I was the centre of attention, constantly entertained. I remember there was one guy who was a brilliant magician. He did this fantastic magic show just for me – the whole lot, rabbits from a hat, card tricks. Later I realized it was more for Bella's benefit than mine – they all wanted to please her – but at the time it was wicked. There was the freedom here that I never really had in town. Bella was pretty relaxed about bedtimes and mealtimes and I was just allowed to roam.'

'Real life would have been hard after that,' Perez said.

'Yeah. I think I've been spending the rest of my life trying to recapture the magic.' Roddy gave a self-deprecating grin. 'Nothing ever quite lives up to it.'

'Did Bella have a serious relationship with any of the visitors?'

'Definitely not serious. I guess she might have slept with them, but I never really knew about that.'

'Do you manage to see much of your mother?' Perez asked.

'We get on OK these days. I was very hard on her when I was younger. Just grief maybe. I couldn't understand how she could take up with another man.

183

Things are still a bit tricky between me and her husband, but we manage to be polite to each other for her sake.'

'The Englishman who died,' Taylor said. 'We think he was the person who was trying to sabotage your aunt's exhibition. Do you have any idea why he would want to do that?'

'Why would anyone?'

'Your aunt doesn't have enemies?'

'Lots of spurned lovers,' Roddy said. 'Bella's always attracted men. Like I said, when I was growing up, Biddista was full of visitors who imagined themselves besotted with her. From spotty students to earnest elderly intellectuals. It was all very amusing for a child. There's nothing a kid likes more than grown-ups making prats of themselves. And even now she still pulls people in. She's flattered by the attention. Sometimes I think she's quite lonely, but she'll never settle down.'

'Has there been a recent admirer?'

'Not that I'm aware of. But I haven't been home for a while. I might not know.'

'She didn't mention anyone?'

'That she was being stalked by an Englishman with no hair and a penchant for weeping in public? No, inspector. And if that was the case she wouldn't need to kill him to get rid of him. She's an assertive woman. She can get her own way without resorting to violence.'

On the beach the wind must have changed suddenly, because the kite twisted and dived into the sand. The little girl dropped the string and ran towards it, arms outstretched, mimicking the zig-zag movement as it had crashed to the earth. Kenny Thomson brought his boat back towards the shore.

Roddy continued. 'If that scene at the party was a stunt to hurt Bella, it was all rather pointless, wasn't it? The Englishman didn't succeed in wrecking the show. All my aunt's London friends were there. They'll still write reviews. The paintings will go back to the galleries. It was just a gesture. An anticlimax.' He smiled again. 'Inspector Perez accused me of being behind the flyers to cancel the party, but if I'd wanted to sabotage the exhibition, I'd have made a far better job of it.'

'Your aunt says you're planning to leave Shetland.'

'I was going to get the ferry tonight, but I don't think I'll make it now. I can't see me getting my act together. I've started packing, but suddenly it all seemed too much hassle and I came out here. Maybe I will. I prefer the boat. Otherwise I'll take a plane first thing in the morning. That would give me another evening. A chance to say goodbye properly to folks here.'

'Is there something urgent to take you south?'

'There's always work of course, but I think it's more that there's nothing to keep me here.'

Taylor thought the boy sounded like an old man, disillusioned and world-weary. Roddy leaned against the wall and looked at the two men, waiting for more questions to come. Taylor couldn't think of anything else to ask.

'If there's nothing more,' Roddy said, 'I'll go, get on with the packing.' Without waiting for a reply, he ran through a gap in the wall and down the grassy slope to the beach. They watched him jog along the tideline until he'd joined the Williamsons. He lifted the little girl on to his shoulders and they walked together towards the houses.

Taylor turned back to find Perez standing by one of the graves.

'This is it. This is where his father is buried.'

The headstone looked less weathered than the rest. The words were still fresh and easy to read. IN LOVING MEMORY OF ALEXANDER IAN SINCLAIR. HE DIED TOO YOUNG.

Taylor thought the same could be said of the Englishman lying on the table in the mortuary. But it seemed there was no one yet to grieve for him.

Chapter Twenty-three

Perez wasn't sure what to make of the conversation with Roddy Sinclair. He thought in a way it had been like talking to a criminal, one of those old offenders who've been questioned so often by the police that they know how to play the game. Roddy spent his life fending off awkward questions from the media. He knew what impression he wanted to give and he stuck to his story. Fran had said she'd met the musician a few times but didn't feel she really knew him. Perhaps he'd been taken in by the hype too, had lost a sense of his own identity. Perez wished Taylor hadn't been there at the graveyard. He'd had a sense that there were things the boy had wanted to say, but Taylor's abrasive style had put him off.

'I'm going to talk to Edith Thomson,' Perez said. They were walking down the road now, back towards the jetty and their cars. 'She's Kenny's wife. She wasn't at the Herring House party, but she was at home that evening. She might have seen something. And she's known Bella for years.'

'Isn't she the one that works in the old folks' home?'

'The care centre,' Perez said. 'I thought I'd catch her there. Would you like to be in on that?'

'It'd make more sense if we separated,' Taylor said.

'I'll stay around here, get more of a feel for the place. I might catch up with Martin Williamson.'

Perez sensed panic in the man's refusal. He thought Taylor would dislike contact with the elderly and infirm. He would prefer not to be reminded of his own mortality. Perez was relieved to have the opportunity to talk to Edith alone. He'd met her a couple of times with Kenny and he'd thought her a proud and dignified woman. She might not respond well to Taylor's approach either.

The care centre was purpose-built, a low modern box with long windows giving a view down the voe to the sea. A minibus specially adapted with a lift for wheelchairs was parked outside, along with the staff cars. Perez walked inside and was engulfed by a sudden blast of heat and the institutional scent of disinfectant and floor polish. In the background a surprisingly appetizing smell of cooking food. It was only eleven-thirty but tables in the dining room had been set for lunch and a woman in a nylon overall was pouring water into brightly coloured plastic beakers. She looked up briefly and smiled at him. On the other side of the front door, he saw the lounge with the long windows. People sat around the walls in high-backed chairs. Some seemed to be dozing. Three men at a table were playing cards. He thought he recognized Willy Jamieson, who had once lived in Peter Wilding's house in Biddista, and gave him a wave, but the old man stared back blankly.

'Can I help you?'

Edith Thomson had come up behind him. She wore black trousers and a blue cotton blouse and seemed to him very neat and professional. He saw that she didn't know him. The voice was polite but rather distant. He held out his hand.

'Jimmy Perez. It's about the murder in Biddista.'

'Of course. Jimmy.' Now she could place him she relaxed a little. This wasn't a work-related visit. He wasn't a relative or a social worker. 'Is it definitely murder then?'

'We're treating the death as suspicious.'

'Poor Kenny,' she said. 'He was so upset when he found the body. And then he got it into his head that it might be Lawrence.'

She, it seemed, didn't share her husband's distress. Perez could tell she would answer his questions briskly and efficiently, but he'd never found the direct approach very helpful. People gave away more if they were allowed space to lead the conversation. It was possible then to get a glimpse of their preoccupations and the subjects they hoped to avoid.

'This must be an interesting place to work,' he said. 'These people have so many stories.'

'We're trying to record them. Keep the tapes in the museum. Life here is changing so quickly.'

'Isn't that Willy in there? I knew him to say hi to at one time, when he lived in Biddista and worked on the roads, but he seemed not to recognize me.'

'On his bad days he doesn't recognize anyone,' she said. 'He's full of stories too, but sometimes they're just a muddle. We can't make head or tail of them and he gets so frustrated. He has Alzheimer's. It developed very quickly. Such a shame. He was always a lively man and even when he first moved into sheltered housing he could manage most things for himself.'

'Could I talk to him later?'

'Sure,' she said. 'He'd be glad of the company.'

'I just need to ask you a few questions first.'

'Of course. Come through to my office. Coffee?'

The office was as neat and efficient as she was. A beech desk with a PC, clear and uncluttered, a tall filing cabinet. On the wall a planner marked with coloured stars. He wondered how she and Kenny got on together. Did he resent her career, the full days away from the croft? She probably earned more than her husband did. Did she try to organize him as she did her staff? There was a filter-coffee machine on a small table in a corner, a Pyrex jug half full keeping hot. She poured him a mug.

'Tell me about the night the man died,' he said.

'I don't know exactly when that was. Was it just before Kenny found him?'

'We assume it was the night of the Herring House party. If not that evening it would have been early the next morning.'

'I have nothing to tell you. I can't help you. I didn't go to the party.' She sat behind her desk, her hands in her lap; not obstructive, interested, but lacking the excitement that most people seemed to feel when they were involved in a murder inquiry.

'But you have a good view down to the shore from your house. Perhaps you saw someone leaving the party?'

'I was in the garden,' she said. 'Each year I think I'll get away with growing a great crop of vegetables, then there's a west wind and the salt ruins them all. But still I'm optimistic and I weed and water. You can't see the Herring House from there. Later I had some work to catch up with. I have an office in the spare bedroom.

If I did all my paperwork while I was here, I'd never have time to spend with our clients. It's at the back of the house. You can't see much but the hill from there.'

'Kenny thought he saw someone running up the track towards the Manse.'

'Then I'm sure he did. He's not one for making things up. And he was on the hill. He'd have a good view from there.'

'Why do you think Lawrence left home so suddenly?'

The sudden change of tack caught her off guard. She frowned slightly. 'Kenny said the dead man couldn't be Lawrence.'

'I know. I'm interested. It seems so dramatic. To leave like that without any warning and never get back in touch.'

'He was a great one for the drama,' she said. 'The grand gesture. Then after a while, I suppose it would be hard to come back. He'd feel so foolish.'

'Do you have any idea why he went?'

'Kenny thought it was all about Bella,' she said, frowning. 'I suppose that could have been it. But he was never the most stable sort of man. Did you ever meet him?'

Perez shook his head. 'I don't think I did. Were Lawrence and Bella having a relationship?'

'I'm not sure. She was always an attractive woman. A bit wilful, but men seemed not to mind that. Maybe Lawrence had hopes and Bella strung him along. She loved having admirers.' Edith paused, looked up at Perez with a grin. 'I think she still does.'

Perez considered. 'Does Bella have an admirer at the moment?'

Edith shrugged. 'How would I know? She's too grand for us now.'

'You'd have heard though.' Perez was quite certain about that. Even if Bella didn't mix socially with the Biddista folk now, she'd be the subject of talk. And if Edith was too proud to gossip, she'd hear the news, from the staff in the care centre, the clients she worked with, from the relatives.

'There was some gossip about her and that writer. Peter Wilding. He followed her up here, they say. Rented Willy's old house just to be close to her.' She looked at him again to gauge his reaction. 'It seems a creepy kind of thing to do to me. I wouldn't want a stranger tracking me down.'

'Do they say what she thought of that?'

'She liked the fact that he went to all the bother,' she said. She sat for a moment in silence, thinking. 'I'm not sure Bella could ever do a real relationship. It would get in the way of the one thing that's most important to her.'

'What's that?'

She gave a brief mischievous smile. 'Bella Sinclair. Her work. Her reputation.'

'Where does Roddy fit into that?'

'He makes her feel good about herself. And he does her reputation no harm at all either.'

'Do you not like him then?'

'Is this relevant to your inquiry?'

'Probably not. But I'm interested in your opinion.'

'Everything's come too easy to him,' she said. 'Looks, talent, money. I don't think that's good for a young boy. He flaunted all he had in front of our kids.

But maybe I'm just jealous. Kenny and me, we had to work for everything we have.'

'Kenny told me Roddy went out with your daughter a couple of times.'

'Roddy always has to have a woman in tow. Just like Lawrence in that respect. Someone prettier came along and he dropped her. That made me angry.'

'He lost his father when he was still a child. And his mother too, in a way.' He's lonely, Perez thought. He's portrayed as a golden boy, but he has no real friends.

She considered for a moment. 'That's true,' she said. 'I didn't know Alec very well. He'd already left Biddista when I married Kenny. But you're right. Maybe I shouldn't be so hard on Roddy.'

'He spent a lot of time in Biddista when his father was ill. He'd have been around the same age as your children. You say he showed off to them. Did they know each other well when they were younger? Even before he took up with your daughter?'

'Sometimes he came on to the croft to play. I didn't like my two going to the Manse. I didn't want them picking up his wild ways and quite often Bella had unsuitable people to stay. Sometimes Willy took all three of them out in his boat.' She paused. 'The children all liked Willy. He was a sort of Pied Piper. When he was home they all hung around with him. Like I said, he was full of stories. He never had kids of his own and he enjoyed having them around. He taught most of the children in Biddista to handle a boat. He took Kenny out when he was a lad. And Lawrence was in a boat almost before he could walk.'

Beyond the office door there was the sound of movement, plates banging, the jangle of cutlery.

'Lunchtime,' she said. 'The high spot of the day. Some of our people only come here for the food. Will you eat with us, Jimmy? Have a bowl of soup at least.'

So Perez found himself sat at a table with Willy, a woman with Down's syndrome called Greta, and Edith. Willy had the look of someone whose clothes had been chosen for him. Despite the heat of the centre he wore a thick jersey over a plaid shirt. He'd shaved that morning but not very well. His hair still had some black in it and was thick and curly.

'Where are you living now, Willy?' Perez asked.

Willy looked up at him, his spoon poised, his mouth slightly open.

'I'm a Biddista man.'

'But that's not where you live now,' Edith said gently. 'Now you're staying in the sheltered housing at Middleton.' She turned to Jimmy. 'A carer comes in twice a day.'

Willy blinked and raised the spoon to his mouth.

'Tell me about the old days in Biddista,' Perez said. 'You kept a boat there, didn't you?'

'The *Mary Therese*,' Willy said eagerly, his eyes losing their blank, clouded look. 'A fine boat. Bigger than anyone else's in Biddista. Some days I had so much fish I could hardly lift out the box.'

'Who did you take fishing with you?'

'They all wanted to come fishing with me. All the lads. Kenny and Lawrence Thomson. Alec Sinclair. The lasses too. Bella Sinclair and Aggie Watt. Though Aggie was a timid little thing, and they were awful cruel the way they teased her. Bella was as strong on the boat as a boy. Nothing frightened her.' He stared into the distance and Perez thought he was imagining

194

midsummer evenings out on the water. The children laughing and fighting, the family he'd never had.

'You stayed friendly with them, did you, Willy? As they got older?'

Willy seemed not to hear. He tore a chunk of bread from the roll on his plate and dipped it into the broth.

'There was Roddy Sinclair too,' he said. 'He liked the fishing when he came to stay at the Manse.'

'That was later,' Edith said. 'Roddy was younger than Kenny and Lawrence. They wouldn't have gone fishing with you together.'

Willy tried to think about that. The soup dripped from his bread on to the front of his jersey. Edith leaned across and wiped it carefully with a paper napkin. Willy shook his head as if trying to clear the pictures in his mind.

'Did you ever have any English friends, Willy?' Perez asked.

Willy suddenly gave a wide grin. 'I liked going out with the Englishmen. They brought a hamper full of food and tins of beer. Sometimes, later, we'd build a fire on the beach to cook the fish and they always had a bottle of whisky. You remember that, Edith, don't you? The summer when Lawrence and me took the Englishmen fishing?'

'I remember that Lawrence always liked a drink,' she said.

Willy grinned again.

'What were the Englishmen's names?' Perez asked.

'It was a fine time,' Willy said. 'A fine time.' He returned to his meal, suddenly eating with great gusto, and Perez thought he was tasting the fresh fish caught just that day and cooked over the driftwood beach fire.

Perez turned to Edith. He didn't want to pull Willy back to the present, to the indignity of slopped food and endless games of cards. 'Do you know who he's talking about? Were there any regular English visitors to Biddista?'

She shook her head. 'Willy used to hire out his boat for fishing to the tourists, but I don't remember anyone regular. Perhaps it was before my time.'

Willy jerked out of his reverie. 'The Englishman came asking me questions, just the other day,' he said. 'But I told him nothing.'

'Which Englishman would that be?' Perez asked Edith.

'There's a writer called Wilding who comes after the traditional stories,' she said. 'Something to do with a book he's writing. That must be who he means.'

Perez would have liked to spend the afternoon there, sitting in the sun flooding in through the windows, listening to Willy talking about fishing and the Biddista children, but he knew he couldn't justify it. How would he account for his time to Taylor? Edith got up from the table and walked with him to the door. 'Come back,' she said. 'Any time.'

In the car, his mobile phone suddenly got a signal again. It bleeped and showed a couple of missed calls, both from Sandy. Perez rang him, could hear the buzz of the incident room in the background. Sandy seemed to have his mouth full of food and it was a moment before Perez could make out what he was saying.

'I've tracked down the lad who gave the Englishman a lift. Stuart Leask. He works on the desk at the NorthLink terminal and he'll be there all afternoon.'

Chapter Twenty-four

Fran was working on a still-life, some pieces of drift-wood and a scrap of fishing net she'd found on the beach. It was more as practice than for a picture to sell. She'd become obsessed by the need to improve her drawing. Even at art school, she thought, she hadn't paid it enough attention.

The phone call came just as she'd taken a break from work and put on the kettle for tea. She thought it would be Perez. He was her lover, the man who had been there at the back of her thoughts for months. But when she heard the English voice at the end of the line, there was a thrill of guilty excitement. She'd looked Wilding up on the internet. He had his own website, which listed the reviews. Perhaps he wasn't bestseller popular, but he was recognized as an interesting and original author. One of his short stories was in production for a feature film. There was in his celebrity the same glamour that surrounded Roddy and Bella.

'What are you doing?' His voice was easy, slightly amused.

'I'm working.'

'So I won't be able to persuade you to meet me for lunch then?'

The invitation reminded her of the spontaneous arrangements that had been part of her city life. A call from a friend. A meeting in a wine bar or over coffee. There'd be gossip and laughter then she'd run back to the office to finish the day's work. Things weren't quite so easy here. Perhaps in Lerwick it might be possible, though the choices of venue were limited. Here in Ravenswick, miles from anywhere, it was all much more complicated. Socializing took place in friends' houses. There was nothing new.

'I've got a hire car,' he said. 'I can pick you up. Half an hour.'

'I'll have to be back at three to collect my little girl from school.' As soon as the words were spoken she realized they'd be taken as acceptance of the invitation.

'No problem. See you soon.' And the line was dead. It was as easy as that. She felt a pleasurable guilt, as if she'd already been unfaithful.

She went back to work, but couldn't concentrate. Where would he take her? Of course they would bump into someone she knew. A friend of Perez's. Or a friend of Duncan's. She started forming the excuses and explanations in her mind. *He wants to commission a piece of art. Of course I had to talk to him. It was just a business lunch.* Should she phone Perez now and tell him what was happening? But then that would give the meeting more importance than it warranted. And how should she dress?

He arrived before she was quite ready and she felt flustered. She had to invite him into the house to wait and was aware how small it was, saw the dead houseplant on the windowsill, Cassie's toys all over the floor, through his eyes. He remained standing while she ran into the bedroom to get her bag. She'd compromised on clothes – jeans with a silk top she'd bought on her last trip south. She'd meant to put on make-up but he'd arrived before it was done and she couldn't cope with the thought of him watching her.

Down in the valley it was lunchtime in Ravenswick School. She could just make out the figures of the children running in the yard.

She wanted to mention Cassie. *My daughter will be one of those. Maybe you can pick her out. She's wearing a red cardigan.* But before she could form the words he'd handed her into the car and they were on their way. She was glad she had no near neighbours to watch.

Away from Ravenswick she began to let go of the guilt. Why shouldn't she have some time just for herself? In the run-up to the exhibition she'd done nothing but work.

He'd taken the road south after leaving Ravenswick, away from Lerwick and any of the restaurants he might have chosen.

'Where are we going?'

'Wait and see.' He turned towards her. 'You're looking lovely,' he said. 'Really.'

In her old life she'd have been able to bat away a compliment like that with a flippant, witty one-liner. Now she felt herself blushing.

He signalled west off the Sumburgh road and they were driving on a narrow track which she didn't think she'd ever been down. There was a cattle grid, then a damp patch with flag irises and a long, narrow loch with a square stone house perched at the end. A grand house for Shetland. Two storeys. Then the land seemed to drop away, so the house almost formed a bridge between the loch and the sea. Fran felt a moment of apprehension. Where was he taking her? What had she been thinking of, getting into a stranger's car?

'Where are we going?' she asked again, keeping her voice even. 'I didn't know there was anywhere to eat down here.'

'Just be patient,' he said. 'You'll see soon enough.'

Perhaps this was a new hotel, she thought, though she surely would have heard about its opening and there'd been no sign on the main road. Besides, when they got closer she could see it was empty, almost derelict. There were slates missing on the roof and the windowframes were rotten, the paint entirely peeled away. Frayed threadbare curtains hung at the windows.

She thought he was waiting for more questions. He wanted her to ask about the house, what they were doing there. She said nothing.

The track came to an end by the entrance to the small garden. Tall double gates, rusting, stood slightly open. Beyond, the vegetation was surprisingly lush and overgrown, an oasis which had somehow survived the battering of the westerlies. There were more irises, a patch of rhododendron.

Fran wondered if he'd taken the road by mistake. She sat, expecting him to turn the car round, but he was opening his door.

'Come on,' he said. 'We've arrived.' Now his excitement was unsophisticated. He was like a child desperate to show off a new achievement.

She followed him. What else could she do? He put his weight behind the gate to make the gap wide enough for her to squeeze through. The long grass behind it stopped it opening further. A path led to another smaller gate at the top of a shallow cliff and steps cut into the rock. The beach below was tiny, a perfect half-moon of sand. Beyond was a flat grassy island.

'Well?' he demanded. 'What do you think?'

She was wondering where they were going to eat. Why had he brought her here? Had she mistaken the nature of his invitation?

Perhaps he could guess what was going through her mind.

'I've brought a picnic,' he said. 'I'll fetch it from the car. I thought we could have it on the beach. That is all right?'

'Of course,' she said. 'It's a lovely idea.'

'I only found this place a couple of days ago and I wanted someone else to see it. It's so perfect.'

'A secret garden,' she said, reassured by his excitement. He wasn't a stranger. He was a famous writer. His photo was on his website along with the jackets of his books.

'Yes! Yes!' He was beaming. 'But you probably know it already. You're a local after all.'

Oh no, she thought. I'll never be a local.

'I've not been here before,' she said. 'Thank you for bringing me.' She could tell he wanted her to be as excited as he was and realized she sounded like a polite child who'd been taken out for an unwanted treat. But the lunch date was turning out to be so different from what she'd been expecting that she wasn't quite sure how to respond. She'd imagined a lunch in a crowded restaurant, conversation about art and books. Not a picnic on the beach.

The food was in a cold-bag. Wilding carried it from the car with a woven rug, which he draped over his shoulder. It made him look as if he was in fancy dress and only added to Fran's sense of unreality.

'I cheated,' he said. 'I asked Martin Williamson from the Herring House to put something together for me. I hope that's OK.'

He set off down the steps in the cliff without waiting for an answer.

On the beach, sheltered from the breeze, it felt very warm. Warmer than Fran could ever remember feeling in Shetland. The sand was white and fine. Seals were hauled up on rocks at the end of the island. Wilding spread out the rug. She lay on her side, propped on one elbow, watching him unpack the picnic. He took out a bottle of wine, still chilled so the glass was misty, pulled a corkscrew from his pocket with a flourish, and opened it. There were real glasses. But Fran thought the heat and the light had made her feel slightly drunk already.

'How did you find this place?'

'I was house-hunting.'

'The house is for sale?'

'Not exactly.' He gave a sudden wide grin. 'Not any more.'

'You've bought it?' It seemed to her an astonishing thing to do on the spur of the moment. He hadn't even been in Shetland that long. She thought of Perez, the agonizing there'd been over his future, where he would live. She admired Wilding's ability to take a life-changing decision so lightly.

'Once I saw it I had to have it. I tracked down the owner and put in an offer. A very good offer. I don't think she'll turn it down. It was left to an elderly woman who lives in Perth and she hardly ever visits. I can't show you round the house. I haven't got a key yet. I'll hear for certain at the beginning of next week. I would like to see what you make of it. It's to be a project. I was hoping you might advise on the design.'

So, she thought, we'll have more excuses to meet. Still she wasn't sure what she felt about that. Of course he hadn't bought the house just to provide an opportunity to spend time with her, but still she felt she was being manipulated, that she, like the house, was one of his projects.

Now the food was spread out on the rug. There were squares of pâté and little bowls of salad, chicken and ham and home-made bread.

'I do hope you're not a vegetarian,' he said. 'I should have asked.' He smiled and she could tell he knew already the food would be to her taste. He must have asked around – Bella or Martin. She supposed she should be flattered that he'd put so much preparation into the lunch, but found the careful planning disturbing. And he had made the assumption that she would accept the invitation to eat with him, since the food must have been ordered before the call was made. But she drank more wine and turned her face to the sun. She wasn't in the mood to pick a fight.

'What a terrible business that murder was,' he said. 'Do the police know yet who he was?'

'I don't know,' she said. 'I haven't heard the news today.'

'But wouldn't you hear before the rest of us?' He reached across her to fill her glass again. 'I understand that you're a close friend of the inspector.'

She sipped the wine. She wished she wasn't lying down. It was hard to challenge him, spread out at his feet. She pushed herself upright, sat cross-legged so she was facing him.

'Who told you that?'

'Hey.' He held up his hands in mock surrender. 'I asked Bella if you were seeing anyone. She mentioned the cop. That was all.'

'It didn't stop you asking me out to lunch.'

'It's lunch. I wanted someone to share this place with me. You didn't have to accept.'

She felt suddenly that she was being ridiculous. 'Sorry,' she said. 'I should never drink at lunchtime. It's always a mistake. This is all lovely.'

'Is it true then? You and Perez . . .'

He was looking at her, squinting into the sunlight.

'I don't think,' she said sharply, 'that's it's any of your business.'

'Does that mean I still have a chance then? Of winning a place in your affections?'

She looked at him. She couldn't make him out. Was he teasing her? Was this innocent flirting? Or something more sinister?

'No,' she said firmly. 'My affections are definitely taken.'

'What a terrible pity. You need some fun in your life and Inspector Perez doesn't seem a lot of fun. I'd help you to play.'

She didn't answer that. He piled mackerel pâté on to an oatcake and handed it to her.

'Does Perez ever talk to you about his work?'

'There's not usually very much to talk about,' she said. 'Nothing interesting.'

'But this is murder. We're all interested in that.'

'I don't think I am. I want the murderer caught, of course. But I didn't know the victim and I'm not involved in the case to any extent. It's Jimmy's job and nothing to do with me.' She wondered now if he'd just brought her here because he was curious about the investigation.

'I'm fascinated. I'd have thought you would be too. You used to be a journalist! And art's about the experience of extremes, don't you think?'

'I'm too chilled to think anything,' she said, smiling, trying to lighten the mood.

He seemed to realize that it would do no good to push it. 'Somewhere in here there's a very good chocolate cake.' And he went on to entertain her with stories of publishers' parties and the sexual activities of famous novelists, so she almost forgot that there'd been any awkwardness between them.

He was the one to say they should make a start back or she'd be late to pick up Cassie. She was surprised at how quickly the time had passed. She stood up and brushed the crumbs and sand from her clothes and followed him up the steps to the house.

'You will take it on, won't you?' he said. 'The house, I mean.'

'I've never done interior design,' she said.

'That doesn't matter. You have an artist's eye. I know you'll make a good job of it.'

205

She stood looking at the house, imagining how she would do it, saw it completed, the windows open to the sound of the waves and the seabirds, full of people for a house-warming party. Another glimpse of her old life. He couldn't have thought of anything better to tempt her.

She laughed and refused to give him a real answer. 'When it's yours we'll talk about it again.'

Chapter Twenty-five

Perez had thought he might go back to Biddista when he left the care centre, call in to the Manse and see if he could find Roddy on his own. He felt he understood the young man a bit better now, still believed Roddy might have information that could help with the inquiry. But the news that Sandy had tracked down the victim's lift made that impossible. How could he justify any delay to Taylor?

He found Stuart Leask at work behind the check-in desk in the ferry terminal at Holmsgarth. He was young and gap-toothed with untamed red hair. The terminal was quiet and echoing. It would be three hours before people would be allowed on to the boat.

'Do you mind chatting here?' Stuart said. 'Only I'm on my own till Chrissie gets back from lunch.'

Perez leaned against the desk. 'Sandy Wilson said you gave a chap a lift to Biddista the night of the Herring House party. Can you tell me what happened there?'

'I was just coming off duty and this guy came into the terminal. I mean the *Hrossey* had long gone and I was about to leave, but I asked if I could help. He wanted to know about car hire. I said he'd left it a bit

207

late, there'd be no one in the office until eight the next morning.'

'What did he look like?'

'Skinny. Pleasant enough. English. He was wearing black trousers and a black jacket. A bit crumpled, but as if it was supposed to look like that. And bald, but as if that was intentional too.'

'And did he seem OK in himself? I mean, not distressed or confused.'

'Not at all. As if it was all a bit of a joke, having missed his lift to Biddista.'

'He said he'd arranged for someone else to take him?'

'Aye, he'd booked a taxi but the guy hadn't turned up.'

'I still don't see how you ended up taking him.'

Stuart looked embarrassed. 'I offered. I know, it was just stupid. Marie, my lass, says I'm just a sucker and people are always taking advantage. But he was a nice guy and I wasn't doing anything else that night and he paid me what the taxi would have charged.'

'Did you go straight from here?'

'Aye, but we had to go and pick up his bag first.'

'He had a bag with him?'

'Like a black leather holdall.'

'Where did you pick him up from? Hotel? B&B?'

Stuart grinned. 'No. From the Victoria Pier. He was staying on that boat that turns into a theatre, *The Motley Crew*. You know the one?'

'It's quite a drive out to Biddista. What did you chat about?'

'He was an interesting man, an actor. He was talking about some of the parts he'd played. Theatre, film.

I mean maybe some of it was bullshit, all the people he said he'd met, but you sort of didn't mind, because he was still entertaining.'

'Did he say what he was doing in Shetland?'

'I asked him that. I'd have gone to see him if he was in a play here. But he said he was looking up some old friends.'

'And all the time he seemed quite rational? He didn't claim he was feeling unwell?'

'Nothing like that. He was brilliant company. It was a really easy way to make a few quid.'

'He definitely took the bag with him? You're sure he didn't leave it in your boot?'

'Absolutely. I thought it was kind of odd.'

'What was?' Perez was glad that he'd decided to interview Stuart himself. By now, Taylor would be beside himself with impatience.

'Well when we got to Biddista I went right up to the jetty to turn round. And I saw the man stick the bag just below the sea wall on the beach. It would have been quite safe there. It was well above the tideline and folks wouldn't have been able to see it from the road. But it just seemed strange. I mean, if he was going to stay with friends, wouldn't he have taken the bag with him?'

'He was going to the exhibition opening at the Herring House,' Perez said.

'Still, you'd have thought he'd keep it with him. I'm sure there'd have been somewhere to leave it.' This detail seemed to fascinate Stuart more than the reason for the man's death.

'Did he say where he planned to sleep that night?'

'I imagined he'd be staying with his friends. He

didn't seem worried at all about getting a lift back to town.'

'Did he tell you who his friends were?'

'No, and I asked him. Aggie who runs the post office is a sort of relative. A cousin of my grandmother, something like that. But he just launched into another story, so I never found out.'

'He must have told you his name,' Perez said.

'Just his first name. And that wasn't anything I'd heard before. I thought maybe it was something popular in the south. Or a nickname.'

'So what was that?' Perez thought that soon even his patience would run out.

'Jem. Not Jim. Jem.'

Before he left the ferry terminal for Victoria Pier, Perez phoned Sandy and asked about the bag. There'd been a search around the jetty at Biddista, but he wasn't sure how far it had extended along the beach. He couldn't believe they'd have missed it, but he needed to check.

He drove too fast into the town. He had a sudden panic that he would arrive at the pier and find the theatre ship had gone, but it was still there, moored near the end of the jetty. A big new banner strapped to the wooden hull read LAST PERFORMANCE SATURDAY.

A young woman was sitting on the deck, sunning herself like a cat. She wore cropped jeans and a long red jumper and there was something feline about the flat face and the green eyes narrowed and lengthened by black eyeliner. She was leaning against the cabin and had a script on her knee but seemed not to be reading it.

'Excuse me.'

She looked up and smiled. 'Do you want tickets for tonight? I think there are a couple left. It's well worth seeing.'

'Are you one of the actors?'

'Actor, set designer, front-of-house manager, general dogsbody. Hang on a minute and I'll fetch the tickets.'

'No,' he said. 'I'm sure the show's great, but that's not why I'm here.' He stepped aboard, thinking this was a lovely old vessel, the timbers weathered, honey-coloured. 'My name's Jimmy Perez and I work for Shetland Police.'

'Lucy Wells.' She remained where she was sitting.

'Did you hear about the guy who was killed in Biddista earlier in the week?'

'No. Shit.'

'It's been all over the news. He was found hanging in the boathouse there. He'd been strangled.'

'It's crazy,' she said. 'Life on the boat. Like living in a bubble. You're rehearsing for the next show during the day and performing at night. The country could have gone to war and I'd not have known about it.'

'Are you missing one of your actors?'

'No.'

He had been so certain that the dead man had been part of the theatre group that the answer threw him.

'A middle-aged man. Shaved head.'

'Sounds like Jem,' she said, 'but he wasn't part of the group. Not really. He was more of a hanger-on. A friend of the management. And he didn't go missing. We knew he was leaving.'

'We think he might be the dead man,' Perez said. 'Would you be able to identify him from a photo?'

She nodded. He saw she had started to cry.

'Are you OK?'

'Sorry, it's just a shock. I didn't even like him particularly. He was a bit of a nuisance. Not his fault, he was pleasant enough, but the accommodation here is cramped as it is and he was foisted on to us. It's horrible to think he's dead. I couldn't wait to see the back of him, so it's almost as if it's my fault. Wish fulfilment.'

'What was Jem's full name?'

'Booth. Jeremy Booth.'

'How did he land up with you?'

'Like I said, he's a friend of the management. He was one of the original team. *The Motley Crew*'s been touring the Scottish coast for donkey's years. Jem needed somewhere to crash and we were told to put him up.'

'What was he doing in Shetland?'

'Who knows? None of us took a lot of notice of him. He was full of himself and his own importance. He made out that he was here on some mysterious mission. The deal of a lifetime. We thought it was all crap and we were just pleased he was leaving.'

'If you could remember exactly what Mr Booth said about the deal, it would be very useful. Even a small detail might help.' Perez paused.

There was a moment of silence. She set the script carefully face-down on the deck. Then she closed her eyes.

'He talked about a weird coincidence. "A blast from the past. A rave from the grave." That was the way he spoke. You know, kind of knowing, self-mocking, but still thinking he was hip. He was a joker, one of those people who are full of gags that never quite make you laugh. He said there was a nice little deal which would set him up for a few years if he could play it right.'

'Did he mention any names?'

She shook her head. 'I'm sure he didn't. Like I said, he enjoyed being mysterious.'

'When did he arrive with you?'

'The twenty-second. Two days after *The Motley* arrived in Lerwick.' And two days before Booth was seen handing out the notices which cancelled the Herring House exhibition to the cruise passengers.

'Did he come on the plane or the ferry?'

'The ferry. It was a tiny bit bumpy when he came across and he was ill. You wouldn't believe the fuss he made. The next day he went off somewhere. He was back that night, then we didn't see him again.'

If he'd arrived on the ferry, Stuart Leask would have access to all the man's contact details, Perez thought. In an hour they'd have a full name and address, a phone number and access to a credit-card account. Their victim was no longer anonymous. The investigation was suddenly more manageable. More ordinary.

'Did he tell you where he came from?' Perez was interested in what the victim had said about himself, to find out how close it was to the truth.

'He ran a drama-in-education company in West Yorkshire. "I've always believed in community-based theatre, darling. Really, it's the most worthwhile work

213

you can do." Which probably means regular theatre wouldn't employ him and he'd conned funding out of the Arts Council to set up on his own.'

'You're very cynical,' Perez said.

'It's the business. We all start off imagining work with the RSC and end up spouting crap lines to three deaf old ladies for the Equity minimum.'

'You could give up. You're young.'

'Oh yes,' she said. 'But I still have the dream. I can still see my name in lights in the West End.'

He couldn't quite tell whether or not she was joking. He pushed himself away from the rail, so he was standing upright.

'Just a minute.' She sprang to her feet and disappeared below deck. When she returned she was holding some tickets. 'Comps for Saturday. See if you can make it. I'm really rather good.'

There was something desperate in the way she spoke. He thought if he rejected the tickets she would see it as a rejection of her. He took them awkwardly, then mumbled that he was very busy, but he'd make it if he could.

When he got into his car she was still watching him.

He phoned the station and spoke first to Sandy.

'Any news on the victim's bag?'

'Well it's definitely not on the beach.'

Perez asked to be put through to Taylor. 'I've got an identity for our victim.'

'So have I,' Taylor said. Perez could hear the smirk, the self-satisfaction. 'Jeremy Booth. Lives in Denby Dale, West Yorkshire. Runs some sort of theatre group. We've just had a phone call from a young woman who works with him. She saw the photo in one of the nationals.'

Perez had nothing to say. Let Taylor have his moment of glory. It was good to have the identity of the victim confirmed.

'I was thinking someone should go down there,' Taylor went on, 'to check out his house and talk to his colleagues. Do you want to do it?'

Perez was tempted. England was still a foreign country. There would be the thrill of exploration. But, he thought, this was a Shetland murder. The victim might have been an incomer, but the answer to his death lay here.

Taylor was obviously becoming impatient. He hated waiting for the answer. 'Well? Or would you rather I go?'

Then Perez realized Taylor was itching to take on the job. This was what he liked best about policing. The chase. He would adore the last-minute flights and hurried arrangements. The overnight drive. Gallons of coffee in empty service stations. And once he arrived he'd get answers immediately, firing away questions, blasting through the uncertainty with his energy.

'You go,' Perez said. 'You'd do it much better than me.'

Chapter Twenty-six

Taylor picked up the last flight out of Shetland that day, then blustered his way on to a packed BA plane from Aberdeen to Manchester. There was a group of oilmen on the flight; they'd just finished a stint on the rigs and were rowdy, determined to celebrate. A couple of them came from Liverpool and, trying to catch an hour's sleep, Taylor felt the old resentment against his home city coming back. Resentment mixed with a strange kind of kindred spirit.

At Manchester Airport he picked up a hire car and as he hit the M62 he realized he was only half an hour from home. Turn west and he could be there before his brothers were back from the pub. How would they receive him if he knocked on the door, a bottle of whisky under his arm and a dopey grin on his face? *Hi, remember me? Any chance of a bed for the night?*

Becoming a cop had been seen as a betrayal. He'd joined up on the wrong side in the class war. Even now that the boundaries were blurred he didn't think that would ever be forgiven.

He took the road to the east. It was dark and he could tell he was climbing the Pennines because of the absence of lights, not because of the view. The motorway was unusually empty and he found himself running over a fantasy in his head. About how he'd track down some fact or relationship that explained Booth's death so far away from home. How his Liverpool relations would see him on the national TV news talking about the arrest. He'd come across as calm and modest, but everyone would know that the conviction was down to him.

On the way into Huddersfield he checked into a Travel Inn, picking up the last room on a cancellation. The adjoining pub had stopped serving food, so he ate all the biscuits in his room and went to bed. Surprisingly for him, he fell straight asleep. It was a relief to have a dark night. Shetland was unnatural, he thought. The spooky half-light which never disappeared really freaked him out. That's why he'd slept so poorly the night before. Perhaps it was the extreme of the dark winters and sleepless summers that made the people so odd. He could never live there.

He woke very early and was on the road before six, picking up a bacon sandwich from a truckers' café and eating in the car as he continued to drive. He'd been given the mobile number of a local DC, a woman called Jebson, but waited until seven before he called.

'I wasn't expecting you till later.' She was brusque and graceless, though he could tell he hadn't woken her.

'Well, I'm here now. Can we meet at Booth's house?'

'If you like.' She sounded less than thrilled. 'But I can't be there till eight-thirty.' He heard a child's voice in the background and thought that was the problem with women in the service. Work never came first with them. It was either their men or their kids. He was about to comment but thought better of it. It would only take one complaint from a lass with a chip on her shoulder for his whole career to go down the pan. He'd seen it happen. And just when he seemed to be getting a bit of recognition that was the last thing he needed. 'OK then,' he said. 'Eight-thirty.'

In Denby Dale he found the house from her directions. 'Director of a theatre company' had sounded quite grand and he'd been expecting something more impressive than a mid-terrace cottage leading straight off the street. He got out of the car to stretch his legs and get a feel for the place.

A neighbour opened her door a crack to bring in a bottle of milk. Through the narrow slit he saw she was wearing a dressing gown which slipped to reveal one bare leg. He couldn't make out her face, just an arm reaching out to the doorstep.

'Excuse me. Police. Have you got a minute?'

He'd startled her. The milk remained where it was. She opened the door a little wider, pulled her dressing gown around her. She was middle-aged but wearing well.

'Could we have a chat?' he said. 'It'll not take long.'

An animal-feed lorry rolled past, bringing with it a strange yeasty smell. 'You'd best come in,' she said. 'I'm hardly decent for talking in the street.'

Her name was Mandy and she was a library assistant in Huddersfield, divorced, the kids all grown up. Today she wasn't starting work till midday.

'What was he like then, the bloke next door?'

Taylor was sitting at the table in the small kitchen. She'd made him tea, very strong, and there was bread in the toaster.

'Why? What's happened to him?' She'd lit a cigarette. 'The first of the day,' she said, relishing it. There were times when Taylor wished he still smoked.

'Didn't you see his picture in the paper?'

'I don't bother with a paper these days.'

'He's dead,' Taylor said. 'He was found strangled in Shetland.'

'Where?' She was curious but she didn't seem terribly upset that her neighbour had died.

'The Shetland Islands. Right off the north of Scotland.'

'Oh.' She finished the cigarette and stubbed it out in her saucer. 'I thought I hadn't seen him lately, but he keeps strange hours. I suppose the house'll be up for sale. I hope we don't get a noisy bugger moving in.'

'Was Mr Booth noisy?'

'Not really. Occasionally he'd have friends in late. I'd hear them talking, maybe a bit of music, but they weren't rowdy. Nothing you could complain about.'

'How long had he lived there?'

'About five years. He moved in after me.'

'Was he on his own for the whole of that time? No girlfriends? Boyfriends?'

'He wasn't gay,' she said seriously. 'At least I don't think he was. He'd been married once. And he'd had a child. But he left them. Quite suddenly.'

'How do you know all that?'

'He told me,' she said.

'Close, were you?'

'No. We lived our own lives. I don't want the whole village knowing my business and nor did he. But one night he'd locked himself out of his house. He'd left all his keys in the Mill. There was a lass who works for

219

him, lives in Huddersfield, and she had a set, but it took a while to get hold of her so he waited in mine. I'd just opened a bottle of wine and we ended up sharing it. It was the only time we really talked. That was the time he told me about his wife. He regretted just walking out on her, but she didn't understand his dreams.' She paused, looked at Taylor. 'Dreams! You're all the same, you men. Selfish bastards.'

Taylor wanted to reply that in his experience it was the women who were the dreamy ones, but he made no comment. 'He didn't tell you he was going away this time, then?'

'No. Like I said, we weren't that sort of neighbours. I just noticed that I'd not seen him around for a few days.'

The toaster popped. She nodded towards it. 'Do you fancy a piece?'

But Taylor didn't have anything else to say and couldn't imagine sitting at her table making polite conversation. That was much more Perez's style than his. He refused the offer and thanked her. As she showed him out she was already lighting another cigarette.

Back on the street, teenagers were coming out of the houses and wandering towards the bus stop for school. How old would Booth's child be now? He wondered if Jebson had traced the wife, if she'd even found out that the man had been married. A small train wound along a viaduct crossing the valley. The sun was already hot enough for Taylor to feel warm in his jacket.

Jebson arrived dead on time. He'd gone into a newsagent's and was sitting in the car trying to concentrate on a paper. She was square with very dark hair and dark eyebrows. He'd have marked her out as CID from a hundred yards, but wasn't sure why. He got out of his car and joined her on the doorstep of Booth's house. She pulled a bunch of keys from her bag.

'Where did you get those?'

'Martha Tyler, Booth's assistant. She's been into the house once. She was worried when he didn't come back. He'd said he'd only be away a couple of days. She imagined some sort of accident.'

Inside, it had the feel of a bachelor household. Tidy enough but not very clean. His place was much the same. He walked quickly through, stopping at the door of each room and looking inside. A small kitchen, the microwave the most prominent piece of equipment, a living room with a sofa and a coffee table a convenient height for eating takeaway food in front of the TV.

'Have you found the wife?' he asked.

'What wife?'

He felt a stab of satisfaction. He'd been here an hour and already he was showing the Yorkies how to do the job.

'According to a neighbour he deserted a wife and child. A few years ago now. Didn't Miss Tyler mention it? You must have asked her about next of kin.'

Jebson shrugged. 'She said she didn't have any contact details for relatives.'

Suddenly he hated being in the small house. It was too depressing, too close to home. If *he* died suddenly, would anyone know who to contact for him? 'We should leave this for the search team,' he said. 'We'll only get in the way. First priority is to check phone

calls and emails. Work computer and home PC. He
had some reason for going to Shetland. He knew
people there, though no one's admitting to it at the
minute, and he must have been in touch to make
the arrangements for the visit. And get into his bank
account. He might have left his wife and child but he
should have been supporting them financially. The
CSA ought to have records.'

'You'll have to check with the boss,' she said. 'The
way he sees it, it's not even our case.'

'Well, I'm hardly going to send a search team from
Shetland . . .'

She shrugged again.

Out on the pavement again, he realized he should
have handled things differently. But he'd used up all
his sweetness and charm with Perez and his team.
'Sorry,' he said. 'I shouldn't have made assumptions.
It's a sod of a case. But you can see we need to know
more about Booth, and you're the people on the
ground.'

'Like I said, you'll have to have a word with the
boss.' She looked at her watch. 'Martha Tyler said she'd
get into work early today. She should be there by now.
I'm due in court at nine-thirty, but I'll point you in the
direction of the Mill.'

Martha Tyler was in the office drinking coffee. Her
hair was tied into one plait, so long that it reached
halfway down her back. It seemed old-fashioned and
at odds with the jeans and the skimpy green vest top.
She watched Taylor approaching across the rehearsal

room and got up to meet him. She looked as if she'd had a heavy night.

'I don't know what to do with the company,' she said. 'The actors are supposed to start a school tour on Monday. Should we carry on?'

'Did Mr Booth have an accountant? A lawyer? Perhaps it would be wise to check the legal position with them.'

'I don't know. I'm only here on a sort of work experience.' She returned to the office, sat behind the desk, motioned for Taylor to take the other chair. 'It even seems odd sitting here. This was Jeremy's domain.'

'Tell me about him.' The sort of question Perez would have asked, which drove Taylor to distraction because it took so long to get relevant answers.

'He was an actor,' she said. 'That's the first thing to remember. I was never quite sure if he was performing, if I was getting the truth or a story. I'm sure he didn't mean to lie. He just liked his version best. He was funny and kind, but there was always this mask. You never knew what was going on in his head.'

'What did he do before he started the company?'

'Bits and pieces of acting, I think. He was full of the people he'd worked with. Maybe some of it was true. But it's such a tough business. Even if you're good, it's all about luck. It's the good people who never make it that I'm most sorry for.'

'And before that? Drama school?'

'I'm not sure. I don't think so. He was quite scathing about the kids who turned up here to work with their degrees in performance and no real experience in theatre.'

'Did he ever talk about his private life?'

'Never. Only about work.'

'No relationships?'

'I think there might have been a few brief flings – young actresses taken in by the bullshit and too much to drink. He liked to be seen with them. It must have been good for his ego. They never lasted, though.'

'They saw through him?'

'No. He was always the one to do the dumping. A couple of them were quite smitten. He was very kind and he did have a certain style.'

Taylor's phone rang. He went into the rehearsal room to take it. It was Jebson.

'The court case was adjourned, so I've made a few calls for you. Work history through the DSS. He's been self-employed for fifteen years, as an actor. I'm waiting to hear back from the tax people about his income.'

'Before then?'

'He was a teacher. A school in Chester.'

'Thanks.'

'One more thing. I've traced the wife.'

Chapter Twenty-seven

Kenny liked Friday evenings. Edith didn't work at the weekend and when she arrived home from the care centre he knew he would have her at home, all to himself, for two days.

She arrived home late, as she often did on Friday, looking tired and a little strained. She said she'd been out of the centre all afternoon doing home visits. She often said the relatives were more difficult than her clients. He took a bottle of wine from the fridge as soon as he heard her car outside, opened it and poured her a glass, so it was ready on the bench as soon as she came in. An end-of-week ritual. She dropped her bag on the floor and took off her jacket, kissed him lightly, then took the wine with her to run a bath. Another ritual. He heard the water run into the tub. When she came out she'd be the old Edith, wearing jeans and a sweater, calmer, more relaxed.

Earlier he'd been on the phone to friends about helping to bring the sheep down from the hill for clipping. The forecast had been fine for the following day. He enjoyed the sense of occasion that came with clipping the sheep; it was one of the days that marked midsummer – everyone walking across the hill together in line, pushing the beasts ahead of them until they reached the dyke, then walking them down towards the croft. It took him back to his childhood, when there'd been more communal work. He liked the banter and the edge of competition as everyone tried to get the fleeces off whole, not nicking the flesh, but keeping up the pace so they weren't at it all day. And then in the evening they'd all come into the house for beer and a few drams, maybe some music.

Edith came into the kitchen all rosy from the bath, not dressed at all, but wrapped in a big white towel. Her shoulders seemed very narrow and her neck very long. She finished the wine and poured herself another glass.

'I was wondering,' she said, 'if it was worth me getting dressed just yet.'

Kenny thought he must be the happiest man in the world.

Later he grilled some of the piltock he'd caught the day before. She sat at the table, dressed now as he'd imagined in jeans and a sweater, and she watched him carefully as he scaled the fish, cut off the heads, sliced the belly and pulled out the guts.

'Was it a bad day at work?' He'd sensed some tension in her.

'I'm worried about Willy,' she said. 'Something's making him anxious. He gets all flustered and confused. I hate to see him like that.'

'Maybe being questioned by Jimmy Perez didn't help.'

'I don't believe it was that,' she said. 'Jimmy was fine with the old man. He's a good listener and he has a gentle way about him.' She paused. 'I'm not sure he's cut out for the police. What do you think?'

Kenny thought Jimmy's mother had a gentle way about her too. But he didn't want to think about her and the strange obsession that had taken hold of him that summer when he was working in Fair Isle.

'Peter Wilding came in to visit Willy late this afternoon,' Edith said suddenly. Kenny thought maybe the visit from the writer had been on her mind all the time, was what had been troubling her all evening.

'That was kind.'

'I'm not so sure,' she said. 'I don't know what he could want with the old man. He's full of questions and demands and Willy gets upset so easily.'

'Perhaps he wants to put Willy into a book.'

'Perhaps he does, but he's like some sort of parasite, sucking the life from him.' She paused and Kenny was surprised to see she was shaking. 'Wilding told me he's put in an offer on a house in Buness,' she went on. 'He wants to stay in Shetland, but Willy's old house in Biddista isn't good enough for him. "Shetland is my inspiration." That's what he told me.'

Kenny wasn't sure what to say. He'd taken Wilding fishing once with Martin Williamson and thought he was a weak, easily scared sort of man. He'd sat white-faced, holding the side of the boat. He wouldn't be sorry if the writer moved to the south of the island. It would be better if a young Shetland family could move into Willy's old house. It would be nice if there was another child around the place, a friend for Alice Williamson, who must get awful lonely.

Edith went into the garden to dig some early tatties to go with the fish and came back, carrying them in a colander with a cut lettuce on the top. She rinsed the light soil from her hands under the tap.

'Would you like *me* to come in and talk to Willy?' he asked when they sat ready to eat. 'It's been a while since I've seen him. We could talk about the old days, and he always wants to know what the fishing's like now and how I'm managing with the boat. I won't suck the life out of him. I promise that'

She looked up at him and smiled. 'He'd love that. You're a kind man, Kenny Thomson.'

She squeezed a quarter of a lemon over the piltock and ate the fish very seriously, almost with respect. He reflected that that was how she did everything.

After the meal he asked if she'd like to take a walk with him over the hill. Some evenings she came with him and he always enjoyed her company. He thought it might help her forget her worries at work. She hesitated a moment before answering, so he could tell she was tempted, but in the end she shook her head.

'I'd like to finish the knitting for Ingirid. Just in case.'

Their daughter was expecting a baby, their first grandchild, and was due in ten days' time. Edith had holiday saved up so she could fly down to Aberdeen as soon as labour started. She was making a shawl for the child. The knitting was so intricate that it looked like one of the wedding veils worn in his grandparents' day. Then, the women had said the yarn should be so fine that you should be able to pull the veil through a wedding ring.

'I might speak to her on the phone,' Edith went on. 'Just see how she is.'

Kenny understood. As the birth got closer Ingirid had become homesick for the islands. It had seemed to them that she'd never missed Shetland before. She had her new life in the south, her friends and her man. Now some nights there were tearful phone calls. Hormones, Edith said, but Kenny thought it was just that she wanted her baby to be born a Shetlander.

He put his boots on at the door, and called to Vaila. Walking up the track his mind wandered and suddenly he found himself near the top of the hill looking down to the sea. A bonxie dived at him, just missing the crown of his cap. They were always aggressive this time of year when they had young. But he was used to the skuas on the hill and he didn't miss a step. He never had to worry about where he was putting his feet. The hill was so familiar and the way he took was the same every evening. If I had paint on my boots, he thought, there'd be one set of footprints on the grass even after a week, because I never vary my path.

It was a clear evening, so still that he fancied he could hear the waves breaking on the rocks at the foot of the hill. There were cars outside the Herring House. Martin opened the café there for dinner on Friday night. It seemed having a murder so close by hadn't put people off coming.

Tonight he thought he would walk on a little further, break the usual routine, check how many sheep there were up near the Pit o' Biddista. And because he knew the hill so well, his thoughts ranged again.

I was nearly unfaithful with Jimmy Perez's mother. I sat on a white beach at the North Haven on Fair Isle in midsummer and held her hand. Her lips were warm and tasted of salt. We told each other we were in love.

He caught his breath, thinking how close he had

come to leaving Edith. He had almost thrown away what was now most dear to him.

I could have been Jimmy Perez's stepfather.

He'd completely forgotten that summer, hadn't thought about it for years, but now, because of the death of a stranger, Jimmy Perez had come into his life again and the memories had returned. He'd never told Edith about it. He wondered briefly if he should, but after all this time it had no importance. Why hurt her?

Now he was on the highest part of the hill, close to the cliff-edge. There was still no wind so the walking had been easy. But he felt a strain in his knee, a dull pain which came occasionally, and he was a little bit breathless. Five years ago he could have done the walk faster. He stopped to look back at his land and despite the familiarity he felt a pride in it.

The grass here was cropped very short by sheep and rabbits. In places there were rough piles of rock; he'd never known whether they were natural or the remains of some ancient people who'd had the land before him. He stood on the rocky bridge between the sea and the Pit o' Biddista. The Pit was a great gouge out of the land all the way down to sea level. When they were children, Willy had told them a story about how it had been made. He said it had been formed by a giant who lost his heart to a Shetland lass. She'd been frightened of him, not realizing he only meant her well, and running way from him, she'd fallen over the cliff. In his grief and rage, the giant had scooped out a hole in the rock and flung the debris into the sea, where it formed the stacks that ran away from the coast. Kenny thought it looked more like the core had been taken out from a huge apple, but a lovesick giant made a better story for children. Willy had entertained generations of them with his stories.

It wasn't a sheer drop into the Pit on all sides. The side nearest to the sea was all rock, an almost flat cliff, cut with ledges where the kittiwakes nested. But the landward side was grass all the way down, pink with thrift and crossed by rabbit tracks. At the bottom of the seaward side a tunnel ran out to the beach and with a very high tide the water was funnelled through it, churning and boiling with the pressure, spitting spray almost to the top. They'd played there when they were children, sliding down the grass slope to the bottom, so their pants were stained green and their knees covered with mud. But never at high water. Then they lay on their stomachs and peered into the hole below.

Looking down, he saw that a ewe had somehow managed to get almost to sea level. She was trapped on a ledge, too stupid to turn round and make her way back. Sometimes he thought sheep were the dumbest creatures in the world. Her fleece was thick and ragged, so heavy that it almost seemed to be falling off her back. She should be clipped with the others the next day.

He began to edge down the slope towards her. He'd try to get behind her and persuade her to scramble up. Although the grass was dry enough it was still greasy underfoot; he was glad of the texture of the thrift to give him grip. He felt suddenly, startlingly, very happy. The pain in his knee was forgotten, it was a fine summer evening and Edith would be home all weekend. And he could still climb down the Pit o' Biddista as he had when he was a boy.

He circled round the back of the sheep, moving

slowly so he shouldn't scare her. He didn't think he'd have any chance of bringing her up if she went any deeper. Then he was there, right behind her, standing on the same ledge, arms outstretched so she wouldn't get past him.

'Go on, girl. Up you go.'

All of a sudden she scrambled up, not following the tracks but taking the direct route to the top, floundering, her feet somehow getting purchase. All he could see was the mucky behind, the loose curls of fleece. Then she was over the edge and invisible to him.

He stood where he was and looked down. Here everything was in shadow, the sun too low to reach this depth. Very few people in the world had seen this view. The only child in Biddista now was Alice Williamson, and her family didn't let her run loose on the hill. Martin and Dawn would have a fit if she climbed down here, though Bella hadn't been much older when she'd first made it to the bottom. She'd been as reckless as any of the boys. Kenny could see the round boulders which had been carried in on full tides, the puddle of brackish water left behind when the sea retreated.

Then he saw a splash of colour against the grey of the rocks. Because he'd been thinking about Alice Williamson, there was a heart-stopping moment when he thought it could be her. That she'd finally broken free from the protective parents, run up on to the hill and lost her footing. He imagined her tumbling over and over down the slope, her head smacking on a boulder, her skull smashing like an eggshell.

But it couldn't be the child lying down there. The

figure was too big. His eyes must be playing tricks. Edith was always telling him he needed glasses and he'd been aware of it himself. He shouldn't be so proud. He should get himself into Lerwick for an eye test. It was probably one of those blue plastic sacks the fertilizer came in. He was tempted to turn his back on it and return up the slope to where the dog was lying on the grass waiting.

As he was thinking that he was slithering further down. The light faded the further he went. There was the smell of rotting seaweed.

Roddy Sinclair was dead. Kenny didn't need new glasses to tell him that. The body was twisted and his head was smashed on a rock, just as he'd imagined Alice Williamson's to be. He knew he should get to the surface again as soon as he could. He should run back to the house and get on the phone to Jimmy Perez. But he wasn't sure how he'd do it. His legs had turned to water and he was exhausted. Only the horror of being here, next to the broken body of the boy, set him on his way.

Chapter Twenty-eight

Perez had spent the day in Lerwick, a frustrating round of phone calls and emails trying to track Booth's movements since his arrival in Shetland. The incident room was airless and overheated and despite the impetus given to the investigation by the identification of the victim, by late afternoon he felt little had been achieved. After work he set off to Ravenswick, to Fran's house. He hadn't phoned in advance to say he was coming and felt ridiculously nervous. He'd been looking forward to seeing her all day and worried, as he always did, that he wouldn't live up to her expectations.

Cassie was sitting at the kitchen table reading a schoolbook. She was frowning in concentration. There was a smudge of paint on her cheek and he thought how she was growing to look very like her mother. He stood awkwardly on the doorstep, afraid of intruding, of doing the wrong thing.

'Is this not a good time?'

'Of course it is.' Fran stood aside to let him in. 'Tea? Beer?'

He sat next to Cassie and asked her how things were going at school, but all the time he was thinking that Fran seemed a little uncomfortable too. He always thought of her as the confident one and wondered what she could be nervous about. She put the kettle on, then told Cassie that was enough homework for one night, and what about a DVD for a treat?

When Cassie was settled they took their drinks outside.

'We've found out who the murder victim is,' Perez said. 'It'll be all over the news tomorrow. I wanted to tell you. He was an actor. A man called Jeremy Booth.'

She shook her head. 'The name doesn't mean anything to me.'

'He comes from Yorkshire.'

'Sorry. I still can't help.'

They sat in silence. On the hill behind them a curlew was calling.

'I met Peter Wilding for lunch yesterday,' she said at last. She was twisting the mug of tea in her hands. He could tell this was the cause of her tension. He wasn't sure how he should react and ended up saying nothing.

'He plans to stay in Shetland. He's put in an offer on a house in Buness. Do you know it? The big place right by the beach.'

'Very nice.' Then, sensing more was required, 'It'll take some work to get it fit for living in.' His head was bursting with questions about what had happened and why she'd gone with Wilding in the first place, but maybe none of that was his business.

'I'm not sure why he asked me to meet him,' she said. 'I think he hoped I might have some information about the investigation. That's how it seemed.'

'And he fancies the pants off you,' he said. 'That might have had something to do with it.'

She gave him a big grin. 'Maybe he does,' she said. 'But there was more to it than that. He has this intense way of asking questions.'

'You believe he might be involved in some way with Booth's death?'

'No,' she said quickly. 'I'm not saying that. He's a writer. Naturally curious. I'm sure that's all it is.'

The thought came into Perez's head that it would suit him very nicely if Wilding turned out to be a murderer. He hated the idea of the man living in Buness, which wasn't so far from Fran. But he knew that was a dangerous way to think. If you hoped for a certain outcome in an investigation, you lost perspective, saw shadows that didn't exist, ignored other possible scenarios.

'Have you eaten yet?' she asked. 'If you can wait until I've got Cassie to bed, I can pull together a meal for us.'

'I'd like that.'

They were at the table when the phone call came. It was on the landline and Perez had no thought that it might be for him. He sliced bread and helped himself to salad while she answered it. She frowned, handed him the receiver. 'It's Sandy for you.'

It was Sandy at his worst. Childish. Full of himself. 'I tried you at home, boss. And I couldn't get a signal on your mobile. Thought I might find you at Mrs Hunter's . . .'

'What can I do for you?' Across the table Fran was pulling silly faces at him.

'There's been another death.' Sandy paused. He'd developed a sense of the dramatic.

'Who?'

'Roddy Sinclair. Kenny Thomson found him at the bottom of the Pit o' Biddista. I sent Robert, the new PC who's based in Whiteness, to confirm it. It's definitely Sinclair. Could have been an accident.'

'A bit of a coincidence.' Perez thought of his sense that Roddy had something to confide and knew that this was no accident. He remembered the walk he'd taken with the boy, the morning they'd found Booth's body. Roddy had grown up there. He wasn't the sort to fall. He pictured Roddy playing the fiddle at the Herring House party, caught in the spotlight of the evening sunshine, dancing. He was as lithe and nimble as one of the feral cats that lived on the cliffs. He'd liked the boy and was overcome by a sense of waste.

'Does Bella know?'

'Not yet,' Sandy said. 'I thought I'd best get hold of you first.'

'Good, I want to tell her.' Roddy had been Bella's golden boy. His death would devastate her. Perez felt a stab of pity, then the thought of work took over. Bella had been playing games with him throughout the investigation. The shock of her nephew's death might persuade her to talk.

'You'd best be quick then. You know how news gets out.'

'I don't think Kenny will be on the phone to her. He and Bella aren't that close and he's not the sort to blab. But don't send anyone on to the hill until I've talked to her. Tell them to stand by.'

'I told Kenny to keep the news to himself.' Sandy seemed extraordinarily proud that he'd thought of such a thing.

Perez smiled. 'Good,' he said. 'Good.'

'I wondered if I should phone Mr Taylor now. He's going to be pig sick, being stuck down in England while everything's happening here.'

'Aye,' Perez said. 'I think maybe you should.'

Fran had been eating, but she stopped now, her fork poised. 'You've got to go, haven't you? And you won't be able to tell me what it's all about.'

'Roddy Sinclair's dead. Kenny Thomson found him at the bottom of the Pit o' Biddista.'

'Poor Bella!' He could tell that Fran was nearly in tears. 'She cared for Roddy as if he was her son.'

'I'm just off to tell her. Can I say you're here if she needs company? I know she was born and reared in Shetland, but it seems to me she doesn't have many friends.'

'Of course.'

He could tell she was pleased he'd told her so much. It was on the tip of his tongue to warn her not to tell Wilding, but he stopped himself just in time.

'Roddy always had so much energy,' she said. 'It was as if he was lit up inside. It's hard to imagine he's dead.' She paused. 'Another death. What is going on here? You do realize the press will go wild over this? He was a celebrity, even in the south. As soon as word gets out there'll be hundreds of journos here.'

'No pressure then.' Perez was thinking there'd be more pressure from the community too. Roddy was a Shetlander. He represented Shetland in the rest of the world. People would want his killer found now. It wasn't the same as some strange Englishman found hanging from the roof.

'Jimmy?'

He was already at the door and he turned back to her.

'It wasn't an accident, was it?'

'No,' he said. 'I don't think it can have been.'

'Suicide? Because he'd killed the Englishman and couldn't face the consequences?'

'Maybe.' He remembered Roddy standing at the top of the cliff, arms stretched wide like a gannet's. It would be the sort of grand gesture he'd go for, killing himself by launching himself into the air. As close to flying as it was possible to get. But he'd want an audience. Without an audience it wouldn't be any sort of performance.

'Come back here when you've finished,' she said. 'It doesn't matter how late it is. If you want to.'

Bella was sitting in her garden when he got to the Manse. A wrought-iron table and chair stood on a terrace by the side of the house and he found her there. The light was diffuse, milky, and he realized it was already ten o'clock. There was a book on the table but she hadn't been reading. Perhaps she'd dozed off. Next to the book was a large glass of wine and a half-empty bottle.

'Jimmy,' she said when she opened her eyes, 'isn't it a lovely evening? So still. There are so few days when we can do this. Have a drink with me!'

He sat on the wall beside her.

'When did you last hear from Roddy?'

'I saw him at lunchtime. He was booked on the last plane south. He'd planned to go yesterday, but you know what the young are like. Time has no meaning for them. It's as if they have for ever. I was expecting him to phone, but he'll have met up with some friends.'

He thought there was no easy way to do this. If he lost someone close to him, he'd want to hear it straight. No platitudes and no prevarication. 'Roddy's dead, Bella. His body was found this evening at the bottom of the Pit o' Biddista.'

Her eyes widened. 'No. No,' she said. 'There's been some mistake. He was on the plane.'

'Did you take him to Sumburgh?'

'I had a meeting in Lerwick this afternoon. He said he'd get himself there.'

'He was going to drive?'

She stood and began to walk backwards and forwards across the terrace, her glass still in her hand. 'I assumed he was, but when I got back his car was still here, so I thought he'd got a lift from a friend.'

'Can I have a look in his car?'

'Of course.' Perez could see she was sure she'd be proved right. Bella Sinclair had never admitted to being wrong in her life. She'd convinced herself Roddy was in some bar in Aberdeen, surrounded by admirers. That was why he hadn't phoned her to say he'd arrived safely.

The car was an old black Beetle, restored. It had probably cost more than Perez's new saloon. It wasn't locked. In the boot he found the bag Roddy must have been packing the day before, when it all got too much for him and he went to visit his father's grave. Lying on top of it was his violin. Perez had left Bella sitting on the terrace, but now she came up behind him. He heard her footsteps, then a throaty cry, so quiet it sounded as if she was just catching her breath. 'So it's true,' she said. 'He's dead. He'd never have left his fiddle behind.' She wrapped her arms around her body and, bending double, she began to weep.

Perez led her into the house and into the kitchen. There was little light now. Sitting on the dark wood bench, she seemed small and very frail, like a child in Sunday school.

'What's been going on here, Bella? The hoax around the gallery opening was one thing, but now Roddy's dead. Who hates you enough to do this to you?'

She took her hands from her face, so he could see her big eyes, red and wet with tears.

'I don't know,' she said. 'Really, I don't know.'

He stayed with Bella until Morag arrived from Lerwick to sit with her. During that time she refused to answer questions. 'I've told you, Jimmy. I don't know anything.' He asked if she'd like him to drive her to Fran's house, but she said she wanted to stay in her own home. 'I need to be here.' He was disappointed. He hoped she might take Fran into her confidence.

By the time he reached the hill, the greyest part of the night had already gone and the sun was starting to slide up from the horizon again. A different sort of dawn. A wren had been singing in Bella's garden when he left the house. The team had managed to get a Land-Rover right up to the cliff-edge and from a distance he saw a number of people at the lip of the Pit. He hoped he wouldn't have to climb down there. It was a crime scene, wasn't it? So it should be preserved. He didn't find the idea as horrifying as being on the edge of the cliff, with space and air all around him, but if he could avoid the climb, he would do.

Sandy was talking to the young doctor who'd called Booth's death as murder. He waved to Perez when he saw him approaching.

'I've called in the coastguard to help bring up the body,' he said. 'That is OK?'

Perez tried not to be surprised at Sandy's initiative. 'Sure, if they've finished down there.'

'I went down with the doctor,' Sandy said. 'I found this. I wrapped it in polythene, didn't get my fingerprints on it, but it was lying near the gully out to the sea, and I thought it might get washed out.' He looked at Perez anxiously, not sure if he'd get yelled at for moving evidence.

'I'd have done just the same myself.' It was a black leather holdall, just like the one Stuart Leask had described as belonging to Jeremy Booth.

'What do you think?'

'I think someone killed Booth, made it look like suicide, then chucked the bag down here in the hope that we wouldn't identify him.'

'What about Sinclair?'

'He could have been the murderer. Maybe he was climbing down to move the bag, or check it was well out of sight, and he tripped.'

'But you don't think so?'

'No. I think the murderer arranged to meet him here. Roddy liked being on the edge. It wouldn't have taken much to push him in. I'm not sure why he had to be killed. Maybe he knew something about Booth's murder. But I'm sure that's what happened.'

Perez stood silently for a moment, imagining what

that must feel like. The shove in the back, the panic as he'd realized he couldn't get a grip, then waiting to hit the ground. He saw that Sandy was staring at him. 'Now all I have to do is prove it.'

Chapter Twenty-nine

Roy Taylor went with Stella Jebson to visit Jeremy Booth's wife. The woman lived on the Wirral, way out of Jebson's patch, but for some reason the DC had seemed keen to go with him. Perhaps like the rest of them she'd become intrigued by the man who'd died, without explanation, so far from home. She wanted to see how the mystery worked out.

'I heard back from the Inland Revenue,' Jebson said. 'Booth's business was on the verge of going under, if his tax returns were anything like accurate.'

Taylor thought that would need looking into. There'd be nothing new in someone self-employed declaring a fraction of what he earned, but if Booth *had* been short of cash, why disappear to Shetland, leaving the business in the care of some sort of student? Had he thought he had a chance of making money there?

Taylor had visited the Wirral when he was a kid. A very young kid, when his mother was still at home, before she'd run away with her fancy man to north Wales. There'd been trips out to the seaside in Hoylake and West Kirby; he remembered them as happy times. Picnics and ice cream, fishing in the rock pools with little nets on bamboo sticks. His dad had never

244

been with them. He didn't mention any of that to
Jebson on the drive across. There was nothing as
boring as other people's reminiscences.

Booth's wife was called Amanda. She'd remarried,
a man called Stapleton, a teacher. Taylor wasn't sure
if the trip would be worth the effort. Booth had run
away years ago. Why would his ex-wife be involved in
his murder after such a long time? Surely she had too
much to lose. Yet Booth had left home quite suddenly.
He'd completely changed the direction of his life and
had relinquished any contact with the child. Taylor
knew that families could haunt you, resentments grow
with time. And why had the relationship fractured in
such a dramatic way?

The family lived on a pleasant estate of 1950s
houses near Arrowe Park Hospital. It was anonymous,
a straight tree-lined road of semi-detached homes. A
place you could lose yourself, Taylor thought. Yet
when they parked he thought the elderly woman
working in her garden opposite had taken note of
them. So it wouldn't be that easy to hide.

It was early evening but Amanda Stapleton was on
her own in the house. She seemed to belong to the
time it had been built. A comfortable blonde in a
sleeveless summer dress and sandals, she made Taylor
think of women with big skirts and permed hair. His
mother had been a great one for the pictures and for
watching old films on the telly in the afternoons. This
woman could have been a minor film star.

'Thank you for your time,' he said. 'I hope it's not
inconvenient.'

'I'm a stay-at-home mum,' she said. 'Sometimes I
think I should look for work now the children are

older, but I love being here for them when they get back from school. John got promoted to deputy head last year, so we can afford it.'

She'd been told about Booth's death, but seemed unaffected. Taylor wondered if she would get round to mentioning it. She took them into a living room at the back of the house. The door was open into the garden.

'I'll make tea, shall I?'

She returned with a tray, home-made biscuits on a plate, a teapot, milk jug, sugar bowl.

'The boys have cricket practice tonight,' she said. 'John will pick them up after work. It's not usually this peaceful.'

'What about your daughter?'

'Oh, Ruthie makes her own way home. She's in her last year at school. A grown-up really, or so she thinks. She'll be here soon. She doesn't know yet that her father's dead. I'm not sure how she'll take it.'

She settled herself on a straight-backed chair, a cup and saucer balanced on her knee, her legs neatly crossed at the ankle. 'I haven't seen Jeremy since he left in the middle of the night more than sixteen years ago. He took one suitcase. Left me with a daughter. And a note which said he was very sorry, but this wasn't the life he wanted.' She looked up at them. 'You can't expect me to be grieving about his death.'

'He'd given you no warning that he was leaving?'

'None.'

'Was there another woman?'

'He didn't mention one in the letter. But there could have been. He was an attractive man. I fell for him, after all.' She paused. 'He was the love of my life.'

Taylor didn't know where to look. He felt himself

flush with embarrassment. He hated people who spilled out their feelings, and this woman had seemed so controlled that it was unexpected.

Jebson leaned forward towards the woman. 'Tell us about Jeremy,' she said. 'We haven't met anyone yet who really knew him.'

'I'm not sure I can help you with that either. I'm not sure Jeremy knew himself. It was all dreams and stories with him. He featured in his own dramas. In his head of course. None of it was real.' She stared out into the immaculate garden. 'He'd have quite enjoyed this. Being the object of so much attention.'

'Where did you meet him?'

'At work. We were both teachers. He taught English and I worked in the technology department, doing craft and cooking. That summed us up really. I was the practical one; he was into fiction, words. He swept me away with his words. In his spare time he ran the school's youth theatre. That was his real passion. He'd done a lot of acting when he was a student, got into the Central School, but couldn't get funding to do the course. He was very bitter about that.'

'We haven't been able to trace any other family. Is there anyone else we should inform about his death?'

She shook her head. 'He was an only child. The classic only child: spoiled rotten and left to play too much on his own. His parents were quite elderly when we married. They're probably dead now.'

Taylor felt he was losing control of the interview. He'd brought Jebson along to observe, not to take over.

'You say you hadn't seen Mr Booth since he left sixteen years ago,' he said. 'Have you communicated with him at all?'

'He's paid maintenance for Ruth since he left. Not a lot. He's never had steady work. Since he set up the drama-in-education company things have been a bit better. I never wanted to make a fuss about the money and we had no direct contact over that. It was as if he preferred not to think about us.'

'Did you try to find him when he left?'

'Of course I did! I worshipped him. But he'd left his job at the school too. Just walked out. Gave no notice, asked for no reference. I thought he must be going through some sort of breakdown, tried psychiatric hospitals, the police, the Salvation Army. I imagined him sleeping on the streets, in some horrible hostel.'

'Did you ever find out where he went after he left you?'

'To his mummy and daddy.' She sounded very bitter. 'Hardly the great romantic gesture, was it? Running home like a scared child. Of course I contacted them but they told me they hadn't heard from him. He got them to lie for him.'

'And there was nothing, really, that precipitated his going?'

'It was when Ruth was born,' she said. 'That was when things started changing.'

She paused, and Taylor wished she'd get to the point.

Perhaps Jebson sensed his impatience, because she cut in with a question. For such a big, ungainly lass, she had a gentle voice.

'In what way did things change, Mrs Stapleton?'

'I don't know what he'd been expecting. He was so excited when I found out I was pregnant. Maybe some ideal of family life. A child who would adore him. Certainly not nappies and crying, coming home to an exhausted wife who suddenly made demands on him. And then Ruth wasn't the perfect baby he'd visualized for himself.'

'In what way wasn't she perfect?'

'She was born with a cleft palate. You wouldn't know now. She's a beautiful young woman. But there have been lots of spells in hospital. And when we first brought her home she was an ugly little thing. I think he was repulsed by her. And disgusted with himself for feeling that way. Perhaps that's what brought matters to a head. He couldn't face the reality, couldn't lose himself in theatre any more. So he just ran away. He pretended she'd never been born.'

'Can you think why anyone would have wanted to kill him?'

'I'd probably have killed him,' she said. 'If I'd tracked him down to his parents' house. If I'd caught him there, being waited on by them while I was struggling to keep things going at home.'

'Did he have any family and friends in Shetland?'

'No family. If he made friends there it was after my time.'

She offered them more tea, handed them biscuits, smiled to show she really didn't care any more. There was the sound of the key in the door.

'Hi, Mum.'

'Shall we leave,' Taylor said, 'so you can talk to Ruth on her own?'

'No. She'll probably have questions. You'll be able to answer them better than me.'

Ruth was, as her mother had said, a beautiful young woman. Dark-haired, full-breasted, with a wide smile. She stood in the door and looked at them. She was wearing jeans and a loose white top, easy with her body. She was curious about who they were, but too polite to ask.

'These people are detectives,' Amanda Stapleton said. 'They have some news about your father.'

The girl looked at them, horrified. 'What about him? What has he done?'

Stella Jebson got up and stood next to the girl. 'Why don't you sit down?' she said. 'We've got some bad news.'

The girl perched on the arm of the nearest chair. 'What's happened?'

'He's dead,' Jebson said. Perhaps she'd realized that Amanda would find it hard to say the words. 'I'm really sorry, love.'

'How did he die? Was he ill?'

'He was murdered. We're here because we're trying to find out who killed him.'

The girl started to sob, taking in great gulps of air. It was hard to tell if it was grief or shock. Taylor thought it was a dramatic way to carry on when she hadn't seen her father since she was born, but that was teenage girls for you. They were all drama queens. Her mother got to her feet, awkwardly put her arms around her daughter, held the girl to her, stroked her hair.

'I've told them you wouldn't be able to help them,' Amanda said. 'But I wanted them to be here if there was anything you wanted to know.'

Again, Taylor found himself disturbed by the show of emotion. 'We'll leave you,' he said. 'I'll give you my number; call me if you think of anything.'

They were standing at the car when Ruth ran out of the door to join them. Amanda was at the front window watching them.

'I want to talk to you,' Ruth said. Her eyes were very red. 'But not here. Not with my mother around.'

'Where then?'

'There's a coffee shop in the main street in Heswall. It's open until seven. I'll see you there in an hour. I'll tell her I'm meeting my boyfriend.'

The last thing Taylor wanted was to kick his heels in the Wirral for an hour, but there was something so fierce about the demand to meet that he couldn't refuse.

The girl turned up ten minutes late, looking harassed and drawn. The coffee shop was one of a chain, all brown leather sofas, piped bland music and hissing machines. Taylor stood up to buy her a coffee and when he got back from the counter with her cappuccino she was already deep in conversation with Jebson.

'Ruth's been in contact with her father recently,' Jebson said. 'That was what she wanted to talk to us about.'

'Why did he get in touch with you?' Taylor asked.

'He didn't. I found him.'

'How?'

'Interact, his theatre company, came to do a gig at school. Drug awareness. You know the sort of thing. He wasn't there but his name was all over the publicity and there was a phone number. I knew he'd gone into acting, thought it was probably a coincidence, but I gave him a ring anyway. Plucked up courage when I had an afternoon's study leave and no one was about.

I didn't tell my mother. I knew she'd go ape. She'd just be worried about him pissing me about . . . And I didn't want to hurt John, my stepdad. I love him to bits.'

'What did you say when you phoned?' Jebson seemed genuinely interested.

'"I think you might be my father." Something like that. I thought, Why not go for the direct approach?'

'Was he pleased to hear from you?'

'I think it was a shock, but yeah, he said he was pleased. We were on the phone for ages talking. It cost me a fortune – it was my mobile and he never thought to call me back. Classic Dad.'

'What did you talk about?'

'Oh, you know, it was just catching up. What he'd been doing. Where I was at in school. Plans for the future, that sort of thing.'

'What were his plans for the future?' Taylor asked.

'He said he was going away. To Shetland. He asked if I'd ever been there and I said I hadn't. To be honest, I wasn't even sure where it was. I went on to the computer later and looked the islands up. He said they were beautiful. Very bleak but beautiful. He couldn't wait to go back.'

'Did he say why he was going?'

'Basically business, he said. He was going to do some work there. Not really the sort of gig he usually took on, but it would give him a chance to catch up with old friends.'

'Did he mention the names of the friends?'

'I don't think so. If he did I don't remember.' She'd been speaking very quickly, answering Taylor's questions as soon as they were asked, but now she paused. 'We'd arranged to meet. He was going to come here when he got back. He said he wanted to be a proper father again, to help me follow my dreams.' She looked up and smiled at them. 'That was how he spoke, the sort of thing he said. I'd emailed a photo of myself, so he'd know me. And there's a picture of him on his website. It was weird to see him after all these years of imagining what he'd look like. There's a resemblance, don't you think? You'd know I was his daughter.'

She paused. 'I phoned him at home a few days ago. I thought he should be back by then. Some woman answered.'

They were on their way back to Yorkshire when Taylor took the call from Sandy Wilson, saying there'd been another death. He dropped Jebson in Huddersfield and began the drive north. Excited to be on the move again, but sick that he wasn't there to take control.

Chapter Thirty

Perez went straight from Fran's house to collect Taylor from the airport at Sumburgh. It was a gusty, showery day, with brief flashes of sunshine, then the shadows of clouds blown across the flat land around the runways. The water at Grutness was choppy, blown into thousands of little waves which scattered the light, but the wind wasn't strong enough to cause a delay. He arrived a little early and sat in the terminal building drinking coffee. A group of Japanese tourists waited for the plane.

Perez had stayed in Biddista until Roddy's body had been lifted out of the Pit on a stretcher. He felt the boy deserved that, and, opening the body bag to look at him, he had the strange sense that for the first time he was seeing Roddy Sinclair in the flesh. Before, it had all been image, glossy and unreal as a magazine advert. By the time he had got to Ravenswick it was four in the morning and as bright as midday. Fran was asleep, must have been disturbed by dreams, because she'd thrown off the covers and lay, naked, on top of the twisted sheet. There was a white blind at the bedroom window and she looked somehow smudged, like one of her own paintings, in the filtered light.

He straightened the sheet and pulled it on top of

her, then slid in beside her. It seemed like an unforgivable intrusion, but he didn't want to wake her and he was exhausted. Her skin was cool and smooth. She stirred and smiled at him, wrapped herself around him. They both slept very deeply and were lying in exactly the same position when the television in the next room woke them. Cassie was singing along to a Saturday-morning children's programme.

'You do realize,' Fran said, 'that this will be all round Ravenswick School on Monday morning?'

'I'm sorry, I should have thought.' He wasn't sure now what he should have thought. She'd invited him, after all. Did she not want it known that they were seeing each other?

'Don't worry. They think I'm a scarlet woman anyway.' And she pulled on jeans and a sweatshirt and went to make tea.

Later they had pancakes for breakfast, with syrup and chocolate sauce. Cassie, still in her pyjamas, was getting silly and excited because of the novelty of the treat. But all the time he was wishing that he knew exactly what Fran was thinking and that he had some rules to follow. This relationship was so important to him and he didn't want to get things wrong. Maybe I should ask her to marry me, he thought suddenly. Then at least I'd know where I was. The idea was at once tantalizing and ludicrous, so he found himself grinning. Fran asked him what he was laughing about.

'Nothing,' he said. 'I'm happy. That's all.'

When Taylor walked into the terminal he seemed surprisingly alive and energetic. He said he'd had a few hours' sleep in the hotel at Dyce and now what he really wanted was caffeine and carbs and he'd be fit for anything. Perez took him into the Sumburgh Hotel. The bar was quiet; the barman, a gaunt Englishman who'd lived in Shetland for so long that he spoke like a native, was chatting in a low voice to an old man sitting on a tall stool. Taylor ordered a burger and a Coke and when that was finished he couldn't stop talking. Perez was reminded of Cassie, bouncing around the kitchen in Ravenswick, full of sugar and E numbers.

'I found Booth's wife and daughter. Nice lass. She hadn't seen him since he left, but recently they'd got in touch. The mother didn't know.'

'Are we sure the mother hadn't found out the girl had tracked him down?' Perez was hesitant. 'It would be a dramatic way to stop the father having contact with the girl, but I suppose we should consider it.'

Taylor paused for a moment. Thoughts chased each other across his face like the cloud shadows outside.

'I don't know,' he said at last. 'I hadn't seen that as a possibility. If the mother *was* involved she's a better actor than Booth ever was. She couldn't have done it personally. She was at home looking after her family.'

'What else did you learn from the daughter?'

'That Booth definitely had friends in Shetland. That was what he told the girl. He was mixing business with pleasure, taking the chance to catch up on old friends.'

'Someone he met when he was here working on the theatre boat, maybe,' Perez said. 'I've contacted the management of the boat, *The Motley Crew*. He did a couple of tours of the northern isles in the early nineties. Must have been soon after he ran away from his wife. The company have no record of him working here after that. But he kept in touch with them.'

'Could he have had a fling with Bella Sinclair?' Taylor said. It had been on his mind. Perez imagined him in the plane working over the scenario. Now his voice was eager. 'You could see it. They're around the same age. Two arty types together. The relationship obviously didn't work out for some reason, but that could be our link.'

'And that's why he tried to sabotage her exhibition?' Perez kept his voice even. Taylor took offence easily and didn't like to be contradicted. 'He'd kept a grudge after all this time?'

'People do,' Taylor said. 'But you're right, of course. Something must have happened to bring him back. But what?'

'Had he had any contact from Shetland? Phone calls? Email?'

'No phone calls to his landline, we know that. I haven't heard about the emails. We need to get that sorted.' Taylor leaned back in his chair and punched a number into his phone. Perez watched from the other side of the table, felt mildly embarrassed as he harangued some poor DC in West Yorkshire to fast-track the information. Which would probably mean, Perez thought, that it would go right to the bottom of the pile. Just out of spite. People wouldn't take to being spoken to like that.

'So where does Roddy Sinclair fit in?' Perez asked. Taylor had subsided in his seat, suddenly quiet after the ranting. 'He'd only have been a child when Booth was last here.'

'We are sure he was murdered?'

'I'm sure,' Perez said, realizing as he spoke how arrogant that might sound. 'Impossible forensically to tell the difference between murder, suicide and accident. He fell and he smashed his skull. But he knew the cliffs very well. He grew up there. And he was all set to get the plane south. You were with me when he talked about it. His car was loaded up. Something must have taken him out on to the hill.'

'The murderer arranged to meet him there?'

'That's how I read it.'

'Nobody saw him that afternoon?'

'They say not. Sandy's been in Biddista this morning talking to people.'

'I'd like to give it another go. I still don't feel I've got a handle on the place.' Taylor leaned forward, his old intense self. 'Come with me, Jimmy. You'll get more out of them than I will on my own.'

So Perez found himself back in Biddista, parked again by the Herring House, all his attention focused on three ordinary families and Peter Wilding, to whom he'd taken an irrational dislike.

Saturday was the Herring House's busiest day. There was a coach outside and a party of elderly Americans was climbing out and trooping into the gallery. Perez supposed there was another cruise ship in Lerwick. Upstairs the café was full. They took one look in and decided it would be impossible to get Martin Williamson's attention now. Perez had expected the place to be closed as a mark of respect, but he suspected Bella hadn't given the gallery a thought and

Martin had decided there were so many people booked in that it would be easier to stay open.

The post office had just shut and they found Aggie at home. She was in the garden taking washing from the line. Perez held out his arms to help her fold the sheets and they stood for a moment in silence, the sheet stretched between them, while Taylor watched as if they were performing a ritual dance. Inside she moved the kettle on to the hotplate.

'You'll have heard about Roddy,' Perez said. He thought she looked very tired, more timid and mouse-like than ever.

'That he's dead. No details. The Whalsay lad that came to talk to me this morning was all questions and no answers.'

'Roddy was found at the bottom of the Pit o' Biddista. You'll have heard that. We don't know how he got there. We need to find out. You do see, Aggie?'

'I do,' she said. 'Poor Bella. I know what it's like to live with uncertainty. But there are some things you can never know.'

'You didn't see him yesterday?'

'Not on the hill. He came into the post office in the morning.'

'What did he want?'

'To buy some sweeties to take on the plane with him,' she said. 'He had a very sweet tooth, you ken, Jimmy. Just like a peerie boy.'

'Did you have any sort of conversation?'

'I asked him when he'd be back. I know he offended people. Dawn didn't like the way he kept dragging Martin into Lerwick to parties; all the young girls threw themselves at Roddy and maybe she

259

thought Martin would get caught up with the same sort of thing. I told her she didn't need to worry. Martin has more sense and he loves her to bits. It's good for him to have a pal. He doesn't get so much company out here. Roddy said he was doing a show in the Town Hall in Lerwick in six weeks' time and he'd be back for that. He was quiet, thoughtful, but he didn't seem depressed. I thought maybe he was starting to grow up.' She paused. 'Have you seen Bella?'

'Only last night.'

'I don't know how she'll cope with this,' Aggie said. 'That boy was her life.'

They left her sitting in the rocking chair in the kitchen, reading a novel, its cover showing a young woman with a shawl thrown over her head, staring into the distance.

In the adjoining house Dawn was sitting with a pile of marking while Alice played with a doll's house on the floor. It was a big house and the front came off completely so they could see all the rooms. The child held a tiny doll in one hand and moved her from room to room, talking to herself as she played out an imaginary conversation in her head. Perez and Taylor watched her for a moment through the window from the pavement. Dawn was frowning at something one of the children had written. Suddenly she became aware of their standing there and waved them to come in. She stood up to greet them and Perez thought he could see the first sign of her pregnancy.

'This'll be about Roddy,' she said. 'Everyone's talking about it. The phone hasn't stopped ringing. Come away into the kitchen. I don't want Alice listening in.'

They followed her into a room the same size and

shape as Aggie's, but about fifty years away in time. There was a microwave on the bench, a juicer and coffee maker. Perez couldn't imagine that anyone would be baking in this kitchen.

'Do you think Roddy was murdered too?' she asked as soon as the door was shut. They could sense her panic. 'What's going on here? I'm even thinking of taking Alice away until we know what's happened. I don't feel safe. I wish it was already the end of term. I could go and visit my parents.'

'We can't know,' Taylor said. 'Not for certain.'

'It's the uncertainty I hate.'

'Booth, the guy who was hanged, came from the same part of the country as you,' Perez said. The thought had come into his head and he spoke without considering how she might take the remark.

'I didn't know him! Yorkshire's a big county.'

'He ran a small theatre company, worked out of a village called Denby Dale.'

Dawn shrugged but didn't answer.

'Did you see Roddy Sinclair yesterday?'

'Sandy's already been here and asked that. I was at work till gone five, came back and cooked a meal for Alice and me, put her to bed and watched television until Martin came in from work. He was at the Herring House all night, in case you want to know what he was doing too.'

She seemed niggly and out of sorts. Perhaps she'd been feeling sick and tired. Sarah had been like that in the early stages of pregnancy. Everyone had said it was a good sign, the hormones working properly. Then she'd lost the baby at fourteen weeks. Perez would have liked to tell Dawn that these questions weren't personal. Everyone would be asked the same. But perhaps at a time like this her feelings weren't so important.

'Do you know why anyone would want to kill Roddy?' he asked. 'He and Martin were friends. Roddy would tell him, wouldn't he, if anything was bothering him?'

'Maybe,' she said. 'When he was drunk. But you'd take everything he told you with a pinch of salt. He was just a little boy showing off.'

Chapter Thirty-one

It had been Taylor's decision to spend the afternoon in Biddista, but now he wasn't sure what good he was doing there. They'd drunk lots of tea, that was certain. He'd be pissing every five minutes by the time he got back to his hotel. It seemed to him that the first two interviews with the women hadn't pushed the case forward at all. Their lives were so quiet and domestic. He thought Perez was wasting his time with them.

After leaving Dawn Williamson they went on to the writer's house. Perez paused for a moment outside before knocking. The Shetlander's hesitancy was starting to get to Taylor. It was as if Perez never had the courage of his convictions. He needs to sharpen up, Taylor thought. He'd never survive in the real world beyond the Pentland Firth. Then it occurred to him that here, in this bizarre, bleak, treeless community, Perez's strange methods might actually get results.

Wilding led them upstairs to his workroom. Beside the computer there was a pile of paper, a typescript covered in scribbled notes. His focus still seemed drawn to it and his offer of coffee lacked any real warmth. It seemed as if he wanted them to go so he could get on with his work.

'I get so caught up in the detail of a book,' he said. 'I lose the overall picture, the story I set out to tell.'

'We're here to talk about Roddy Sinclair,' Taylor said. How self-centred could you get? he thought. A young man was dead and this guy was stressing about a fairy tale. Taylor was an obsessive himself and recognized the signs.

'How can I help?' For the first time Wilding seemed to give them his full attention. 'It's such terrible news. I can't imagine what Bella must be going through. I wondered if I should call on her. What do you think? I don't know what the convention is here.'

'She'd probably be glad to hear from you,' Perez said. 'Maybe leave it for another day.'

'I spoke to your colleague this morning. I don't think I can help any more.'

'He'll have asked, I expect, if you saw Roddy yesterday.'

'I saw him in the morning. From the window here. He walked down the street to the post office.'

'And then he came back?'

'I didn't notice that. He was probably chatting to Aggie and then I was concentrated on my writing. This problem which has been haunting me for several days.' Again his eyes flicked to the manuscript on his desk. 'He must have come back. There's no other way to the Manse, but I didn't see him.'

'We've identified the man who was killed here at the jetty,' Perez said. 'His name was Jeremy Booth.'

Taylor thought Wilding expressed a brief moment of recognition. 'Do you know him?'

Wilding frowned. 'The name sounded familiar for a moment. But I had an agent called Booth once. Perhaps that was it. I had to sack him. His name was Norman. Probably no relation to the victim.'

'This is a serious matter.' There was an edge to Perez's voice which surprised Taylor. 'Are you sure you've never heard of the man?'

'No,' Wilding replied. 'I don't think I have. Sorry. I didn't mean to sound flippant.'

Taylor thought he didn't sound sorry either.

'How did you come to live in Biddista?'

'I think I explained before that I've always admired Bella's work. I wrote to her years ago to tell her how much pleasure I took from her paintings and we began a correspondence.' He paused, saw that more explanation was required. 'I've recently separated. My partner left me. It was unexpected, to me at least. I'd thought we were happy. But she'd been seeing someone else. I had a sort of breakdown. I even spent a couple of weeks in hospital.' He stopped and looked over to where they were sitting. 'Perhaps you know all this already. I suppose you check the backgrounds of people close to a murder case.'

Not well enough, Taylor thought. Obviously. He felt the old anger at a job not properly done.

Wilding continued. 'I suppose I behaved rather badly. I followed my partner. Sent her flowers and presents. Tried to persuade her to change her mind. Her lawyer called it harassment, though I didn't see it that way. I was never charged with an offence but she took out an injunction to stop me bothering her. I thought it would be safest to move away.' He smiled briefly at Taylor, who seemed the most sympathetic of his listeners. 'Shetland was about as far away as I could get.'

He seemed strangely unemotional now, talking about the obsession, the injunction. He could have been describing someone else.

'What was your girlfriend's name?' Taylor tried to keep his voice even, but he allowed himself a tentative excitement; this held the possibility of some sort of motive.

'Helen. Helen Adams.'

'And her new partner?'

'Jason Doyle. A rather vulgar name, I thought. It was a surprise when I found out he was a lawyer. I'm sorry to disappoint you, inspector. He wasn't called Booth, and he's a creature of the inner city. I don't suppose he'd ever choose to visit Shetland. I haven't killed anyone.'

'What are your plans for the future, Mr Wilding?' Perez again, crisp and clipped. He was being sharp enough now, Taylor thought. Perhaps it was because he was dealing with an incomer and he wasn't so involved.

The writer answered immediately. 'I'd like to settle here. Make a fresh start. My partner and I never had children. There's nothing to take me back.'

'How did you come to rent Willy's house?' Perez dropped in the question as an afterthought.

'Didn't you know? Bella owns it. The council sold off all these houses some years ago. Willy was given the option to buy, but he'd already retired and couldn't raise the mortgage. She gave him the money. Security and a rent-free home for the old man, and an investment for her. He doesn't have any family. Recently he moved into sheltered housing. When I emailed her that I was looking for a short-term let in Shetland, she offered it to me.'

Taylor wondered why that fact hadn't come to light before. Perez was supposed to know these people, everything about them. But then, could it have any importance? Another small domestic detail. Nothing likely to lead to murder. It was time to move on.

Perez, though, seemed reluctant to leave the writer.

'Did you go out yesterday evening?'

'Not on to the hill. Only for a walk on the beach.' Wilding looked directly at the Shetlander. 'If I could help you, inspector, I would. I liked Roddy. He was young and irresponsible, but he didn't take himself too seriously. He made people laugh. More than that, Bella doted on him and I'd do anything in the world to make her happy.' His face softened. Taylor thought he was besotted. That obsessive streak again.

He moved over to take a seat in front of the computer, to show them that he wanted to go back to work.

Outside on the road, Perez said abruptly that he needed to get back to Lerwick. He had an appointment he couldn't cancel. If Taylor wanted to continue questioning the community, he'd arrange for a car to pick him up later. Of course Sandy had already spoken to everyone. The implication was that Taylor was unlikely to come up with anything new and it was all rather a waste of time.

Taylor forgot that earlier he too had thought there was little to be gained by talking to the Biddista residents. He saw this as a chance to beat Perez on his home ground. He sensed an edge in the competition. 'I'll just pay a visit to Miss Sinclair,' he said. 'I know you talked to her yesterday, but she should be calmer now. She might remember more.'

It was late afternoon on a Saturday. In Inverness Taylor hated the weekends when he wasn't working. He didn't know what to do with himself. He hadn't made friends there; somehow he'd always known he wouldn't be staying and that had made him keep people at arm's length. Suddenly the exile in the highlands seemed pointless. What was the point of spiting his father, even though he was no longer alive?

He was so wrapped up in these thoughts that he arrived at the Manse without realizing. He rang the bell and heard the tinny ring inside. The door was opened by a woman he didn't recognize. She was wiry, smartly dressed. His first thought was that she might be a housekeeper or cleaner, but that was dispelled by the calm air of authority when she spoke.

'If you're a reporter, Miss Sinclair isn't speaking to anyone.'

Taylor thought the woman could be a member of Perez's team, an officer he hadn't yet met. He introduced himself and she invited him in. As if she were doing him a favour, not that he was there by right.

'We haven't met,' she said. 'I'm Edith Thomson. I thought Bella needed someone with her.'

'Of course. A time like this she'll need her friends.'

Edith looked at him thoughtfully. 'We're not exactly friends. But I couldn't leave her alone at a time like this. I was imagining how I'd feel if I'd lost one of my children.'

'He was her nephew,' Taylor said. 'Not quite the same.'

'It felt the same to her.'

'Your husband found the body. Both bodies.'

She looked at him. Through him. Decided to ignore the challenge under the words. 'I know. It'll haunt him for ever. He's already having nightmares.'

'Can I speak to Miss Sinclair?'

She shrugged. 'You can try. She's been drinking.'

They went into a room Taylor hadn't seen before. A rather grand living room at the front of the house with a view over the water. The windows were long, with folded shutters in the French style. The furniture was old and a little shabby. Bella was half sitting, half lying on a chaise-longue. There was a small table with a glass and a bottle beside her. She was drinking whisky.

When she saw Taylor, she half stood, an attempt at the old charm, then fell back on to the seat.

'Inspector.'

'Would you like me to leave you alone?' Edith asked.

'No, stay.' Bella made an extravagant gesture with her arm. 'Please stay. Edith and I have known each other for years, haven't we? Do you remember when you first came to Biddista? Weren't we all pals, the six of us?'

'Six of you?' Taylor was still finding it hard to come to grips with the relationships within the place. I should write it all down, he thought. Make a chart. The sort of list Wilding had on his desk for all his characters.

'My brother Alec, Aggie Watt, Kenny and Edith and Lawrence and me.'

Taylor turned to Edith. 'Who's Lawrence?' The name was familiar but he couldn't place it.

'He's Kenny's brother. He left Shetland years ago. We've lost touch.'

'Of course. I should have remembered. Your husband thought he might be the man who was hanged. Why did he leave Shetland? Some sort of family feud?'

'No,' she said awkwardly. 'Nothing like that.'

'They think it was my fault that Lawrence left.' It was Bella, talking too loudly, as if she were giving a performance. 'They think he was madly in love with me and I spurned him and he was so heartbroken that he ran away.'

'Well?' Edith asked. 'Wasn't it a little like that? Kenny could never understand why Lawrence left like that, so suddenly. He still misses him. When the phone rings he thinks it could be his brother. He doesn't say anything, but I can tell what he's thinking.'

Taylor had a picture of Kenny Thomson standing in the mortuary, his relief when he discovered the body looked nothing like his brother.

'No,' Bella said. 'It wasn't like that at all.'

'So tell us,' Taylor said. 'What was it like?'

'I loved Lawrence. If he'd asked me to marry him, I'd have accepted. I had my wedding dress designed in my head, and the hymns for the service chosen. But he never asked me. We were great friends, but he wasn't the marrying kind. He wanted to see more of the world than Shetland and I wasn't going to leave. The islands were my inspiration, and besides, I had Roddy to think about. If Lawrence was crazy about me, as everyone says, why didn't he want to settle with me and make a family with me?'

She looked at them with a haunted desperation, which was only partly to do with the drink. Taylor thought how much energy she must have put in over the years, putting on a brave face. It suited her for people to think she'd been the one to reject Lawrence Thomson. At least that way she'd managed to maintain her pride.

'He never contacted you either?' Edith asked.

Bella shook her head. She'd started to cry. 'Kenny's not the only one who has a flicker of hope every time the phone rings.'

She wiped her eyes. Taylor found himself thinking that part of her was enjoying the drama. He wished he knew how much of it was real.

'Tell me about your relationship with Mr Wilding,' he said.

'I don't have a relationship with him.'

'He's your tenant?'

'Yes.'

'But that's Willy's house,' Edith said.

'It's Willy's house but I gave him the money when the council gave him the right to buy. He gave me the house when he moved into the sheltered housing. All legal and above board. I wanted to give him a bit of security. I didn't need his rent. I told him he was looking after my investment for me.'

'I didn't know.'

'There are lots of things about me folk don't know.' Bella dabbed at her eyes with a tissue. 'I gave him the money. He got into a state when the council gave him the right to buy, thought they might throw him out.

ANN CLEEVES

He said he wanted to stay there until he died. Such a
shame he couldn't manage on his own in the end. It
was Roddy's idea to give him the money to buy the
house. He loved Willy. The nearest he ever had to a
grandfather, I suppose. You know how good he was
with the children.'

'Yes,' Edith said. 'He was the same with Kenny and
Lawrence and then with our two. Perhaps it was
because he'd never quite grown up.'

'Why did you suggest Mr Wilding live there?'

'Willy had moved out and I didn't know what to do
with it. I didn't want to sell. Not while Willy was alive.
I always told him it would be there for him to move
back when he felt more himself. And I suppose I
hoped Roddy would want to settle in Shetland one day.
It would be a good home for him to start with. Then I
had the email from Peter Wilding asking if I knew anywhere he could rent for a short while. He'd not been
well and he needed somewhere quiet to stay. I thought
why not?' She paused. 'Besides, he was a fan. As you
get older, it's good occasionally for the ego to have an
admirer close at hand.'

'How did Roddy get on with him?'

'I don't think Roddy liked him particularly. Sometimes he took against people for no reason. Roddy said
it always made him feel sad to think of that house
without Willy in it, but that was hardly Peter's fault.
Roddy loved the old man and visited there whenever
he came home from tour. Take a bottle of whisky and
stay up half the night talking about old times. He said
he'd heard Willy's stories hundreds of times but he
never tired of them. He still kept in contact even after
Willy moved into the sheltered housing. That's a part

of his life the press never picked up on.'

Suddenly she got to her feet, more sober than she'd seemed throughout the rest of the encounter. She carried the whisky bottle to a sideboard and put it away. 'I'm going to make coffee,' she said. 'Would anyone like one? Edith, you don't need to stay, you know. I'm quite used to being on my own.'

Chapter Thirty-two

The appointment Perez couldn't miss was the final performance on *The Motley Crew*. He'd invited Fran and Cassie before Roddy's body had been discovered. Fran would understand if he cried off but he'd decided, suddenly, sitting listening to Dawn, that he should be there. If he pulled out this time it would set a precedent for other occasions, other times when there were pressing things to do at work. He wanted to be part of a family again.

He collected them from Ravenswick. Cassie was wearing a new pink cardigan and Fran had put on make-up and the earrings he'd given her for her birthday. I should have made more of an effort, he thought. It seemed as if he'd been wearing the same clothes for days. The show took place in the saloon below deck, so the audience were crammed into seats very close together. As Lucy Wells had said, it was packed. Mostly families, mostly visitors. It still smelled of a boat, wood with a hint of tar. And they could feel the movement of the water under them.

The show was an environmental piece aimed mostly at the children. There were songs about the rainforest and melting ice floes, but enough of a pacy story to keep Cassie enthralled. Lucy played a green fairy, dressed mostly in emerald Lycra with a couple of wispy wings. Perez found his eyes drawn towards her, became lost for a moment in a sexy fantasy, thought of the possibilities that would be closed to him if he was committed to Fran.

After the show the actors jumped down from the low stage and mixed with the audience, following up some of the issues raised in the piece. Lucy came up to Perez.

'You made it,' she said. 'I didn't think you would.' She seemed extraordinarily pleased to see him. Perhaps that's what actors do, he thought, disconcerted. They exaggerate without meaning to. She was playing with some green glass beads she wore round her neck and he saw that her hands were plump and soft.

'Did you enjoy it?'

'Very much.' He paused and saw that a compliment was in order. 'You were very good.'

'It's not a role that requires much characterization,' she said, smiling. 'Fun, though.'

He was flattered by her attention. There were all these people to speak with and she'd chosen him. Beyond her, he could see Cassie and Fran chatting to friends.

'When do you leave?' he asked.

'Tomorrow afternoon.' Something in her reply made him think that if he suggested they might spend the evening together she would agree. That she'd be delighted. He was horrified that the thought had even crossed his mind.

'Good luck,' he said to Lucy. 'I hope everything goes well for you. When you're famous, I'll be able to tell folk I met you.'

He moved away from her and put his arm around Fran's shoulder, asked her in a whisper if she was ready to leave. Later, he wondered if it was a good thing he'd done, walking away from a lonely young woman who wanted his company, or if he was just a coward.

That night he stayed at Fran's place again. While she prepared supper he sat on Cassie's bed and read her a story. She was asleep by the time it was finished and he stayed for a moment, thinking how it must be for her, having a new man in her mother's life. And how it would work for him, sharing her with Duncan Hunter, her father, a man he didn't much care for, though once they had been best friends.

Back in the kitchen Fran was draining rice. Her face was flushed. She'd taken off her jacket and was wearing a sleeveless white T-shirt. He could see the lacy pattern of her bra in relief through the fabric. Distracted, he returned to the subject of her ex-husband.

'What will Duncan make of us seeing so much of each other?'

She tipped the rice into a brown earthenware bowl.

'I like everything I've seen of you. If you're talking literally . . .'

'I'm being serious.'

'You're way too serious. It's my mission to get you to lighten up. Anyway, who cares what Duncan thinks? It's none of his business.'

'Cassie's his business.'

'I'd never stop him seeing Cassie and neither would you.'

He could tell she thought he was making difficulties where none existed. In London she'd been surrounded by unconventional families. She'd told him about close lesbian friends who'd fostered a son; many of her colleagues were divorced and remarried, and for them weekends had been a time of shared parenting, the entertainment of visiting stepchildren. He was used to more traditional ways, but didn't want to question her judgement. He didn't want her to think him narrow-minded.

The subject must have been on her mind throughout the evening, because at the end of the meal she returned to it. She reached across the table and took his hand.

'It was because of Cassie I didn't rush into this. We come as a package. You understand that, don't you? If you want me, you take her on too.'

He said that of course he understood. He wanted to tell her that he wanted above all things to make a family with her and Cassie, but he thought that would have sounded sentimental. She hated it when he was soppy.

He left early the next morning to go into Lerwick, to his narrow house on the waterfront. Despite the weather, he could smell the damp as soon as he unlocked the door. It was as if he'd been away for weeks. He loved the house, which was just as well, because no one else would be foolish enough to pay good money for it. He opened all the windows to let in the salt air, and checked his answer machine. There was a message from his mother, easy and chatty with news of Fair Isle. He wondered when he should take Fran home to meet his folks and what they would make of her. They didn't have much experience of people who'd grown up in the city. He made a jug of coffee and sat by the open window, watching the terns diving into the shallow water.

Later he went into the station to check if they'd had any report back on the bag belonging to Jeremy Booth, which had been recovered with Roddy Sinclair's body from the Pit o' Biddista. Sandy was on his way out, scrubbed and smart. Every week he went home to Whalsay to take Sunday lunch with his parents.

'Have you seen the TV news?' he said. 'Roddy Sinclair was all over it.'

'No.' Perez didn't keep him. He knew Sandy would be on his way to Vidlin for the ferry, and anyway he wasn't the best person to ask about the bag. He was never brilliant at detail.

The incident room was quiet, flooded with midday sunshine. Taylor was at his desk in a corner, drinking coffee, looking as if he'd been there all night.

'Good night?'

Perez couldn't quite tell if he was really interested or if that was a sneer. 'Sorry, to leave you in Biddista. Like I said, it was something I couldn't get out of. How did you get on with Bella?'

'She was pissed. Talking about old times. Lost loves.'

'Oh?'

'Kenny's brother, Lawrence.'

'The way I heard it, he loved her, not the other way round.'

'Not according to Bella Sinclair.' Taylor crushed the polystyrene cup in his fist and hurled it across the room into a waste basket. It hit with such force that it bounced out. 'According to her, she'd have married him like a shot if he'd asked. But he never did.' He got up and retrieved the cup. 'I finally met Kenny's wife. Edith. She seemed surprised by the new twist on the old story too. Hardly bosom pals, those two, are they?'

'Those sorts of communities, people come together if there's a tragedy.' Perez spoke without really thinking about it.

'Nobody seemed much concerned about Booth.'

'He was an outsider. A bit different.'

'That stuff about the past doesn't help much anyway,' Taylor said. 'If any of them met Jeremy Booth when he was here on *The Motley Crew* all those years ago, they're not saying.'

'Maybe they don't remember. People change in fifteen years.' Perez still thought there was a history to this case.

'Perhaps.' But Taylor sounded sceptical.

'Anything on the contents of Booth's bag?'

'I've just had the report. It gives us a definite confirmation that he was the person handing out the flyers cancelling the art exhibition. The found the costume and the sequinned bag some of the witnesses described. Nothing else of much use. Just a few clothes and toilet things. No letters, no address book. No mobile.'

'Booth didn't have a mobile with him when he staged that scene at the Herring House,' Perez said. 'I checked his pockets for ID.'

'Could it have been thrown separately down the hole?' Taylor asked.

'Maybe. Then sucked into the tunnel. Or washed out to sea.'

'Worth getting a search team down to take a look? Even if the phone's damaged, there's a chance the SIM card is still intact. Might be quicker than trying to track down his account with the phone companies, especially if he had one of the pay-as-you-go deals.'

'I know a couple of climbers,' Perez said. 'I'll ask them to go down for us. I could scramble to the bottom of the grass slope myself, but I'd not be confident to go through the tunnel, and it could be wedged on a ledge in the rockface.' He knew he should have thought of the phone himself. His head was too full of personal stuff. He was losing concentration.

Before he could forget, he went through to his office and called a friend who volunteered with the Cliff Rescue. She couldn't make the climb that day, but said she'd sort something out for Monday if that would do. The tides were low now, so if the phone was down there it wouldn't be shifting anywhere.

Back in the incident room, Taylor was still at his desk, staring at the computer screen as if he could force it to provide answers just through the effort of his will.

'We need to find a link between Booth and some-one at Biddista,' he said. 'That's all it'll take.' He swivelled round in his chair so he was facing Perez. 'Fancy a pint? I'm going crazy sitting here.'

Perez hesitated. In the previous case they'd worked on together, he'd enjoyed the informal con-tact, Taylor's relentless energy. But Fran would be waiting for him. 'I thought I'd take a run out to the Sunday teas in Middleton, see if I can find the lass who sold the masks. Maybe it's not so important now, but it'd tie up a loose end.'

He waited for Taylor to ask if he could come too. He was like a hyperactive boy who needed constant stimulation. But the Sunday teas were too tame for him and he turned back to the computer screen.

The hall in Middleton had been the school before the new smart place was built. Perez parked in what had once been the playground, next to a row of trestle tables where a big woman was selling plants. Fran was with him. Cassie was spending the afternoon with Duncan.

He'd asked Fran the night before if she'd like to come with him to the teas. He hadn't thought she'd be interested. Usually she spent the days when Cassie was away working, and he'd thought she'd be used to more sophisticated entertainments. 'Are you joking? Of course I want to come. It's shopping, isn't it? I'm a shopaholic and I've been seriously deprived since moving here.'

And as soon as they got out of the car she pulled him over to look at the plants, although she had no garden in Ravenswick. Her house was surrounded on all sides by the hill.

Inside the hall there were more stalls. Junk and bric-à-brac and hand-knitted sweaters. At the other end of the room tables were laid out for tea with plates of home-bakes. Middleton women in aprons were wielding huge metal teapots. Urns hissed. It reminded him of the dances at home. Pooled baking and flustered women serving the men. What would Fran make of that?

Again she went immediately to the stalls, picking up pieces of china to look at the marks on the bottom, shaking out a jumper to see if it might fit Cassie, chatting to the women who were selling. Dawn Williamson came in with Alice holding her hand. She saw Fran and went up to her. By now the noise level in the hall was so high that Perez couldn't make out what they were saying. It was like watching a mime. Suddenly Fran threw her arms around Dawn. Dawn's told her about the baby, he thought. What is she feeling? Then the two women separated. Dawn sat Alice at one of the tea tables with a carton of juice and a biscuit and Fran came back to him.

'Dawn's pregnant,' she said.

'I know. She told me when I went to the school to talk to her.'

'Lucky thing,' she said. But there was no passion behind the words so he didn't feel the pressure of expectation.

'The woman with the masks isn't here.' He was disappointed, but thought that since they'd found Booth's bag it didn't matter so much. Booth could have bought the mask anywhere. He'd have had it in the bag he'd left on the beach before the Herring House party. The murderer would have found it and put it over his face. Why anyone would want to do that was a different matter entirely.

'No,' Fran said. 'She just came that one week with all sorts of novelty goods. She doesn't live in Shetland. She was up visiting relatives for a few days. They let her have a stall because she was raising money for a children's hospice. Her mother-in-law is the lady who knits the sweaters and she'll give you the phone number if you ask. But she says she'd probably not be able to give you the names of the people who bought from her. Because she's not from here, she wouldn't be able to recognize them. One interesting thing though. The daughter-in-law lives in Yorkshire. So that might be where Booth bought it.'

'How did you find all that out?'

'I asked,' Fran said. 'Now I want a cup of tea. And home-made meringues.'

Chapter Thirty-three

Kenny postponed the clipping of the sheep until Monday. He couldn't have done it on Saturday, just after he'd found Roddy's body. He might not have thought much of the boy, but it was a matter of respect. Some things had to be done properly, whatever he made of the personalities involved. In the same way, it had been the right thing for Edith to spend Saturday at the Manse with Bella. She was grieving and couldn't be left on her own the state she was in. Edith was the only person in Biddista to calm her. Aggie was frail and nervy herself and Dawn, though she was capable enough, came from outside and wouldn't really understand what was needed.

He would have been able to get more of the boys out on Sunday to help, but he had a kind of superstition about working on Sundays. When he'd been growing up, nothing was done on the Lord's day. The women wouldn't have considered hanging washing on the lines and most of the preparation of the dinner was done the day before. Certainly there was no work outside on the croft. Kenny wasn't religious himself, but he liked to keep the old traditions. If Willy had still lived in his house it would have upset him to see the line of men crossing the hill on a Sunday morning.

He'd been a regular at the kirk in Middleton. One of the congregation would collect him each Sunday. Willy would be ready and waiting at the door, dressed in a suit which was quite shiny with wear. Kenny wondered if they still took him to the kirk from the sheltered housing. He hoped they did.

So there would be fewer men available to help on the hill on Monday; they all had their own work to go to. But if they missed a few sheep, he could go back later in the week and fetch them in. Edith had arranged to take the day's leave from the care centre so she would be there to help. He was grateful for that. He knew she'd been saving as much holiday as possible to go south when their grandchild arrived.

Martin Williamson came along. He'd opened the Herring House on Saturday, because it was always so busy and he'd heard nothing from Bella to the contrary. But when she'd found out she'd been furious and had insisted on closing the gallery and the restaurant for the rest of the week. He said he didn't mind as long as she continued to pay him and he'd be glad to help with the sheep. Kenny was surprised by his flippancy. He'd thought Martin and Roddy had been friends of a kind. But perhaps that was just the way he was, always making light of things. And there was a group of retired men, all from Unst, who still worked a bit of croft land as a hobby. They turned out for events like this and stood now outside the house, identical in their caps and boiler suits, talking about the old times, their dogs panting at their feet. Kenny could tell the men were happy to be there. It was such fine weather and they were glad to be useful.

Although he knew exactly what he planned to do

when he got on to the hill – he had almost as much experience as them – he asked their opinion, and nodded seriously when they told him the best line to take. Edith came out of the house to join them. She was wearing overalls and boots and had her hair tied away from her face. She'd caught the sun in the last few weeks of good weather and there was a pale mark where her hair usually hung. She carried the stick that his father had always used.

At the last minute Peter Wilding turned up. They'd just started up the track and he chased after them.

'I heard from Martin what you were up to. I wondered if you could use an extra pair of hands.'

'Of course,' Kenny said. 'The more the merrier.' It was true that the more people there were to cover the hill, the easier it was to round up all the sheep. There was less chance for the odd beast to escape. But he couldn't quite take to the man and he wished he wasn't there. He thought the writer was like some sort of parasite. He only wanted to be on the hill so he could write about it later. It was the first thing to spoil the day for him.

The second was seeing Perez and a young couple on the lip of the Pit o' Biddista. They weren't in the way to scare the sheep – Kenny and the others would be walking the animals away from them – but Kenny found them a distraction. He'd hoped today to forget about the man hanging in the shed on the jetty and Roddy Sinclair's twisted and broken body.

While the others lined up down the length of a gully to begin the walk, Kenny went up to talk to Perez. The young couple had climbing gear. He didn't understand that. If they wanted to get to the bottom, why not just go down the grass slope? They were young and fit.

'What are you doing?'

Perez turned very slowly to him. Kenny thought he was probably working out in his head how much to tell him. Instead he ignored the question.

'You're clipping today,' he said. 'If we get finished here in time I'll come and help you.'

'What's going on here?'

He thought Perez would refuse to answer again. But he said, 'I want a thorough search. Of the rockface and the tunnel at the bottom. There are some items that are still missing.'

'How long will this go on?' Kenny demanded. 'When will we be left in peace?'

'When I know what happened,' Perez said. 'When I know who killed two men.'

The young people had been ignoring the exchange and preparing for their climb. The woman was already at the edge of the cliff, leaning out, held by the nylon rope. Kenny turned away; if he had his back to them, perhaps he could pretend that none of this was happening.

He ran to catch up with the line of people walking slowly across the hill. The dogs chased between them, filling in the gaps. The men had their arms outstretched and whooped and called to move the sheep ahead of them. The ones at the end seemed a long way off, their voices lost in the thin air. Kenny stood beside Edith, who was waving the stick and yelling like the rest of them.

'What's going on up there?' She had to shout to be

heard above the noise of the men, the dogs and the sheep.

'Some sort of search. I don't know. I hate it. I hate all this happening so close to home.'

She seemed to be shouting back some words of comfort, but he couldn't make them out because of the noise.

They had the sheep gathered up in a circle of dry-stone with a rough wooden gate held across the gap and let them out one at a time for clipping. The old men sat with an animal each, turned on its back, the front legs held firm, and hand-clipped with sure firm bites until the fleece was free. Then the poor bald beast was let loose to run away. The men's hands were brown and soiled and calloused. Kenny looked at his own and saw that they were going much the same way. Edith's hands were soft and he thought she'd have a few blisters by the end of the day, but she was just as accurate as the men, and as strong as most of them too. She had a fine deft way with the clippers and she could keep her sheep calm. But she wasn't as quick as they were. Sometimes they looked over and teased her about how slow she was and she laughed back at them, not minding at all.

At midday she brought out flasks of tea and thick sandwiches made with cheese and a ham which she'd cooked herself. They ate, although their hands were still greasy with lanolin, just rubbing them on the cropped grass to get rid of the worst of the muck. Peter Wilding sat with them, but didn't join in much. He tried to clip one but held it away from him as if he was scared of it. Edith took it from him and finished it in the end. Kenny thought he was just listening to all the conversation. It was as if he was making notes in his head. Later he lay back in the grass with his eyes shut. He probably wasn't used to working in such a physical way.

Then the gate was opened and another animal released. When Edith had finished doing a dainty black ewe, she held the fleece up to show Kenny. 'I might have a go at spinning this,' she said, 'knit something for the baby, a soft toy. What do you think?' She was always thinking of what she could make for the children, things to remind them of home. In the shed at Skoles there was a skin she'd been preparing for the baby's bedroom. She'd rubbed it with alum to preserve it; later she'd comb out the wool until it was soft. On the floor of their living room they had three rugs she'd made in the same way.

They finished late in the afternoon. From where they'd been working there had been no view of the Pit o' Biddista and the climbers. Walking back to the house, Kenny expected Perez and the people to be gone. How long could it take? He hadn't taken seriously Perez's offer to help with the sheep. But when they rounded the curve in the land so they could see the cliff ahead of them Perez was still there, and there was a police Land-Rover, which had been driven as far as it could possibly go up the track. People standing in a· huddle as if they were waiting for something to happen. Kenny recognized the English detective who had flown up from Inverness.

Again he decided to pretend that none of this was happening and continued on his way towards the house. The old men took his lead and though they shot glances at the group by the cliff and whispered among themselves they didn't talk about it to him.

Wilding, though, was too curious just to walk past. He stared at the group of police officers and finally sauntered up to them, all arrogant as if he had as much right to be there as they did.

The rest of them were halfway down the track, too far away to hear the exchange, but they stopped to watch what was happening. In the end Kenny turned to watch too. He would look foolish, striding on down towards the house on his own.

The English detective moved away from the rest of the group and stopped the writer before he could get anywhere close to the edge of the hole. There was a brief conversation, then Wilding was sent away. With a flea in his ear, Kenny thought with some satisfaction.

'Well?' Martin asked. 'What are they all doing up there? Is it the giant's lassie they're after?'

Wilding obviously hadn't heard the story, because he just looked at Martin as if he were soft in the head. The old men chuckled.

'They won't tell me anything,' Wilding said. 'It's a crime scene and everyone should keep out. That's all the man would say. Actually, he was rather rude.'

Usually after a day on the hill Kenny slept suddenly and deeply, despite the light outside. But tonight he was unsettled. Edith had been restless as she always was, but at last had fallen asleep. Afraid of waking her again with his tossing and turning, in the end he got up. He pulled on his clothes and his boots and went

outside. It was as near to dark as it would get, everything grey and shadowy. He walked out on to the hill
a little way.

At night at this time of the year storm petrels and
Manx shearwaters flew into the cliffs to the nests they
made in the old rabbit burrows. When he was a boy,
Willy had taken him to show him. Kenny tried to picture the tiny petrels, small and ghost-like like bats in
the gloom, and thought he might walk up now to look
at them again. But as he approached he was aware of
a faint mechanical hum coming from the direction
of the Pit. A generator. The police must still be up
there. During the evening he'd heard vehicles coming
up and down the track. He couldn't face seeing them
and walked back towards his home. The noise of the
generator was faint, but Kenny found it menacing.
He wouldn't be able to clear his mind of it even inside
the house. He knew it would keep him awake all night.

Chapter Thirty-four

Perez had watched Kenny Thomson and his team of helpers cross the hill with envy. Bringing in the sheep for clipping reminded him of home. Fair Isle, the furthest south and the most remote island of the Shetland group. Famous for its knitting and for being an area on the shipping forecast. When he'd worked in the city, he'd lie awake at night and listen to the measured voice on the radio. *Fair Isle, Faroes, south-east Iceland. Easterly five to six, light rain, good.* And he'd picture Dave Wheeler, who farmed at Field. The man had come to the Isle after working in the South Atlantic and since Perez could remember had been the met. officer on the island. Before his retirement he'd looked after the airstrip and been one of the firefighters.

At one time Perez had thought Fair Isle was where his future lay. He'd take a croft there and when his father retired he'd become skipper of the mail boat, *The Good Shepherd.* His children would grow up on the isle and know it as well as he had done. Then earlier in the year the opportunity had arisen for him to move back. A croft had become available and he'd have had a good chance of getting it. His mother had been desperate to get him back, but he hadn't put in the application. Lethargy perhaps. A reluctance to leave his little house by the water. But more than that. He wasn't ready yet to give up his work. Policing was a challenge, even in Shetland, he'd realized. And although he'd only just met her, he'd dreamed even then he might get together with Fran. He didn't have any regrets.

The offer to help Kenny with the clipping had been an impulse, but he'd meant it. He'd enjoy the physical exertion after the stress of the inquiry. It might free his mind, pull out the tightness in his muscles. He turned back to the climbers, hoping that they wouldn't be long. If Booth's phone was there, surely they'd find it soon enough. The search area wasn't huge.

The climbers were a married couple called Sophie and Roger Moore. They'd come to Shetland first as students, liked it and stayed. Sophie was an accountant with Shetland Islands Council; Perez wasn't sure how Roger made a living. He watched them slide over the edge in turn. They moved slowly, stopping to pass a hand across the ledges where thrift or the mess of a bird's nest could be hiding the phone they were looking for. When they'd first arrived at the site they'd said it was easy enough, good practice, though Perez had convinced himself that it would be a waste of time for them. He was going through the motions to satisfy Taylor. He couldn't see that anything would be found. It was a sort of superstition for him, not to be too hopeful at times like this. He was glad Taylor had decided to have a day at his desk, pulling together all the information that had already come in. The wait would drive the Englishman frantic. Perez imagined him standing at the top, shouting ridiculous, meaningless instructions to the climbers below.

When they were out of his view, Perez moved around to the landward side of the Pit, where the grass slope was, so he could see them better across the space. He couldn't hear what the climbers were saying to each other. They were well down the cliff and although there was only a scattering of kittiwakes there, the birds were making a lot of noise. He thought now that there was probably some law about disturbing the birds in the breeding season. Should he have got permission? The thought distracted him for a moment – the numbers of breeding seabirds had declined, he didn't want to add to their problems – and when he looked again the couple had reached the floor of the cavern. He moved carefully to the edge of the grass slope and sat, looking down at them. Even here he felt slightly dizzy. The beginning of panic. He had regular nightmares about falling into space, about being sucked to the edge of a cliff.

Roger and Sophie were moving into the tunnel between the hole and the beach. It was dead low water, so there was no danger of being swept out to sea. The channel was narrow, but quite high, certainly tall enough for a man to walk along without stooping. It bulged slightly in the middle and from this view was shaped, Perez thought, like a giant eye of a needle. The bridge of rock that separated the Pit from the shore was about twenty feet thick, so that was how long the channel ran for. In the middle it would be dark, and the climbers had torches. Claustrophobia didn't hold the same terror for Perez as vertigo, but he was glad he wasn't with them. They waved to show they were on their way in.

While he waited for them, Perez worried at the

case. The sun was warm. In the far distance occasionally he could hear Kenny's party calling at the sheep.
He needed to find a motive for Booth's death before he
could move forward. Roddy's could be explained
because he'd been a witness to the first murder, or to
something leading up to it. But why would a Shetlander want to kill an Englishman who hadn't set foot
on the place for years? It made no sense. He thought
it must have been a Shetlander. They'd traced all the
outsiders who had been in Biddista that night. That
had been the focus for much of the work. The team
sitting in the incident room in Lerwick, on the phone
for hours at a time. 'I understand you visited the Herring House on midsummer's evening. Could you tell
me who was with you? What time did you leave? Did
you see anything unusual?' Then the alibis had to be
checked and cross-referenced. And they all checked
out. Every one.

He must have started to doze, because the shout
from below startled him. He realized suddenly how
close to the edge he was and could feel his pulse
racing. He put his palms flat on the grass at his side,
to make sure he was safely anchored to the ground.

'Jimmy! I think you'd better come down.' It was
Sophie. From this angle she looked all head and no
body. Her mouth was open very wide as she yelled to
him. A monster from the deep. The giant's mistress,
he thought, remembering the legend.

'Why?' He'd given them gloves and plastic evidence bags in case they found the phone.

'Really, Jimmy, you have to come down. You can
manage down the grass, can't you? You don't need a
rope if you come that way.'

Perez had avoided the climb when Roddy Sinclair was found. Sandy had taken care of the crime scene then. Now he saw he had no choice. Sophie was still looking at him.

He took off his jacket, folded it carefully and placed it on the grass, feeling a little like a man who decides to commit suicide by drowning. Then he slid over the lip of the Pit on to the first of a series of rabbit tracks that crossed the slope. He kept his centre of gravity low and tilted his body into the slope, so one hand was always on the grass. There was no danger of his falling – Sophie would bound down it. He could imagine her confident and upright, jumping from one path to the next, facing forwards all the way down, only needing her heels to grip. He knew he was being painfully slow. Occasionally he stopped and glanced up so he could see how far he'd climbed. He didn't think it was sensible to look down.

He knew he was approaching the bottom because he could hear Sophie, shouting through into the tunnel to Roger. Her words were blurred by echo, but he could tell she was standing quite close to him. Then he did turn and saw he was only six feet from the ground. He slid it on his backside and landed beside her, one foot slipping on a slimy rock into a pool. There was no direct sunlight there; a strong smell of rotting seaweed, organic and salty. It was somehow prehistoric. He tried not to think about the return to the real world.

'What have you found?'

'We didn't like to touch it. This way.' She led him into the mouth of the tunnel.

The floor was uneven – shingle, solid rock which

formed crevasses and pools, and small smooth boulders which must have been washed in from the beach. Too late he remembered a directive he'd received a couple of months ago about risk assessment. He wondered what Health and Safety would make of this. Roger and Sophie weren't even employees.

At this point the tunnel looked like a cave. It must curve further in and the gap leading to the open water must be very narrow, because no natural light showed from the other end. Roger had put on his torch and was waiting for them, haloed in a yellow glow. He was sitting on an outcrop of rock which jutted from the channel wall, eating a bar of chocolate.

'Sorry,' Sophie said. 'Jimmy was a tad slow.'

'Have you found Booth's phone then?' Perez thought they were playing a sort of practical joke on him. They knew he was uncomfortable with heights and had dragged him down here under false pretences. They'd pull out some ridiculous object that had been washed in – a pair of false teeth, an old boot – and expect him to find it amusing.

'No,' Roger said. 'But we found this.'

He shone his torch into a pile of debris which had been lifted on to a shelf in the rock. There were scraps of fishing net, shell and seaweed, two of the plastic rings which hold four-packs of beer and, creamy and smooth, a piece of bone.

'Very funny,' Perez said. A sheep had become trapped down here, starved to death. It wouldn't take long for the flesh to rot and be eaten away by fish and other creatures. When it was exposed to the air the bonxies and the rats would have it. The tide would have lifted the small piece of bone on to the ledge.

297

'What do you think it is?'

'Sheep? Dog maybe?'

'Look closer,' Roger said. 'I think you're wrong. If I'm not mistaken it's a human thigh bone.'

'Roger works as a physio,' Sophie said. 'He knows about human anatomy.'

Perez could tell she was enjoying herself. It was that excitement around unexplained death again.

'It must have been pushed up to the ledge on a really big tide.' Roger played the torch along the tunnel wall, half a metre below the ledge. 'You can see this is the normal high-water mark.'

'So it could have been flushed in from the open sea?' Perez said. He wondered how many men had been lost in the seas around here over the years. The currents were so fierce that it wasn't unusual for the bodies from wrecks never to be recovered. The bone was worn shiny and smooth. It had been here for ages.

'It wouldn't take very long for it to get like that,' Roger said, seeming to read his thoughts. 'I mean not decades. Not necessarily. Not down here. Think of the action of the sand and the shingle.'

'When was the last really high tide? I mean, when do you think it was lifted on to the ledge?' Perez found his thoughts moving very fast. It was as if he'd had a shot of caffeine.

'This year,' Sophie said quickly. 'Spring equinox. Don't you remember, those wonderful photos in the *Shetland Times* of the waves at Scalloway? It could have been here in the tunnel before that but washed on to the ledge then.'

'I need to get right to the end of the tunnel.' Perez

had forgotten any question of risk assessment. 'I need to know how big the entrance is on the seaward side.'

They walked in single file with Roger in the front, Perez in the middle and Sophie at the rear. The way into the tunnel from the Pit was wide enough for them to stretch out their arms, but it narrowed as they approached the shore. A slit of natural light appeared ahead of them, and there was a gust of salt fresh air from the sea. Now they were clambering over solid rock. Before they could reach the gap the tunnel had become so tight that they couldn't move further forward. Sunshine shone through the strange vertical crack, picked out the colour in the rock at their feet in a sparkling strip.

'A body couldn't have been washed in there,' Perez said. 'Even with the force of the tide behind it. There's no room.' Sandy needn't have worried about leaving Booth's holdall down here. There was no way it would have been washed through the tiny gap.

'Couldn't the body have broken up at sea? A bone the size we found could just about have been sucked in.'

Still Perez's thoughts were racing. 'That's possible. But if we find any more than that, it would be more than chance. Think of all the places along the coast where they could be washed up. And if we discover part of a corpse which is bigger than the piece we found, it couldn't have come in this way.' He looked at them. 'Could it? The gap's too narrow. If we come across more bones, or a bigger fragment of bone, it means the body was tipped down from the top of the Pit. Like Roddy Sinclair. It means another, older murder.'

Chapter Thirty-five

On Monday afternoon Fran went to visit Bella. She'd been thinking all weekend that she should go. She wasn't sure what she could do to help, but the death of someone so young and beautiful needed marking. It demanded a certain ritual. She knew Bella would see things that way too. Fran thought she would be waiting in the Manse, queenly, expecting visits. That didn't mean Bella would be feeling the loss any less – Roddy was as much a child to her as Cassie was to Fran – but she would want his going dramatized, turned into art, made splendid.

There was a small group of reporters at the entrance to the Manse. None of them looked local. They seemed content to sit in the sun and take photos of the Manse with their long lenses. A uniformed policeman stood there too, and he seemed to be enjoying the banter with the journalists. He let Fran through with a wave when she said she was there to see Bella. She thought she'd seen him before at one of Duncan's parties. Those days seemed a long time ago.

Bella opened the door to her and as Fran had expected she was dressed to meet guests. Her clothes always tended towards the theatrical. Today she was wearing a long skirt, gathered and full, in a plum-coloured muslin, and a white embroidered cotton top. The effect was exotic – flamenco or gypsy. Fran despised herself for considering such trivial matters as dress, but Bella would want it to be noticed. Fran wondered if it would be tasteless to say how nice the artist looked and decided that it would be. Besides, she would know she looked good.

'I wanted to come,' she said. 'I probably can't do anything, and if you'd rather be alone, do say.'

'No.' Bella stood back, so she was framed by the light through the old kirk-style window. 'Company helps. It stops me brooding quite so much. Have you had lunch? Aggie Williamson keeps bringing me food. Either things she made or wonderful little goodies Martin's cooked, but I can't face eating.'

And Fran saw that she did seem to have lost weight. Her eyes were hollow and her cheekbones angular beneath the fine skin. She had put on make-up though, a very subtle foundation, a smudge of shadow on her eyes. I would do the same, Fran thought. It would keep me from falling apart altogether.

Bella was continuing. 'Shall we have tea then? And perhaps a slice of cake. Do you mind sitting in the kitchen?'

Fran was reminded of the last time they'd sat here, discussing the fake notices which had been circulated to cancel the exhibition. How fierce and angry Bella had been then. How important the launch had seemed.

'Do the police know yet why Jeremy Booth put out all those flyers?' she asked.

'Surely you'd know that better than me.' For a

moment it was the old Bella, amused, sharp. 'Haven't you taken up with Jimmy Perez?'

'He doesn't discuss the case with me.'

'I've been trying to think where I might have met Booth,' Bella said. 'I've been thinking a lot about the past in the last few days. It's suddenly become sharper, somehow more vivid. It's more pleasant than the present, and with Roddy gone there's really not much future left. Nothing worth caring about, at least. It is possible that I knew him.'

'There's your work.' That would hold me together, Fran thought. That and the pride of keeping up appearances.

'Oh yes, there's always that.'

'Any idea where you might have met Booth?'

'There were occasional visitors,' Bella said vaguely. 'People who drifted into my life for a few weeks and then disappeared. Students and other artists. I liked the energy of the people who came and sometimes I asked them to stay. I'd bought this big house. And I loved parties. Just like your ex-husband, my dear. So why not?'

'You think Booth might have been one of your stray guests?'

'Perhaps.' She nibbled at a piece of fruit cake. 'I think Peter Wilding might have been one of them too. I hadn't realized before. It's only since Roddy died, this strange escape into the past, living the old days in my head. If it's the man I'm remembering, he doesn't even look very different. But the summer I believe he was here wasn't a very happy time for me. I've been trying since then to put it out of my mind. Besides, I can't be sure.' She seemed to realize she was rambling, looked up and gave a quick, wicked smile. 'Will you pass all this information on to Jimmy Perez?'

'Would you rather I didn't?'

She gave a shrug. 'Just tell Jimmy I can't be certain. And Wilding never mentioned having been here. That does seem odd, doesn't it? When he first started writing to me, telling me how much he enjoyed the paintings, he didn't bring that up. His letter was very flattering, of course. We all enjoy being flattered. But you'd think he'd say something, wouldn't you, if he'd been a guest in my house? Something self-deprecating and hopeful. *I don't suppose you remember but you were kind enough to put me up one summer.* I'm not sure how accurate my memories are. It could all be make-believe. I think grief makes everyone a little bit mad. That and the simmer dim.'

'Do you think Jeremy Booth and Peter Wilding were here at the same time?'

There was a long silence before Bella answered.

'You know, I rather think they were. It was this time of the year. An unusually warm summer. The house was full. Roddy's parents were still living in Lerwick then, but he came over to see me most weekends and there were a couple of weeks when Alec was away in hospital. I remember swimming with him from the beach here. I taught him to swim. There aren't many days when it's warm enough to do that. And at night we had parties on the beach. Bonfires and music. There was usually someone who could play. Too much drink and too much dope. It was long after the sixties, of course, but perhaps we were trying to recreate that sort of sense. The creativity and the freedom. We wanted to believe that we were young.' She paused.

303

'And I was in love, with Lawrence Thomson. I'd been in love with him since I was thirteen. Probably before that. I remember playing kiss-chase with him in the little school in Middleton. All these people who stayed, none of them could match up to him.'

Fran had dozens of questions, but kept them all to herself. Bella shook her head, as if to force herself back to the present.

'Everyone went, of course,' she said. 'As soon as the weather changed and the rain started. They didn't want to make a life in the real Shetland. They talked about authentic culture, but there was nothing authentic about their experience.' There was another moment of silence. 'Even Lawrence went.'

'I don't suppose you have any photographs of that time?'

Bella didn't seem to hear. 'But I had Roddy,' she said. 'He more than made up for losing all the summer hangers-on. And after Alec died and his mother ran away with her oilman, I had him all to myself. Did he make up for losing Lawrence? I'm not sure about that.'

'Do you have any photographs?'

Again Bella gave the little shake of her head to disperse the images of previous times.

'I'm sure there are some,' she said. 'Roddy was looking at them not very long ago.'

'Would you mind showing me? If it wouldn't be too upsetting.'

'I'm not sure where they are. And I really don't think I have the energy to look.'

'I'll go,' Fran said, 'if you tell me where they might be.' She found herself fascinated by the idea of the summer house party. The long white nights. The artists and actors and writers attracted to Shetland, but more especially to Bella like moths to a very bright candle, and the woman who had no interest in any of them. She wanted Lawrence, her childhood sweetheart, her golden boy. What a brilliant film it would make! she thought. All those beautiful people in this stunning setting.

'They're in an old shoebox,' Bella said. The answer came so quickly that Fran thought she'd wanted the photographs found all the time. She was too lethargic or too sensible of her own importance to look for them. 'I think they might be in the cupboard in the studio. Do you know where that is?' She leaned back in her chair and waved her arms to give directions.

Fran enjoyed walking through the house on her own, the glimpse into other rooms through half-open doors. She had, at times like these, a sense of images stolen and saved for future use in her painting.

The photographs were exactly where Bella had said they would be – in a battered shoebox on a shelf in a tall dark-wood cupboard. Fran wondered if she'd been looking at them herself. All the photos were loose and seemed to be in no chronological order. Many were in poor condition, the edges tattered, the corners bent, the print faded and discoloured. She was tempted to sit there, on the floor, and to spread them out until she found a pattern, or people she recognized. But they belonged to Bella and that would have been an intrusion too far.

In the kitchen Bella cleared the table of the teapot and mugs and Aggie Williamson's fruit cake. 'Now,' she said. 'Let's see what we have here.'

Fran would have tipped out the photographs in a

heap, fanned them out like playing cards, but Bella
kept them in the box and took out one at a time. The
first was of Roddy as a child, wrapped in a towel, his
face brown from the sun and freckled with sand. Many
were of Roddy, and Fran had to hear the story behind
each one. At one point Bella started to cry. Fran went
up behind her and put her arm around her.

Going back to her place at the table, she stole a
look at her watch. Of course she was sympathetic, but
she'd have to leave very soon. Cassie was going to play
with a friend after school, but still she'd need collect-
ing before teatime. She'd phone Perez about the
photographs. This wasn't really any of her business.
She'd have to learn not to meddle in his work, not to
ask questions, if they were going to make their relationship work.

Then at the top of the heap in the box there was a
picture of a group of adults. They were wearing party
clothes. It had been taken in the garden with the house
in the background. Everyone looked stiff and formal.
Beyond the house a cloudless sky. And all of them
held in their hands masks, glorious, elaborate affairs,
fastened to a cane. Fran felt suddenly very cold.

The implication of the masks seemed lost on Bella.
She left the photo where it was and stared at it.

'I remember that night,' she said. 'It was the
evening before most of them went. We held a real
dinner party to mark their leaving. I made everyone
dress up, set the big table in the dining room. I wanted
something special and came up with the idea of the
masque. How pretentious I must have seemed! I
thought we were so sophisticated. We're none of us
very young there, are we? I remember it as a time

when I was young, but that's not true at all.'

'Where did you get the masks from?'

'I hired them from a theatre company. The one which still turns up in Lerwick every year on the boat. I made friends with one of the actors.'

'How long ago was it?'

Bella stared into space. 'Fifteen years? Roddy had his sixth birthday the next day. He came here to collect his present and those of us who were left had such hangovers.'

'Do you know who everyone is?'

Bella lifted out the picture. It was larger than most of the others, which were just snaps, and almost covered the area of the shoebox.

'This is me. Right in the front. Of course.' She was wearing a red silk halterneck dress. Her hair was cut very short, almost exactly the same style as she wore today. Fran was reminded of the self-portrait that had caught the attention of Jeremy Booth at the Herring House party.

'You look lovely.'

'I made an effort,' she said. 'Oh how I made an effort! I'd got it into my head that Lawrence would propose that night.'

'Is he in the photograph?'

'No,' Bella said briefly. 'I'd invited him to the dinner, but he never appeared.'

'Isn't this Peter Wilding?' Fran turned the photograph round so she was looking directly at it. 'This man standing beside you.' He was very dark, handsome in a sulky sort of way.

'Do you think it is? He's put on a little weight, if

it's him. I suppose it could be. The shape of the nose is the same.'

'Are you sure you didn't recognize him when he turned up to rent the house from you? He hasn't changed that much.'

'Don't you think so? I certainly didn't know him. I've already explained, I had no reason to want to remember that summer. Besides, there was no need to go back to the past. I had a future through Roddy.'

Fran thought that Bella had put too much on to the boy – the responsibility for all her happiness. 'Is Jeremy Booth there?'

Bella swung the picture back. 'It's difficult to tell, isn't it? I only saw him briefly at the Herring House the other night. Where is it? I wondered if this could be him.'

'Where?'

'Here. I thought the long face, rather narrow nose. He has more hair here, of course. It's unfashionably long, even for the time. And he has a beard. Very much the bohemian.'

'And you really don't remember anything about him? Not even the name?'

'I don't think he can have been here for very long. Perhaps not more than a few days. That happened. People came for a while and then moved on. I spent quite a lot of my time in Glasgow, visiting lecturer at the art school. I'd get pissed at parties and invite people to stay.'

She leaned back in her chair with her eyes half closed. Fran thought she was reliving that summer in her mind.

'I think perhaps he was the magician,' she said. 'He

put on a magic show for Roddy, who was completely entranced. It seemed such a kind thing to do. I rather fancy he was my actor. He told me he was in love with me.' As if this was of no consequence at all, a common occurrence. She paused. 'He was given to practical jokes, I remember, and not always in good taste. The flyers cancelling the party would have been just his style. A way of getting his own back. But why wait all this time? Surely he didn't come to Shetland just to upset me.' There was a note of satisfaction in her voice. She liked the idea that she had haunted him for years.

'Did anything happen that time they were all here at the Manse?' Fran asked. 'Something that could have triggered this violence so many years later?'

'No,' Bella said. 'The night that photograph was taken was an anticlimax. We dressed up and ate dinner. The next morning I was left with a hangover and a pile of dirty dishes. No drama. Nothing.'

'Can I have the photo to show Jimmy?'

'Why not?'

She sounded very tired, as if nothing really mattered any more.

Chapter Thirty-six

Taylor had been at his desk since eight and was finding it impossible to concentrate. He'd been restless even as a child, could see now that he must have driven his father to distraction with his fidgeting and his demands for attention. His father had been a foreman in the docks and used to a bit of respect. Taylor hadn't been prepared to make the effort.

Since the trip to the Wirral, he'd been thinking more about his family. He should have been in touch with them, at least let them know he was safe and well. Everyone thought Jeremy Booth had been a selfish bastard, walking out on his wife and baby. Maybe they were saying the same things about Roy Taylor. *You'd have thought he could pick up the phone and let his mother know he wasn't dead.* This case had too many resonances with his own life. It seemed Lawrence Thomson had just walked out too. Because he was bored, or being pressured to take on the commitment of a wife and family. Perhaps he just needed the space to make his own decisions and live his own life.

Taylor left the building and went out into the street. He needed exercise and fresh air and a decent cup of coffee. Another huge cruise ship was sliding

310

into the mouth of the harbour, blocking out the view of Bressay, dominating the town. Taylor thought cruising was like his idea of hell. Being shut up on a boat with a load of people whose company you hadn't chosen, having to be pleasant to them, never being able to escape. Like a family, he thought. And he thought that though he hadn't spoken to his relatives for years he had never really escaped them either. Resentment against his father bubbled inside him, fuelling his ambition, pushing people away.

He walked down the lane into the Peerie Café. He'd come here with Perez when he was last in Shetland. They'd drunk coffee and discussed the case, united against a general assumption that the murderer had already been found. He missed the easy relationship they'd had then. He seemed to remember laughter. They'd been more like friends than rivals. Why did Perez irritate more now than he had on the earlier visit? Was it because he'd taken up with Fran Hunter? Was Taylor jealous because he had a woman? An attractive woman.

There were two middle-aged women in the queue ahead of him – English tourists in walking gear. He tried to curb his impatience as they dithered about whether it would be *terribly* wicked to have cream with their scones. He was tempted to turn round and walk out, but the smell of the coffee held him.

He'd just put in his order when the phone call came from Perez.

'I'm in Biddista. You might want to get over here.' There was never any urgency when the Shetlander spoke, but Taylor could sense in his voice that this was important. 'The climbers came across something . . .'

The Englishwomen were back at the counter, hovering at his elbow, fussing with napkins. They were chatting and Taylor found it hard to hear what Perez was saying.

'I'll be on my way. You can tell me when I get there.'

He asked for the coffee to be tipped into a cardboard cup so he could take it away and felt as close to joy as he ever did now that he was grown-up. He had a function, an excuse for activity. For a few hours at least he wouldn't be bored. In the car he played Led Zeppelin so loud that it pushed thought out of his head, and drove one-handed as he drank the coffee, which was still too hot. He reflected that the fear of boredom had driven him the whole of his life.

He went as far as he could up the track then pulled on to the grass and walked the rest of the way. Perez and the climbers were sitting at the top of the Pit o' Biddista waiting for him. The sight of them, lying back with their faces to the sun, irritated him all over again. Did they have nothing better to do? Did Perez think a murder investigation was just a holiday from the routine and the mundane business of policing this wind-blown, godforsaken place?

'What is it?' He felt at a disadvantage, breathless and sweaty after the walk on to the hill. 'Have you got Booth's mobile?'

'No,' Perez said. 'We didn't find that.'

'What then?'

'A human bone.' Perez frowned. 'Old. Not fresh, at least. I'd need an expert opinion. I wanted to know what you thought we should do next. I didn't feel we could continue without clearing it with you first.'

Taylor tried to keep his temper. It would be a wonderful indulgence just to let rip, to blast away at Perez for his incompetence. The Shetlander had managed the original crime scene after the body of Roddy Sinclair had been found. Why had no proper search been done immediately? Why had it taken a suggestion by Taylor to get things moving? He felt the warm glow of the self-righteous. The day was turning out well after all.

'What are you saying has happened here?' Keeping his voice even, reasonable. Holding the moral high ground. He was competitive even in this.

'I think another murder,' Perez said. 'The cause or trigger maybe for the recent incidents. At first we thought the bone was washed in from the sea. There have been men lost here over the years. It wouldn't be so unusual. Then we found another. Part of the shin, we think. There will probably be more.'

Taylor looked at the Shetlander. It seemed a mighty big leap in logic to deduce a murder from a couple of fragments of bone. Perez had a theory, believed he knew what had happened here. That didn't mean he was right.

'The body couldn't have been washed in whole and disintegrated in the Pit, without anyone seeing it?'

'No one would see.' Perez nodded his agreement. 'Folk don't go down there very often, that's for sure. When there were more children living here and running around the hill, that was a different matter, but not now.'

'So that's a possible scenario?'

'No. The crack into the tunnel is too narrow. A

313

body wouldn't be washed in there. Not even the body of a child, and this is an adult.'

'What are you saying, Jimmy? I don't have all day. Help me out here!'

'I think this is the body of a victim who was killed and then thrown down the Pit. The same means of death and disposal of the body as with Roddy Sinclair.' He squinted against the sunlight. 'It suggests, wouldn't you say, the same murderer?'

'But Jeremy Booth was killed in quite a different way. Are you saying someone else strangled him? Two separate murderers?'

'I'm not sure. I'm feeling my way.'

You think you know what happened here, Taylor thought. But you won't commit yourself.

'We should have done a thorough search of the crime scene when Sinclair's body was first found.' Taylor thought he could allow himself that. The comment was measured and moderate, but Perez would pick up on the criticism.

'You're right. We should.' Perez paused. 'What should we do now? Wait for a specialist search team from the mainland? There are no high tides forecast. We're unlikely to lose more than has been lost already.'

Taylor tried to imagine how long that would take. Tracking down the right people and getting them here.

'What's the alternative?'

'Us!' It was the young woman. The climbers had been sitting slightly apart, obviously listening in but pretending not to. 'We're free for the rest of the day. Tell us what to do and we'll do it. You can get one of your experts to talk us through it if you want.' She had frizzy fair hair and she'd tipped back her head to appeal to him. She wore a sleeveless vest with a fleece thrown over it, and he found it hard to keep his eyes away from her breasts. 'You wouldn't even know that there was anything down there if it hadn't been for us.'

And he agreed, because he couldn't stand the thought of more hanging about. And because if there was a team brought in from outside, they'd have their own leader and he wouldn't be in control any more. To this couple he was the expert. They'd do what he said.

'Yeah,' he said. 'Why not?'

The young woman grinned at him, excited, like a little girl.

When Taylor turned back to Perez, he smiled too, complicit. It was like the time in the winter, when it had been them against the system.

Later he thought the Shetland climbers were as careful and meticulous as any professionals would have been. He and Perez stayed at the top and watched them quarter the base of the cavern in lines, sifting through the shingle and the seaweed with their fingers. They found one new bone very quickly. It was only a fragment. Perez wondered if it could be animal, but Roger seemed to think it was human. Then nothing happened for a long time. Taylor called down to them:

'Are you OK?'

'Apart from being starving.'

Taylor was torn. He didn't want to miss anything but boredom had set in a long time before. 'I'll go and see if I can rustle up some coffee and food for them,' he said to Perez. 'And for us.'

'I'll go.'

'No. You're the local. You stay here.'

The Herring House was closed to visitors, but he could hear movement inside and banged on the door. There was no reply but he persisted.

'For Christ's sake, man. Can you not read? The gallery's closed.' He'd been expecting Martin Williamson, but it was Aggie, his mother. Because he'd never seen her in the Herring House before it took Taylor a moment to place her.

'I know,' he said.

She blushed when she saw who it was, seemed to feel some explanation for her presence there was required.

'I don't open the post office on a Monday afternoon,' she said. 'I'm helping out with a bit of spring cleaning here while the place is closed.'

'I'm surprised Miss Sinclair is thinking about the business at a time like this.'

'Bella didn't ask me,' she said. 'Martin did. She leaves the restaurant to him. He's out today helping Kenny Thomson with the hill sheep. It seemed a good time to get in.' She seemed to Taylor to be very flustered. Perhaps his banging on the door had scared her. He supposed everyone in Biddista would be scared by loud noises and unexpected visitors until they found the killer.

'Would you be able to put me together a couple of flasks of coffee?' he asked. 'Some sandwiches. Of course I'd pay.'

'I don't know. This is Martin's business.'

'He wouldn't begrudge us a couple of rounds of sandwiches.'

She flinched at the sharpness in his words.

'I expect I can find you something,' she said.

She didn't invite him in, but he followed her into the restaurant and through into the kitchen. He thought she seemed at home there. 'Do you help Martin out often?'

'If he's busy. Preparations for events.'

'Did you help out before the opening of Miss Sinclair's exhibition?'

'Just arranging tables in the afternoon. Folding napkins, that sort of thing. Not on the night. I used to help Bella when she had parties at the Manse, but always behind the scenes.'

He thought she would be too timid to serve the public. 'What were the parties like?' he asked. 'I guess they'd be grand affairs.'

'You could never tell.' She gave a little smile. 'Sometimes I'd turn up expecting champagne and canapés and they'd all be eating beans on toast round the kitchen table. I'm not sure what her guests made of it.'

'Do you remember any of the guests?'

'No, not after all this time. The big parties stopped long ago.' But she spoke so quickly that he wasn't sure he believed her.

'Did everyone from Biddista go too?'

'Mostly it was the men who got the invites,' she said. 'Alec, of course, when he was well enough. He was Bella's brother. And Kenny, though he wasn't so keen. And Lawrence. Bella always preferred the company of men.'

'Tell me what it was like,' he said, 'growing up in a place like this. I just can't get my head round it. Everyone knowing your business.'

'Oh, we all hang on to our little bit of privacy. It's the only way we keep sane.'

She seemed embarrassed then to have spoken so freely and opened the door of the big fridge. 'I could do a round of cheese and a round of ham. Maybe some pâté if you'd like it.'

'Can you make it a couple of each? There are a few of us.'

'I thought you'd finished up on the hill.' She was slicing bread and stopped, the knife poised, watching for his answer.

'Not quite,' he said easily. Then added, just to see her reaction, 'Something's come up.'

'Why?' she asked quickly. 'What have you found?'

'I'm sorry, I can't discuss the investigation with anyone.' He tried to smile reassuringly. She was so anxious, he wanted to put her at her ease, even though he'd provoked the response. He could feel the tension in her like an infection which he was already catching. 'Is there anything you think we should know?'

She bent her head over the sandwiches, so he couldn't see her face. 'No,' she said. 'Of course not. We just want it to be over.'

He wondered if he should push it, imagined again the whole valley in a conspiracy of silence. But she seemed so closed off from him that he didn't think it would be any use.

She made a flask of tea and another of coffee and wrapped the sandwiches in foil and cut half a fruit cake from a tin. She wouldn't take any money. 'I'm sure Bella would want me to help you.'

She stood at the door of the gallery and watched

him walk up the road, as if she wanted to be sure that he'd really gone.

By the time he got back to the hill a large piece of jawbone had been found. This fragment had two teeth attached. But the climbers said they'd only just started. Perez was on the phone to track down a generator and lights. They thought they'd be at it well into the night.

Chapter Thirty-seven

When Perez arrived at the house in Ravenswick it was half-past midnight, but Fran was still up. She'd said that she would be. There'd been a brief guarded phone call with Taylor listening in. He was on the hill and his mobile reception was dreadful, so her words kept breaking up.

'I need to talk to you,' she'd said. 'It doesn't matter how late it is. I've been to see Bella. It's important.'

She would have told him over the phone what was troubling her, but Perez didn't want that. He was focused now on the climbers sifting through debris and he didn't want to prolong the conversation. Taylor was critical enough as it was. He was right: Perez should have organized a more thorough search of the cliff and the cave when Roddy's body was found. This wasn't the time for a personal conversation.

When he got to her place, she was sitting at the table reading. The house was quiet. No music. He watched her through the window, one side of her face caught in the glow of a table lamp. She must have heard his car as a background noise in her head, but she continued to read, frowning with concentration, her attention held by the words on the page. She only turned when he tapped at the door and walked in.

Then she stood up and put her arms around his neck and pulled him to her.

'You're cold,' she said. 'The water's hot if you want a bath.'

'I'm sorry I couldn't talk earlier.' On the way back he'd wondered what she could want to talk about. It sounded ominous. 'We need to talk.' Sarah had said that when she'd told him she was leaving him. It had come as a complete shock. Perhaps he should have seen it coming, but it had never occurred to him. He'd known she was sad, but had thought it was the miscarriage. She would need time to get over that. He needed time himself to come to terms with it. He hadn't realized he was the problem.

'It's about the case,' Fran said now. 'I think it could be important.'

He felt relief, followed by irritation. He'd hoped he could forget the case for the night.

'I went to see Bella. She thinks she knew Jeremy Booth after all.'

'She recognized the name?'

'Perhaps that was partly it. I think it's more that she's been hiding in the past. Escaping from Roddy's death by living in her memories. She remembered seeing him. Her memory will be very visual, and although he'd changed a lot something about his face came back to her.'

'Where did she know him from?'

'Shetland. Biddista. One summer she seems to have run a sort of artists' commune in the Manse. He turned up and stayed. I don't think she can remember how she came to invite him, only that he was there.

321

And that he was an actor with a fondness for practical jokes.'

'When was that?'

'About fifteen years ago. That was what she said, but she was very vague about the details.'

'Why would he have wanted to spoil the opening of her exhibition after all this time? Does she know?'

'He'd told her he was in love with her, apparently! But she hadn't heard from him since then. She said she didn't recognize him on the night of the exhibition.'

'Are you sure? It seems a bit odd, memories of that summer only coming back to her now.'

'Bella *is* a bit odd, don't you think? Especially now, with Roddy gone. She told me she'd put that summer out of her mind – I suppose because it was when Lawrence left. I'm not sure. I think she's reliving happier times now – when Roddy was a child – and former glories. All those men besotted with her. It's an escape from the grief.'

'But nobody else in Biddista remembers Booth.'

'It was fifteen years ago. That summer strange people were coming and going to the Manse all the time. I'd have been astonished if anyone *had* recognized him.'

He was surprised that he didn't feel more tired. Driving to her house, his mind had been clear, as if the evening was just beginning, as if he'd just finished a normal day's work. 'Would you mind if I had a drink?' he asked.

'Of course. What would you like? Wine, beer whisky?'

'White wine please.' The drink of summer afternoons. He imagined the house party at the Manse all those years ago. Bella's guests would have been sitting in the garden drinking chilled white wine, talking painting and politics.

'That wasn't all Bella said.' Fran must already have had a bottle of wine open in the fridge. She poured a glass for them both. 'She thinks Peter Wilding was there that summer too.'

'Is the woman mad? Playing some sort of crazy game?'

'Really,' Fran said, 'I don't think so.'

'It's so fanciful. Suddenly all these people who seemed unrelated turn out to have been in the same house at the same time. And Bella, who claimed not to know them, remembers as if by magic.'

'I know,' Fran said. 'But I do understand what she's saying. She's been so caught up in the present that she's had no reason to revisit those days. You know how self-absorbed she is. I understand what it's like when I'm working. The art is all I think about really, even when I'm reading a story to Cassie, even when I'm spending time with you, it's at the back of my mind. You're the same when you're working on a big case. She had no reason to think about the past. Now her memories of those times have become very clear. It's her way of blocking out what happened to Roddy.'

'It still seems preposterous to me.' Perez drank some wine. 'Like a kids' game. Or Up Helly Aa after the parade. The guisers all wearing masks and running from one hall to another. I'm never part of the squad, so I bump into people and can't quite recognize them, though I know they're familiar. That's how I feel now; I'm losing track about what's real and what's pretend.'

'I know,' she said again.

'Am I talking rubbish?'

'I think I know what you mean.' She paused. 'There's a photograph. That might help pin things down. And masks figure there too.' She laid a faded colour photograph on the table and turned the lamp so it was fully lit.

'They're dressed up for a dinner party,' she said. 'Fancy dress too, in a way. The masks must be significant, mustn't they?'

Certainly that, Perez thought, but I'm not quite sure how. He'd thought he was inching towards a solution. Had he been wrong?

'That's Wilding,' Perez said, pointing to the dark man. 'He's hardly changed. How can she not have recognized him?'

'It was a long time ago, in a different context. But he must have remembered being here. Why didn't he say something to Bella when he asked to rent the house from her? That seems most odd to me.'

'And there's Bella. She always wore red in those days. It was her sort of trademark.'

'You knew her then?'

'Knew *of* her, certainly. She was a local celebrity even in those days.'

'Bella thinks that's Booth.' Fran pointed to a figure on the back row. With his long hair and beard, his rather thin face, he looked like a Renaissance representation of Jesus. The Last Supper, Perez thought.

'Who are the others?'

'I don't know. She didn't say and I didn't ask. Lawrence isn't there, though. She expected him to come. She thought he would propose to her that night, but he didn't turn up. Isn't it sad?'

'It is if it's true.'

'You don't believe her?'

'I've told you, I don't know who or what to believe.' He drank more wine, a good mouthful, not a sip. 'I should tell Taylor.'

'Won't he be asleep?'

'I don't think he ever sleeps.' He took another drink. 'Could I ask him over? We won't disturb you.'

She didn't hesitate. 'Of course.'

And Taylor did pick up his mobile after the second ring, and his voice was as strong as it always was, the accent deepened somehow over the phone. Perez explained as best he could, realizing that he was stuttering slightly. 'There's a photo,' he said. 'It's interesting. It would wait until the morning but you'd be welcome to come over if you like. You know where Fran lives.'

A moment of hesitation. Perez was preparing himself for a rebuff. Then Taylor's voice came again, stronger than ever. 'I'll be there. Half an hour.' Another pause. 'Thanks.'

Fran took herself to bed before Taylor arrived. She set out a plate of food for them – cheese and oatcakes and a tin with home-made biscuits.

'There's no need for that.' Perez reached out and touched her hand.

'I think I've been in Shetland long enough to know how to behave with visitors.'

He heard her move around the bedroom, pictured her taking off clothes, pulling out the long earrings, reaching behind her head to unclip her bead necklace.

Then she stood at the door in a long white cotton nightdress he'd never seen before.

'I'll be asleep before you come in,' she said. 'Sorry.'

'My fault. I shouldn't have asked Taylor.'

He thought this was a crazy way to begin a relationship. They floated into each other's lives when they were too exhausted to make sense. Ghosts passing in the white nights. Sarah would never have put up with it. She'd wanted more of his attention and his energy. Fran, surely, would tire of his preoccupation with work in the end. But then, as she'd explained, she had her own obsession too, with her art.

He most have dozed off because he didn't hear Taylor's car, only a tap at the door. Outside, the darkest of the night had passed. The grey light in the east showed the black silhouette of Raven's Head. He filled a kettle and made coffee. They started talking in whispers. Perez set Bella's photograph on the table.

'See the masks,' he said.

Taylor frowned. 'So that was significant. A message?'

'Perhaps. But who from? Booth, who wore it to hand out his flyers? Or the murderer?'

They considered this for a moment in silence, reached no conclusion.

'Is that Jeremy Booth, do you think?' Perez asked. 'It looks like him to me and Bella seemed sure. I'd already checked dates with the management of the theatre ship and that was the summer he was here. I'm not sure we'll ever be able to prove how they met unless she tells us. Perhaps she went to the show. They cater for a family audience. Roddy wasn't staying with her then but she spent a lot of time with him.

It's the sort of thing a doting aunt would do, take her nephew to the theatre for a treat. And I can imagine her sweeping all the cast back with her to Biddista. For dinner or a few days at the end of the run.' He thought of Lucy, the young actress. He could see that they would want to celebrate the end of a show. All those nerves. All that excitement. 'And she told Fran that she hired the masks from the theatre company. Another connection.'

'We can show the photo to the theatre management,' Taylor said. 'Perhaps they can identify the other people there. We can chase that up, confirm Booth's presence.'

'That's definitely Wilding.' Perez pointed to the dark-haired man. 'He hasn't changed as much as Booth.'

'So Bella Sinclair's been lying?'

Perez shrugged. 'Or she'd genuinely forgotten. She didn't have to tell Fran about that summer. Why would she if she has things to hide?'

'*He* would remember though,' Taylor said. 'I can go along with Bella forgetting a house guest who turned up briefly with a load of other people. But to travel to Shetland and spend days in the company of an artist you admire . . . No way did that just slip out of Wilding's mind.'

His voice rose. Perez imagined Cassie stumbling into the room, woken by the noise.

They continued the conversation outside, the food on the white bench between them, fresh mugs of coffee at their feet. It was still chill and they sat huddled in their coats.

'So what happened that summer?' Taylor demanded. 'Why have two people died?'

'There was a murder.' Perez was quite certain about that. 'The bones at the bottom of the Pit. It would be good if we could date them. Any chance, do you think?'

'Not sure. We should get an ID eventually. A DNA match from a relative maybe. And the teeth will help.'

'Oh I think I know who it was,' Perez said. 'Lawrence Thomson disappeared that summer. He told Bella he was leaving the islands, but he's never been heard of since. If you listen to Kenny you'd think his big brother was a saint, but he had a record of fighting.' He'd checked that too.

'What are you thinking? Too much drink and a brawl that got out of hand and they tipped the body down the Pit? Then they all agreed to keep quiet about it?'

'Perhaps.' Perez could see that might have happened. It would be a heady mix. An unusually warm summer. The excitement of new and exotic strangers in the community. All the men showing off for Bella. The tribal hostility between incomer and outsider. Then a pact of silence.

'So what's changed? They'd got away with it. Even if those bones had been found now, people would have thought they'd been washed in from the sea. Some old dead sailor. Without the other deaths we wouldn't have given them a thought.'

'Perhaps someone got greedy,' Perez said.

'Blackmail?'

'Maybe.'

'I can see Jeremy Booth trying it on. He was a bit

of a chancer. But again, why now? He'd always had money problems, but I've had a look at the company figures. It was solvent. Just. He'd recently found his daughter again. Why risk all that? And I can't believe Roddy Sinclair was short of a few bob. He'd not need to resort to blackmail.'

'Perhaps Wilding coming back triggered the series of events,' Perez said. 'His arrival's the one thing that's changed in Biddista recently.'

'You're right. And he was at the opening of the exhibition at the Herring House, when Booth played his stunt.' He paused. 'What was that about anyway? A warning? A threat? Did the flyer he was handing around talking about a death in the family refer to the poor sod we found in the pit? Only Lawrence wasn't family, was he?'

'Not quite.' Perez paused. 'Roddy's father died later that summer. He was Bella's brother. It would be a death in the family. But he had cancer. We know there was nothing suspicious about his death. We've seen where the body was buried in the graveyard just up the coast from the Herring House. My father was a kind of relative and went off Fair Isle to the funeral.' He'd only just remembered that. His father in his black suit, flying out with Loganair. Some memories did stay hidden and it just took a trigger to resurrect them. He felt more at ease with Taylor than he had since he'd collected him from the plane in Sumburgh. Perhaps that's why he said, out of the blue, 'I was quite glad to see him go for a few days. It gave us a bit of peace. Strange how things were always calmer at home when he wasn't around.'

'My dad was an awkward old sod too.' There was a moment of silence, of shared experience.

'So what do we do now?' Taylor stood up. It was four in the morning, yet Perez could see he was eager to be thumping on doors, shouting down phone lines, making things happen. But despite the flash of energy, it was obvious the man was so tired he could hardly stand.

'We sleep,' Perez said. 'You can't drive back to the hotel. Stay on the sofa. Fran won't mind.' He'd built a few bridges this evening. He and Fran understood each other better too. 'Later we'll talk to Wilding, find out why he lied to us.'

'You talk to Wilding,' Taylor said. 'We don't want to go in too heavy. That's what you're good at, making people believe you're a friend. People like you.'

Not Wilding, Perez thought. He doesn't like me. But he nodded. He was glad of the chance to talk to Wilding alone.

Chapter Thirty-eight

Perez phoned Wilding in the morning to arrange a visit. He thought a formal appointment might increase the pressure on the man. It might give the writer time to prepare a story, but while he was waiting for Perez to arrive, surely he would be becoming more anxious. He'd have heard by now about the bones in the hole. Even if he hadn't picked up on the Biddista gossip, a press release had been issued that morning. It was bland and unspecific, but if Wilding had already known there was a body in the Pit, by the time Perez called he'd be quite sure that it had been found.

Taylor had gone out before Perez and Fran woke up. He'd collapsed on the sofa after Perez had forced him inside from the cold dawn. By then they were both shivering but exhilarated. Things were right between them again. Taylor had fallen asleep immediately: Perez had heard the gentle snoring while he was cleaning his teeth. Fran hardly stirred as he climbed in beside her. He didn't like to wake her. There was an excitement lying next to her, knowing that he wouldn't touch her and the thought of that, the anticipation, kept him awake for a while. Sexy images spinning in his head as the light behind the blind changed colour from grey to a milky yellow. Then he slept too.

Taylor must have left very quietly, because none of them heard him go. He'd left a note on the kitchen table. *Thanks. Good luck.*

Wilding answered the phone very quickly.

'Yes?' As if he'd been expecting a call.

'It's Inspector Perez. I wondered if I might come round. There are a few questions . . .'

There was a moment of silence. This obviously wasn't the call Wilding had been expecting.

'I'm afraid it won't be convenient today, inspector. I'm just on my way out. I've bought a property in Buness. I'm on my way over there with a builder to see what needs to be done before it's habitable.'

'I can meet you there,' Perez said. 'I know the place you mean.'

'Of course you do, inspector. I should have realized. There are no secrets on Shetland.' He gave a little laugh. 'Very well, I'll see you in my new house. You'll be my first real visitor. But give me an hour or so to talk to the builder and the plumber. I don't need the news getting out that I'm being questioned by the police.' He waited for a response from Perez, an answering laugh perhaps, or a reassurance that of course he wasn't a suspect, this was just a matter of routine. Perez said nothing. 'Well,' Wilding continued awkwardly. 'I'll see you there in a little while.'

As Perez replaced the phone Fran came in after dropping Cassie to school. She was flushed from walking up the hill.

'I'm glad you're still here,' she said. 'I thought you

might have gone. I bumped into Magnus at Hillhead and you know how hard it is to get away from him.'

He kissed her to stop her talking and led her back to bed.

Later he made coffee and took it to her. 'What are your plans for the day?'

'Work,' she said. 'Yours?'

'Work.' He considered how much he should tell her. 'I'm off to see Wilding in his new house.'

'Be careful,' she said. 'He's kind of creepy. An obsessive, I think. One of those people who've never quite grown up, can't do real relationships, only teenage crushes.'

'Did he have a crush on you?'

'On me. On Bella. Maybe on any woman who fits in with his fantasy of the time. I was almost tempted to work on his house, though. It's a lovely place.'

Driving down the island, Perez tried to separate his prejudice from what he knew about Wilding. He was definitely a writer. Perez had checked on Amazon. Fantasy novels, quirky, funny but with a dark edge. He'd read some of the reviews. And he'd checked other things too. Wilding had spent a short time in the psychiatric unit of his local general hospital after his girlfriend had left him. He'd made a nuisance of himself, had become obsessed with her. Never violent though. Taylor had talked with the officers who'd taken the complaints. The woman hadn't been frightened by him, just irritated and annoyed. They'd thought him weak and ineffectual, had never believed he'd cause her harm.

Usually that sort of history would have made Perez sympathetic. In his previous job he'd been famous for being soft on nutters. But he couldn't like Wilding. Perhaps it was the money that repelled him. It was hard to feel sorry for a man who was very rich. One of the articles he'd tracked down on the internet had named the sum paid to Wilding as an advance on his last book. He certainly wouldn't need to resort to blackmail.

Perez turned off the main road south, crossed the cattle grid and drove along the side of the thin loch that led towards the sea. It was another lovely day. Perhaps it would continue to be a hot dry summer. His thoughts turned to the photo of the group in the Manse garden, the men in smart clothes, Bella in her slinky red dress. Behind them a perfect sky. It had been hot then too. For the first time it hit him that Bella was the only woman in the picture. Of course he'd seen that, but he'd accepted it as natural. In most gatherings, even now that she was older, Bella was surrounded by men.

A white van came down the road in the opposite direction. Perez pulled in to the verge to let it past, waved at the driver. Davy Clouston, the builder Wilding must be using to do up the house. A good choice. Clouston was a fine workman. Not cheap, but reliable. Perez wondered how Wilding had persuaded him out at such short notice.

The writer would be alone in his new house now, ready to greet visitors. He could have arranged to see Perez later in the day at Biddista, but perhaps he'd wanted to show off the impressive building.

The wrought-iron gates had been pushed open so Perez could pull on to the drive. The gravel was so pierced by weeds and flowers that it looked like an alpine garden. He parked in front of the house and saw Wilding standing at the front step. Like an English laird, Perez thought. And he was wearing corduroy trousers and a tweed jacket to complete the picture. The man was beaming. If he had any anxiety about the interview he was hiding it well.

'Come in,' he said. 'I'm so excited that this place is mine. I fell in love with it the minute I saw it. I know it's dreadful to feel like this when other people are grieving, but I've dreamed of having my own place on Shetland since I first saw Bella's paintings. I never thought I'd get somewhere so delicious.' He opened the double doors and let Perez into a wide hall. Specks of dust twisted in the sunlight. 'I've brought the essentials,' he said. 'Coffee and biscuits, and I've arranged for the electricity to be switched on.'

He led Perez into a room, which was empty except for an unidentifiable item of furniture shrouded by a dust-sheet. It wasn't such a big house, Perez saw now. Two living rooms facing the sea, with a kitchen and bathroom at the back. Probably three bedrooms upstairs. Smaller certainly than the Manse. Wilding was bent over a kettle, which he'd plugged into an ancient socket close to the floor. He spooned coffee into a jug, added the water carefully. 'You do have it black, don't you, inspector? You see, I remembered.' He polished a mug on his shirt and poured the coffee through a fine strainer. 'The best I can do in the circumstances, but I'm sure you'll enjoy it. Shall we take it outside, make the most of the weather?'

They sat on a drystone wall looking down over the beach and the flat island at the mouth of the bay.

'Why didn't you tell me you'd been to Biddista before?' Perez looked at the horizon.

'I'm not sure that you asked.'

'You didn't tell Bella that you'd met before, that you'd been a guest in her house?'

'Well, I thought that might be a little ungallant.' Wilding turned to Perez and smiled. 'It might imply that her memory was failing her. Or that I should mean more to her than I obviously do. I thought too that she might prefer to forget that summer.'

'Why would she want to do that?'

'It was a rather wild time. Frantic. We all have a little more dignity these days.'

'How did you come to be there?'

'She invited me. We met on a train. The sleeper which went then from London to Aberdeen. Perhaps it still does. I was on my way to Dundee to talk at a literary lunch and she was going home. Neither of us had berths booked and we sat up all night drinking and talking. One of those memorable, strange encounters that can change your life. "Come and stay. I love creative people." She was, still is, so charismatic, don't you think? I was bewitched. So after the gig in Dundee I went on to Aberdeen and got the ferry north, took her at her word. The old *St Clare*: oilmen boozing in the bar and kids dossing on deck in sleeping bags. When I turned up at the Manse I'm not entirely sure she knew who I was even then. She'd had a lot to drink in the train. I'd imagined a love affair, that she'd invited me because we were in some way kindred spirits, but the house was full of people.'

He turned to Perez and smiled. 'It was a little humiliating. I turned up on the doorstep with champagne and chocolates and there was a blank stare before she welcomed me in. You can see why I didn't want to repeat that experience a second time. If she wasn't going to know me after two days, she was hardly likely to remember after nearly fifteen years.'

'Who else was staying that summer?'

'I'm not sure. A couple of young men, art students from Glasgow.'

'Jeremy Booth,' Perez said. 'He was there.'

'The man who died at the Biddista jetty?' Wilding seemed genuinely surprised. 'Was he?'

'You don't remember him?'

'No.'

Perez laid the photograph of Bella's party on the wall between them. 'Perhaps this will jog your memory.'

Wilding looked at the photograph. 'Good God, I can't even remember this being taken. I don't think I ever saw it. Doesn't Bella look wonderful? But rather unhappy, I fancy.'

'That's you, I think.' Perez pointed to the dark man, standing in line.

'So it is, of course. That's still how I remember myself. It's always a shock when I look in the mirror.'

'What were the masks about?'

'A whim of Bella's. Her idea of a sophisticated evening.'

Perez pointed again. 'We think that's Jeremy Booth. Do you recognize him?'

Wilding considered. 'Perhaps I do. You know, the name seemed familiar when you first told me it. He was an actor, just as you said, and he was there that summer. Not for long though. I was obsessed and I couldn't leave until everyone else did, but he was only there for a few days. He arrived right at the end of my stay. Bella had picked him up in much the same way as she'd collected me from the train. I think he had the same expectation as me of romance, a sexual encounter at least, and was similarly disappointed. He followed her round like a lovesick puppy, but nobody could take him seriously. He looked very different then from his picture in the paper and the man who caused the scene in the Herring House. He had long hair. Jem, he called himself. We got on rather well. I can't believe that Bella remembered him. She had so many admirers.'

'She had this photograph. Something triggered her memory.'

'It was taken at the farewell dinner,' Wilding said. 'We told each other we didn't want to go and yet most of us seemed relieved it was over.'

'You came back, though, after fifteen years. The place must have held some importance to you.'

'Ah, this time I was in Shetland with quite different expectations. I wanted peace and an escape from my girlfriend. At least an escape from my obsession with my girlfriend. I met Helen soon after my stay at the Manse. She's very different from Bella. Frail, rather shy. Though she haunted me too.'

'You don't look very haunted.' It was an unprofessional comment but Wilding, with confidence and his precise, arrogant words, sitting on the wall with a chocolate biscuit in one hand and his coffee in the other, seemed incapable of such sensibility.

'I've had to toughen up, inspector. I've learned it's the only way to survive.'

'Why Biddista? You could have gone anywhere in Shetland.'

'I think I explained that before. I did still love the paintings. Bella's work got better, much stronger, as she got older, and I renewed my contact with her by email. I hoped of course that she'd recognize my name but she didn't. When I said I wanted a break in Shetland, she offered me the house in Biddista to rent.'

They sat for a moment in silence.

Perez spoke first. 'You went to visit Willy in the care home. Did you talk about that summer?'

'Of course not, inspector. Willy can't remember what happened last week. I enjoy hearing his stories, that's all.'

'What happened that night fifteen years ago? The night the photograph was taken?'

'Really, inspector, can it have any relevance to your present investigation?'

'I think it can. It might tell us why Jeremy Booth came back.'

'We all drank too much and made fools of ourselves.' He paused. 'At one point Bella was weeping. I'd never seen her lose control in that way before. The tears were rolling down her cheeks, her face was all red and blotchy. She was ugly. It was horrible. It was that image I think that persuaded me to leave with the others. I didn't want to know that she was human.'

'Why was she crying?'

'I don't know. Someone said something to offend her, perhaps. She could take offence very quickly.'

'Was there a row? An argument?'

ANN CLEEVES

'No. We were all too drunk and stoned to fight.' He
paused. 'We didn't see her the next day. She stayed in
bed. We joked that she must have a massive hangover,
but really I think she was embarrassed that we'd seen
her like that. We went without saying goodbye.'

'Nobody thought to check that she wasn't ill?'

'The boy, Roddy, was there. I suppose he'd stayed
all night, gone to bed before the festivities started. Or
perhaps his parents dropped him off in the middle of
the morning. I don't remember. He spent a lot of time
in the Manse that summer. He was quite young then,
but a bright little thing. We sent him into Bella's bedroom to see how she was. How cowardly we all were!
We couldn't face her. He came back to the kitchen
where we were all sitting. "Auntie says, 'Piss off the lot
of you!'" It was so much the sort of thing that Bella
would have said that we went with a clear conscience.
We always did what she told us.'

'Booth left with you too?'

'Not exactly the same time. Willy gave him a lift to
Lerwick in his van. I'd been in Willy's van before.
There were no real seats in the back. I remember the
bruises. I decided to leave Biddista in style and
ordered a taxi from Lerwick.'

'We've found another body in the Pit o' Biddista.'

Wilding turned sharply. 'I heard you'd found
bones. Couldn't they have been there for generations?'

'You have no idea who it could be?'

'Of course not!'

'And you're quite sure you didn't recognize Booth
when he made the scene at the Herring House?'

'Would you remember someone you'd seen briefly
fifteen years ago? And he'd changed so much.'

340

'Did he get in touch with you? You're pretty famous now and you've written about the move to Shetland on your website. An email perhaps. *I'll be in Shetland, can we meet to talk about old times?* We know he intended to catch up with friends when he was here.'

'Not me, inspector.'

Perez thought Wilding would stick to whatever story he'd created. Perhaps he even believed it. Perhaps it was true. He stood up. 'Thank you for your time, Mr Wilding. If you remember anything, please get in touch.'

'Of course.' Wilding was playing the good-natured host once more. He took Perez's mug, walked with him back to the car. There he stood for a moment and gave a malicious grin. 'I've asked Fran Hunter to manage the interior design of the house for me. I can't think of anyone better, can you?'

'No,' Perez said. 'I don't think I can.'

Chapter Thirty-nine

Kenny heard the news about the bones in the Pit o' Biddista on Radio Scotland while he was washing up the breakfast dishes. Edith had already left for work. Now the gathering of the people on the cliff the night before made sense to him, and since hearing the radio report he'd been waiting in the house all day for the police to turn up. Because the bones must belong to Lawrence, mustn't they? That would explain his sudden disappearance. Lawrence might have told Bella that he was leaving the islands, but something had happened before he could get on the ferry or the plane. Not an accident. Lawrence had grown up on the cliffs, had been more sure-footed than any of them. Nor suicide. Kenny knew Lawrence too well to believe that. But an act of violence. That would explain his absence, the years without a letter or a phone call.

Kenny was almost pleased that the body had been found. Thinking that a few bones, like the carcase of a sheep in a ditch, was all that was left of his brother made him feel ill, but still it was a kind of relief. What had hurt most since Lawrence had disappeared was thinking he hadn't cared enough about him to keep in touch. He'd pictured Lawrence in a strange town, a strange country even, with a new family. A blonde wife, because Lawrence liked blondes, two sons. He'd be older, his hair grey but still thick and curly. They'd be sat together at the supper table, laughing at one of Lawrence's silly jokes, not thinking at all about the family back in Shetland. But if Lawrence had died without leaving the islands there had been no perfect family, no laughter.

By ten o'clock he'd still not heard from the detectives working the case. Kenny phoned the police station in Lerwick and asked to speak to Jimmy Perez. A young woman said he was out. Could another officer help? Kenny tried to imagine talking to someone else about Lawrence, that big Englishman for example, but the idea horrified him. He asked the young woman to tell Inspector Perez to call him back as soon as possible. He gave her his phone number in Skoles and his mobile number, made sure she repeated them.

'It's urgent,' he said. 'Tell him it's urgent.'

By midday there was still no word from Perez. Kenny had gone out briefly to finish singling the second field of neeps, only because he knew there was mobile reception there, and he could see the road right to the end of the valley. He thought Perez might drive out to talk to him, rather than phone. If they'd found out that the bones belonged to Lawrence they would want to tell him in person. Kenny couldn't quite explain the excitement he was feeling. It was different from when he'd asked to see the body of the hanged man. He'd known deep down that person wasn't Lawrence and, even if it had been, he would still have to live with the thought of his brother abandoning him. This time he thought there really might be an end to the waiting and to the feeling he'd been rejected for all these years.

He went to the house, intending to phone the police station again, but instead he found himself phoning Edith at the care centre. She answered with her calm, businesslike work voice.

'Edith Thomson speaking.'

He could picture her in her office, behind her desk, with the photo of Ingirid and Eric on the windowsill behind her. The photo of him which she said she liked the best, pushing his boat into the water.

Now, he wasn't quite sure what to say.

'I wondered if you might like to have lunch with me.' Suddenly he wanted to see her. He felt like a young man asking a woman out for a date, all shaky and nervous. He'd felt a little that way around Jimmy Perez's mother.

'What's happened?' Her voice was alarmed. He had never before offered to take her out to lunch when she was working. Not even on her birthday or their anniversary. He knew she liked to eat with the people who used the centre. She said it kept her in touch with how things were going there.

'Have you not heard the news on the radio?'

'No,' she said. 'I've been very busy today. I've hardly moved out of the office.' He could imagine her, frowning with concentration, tapping away on her computer.

'There's been another body,' he said. 'An old one.'

There was a pause at the end of the line.

'And you think it might be Lawrence?'

'I think it must be.'

'I can't get away,' she said. 'You can come here if you like, though. Of course you must come here.'

But just having spoken to her had calmed him. 'Maybe later. I know you're busy at lunchtime.' He replaced the phone, thinking there was nothing after all to be anxious about. Nothing had changed, except his idea of what might have happened to Lawrence. He looked in the fridge for something to have for his lunch, but there was nothing there that he wanted to eat. He thought he would go to the shop and buy something. A pie or a burger, and a cake. Aggie didn't close until one and he would get there just in time. It would do him good to get away from the croft, even if it was only for a while.

The shop was empty and Aggie sat reading, just as she always did if she was on her own. She was surprised to see him.

'Kenny. What can I do for you?' They'd known each other since they were babies and yet she always kept her distance from him. A certain formality. Had she been that way even when she was a child?

'I fancied something tasty for my dinner,' he said. 'Edith buys all the healthy food. Today I thought I'd like something a bit different.'

'Comfort eating,' she said, and smiled.

He knew then that she'd been thinking exactly the same thing as him about the bones the police had found.

She looked at her watch. 'There'll be no one else in the shop now. Why don't you come next door with me? I could do you sausage, egg and chips. Would that suit you?'

The invitation shocked him. She'd come to Skoles

when they'd had a bit of a party at Christmas or New Year, but she'd never invited them into her house. Aggie and Edith had got on well enough when they were young, but the women had never been great friends, at least not since Lawrence had gone. Lawrence had seemed to hold the whole of Biddista together.

'I'd like that very much,' Kenny said. 'If it's not too much trouble.'

'Not at all.' She smiled, and he saw that she had quite a pretty face. 'I like comfort food myself.'

She brought up the subject of Lawrence while she was cooking the chips. She cooked them the old-fashioned way, with oil in a big pan and a basket, so there was the noise of them frying. She had her back to him, so it was hard to tell what she was thinking. The sausages were in a frying pan and they smelled very good. She'd made him a big mug of tea as soon as they got into the kitchen and he sat with his boots off at the table, drinking it. He was just thinking it was a pity she'd never remarried when she started speaking.

'Have the police been in touch with you?'

'About the bones in the Pit? No. I phoned Jimmy Perez this morning but he was out.'

'You think it's Lawrence?'

'I think it was too much of a coincidence for it not to be.'

'I suppose they'll be able to tell,' she said. 'All those things you read about. Forensics.'

'I just want to know,' he said.

She cracked three eggs on the side of the pan and

added them to the sausages, lifted the chip basket so it rested just above the oil, then turned round to him.

'I felt that way when Andrew drowned,' she said. 'But sometimes I think hope is better.'

'Do you remember that summer when Lawrence disappeared?' he asked. 'I wasn't here. I was away in Fair Isle, working.'

She took two plates from the warming oven at the bottom of the Rayburn, carefully lifted out the eggs – two for him and one for her – and the sausages, then shook the oil from the chips and tipped them on to the plates.

'I wasn't here then. I was in Scalloway.' She pushed a knife and fork across the table to him. He couldn't tell what she made of the question. He didn't know what she was thinking at all. 'Eat up while it's hot.'

'But you'd hear what was going on. What were folks saying?'

'Just what they've been saying ever since. That he asked Bella Sinclair to marry him and she turned him down, so he took a great temper on him and left the islands.' She picked up a chip with her fingers and blew on it before putting it into her mouth. Then she frowned. 'He did have a temper, Kenny. You know he did. You remember when we were children, him scrapping in the schoolyard. The teacher having to pull the boys apart. He always had to be the best, the strongest. Always in competition, even with you.'

Kenny thought of the two of them racing to finish singling the neeps. Lawrence was the quickest, but his own rows were the neater. He wasn't sure there was much of a competition, but it was true that Lawrence always wanted to win.

'You never heard anything else? That he'd picked a fight over work? Fallen out with anyone?'

It occurred to Kenny that he might have to apologize to Bella when all this was over. Perhaps she'd had nothing to do with his brother's disappearance after all.

'No,' Aggie said. 'I heard nothing like that.'

Chapter Forty

Back in the house, Kenny sat in his chair in the kitchen and dozed. He wasn't used to eating such a big meal at lunchtime. The telephone woke him with a start. He rushed into the hall, thinking it would be Jimmy Perez, but it was Edith. He looked at his watch and saw that it was three o'clock.

'Are you OK, Kenny? Is there any news?'

He felt guilty then. He should have phoned her. She'd have been worrying about him all afternoon.

'No news,' he said. 'But I'm fine.' He didn't tell her about the big fried meal Aggie had cooked for him. He'd enjoyed the meal so much that it seemed like a guilty secret. He knew Aggie wouldn't tell anyone about it.

'Do you still want to come over?'

'Yes,' he said. He didn't feel panicky any more, but the lunch with Aggie had given him a taste for company.

When he walked into the care centre through the big double doors and saw the people sitting in the sunny room, dozing or chatting, he thought maybe it wouldn't be so bad to end his days here. He would be with people he knew, people he'd grown up with. He waved to Willy, who sat a little apart from the others, staring out of the window. Willy waved back at him with a great silly grin, and Kenny gestured with his hand to show that he'd come back to chat to him later.

Edith came out into the hall to greet him. He thought what a nuisance he must be to her, more like a child at times than her man.

'Come into the office,' she said. 'I've asked Sandra to make us some tea.'

He sat in the easy chair on the other side of her desk. He thought this was where people would sit when there was a problem with a relative she was looking after. Maybe even if a client had died. He supposed she would arrange for tea to be brought then. She would pour it out for them, from the china teapot which sat there on its tray. She thinks the bones belong to Lawrence too, he thought. She's treating me like a grieving relative.

'I wish Perez would phone and let me know what's going on,' he said.

She reached out and squeezed his hand. 'Maybe he doesn't want to talk to you until he has information. It can't be easy identifying a body from a few scraps of bone.'

Kenny considered this. Sometimes he watched police shows on the television. In those shows test results seemed to come back within hours. But those programmes weren't set in Shetland. Perhaps there was no one here competent to do the tests. The samples would have to be sent south and that would take time.

He sipped from the cup, which seemed very fragile in his big hand. There was a plate with little square biscuits covered in sugar. He took one and dipped it into the tea. It tasted of coconut.

'Do you remember anything of that time Lawrence disappeared?' he asked.

She poured tea for herself. 'I've been trying to think ever since you phoned. Bella had a heap of people in the Manse. Sometimes Willy took them out fishing. They'd come back and build a fire on the beach to cook the fish. They all drank too much. Lawrence spent quite a lot of time with them. You know how he liked a party.'

Kenny nodded.

'I was so busy then,' she said. 'With the children and your father and trying to keep things tidy on the croft. You were in Fair Isle. It wasn't easy.'

'I shouldn't have gone,' he said. 'I see that now.'

She gave a little laugh. 'We needed the money. Don't you remember all the plans we had? And it was worth the work, wasn't it? We have a lovely home now.'

Kenny thought he would give up the lovely home to have been in Biddista when Lawrence disappeared. He'd gone to Fair Isle with Edith's encouragement. She'd wanted their children to have the things her parents had never been able to afford for her.

'I just think you have to wait,' Edith said. 'Perez will get in touch with you as soon as he knows anything. After all these years you can wait a few hours.'

He knew she was right, but he couldn't face going back to the croft and just sitting there, hoping the phone would ring.

'I'll have a talk to Willy, see if I can cheer him up.'

'You do that. But he's quite confused today. A bit agitated. Don't be upset if he doesn't know you.'

'Has Wilding been in to see him again?'

She frowned and he remembered how Wilding's visit to the centre had upset her. 'Not here, but he could have visited him at the sheltered housing over the weekend.'

'Do you think I should call in on Wilding, ask him what he wants from the old man?'

'I'm overreacting, I expect. It's probably nothing. Just a writer's curiosity. I'd like to know what he's up to, but I wouldn't want you going to see him on your own. Not with everything that's happened since he arrived. Wait until Martin can go with you.'

'Wilding's a weak sort of man. I can't see him killing anyone.'

'I'm not sure,' she said. 'Don't you think it's the weak ones who are most violent?'

There was a knock at the door. 'I'm sorry,' she said. 'I'll have to go. There's a meeting. Something I can't cancel. My boss has come up from Lerwick.'

He leaned across her desk and gave her a peck on the cheek. 'I'll see you at home.'

Kenny sat beside Willy in the lounge. The staff were bringing round cups of tea on a trolley, stopping beside each person in turn. Willy already had his, but it sat untouched on the table beside him. His chin was on his chest and his eyes were half closed. It was very warm in the room and Kenny could see why some users of the centre spent all day dozing. He could feel himself nodding off too. He patted Willy's hand just to wake him, though he didn't seem properly asleep, just daydreaming. He was surprised at how cold the hand felt.

352

'Hi Willy. It's Kenny. You mind me from Biddista? You taught me everything I know about boats.'

The old man turned very slowly, opened his eyes and smiled.

'Of course I mind you, man.'

'I've just come to see how you're feeling.'

'Not so well. Things are such a muddle in my head these days. Don't get old, man. There's no pleasure in it.'

'We had grand times, didn't we, Willy? Those summers when you took us all out fishing. There was the group of us. Bella and Alec Sinclair, Aggie Watt, my wife Edith, who looks after you here, and Lawrence and me.'

Willy sat quite still, staring into space with a sort of fierce concentration.

'You *do* remember Lawrence, Willy? My brother Lawrence?'

There was a moment while Willy stared into space.

'He left Shetland,' Kenny said. 'We all thought he left Shetland because Bella Sinclair turned him down.'

'No,' Willy said firmly. 'He's still here.' He raised a shaking hand to grasp his tea. 'He didn't go anywhere.'

'Where is he?'

But Willy seemed not to have heard the question. 'He's a great one for the fishing,' he said, and he started a story about taking the boat out with a couple of Englishmen. It was all about a big party Bella was holding and how she wanted fish to serve her guests. Willy gutted them for her and took the heads off. He described that in great detail, the gutting of the fish, as if Kenny had never done it for himself. In the end Kenny only listened with half his mind.

353

'Was Lawrence there that night?' he asked in the end. He wanted to get home in case Jimmy called at Skoles.

'Of course he was. He wanted fish too.'

Willy closed his eyes again, then opened them slowly. 'That Englishman came to see me,' he said. 'Full of questions. But I told him nothing.'

Kenny was going to touch his hand again, to prompt him back to the present, when the mobile in his pocket started to buzz. He fumbled to get it and answered just before the message service cut in. It was Jimmy Perez. Kenny stood up and walked with the phone out into the car park. Willy seemed not to notice his leaving and the other people watched him go without interest. There were a couple of gulls, very noisy, fighting over a scrap of bread, and for a moment he was distracted. Soon he realized there was no real news.

'I'm sorry it's taken me so long to get back to you.'

'I heard about the bones you'd found.'

'I should have come to tell you, Kenny. But we were so late finishing last night I didn't want to trouble you. And this morning I've been working on the case.'

'Is it Lawrence?'

'We won't know for a while.'

There was a pause. Kenny could tell he was going to add something more, but couldn't help interrupting. 'Can't you do something with DNA?'

'We'd need bone marrow to do a standard DNA test, and because of where the bones were found we don't have that. There is a tooth and it's possible that we could get some dentine. But there's another test.

354

Mitochondrial DNA. It's passed down the maternal line. It means you and Lawrence would share it.' Kenny was trying to focus, to take all this in, but found his thoughts swimming. This is what Willy feels like. He can't keep a hold on what's happening around him. He forced himself to listen again to what Perez was saying.

'Could we take a DNA sample from you? Do you understand, Kenny? We need your DNA to identify your brother.'

'Of course you can. Of course.' Kenny felt ridiculously pleased that there was something he could do to help.

'I'll come in this evening to take a swab. But it might be very late. Or I could send someone else . . .'

'Don't worry, Jimmy. I'd rather you came. I'll just stay up until you arrive. It doesn't matter how late you are.'

'And Kenny, it's going to take longer than we'd like to get an answer. About two weeks, because it's not a standard sort of test. I'm sorry.'

Kenny stood for a moment. He was tempted to go back to Willy, to find out what he knew. Then he realized there were other people in Biddista who should be able to tell him.

Chapter Forty-one

When he came back from seeing Wilding in Buness, Perez returned to the station. He phoned the pathologist in Aberdeen to check the situation on identifying the fragment of bone, then called the Thomson house. Nobody was at home. He knew what Kenny would be thinking and when finally he spoke to him on his mobile he could sense how much he needed an answer.

'I'm sorry, man. I wish I could make it happen more quickly.' Perez felt helpless because the test was completely out of his control. But all the time he was thinking that really it didn't matter. He had a sense of events moving quickly, racing away from him. He thought the case would reach a climax before the results of the mitochondrial DNA test were returned.

He found Taylor at the desk he'd taken over in the incident room. He'd just finished a phone call and an A4 pad covered with scribbled notes lay in front of him. Taylor was hunched over them.

'I've been on to Jebson in West Yorkshire to see if they've had anything back yet on emails to and from Jeremy Booth. Post too. They had a search team going through the house. The bin hadn't been put out since he left and they thought they might find a letter.'

'Anything useful?'

'No mail. Jebson did come up with an interesting email contact though. A woman called Rita Murphy who runs a theatrical agency. I've just been talking to her. Booth was on her books, had been for years. She comes from Liverpool, like me. We hit it off and she's been dead helpful.'

Taylor took a swig from a can of Coke. Perez thought he must be exhausted, running on caffeine and will power. 'It seems Booth hadn't done much through her in the last few years – most of his time was spent running his own business – but Rita said he liked to keep his hand in by doing bits of theatre if it was offered. They kept in touch, anyway. It sounds as if they'd become good mates.'

'Was she representing him when he took on the work with *The Motley Crew* fifteen years ago?'

'Yeah, she was just starting up then. She'd seen him in an amateur play and thought he was good, offered to take him on.'

Perez remembered the performance in the Herring House, the tears. Oh, he was good, he thought.

'How did the work on the boat come about?'

'She'd been in college with the guy who dreamed up the idea of the theatre in the boat and he asked her to find him a couple of actors. It was Booth's first professional work. That's why she remembers it.'

'I don't suppose he talked to her about it afterwards? Or that she remembers what he said?'

'No detail. He called in to see her when he got back. She said he'd enjoyed the acting, travelling round the coast, but he seemed a bit low. She'd expected a blow-by-blow account of the season but he didn't want to talk about it much. She put that down to the recent separation from his wife and daughter. But if Bella sent him away with a flea in his ear, perhaps that explains it.'

'Did he tell her that he was planning to come back to Shetland?'

'He went over to Liverpool a few weeks ago. It was about the time that his daughter got in touch with him. Perhaps he was curious to see the girl before he made a commitment to meet her. I can imagine him hanging around the school, waiting to see what she was like.'

What would he have done if he hadn't liked the look of her? Perez wondered. Made some excuse? Run away again?

Taylor was still sketching out the possible scenario. 'He went to see Ms Murphy while he was in Merseyside. We'll probably never know if that's why he was there, but anyway, they met for lunch in a bar. Rita said Booth was really elated. It sounds as if they had a lot to drink. He told her then that he was taking on a bit of work in Shetland. "Don't worry, darling. You'll get your ten per cent. But this is a bit of private enterprise."'

'Did he say what sort of work it was?'

'"Promotional street theatre".' Perez could hear the quotation marks in Taylor's voice, thought that might describe the pantomime at the cruise ship and in Lerwick. He wasn't sure it covered the drama at the Herring House though.

'Rita thought it was weird that he'd consider doing work like that. She said usually he was a bit picky. He liked real theatre, not the arty stuff. She thought it would be some sort of conceptual theatre – whatever that is – because he said it was linked to an art gallery. When I told her what was actually involved she said she was surprised he hadn't just left and come home. It wasn't acting at all. A kid straight out of school could put on a costume and hand out a few flyers. And Booth could be very arsy when it came to work.'

'So she thought he'd been hired to do the work by the gallery?'

'That was the impression he gave at first. Later he said what a great opportunity it was – a chance to get close to a real celebrity. "This could be my big chance, darling. The time to hit the jackpot. My little bit of luck. And if I hadn't been watching the telly the other night, I'd never have known." He went all mysterious on her after that. She didn't really take any notice. He was always talking about hitting the big time. All actors do.'

Perez sat for a moment in silence, wondering how this information fitted in with his ideas about the case.

'Do you have any idea which television programme he was talking about?'

'Wouldn't it have been that documentary about Roddy Sinclair?'

Perez didn't watch much television, but the uncertain theories in his head about how Booth had died suddenly shifted and came into focus.

'What documentary would that be?'

'It was one of a series. Sort of a fly-on-the-wall look at contemporary artists. The cameras followed Roddy round for a week.'

'I think I read about it in the *Shetland Times*,' Perez said. 'The BBC came here to film him during the music festival last year.' Then he remembered that Kenny had talked about it and been involved in it too.

'Some of it was set in Glasgow. Him playing at a folk club, meeting up with his friends, talking about his music – but there were a couple of scenes in London and quite a long piece filmed in Shetland. The Herring House featured, I think, and there was an interview with Bella. I remember one part where they followed Roddy into the Biddista shop – there was a bit of banter with the customers – and another of him playing music in the school where he used to go.'

'The high school?'

'Nah, these were little kids. It must have been the local primary.'

'In Lerwick?

'Out in the wilds somewhere, I thought.'

'Can we track down a copy of the film?' Perez asked.

'If you think it's important.'

Perez didn't answer, but he was thinking it would confirm to him who'd killed three people. Proving it, though, would be quite a different matter.

Perez arrived at Middleton School just as the children were leaving. He'd asked Taylor if he'd like to come too, thought Taylor could do with a break from the incident room, some fresh air, cold turkey from the caffeine. And if Perez did the driving he might even catch some sleep in the car. But the conversation with Booth's agent seemed to have had a strange effect on Taylor. He sat at his desk, frowning, oblivious to the activity around him. He was quite still. The restlessness and fidgeting seemed finally under control. He didn't even ask why Perez wanted to go to Middleton. He seemed preoccupied with concerns of his own.

'Are you OK?'

Taylor turned then, flashed a grin, which immediately disappeared.

'Yeah, fine. Things on my mind. You know. Nothing to do with this case. Work-related, stuff happening back in Inverness.'

Perez didn't think he could push it. They'd reestablished a delicate balance in their friendship. He wanted to keep things that way.

It was classic Shetland weather, breezy with flashes of bright sunshine, and as Perez got out of his car a group of children ran out of the school into the wind, arms outstretched, yelling and laughing. He envied their energy. He waited until the playground was empty before he went inside. Dawn Williamson was in the school library, sitting on one of the small chairs in front of a computer. He stood for a moment watching her, but her body blocked his view of the machine so he couldn't see what was on the screen.

'Don't you have a PC at home?' Everyone did now. Most Shetlanders shopped online. One time, when you went south, people gave you a list of goodies unobtainable in the islands to bring back. Now people bought their CDs, books, clothes and even household items on the internet.

She turned, startled by his voice, then smiled, reassured, when she recognized him.

'The hard drive's crashed,' she said. 'I've only had the bloody thing for six months. It's a real nuisance.

361

Martin used it for work. Even Aggie had become a convert – she's really interested in family history and there's loads you can do online. I've just sent it back to the manufacturer. It was still under warranty and I couldn't get anyone to come out to fix it.'

'I'm sorry,' he said. 'I've a few more questions.'

She stood up and leaned against the desk so she was facing him. Something about his expression seemed to panic her.

'Is anything wrong, inspector? What's happened now?'

'There's nothing new,' he said. 'Just questions.'

'We're all so jumpy. I heard you'd found another body down the Pit. It's horrible, unbelievable. What do I tell Alice? I hoped she'd be protected, growing up here.'

Perez thought of the bullying he'd endured when he moved from the small Fair Isle school to the hostel in Lerwick. Kids were cruel wherever they lived. He didn't think people were so different because they lived in Shetland. Not the children or the grown-ups.

'It's about the television documentary on Roddy Sinclair. You remember it?'

'I'll never forget it,' she said. 'You won't believe the excitement it caused, the BBC coming to the school. They were here for three days and in the end the scene only lasted for about five minutes. The kids loved it.'

'Roddy was never a pupil here, though, was he? He lived in Lerwick when he was in the primary.'

'Dramatic licence, I suppose. Middleton's a bit more scenic. And I think he did come here for a few weeks when he was very young. It was when his father was first diagnosed and had to go away to Aberdeen to hospital. His mother went too and Roddy stayed with Bella. He has come in to do some music with the kids since he started recording. They loved him, of course. There was enough of the rascal in him to appeal to them.'

'How long did the BBC spend filming in Biddista?'

'Quite a lot longer. More than a week. In the end the documentary was as much about the community as about Roddy himself.'

'What did the Biddista folk make of that?'

'Oh, they all pretended to be very cool, but they made sure they were out and about whenever the BBC were filming.'

'Everyone?'

'Well, Aggie's always been a bit shy. She got Martin to stand in for her the day they did the bit in the shop. We persuaded her to pretend to be one of the customers, so the whole community was captured.'

'Was Willy still living in Biddista then?'

'He was. He was there on the film. Although it's not long been shown on the television, they shot it last spring.'

'So it was before Peter Wilding moved into his house?'

'Yes, it was. Willy was managing quite well on his own then.' She looked directly at Perez. 'What is all this about? You can't think one of us is a killer.'

He didn't answer. He stretched and felt the tension in the muscles in his back. I need a bath, he thought. A long hot soak. Real food. Why do I think I enjoy doing this job?

'I'm really sorry to have troubled you at work again,' he said.

'Is that it?' she demanded. He saw that her nerves were tattered and she was having trouble holding things together. 'No explanation for all these questions?'

'Sorry,' he said again.

He could see she wanted him to leave, but he hesitated, wondering if he could risk one last question. The question that had been in his head since he'd come to the school. 'Have you any idea who the murderer is, Dawn?'

She stared at him. 'I can't believe you asked me that.' He saw he'd pushed her too far, but couldn't help continuing.

'You might have heard something. People talking. I know you weren't involved. You weren't living in Shetland when all this started. But someone in Biddista knows.'

'I can't talk about this now. I want to get home, spend some time with my daughter. If you have more questions come to Biddista later when she's asleep. I'd rather have Martin there anyway. I know it's pathetic, but I can't do this on my own.'

Perez thought how Dawn had been when he'd first met her. A strong and confident woman. This is what violence does, he thought. It makes victims of us all.

Chapter Forty-two

Perhaps it *would* be better talking to Dawn and Martin together, Perez thought. He drove out of Middleton a little way on the Lerwick road. He didn't still want to be parked in the playground when Dawn came out of the school. She was jumpy enough and he didn't want to scare her, didn't want her thinking he was watching her. He pulled in to the side of the road, next to a few scrubby trees someone must have planted years ago as a windbreak, and made plans for the rest of the evening.

He thought he should call in on Kenny while he was waiting for Dawn to get Alice to bed. He could take the swab for the DNA. But didn't think he could face talking to the crofter just yet. It came to him again that he needed hot food and a bath. And that would give him time on his own to order his thoughts. He was groping towards a solution but had no evidence. He still couldn't see any way of obtaining sufficient proof to allow an arrest.

He drove back to Lerwick and parked in the lane outside his house. Inside he opened the windows, so the breeze blew the curtains and rattled the doors. A neighbour had the radio on and the sound blew in too. Perez recognized a track from the latest Roddy Sinclair album. He scrambled eggs and made toast and coffee and ate the food with the plate on his lap, perched in the window seat, watching the Bressay ferry make its way across to the island. Then he ran a deep hot bath and lay in the water, almost dozing, letting various scenarios around the case play in his head. He wasn't usually one for conspiracy theories, but this time he allowed himself to consider the most preposterous ideas. Investigation was all about 'What if . . .' He thought Wilding must play the same games while he was writing his stories.

Before leaving the house he phoned Taylor, using his mobile number because he thought surely by now the man would have left the police station. The Englishman was staying in exactly the same room in the same hotel as in the previous investigation. Perez had picked him up from there once and it had been as tidy as a cubicle in a military barracks. It was hard to believe the bed had been slept in; his clothes were neatly folded. On the dressing table a pen, a brush and a notepad had stood in a precise line. Perez wondered whether Taylor ever relaxed.

Certainly he wasn't relaxing now, because it was clear from the background sounds that he was still at work.

'Yes?'

'Did your friends in West Yorkshire mention finding any photographs in Booth's house?' Perez had returned to his seat at the window. 'Someone was obviously taking pictures that summer because we have the group photo with Bella and the men. I wondered if there were any others.'

There was a silence. Taylor was trying to follow his

reasoning. 'Is there something you're not telling me, Jimmy?'

Now Perez hesitated. 'I need to talk to the Williamsons again,' he said. 'Then I'm going in to get that swab from Kenny. Do you want to meet me in Biddista later? Or maybe you'd rather get to your bed?'

'No point,' Taylor said. 'I thought winter was bad enough here, but I'd survive that better than these crazy light nights. I know I've not been the easiest person to work with on this case. Put it down to being halfway to the Arctic Circle and getting no sleep. If I can track down any photos, I'll get West Yorkshire to scan them and send them as attachments. I'll print them out and bring them with me.'

'Have you managed to track down a recording of the TV documentary?'

'Apparently Sandy's mother has one. She taped it because of the Shetland scenes. He's gone to Whalsay to fetch it, hopes to get the last ferry back.'

'Good.'

There was a brief hesitation. 'Jimmy?'

'Yes?'

'Doesn't matter. I wanted to ask your advice about something. But it'll keep. You need to get off.'

Perez replaced the phone and then realized they hadn't decided where they should meet. It didn't matter. Biddista wasn't such a big place. Taylor would find him, and anyway he wasn't sure yet where he would be.

When he arrived at the Williamson house, the child was in bed, but all the adults were there. Even Aggie had been brought in from next door. Perez hadn't been expecting that and wasn't sure how it

367

would work, but didn't think he could send her back to her house. He didn't want to start off the interview with a confrontation. Besides, he needed to talk to her. They sat in a row on the sofa. Martin opened the door to him, then returned to his place.

'What is all this about, Jimmy? I didn't have you down as the sort to go in for bully-boy tactics. You shouldn't have gone to the school and harassed my wife in that way.'

'I have to ask questions. That's what I do for a living.'

'You accused Dawn of knowing who the murderer is.'

'No,' Perez said. He hated being thought a bully. There was a pause while he considered if he could have played it any differently, then decided they had to know this was serious. 'I asked her if she had any idea. That's rather different. If I *believed* she knew what had been going on here she'd be under arrest for perverting the course of justice.' He paused. 'I wanted Dawn's opinion because she's relatively new to the place, more objective. Nothing more than that.'

Dawn had been sitting quietly throughout the exchange. Now she spoke. 'I'm sorry,' she said. 'I over-reacted in the school. But this is horrible. The violence going on just outside the door. It was close enough to home already. Now it seems personal, as if it's come in and become a part of our lives. Is there someone out there who hates everyone who lives in Biddista?'

'No,' Perez said. 'I don't think it's that.'

They sat for a moment in silence.

'What about you, Aggie?' he asked. 'Can you tell me what's been going on?'

She sat very upright in the sofa and shook her head. The rest of her body was frozen and the movement seemed unnatural. It reminded Perez of a mechanical doll.

'What were you doing fifteen years ago?'

'I was living in Scalloway with my man, running the hotel and minding Martin here.'

'Your mother was still living in Biddista then?'

'Aye, she was still in this house. My father was dead by then. I moved back here when she died.'

'So you visited quite often?'

'I was here a lot,' Aggie said. 'Somehow I never quite settled in Scalloway. Maybe it was my fault that my husband was the way he was. My heart was never in it – the marriage or the work.'

Perez looked at Martin, expecting some sort of reaction – a defensive comment or an attempt at humour – but there was nothing.

'What about you, Martin? Did you spend much time in Biddista?'

'I was a teenager,' he said. 'Into hanging around with my mates, football, music. There wasn't much to bring me to Biddista. And I liked the hotel in Scalloway, talking to the visitors, helping my father in the kitchen. It suited me fine.'

Perez returned his attention to Aggie. 'Did you keep in touch with Bella too?'

'Oh, aye. I'd go and visit her at the Manse. She liked to have me as an audience when there was nobody better around. She liked to show off her fancy house and her fancy furniture. Having me there made her realize how much she'd moved on.'

'You sound quite bitter.'

'Do I?' She seemed surprised by the thought. 'No, I was never jealous of Bella. She wasn't a contented woman. However much she had, it was never enough for her. And she never had a child of her own. I know she wanted that. Physically, like a craving or an addiction. She talked about it to me. She had all those new friends around her, all those men to admire her, but it was her old pals she confided in. These days having the baby she wanted would be easier. She'd have been able to arrange it. Then things were more old-fashioned and Bella always wanted to do things the traditional Shetland way. You needed a husband before you had a child and Bella couldn't get herself a husband. Not one who would suit, at least. There were lots of men, all drawn to her, but none of them wanted to marry her or give her a baby.'

'Did you ever get invited to Bella's parties?'

'Not as a guest.' Aggie smiled. 'And I wouldn't have wanted that. I've never been easy talking to strangers and Bella's parties were full of folks I didn't know. It would have been like the hotel in Scalloway, only worse. I've always been kind of shy.'

'But sometimes you were there?'

'Aye, sometimes I'd help out. Prepare the food, clear up afterwards.'

'You worked, skivvying for Bella Sinclair?' Martin sounded horrified.

'Well, isn't that what you do, son, in the Herring House restaurant? And it wasn't really work. It was just helping out, if I was around.' Aggie smiled. 'I didn't even get paid that often – not a real wage. Bella would bring me back a present from her travels – something pretty I'd never get the chance to use – or she'd put a twenty-pound note in a thank-you card. We'd been at school together. We'd gone our separate ways but we were friends.'

'What about the other people in the valley?' Perez asked. 'Did Bella employ them too?'

'Edith came in occasionally when there was a big party, but not so often. She never really got on with Bella. She'd had two children very close together and though they were a bit older by then she still had her hands full with them. And Kenny's father was still living. He was a demanding old man.'

'Anyone else?'

'Well of course Bella paid Lawrence and Kenny to work on the Herring House. It was one of those jobs we thought would never get finished. When she bought the building first we all decided she was mad. It was just a shell with a rusty corrugated-iron roof, nowhere near the size it is now. They almost built it from new, just using the old stone and some of the old timber. And now look how lovely it is, with the gallery and the restaurant.'

'The restaurant's a recent feature,' Martin said. 'It only opened five years ago.'

'What about the gallery?' Perez asked. 'When was that completed?'

'The boys worked on it in stages,' Aggie said. 'Because they could only do bits and pieces in the evenings. Kenny had the croft and Lawrence was doing building for other folks in the day. Folks who were willing to pay. It was almost finished when Lawrence left the island. We decided he waited until it was done before he went. He couldn't bear to leave it half finished.'

'Did he tell you he was going?'

'No, but I wasn't surprised when he went. He'd been kind of restless all that summer.'

'That was the hot summer, the summer Bella had her house parties.'

'That would have been the one. Kenny had some work away for part of it. He wasn't around so much. But Lawrence was there. Bella would invite him as a guest to the parties.'

'What did he make of it all?'

'He behaved like a great court jester, playing to the gallery. I hated to see it. He was a good man but he had a sort of short fuse on him. He should have carried himself with a bit more dignity. He believed all those fancy artists and writers thought he was such a clever, witty fellow, but they were laughing at him behind his back. Calling him a clown.'

'You sound as if you were very fond of him, Aggie.'

She blushed. Very suddenly, so he felt as if he'd hit her with his words, marked her face.

'I didn't mind him playing the fool. Better that than when he lost his temper. Besides, he didn't try so hard for me as he did for the soothmoothers.'

'Were you ever more than friends, Aggie?'

He thought she would blush again, but she answered with great dignity. 'We were friends. Nothing more than that. All that showing off wouldn't have suited me, and I was married to Andrew.' Then she paused. 'I always felt a little bit sorry for Kenny. He was the one playing second fiddle. He was the quiet one, the dark horse; Lawrence was full of laughter and sunshine, all show.' She looked up at him. 'Take no notice of me. I'm just being foolish.'

But that summer Kenny was in Fair Isle, Perez thought. A boat or plane ride away.

'Tell me, Aggie, did Roddy spend much time in Biddista then? He'd only have been a boy. How old? Five? Six? At school in Lerwick during the week, but he'd maybe come to visit at the weekends.'

'Most weekends. And sometimes during the week too. He could twist Bella round his little finger even then. "I've got a tummy ache, Auntie. I can't go to school." And there was one period when Alec was away in the hospital and he went to the school in Middleton. Aye, he was always in the Manse, getting under my feet when I was trying to get things ready for the people who were staying.'

'Do you remember any of the visitors, Aggie? Any of the men who came up from the south to stay with Bella?'

'I never really met them,' she said. 'They were so loud and full of opinions I wouldn't have known what to say to them.'

'You never met any of them again?'

'How would I do that?'

'Two of them came back,' Perez said. 'Peter Wilding was one. He lives in the house next door. He uses the post office. He hasn't changed so much. Did you never recognize him?'

'No,' Aggie said very quickly. 'How would I remember him after all this time?'

'And he never said anything to you? Not a hint about the old times?'

'Nothing. He'd certainly not mind me, after all. I'd be pouring the drinks and clearing plates. Would you remember the face of a waitress who served you in a restaurant fifteen years ago?'

'No,' Perez admitted. 'Probably not.'

'Who was the other man who came back?' Martin broke into the conversation abruptly. It was hard now to believe that he was a man famous for his jokes, for laughing at his father's funeral.

'That was Jeremy Booth, the man who was found hanged in the hut on the jetty. He was here that summer too.'

Chapter Forty-three

Perez left the house and stood in the street. It was very quiet. The wind had dropped with the full tide. A family of eider duck floated on the water near the shore. He walked back past the Herring House. There was a path that led that way up towards the hill and back down to Skoles. It would save him having to pass Wilding's place; he couldn't face being a subject of the writer's voyeurism tonight. But perhaps Wilding wasn't at home. Perhaps he was in Buness, supervising some work to his new house. Perez thought Fran could be there too, discussing flooring and wallpaper, and the idea gave him a chill of unease. Then he thought she wouldn't be so foolish. Not until the investigation was over.

He walked out on to the open hill to the sound of skylark and curlew and into a raw orange light. It must already be late in the evening, because the huge ball of the sun was dipping towards the cliff-edge. There too, silhouetted, was the figure of a man, unrecognizable at this distance. A gothic figure against the setting sun.

Although he couldn't make out the man's features, had to squint against the light to make him out at all, Perez knew who it was. He wasn't prepared for the encounter. Things had moved more quickly than he'd expected. He was tempted to turn away, to wait for Taylor, who might have evidence. But the man was right at the edge of the cliff, on the narrow bridge of rock between the Pit o' Biddista and the sea. Perez thought the hot summer fifteen years before had resulted in enough loss. He'd allowed Jeremy Booth to run away from him to his death after the Herring House party, and was still troubled by a nagging guilt. How much worse would that be if he made no effort to stop this man jumping?

He walked quickly over the grass, swearing under his breath when he twisted his ankle on a clump of heather. As he approached the cliff-edge, the sound of the seabirds got louder and the orange light stronger, so his head seemed filled with the noise and the light and he couldn't think clearly at all.

Kenny Thomson didn't hear Perez approaching. Perez thought the man was so wrapped up in his own thoughts that if Perez had been accompanied by the whole Up Helly Aa marching band, he still wouldn't have noticed. Kenny stood very close to the cliff-edge, with the Pit at his back. Perez called to him.

'Come away, Kenny. Come here where I can talk to you.'

The man turned slowly.

'I'm fine where I am. And I've nothing to say.'

'I can't shout at you across all this space, man. Not about this. Not about Lawrence.'

Kenny turned again, so once more he was facing the sea.

Perez inched closer, felt his stomach tilt and turn. Now he could see the waves breaking on the outlying stacks. The sound of the water seemed to take a long time to reach him. He had an image of Roddy's body, smashed in the Pit. He stumbled, and although he was still yards from the edge his heart seemed to stop. A pebble, loosened by his foot, rolled and bounced down the rock until it was lost in the spray at the bottom.

'Kenny, I can't do this, man. Why won't you come here where I can talk to you?'

Perhaps Kenny heard the panic in his voice, because for the first time he looked directly at Perez.

'There's no need for you to be here.'

Perez struggled to find some connection between them, some way of holding the man back from the cliff with his words. 'Do you mind that summer when you were working on Fair Isle, Kenny? The harbourworks in the North Haven. I've been thinking about that since we met up again.'

'Have you?' Kenny frowned, willing to be distracted, for a moment at least, from his own thoughts. Perhaps he was glad to be distracted.

'You came to stay with us in my parents' house, then you moved back to the hostel. I wondered why you might do that.'

'Did your mother ever talk to you about me?'

'Not since. When you were staying on the Isle, I could tell she liked you. She had nothing but good to say about you.'

'I thought I loved her,' Kenny said. 'A bit of summer madness.' A pause. 'I did love her.'

Perez felt his stomach tilt again, only this time it had nothing to do with the height of the cliff. His mother was his mother. She wasn't a woman for men to fall in love with. He didn't say anything.

'Nothing happened,' Kenny said. 'We weren't lovers, though I would have liked us to have been. That was why I moved back to the hostel. It drove me mad being in the same house as her. I couldn't settle. I couldn't sleep. Now I know it wasn't a lasting thing. Edith was the woman for me.' He gave an odd cry, which was lost in the noise of the seabirds.

'Did my father ever know how you felt about each other?'

Kenny didn't answer and seemed drowned again in thoughts of his own.

'Why don't you move away from the edge, Kenny? So we can talk properly. Not about Fair Isle, but about Lawrence.'

Perez saw that the man's face was streaming with tears. Molten copper in the orange light. Watching him standing there sobbing, Perez found he was holding his breath. He felt his heart thumping against his ribcage. A couple of steps and Kenny could be over the cliff.

'Don't you see?' Kenny said. 'There's no point in talking. Not any more.'

'I think I've worked out what went on.' Perez sat on the grass, felt the thrift rough against the palms of his hands, and he started to breathe again. 'Why don't you sit down too, Kenny? Sit here with me.'

Kenny remained standing. Perez could see that he wasn't getting through to him. 'When did it start?' he asked urgently, shouting out the words, willing Kenny to listen. 'Did Lawrence always want what you had, Kenny? Even when you were boys?'

'He was older than me and brighter than me,' Kenny said. 'That was only right.'

'Come away here,' Perez said again. Kenny was rocking with grief. He'd always been a controlled man, quiet, understated, repressed even. Now he seemed taken over by emotion, unaware of how close he was to the cliff-edge. If he continued like that it would be only a matter of time before he fell. Perez kept his voice light and easy, speaking just loudly enough to be heard above the kittiwakes. 'But to take Edith away from you, Kenny. That was never right, was it?'

Kenny threw back his head and screamed. 'What does any of that matter now? Can't you see, man? It's all over.'

Something made Perez lean forward and look down to the beach made of rock and shingle at the bottom of the cliff. A small, white figure lay there. Edith. Kenny's wife. His love.

Chapter Forty-four

Kenny crouched and put his head in his hands. Perez got slowly to his feet and inched towards him across the bridge of rock, keeping his eyes firmly on the man and not looking down, feeling the rush of air on all sides. At last he was standing right behind him. He put his hands around Kenny's shoulders and pulled him upright, led him to safety away from the cliff-edge. Then they walked together in silence back to Skoles.

In the house Kenny took him through to the sitting room, seeming to think that something more formal than the kitchen was called for, though with its big window looking out over the bay, the sheepskin rugs and the comfortable chairs, this was hardly a standard interview room. On the mantelpiece stood pictures of the Thomson children, smiling, gap-toothed. A wedding photograph. Still Kenny didn't speak. Perez knew he should telephone Roy Taylor to let him know what had happened, and arrange for Edith's body to be collected, but all that could wait.

'You'll take a dram, Jimmy.' Kenny was quite composed now, though very white and strained. The outburst on the cliff might never have taken place.

Perez nodded. Kenny took a bottle of Highland

Park from a cupboard built next to the chimney and poured out two glasses. They sat looking at each other.

'I tried to stop Edith jumping,' Kenny said. 'In the end she just slipped away from my grasp.' He shut his eyes. Perez thought the picture of Edith, stepping over the cliff-edge into space, would never leave him.

'When did you find out that Edith and Lawrence were having an affair? Did you know at the time?'

'No,' Kenny said. 'It never crossed my mind. Not while I was on Fair Isle. I was too wrapped up in my own business there. How did you know? Did Edith tell you?'

'You know Edith would never do that, Kenny. It's been her secret. She had too much to lose.'

'I never thought she would be the sort of woman Lawrence would go for,' Kenny said. 'She was quiet, homely then. Not a beauty. Not pretty in the way that made her stand out. But maybe that was what he took a fancy to. The quietness. The determination. He could have had showy Bella, but he decided in the end that wasn't what he wanted.'

'He didn't want Edith just because she belonged to you, Kenny? I wondered if it was about that? A jealousy thing between brothers. Rivalry.'

'No,' Kenny said. 'I don't think it was that. Lawrence didn't want to hurt me. He couldn't help himself.'

'How do you know that?'

'I don't know it. Not for sure. It's what I think – what I want to think, I suppose.' Outside the sun had dropped further, was chopped in half by the horizon, the outline broken by some twisted threads of purple cloud. The light was softer, less lurid. 'How did you find out about the pair of them if Edith didn't tell you?'

ANN CLEEVES

'I worked it out from what people said.' Perez took
a sip of the whisky. 'Edith mentioned something herself. She told me that Lawrence was like Roddy, had
to have a woman in his life. I knew he was spending
all his spare time in Biddista that summer. He wasn't
seeing Aggie or Bella, so it must have been Edith.
Then Aggie said something similar tonight. "I always
felt sorry for Kenny, having to play second fiddle."'

'Did the whole valley know?' Kenny was angry.

'Not the details,' Perez said. 'But that Lawrence
liked Edith, most of them would know that. It was just
you and Bella in the dark, and I think Bella suspected
something. It was just her pride stopped her seeing it.'
He paused. 'And how about you, Kenny? How did you
find out?'

'I worked it out in the end, a bit like you. I went to
see the writer, Wilding. He remembered something of
what went on. All those parties. Lawrence must have
talked to him. He always did get sentimental when he
was drunk. You're right: Wilding tried to tell Bella at
the time that Lawrence had no interest in her, but she
didn't want to hear it.'

'Jeremy Booth must have known too.' Perez took
another sip from the whisky. Later he would need all
this in a statement. Now he just wanted things straight
in his own mind.

'Booth was on the hill when Lawrence went into
the Pit,' Kenny said. 'He saw what happened.'

'What did happen that day, Kenny? Did Edith tell
you?'

'It was the middle of summer, a steaming hot
night. Airless. The evening of the grand party at the
Manse. Lawrence asked Edith to meet him on the hill

382

while the rest of them were dressing up in their fancy clothes and their masks. Edith must have been flattered by him, don't you think? Is that why she fell for him? Lawrence, the man all the women fancied, wanting her. He said he needed to talk to her. Anyway she left my father minding the children and went out to see him. Lawrence said he'd told Bella that he could never love her, never marry her, never make a family with her. "I've said I'm going away on my travels, I'm leaving Shetland." He asked Edith to go with him. "Just bring the children. We'll go to Sumburgh tonight and get the first plane south." That was Lawrence for you. No sense of the practicalities, of where they might stay.'

'But Edith wouldn't go with him?'

Kenny looked up at Perez. It was as if he'd forgotten he was there.

'No, she wouldn't go. She enjoyed being with him; maybe she even fancied herself in love with him; but she was married to me. By then they'd walked to the top of the hill and were standing right by the Pit. Lawrence tried to take her in his arms. Edith told me she was worried that if he touched her she might be tempted to give in and go with him.' For the first time Kenny let a trace of bitterness into his voice. 'He always did have that effect on women.'

'Tell me what happened, Kenny.'

'Edith pushed him away and he slipped into the Pit. Hit his head on the rocks at the bottom. She climbed down after and could tell he was dead. She pulled him into the tunnel so nobody could see the body from the top. She always was a strong woman. She could keep up with me in the work on the croft.' He paused. 'The rats and the birds and the tide will have done the rest.'

They sat for a moment in silence.

'Did Jeremy Booth confront Edith that night about Lawrence?'

Kenny shook his head.

'She saw Booth when she climbed back up after hiding the body. He was at the bottom of the hill looking up at her. She hoped he hadn't seen the scuffle between her and Lawrence. The next day he disappeared. She must have thought it was all over.'

'That she'd got away with it?'

'Aye. But she never did really. Every summer she lay awake. I thought it was the white nights, but it was dreams of Lawrence.' He set down his glass. 'She should have talked to me. What did she think? That I'd hate her for it?'

'When did Booth get in touch with her?'

'A couple of weeks ago, by email. It went to her address at work, but she picked it up here. She was always working in the evenings on that computer of hers. He'd seen that television documentary about Roddy and Bella and Biddista. It mentioned that Edith worked in the care centre and made us out to be much more wealthy than we really are. He needed money, he said. To give to his daughter. To make up for all the years they'd never had.' He looked at Perez. 'What about *my* daughter? What will I tell her?'

Perez shook his head to show that he had no answer.

'Then Booth turned up at Edith's work. Imagine how shocked she was! She'd thought he was in England, but he was standing there, claiming to be an old friend of Willy's, looking quite different. He was chatting away to the old man when she found him. "You know what happened, don't you, Willy?" Booth was saying. "You guessed at least." But Willy wouldn't talk to him.'

'Willy said an Englishman had been asking him questions,' Perez said. 'At first I thought he meant Wilding. When I realized it was Booth, I wondered why Edith hadn't mentioned him visiting. What happened next?'

'Booth said he was going to come out to Biddista for the opening night of the exhibition. He'd put on a bit of a show, have some fun, kill two birds with one stone. Bella had always been a snooty cow. She'd invited him into her home then treated him like dirt. It wouldn't hurt her to know what rejection felt like. He just enjoyed making mischief, I think. The mask, the dressing up, he'd have loved all that. Edith didn't ask what he intended to do. She just wanted him to go away without a fuss. He said he'd pick up the money from her at the same time. He'd meet her in the hut on the jetty.' Kenny got to his feet and poured more whisky into Perez's glass and then into his own.

'Why didn't Edith just pay him?' Perez asked gently.

Kenny gave a little shrug. 'She said she didn't trust him. He might come back for more. And she resented it. We've always worked hard for what we have. That's what she said, but I could tell her nerves were shot. All those sleepless nights. She wasn't thinking straight.' He held on to his glass with both hands, but still they were shaking. It was taking an effort to keep his voice even. 'She told me how she waited for him in the hut in the dark. He'd picked up his bag from the beach and had put that stupid mask over his head. Playing the fool again. Wanting to startle her, maybe. Perhaps she wouldn't have strangled him if she'd been able to see

ANN CLEEVES

his face – he didn't look human with that thing on –
but I'm not so sure. Edith was always determined once
she'd made up her mind. She surprised him in the
dark, strangled him from behind. She made it look like
suicide and was back in the garden by the time I came
down from the hill.' He paused and looked sadly at
Perez. 'I didn't have any idea what had happened. We'd
been married all that time and I didn't guess a thing.'

'Where did Roddy come into it? He was only a boy
when Lawrence died.'

'He saw Edith walking back from the jetty the
night Booth died. He was watching from the Herring
House window.'

'Of course he was. I remember seeing him.'

'Sounds like Roddy didn't think anything of it until
she put it about that she'd never left Skoles. It must
have been troubling him. He came to the care centre
to visit Willy and passed a comment that got her
scared. "What were you doing out on the shore, Edith?
Who did you meet that night?" She told him some
story, but she could tell he wasn't taken in.'

Perhaps, Perez thought, a memory had come back
to him, of something he'd seen when he was a boy,
like it did to Bella. 'So she killed him too.'

'Yes,' Kenny said. 'She killed him too. Poor lad.
Whatever I thought about him, he didn't deserve that.
Edith always said he reminded him of Lawrence. She
persuaded him to meet her up by the Pit and she killed
him in just the same way. She told the care centre she
was out doing home visits.'

'I know,' Perez said. 'I checked.'

Kenny set down the whisky, put his head in his
hands as he had on the hill, and began to weep again.

Chapter Forty-five

This time they talked in Perez's place, which always felt more like a boat than a house to Taylor, with the water lapping against the outside wall and the gulls on the roof. Perez was making coffee and Taylor was shouting through to him from the living room, where he was lying on the floor. It was his back, he said. He had recurring problems with his back. An old sports injury. Sometimes this was the only way he could get comfortable.

'I should have worked it out,' Taylor yelled. He sounded furious with himself. 'There was a photograph of Edith and Lawrence in Booth's house. West Yorkshire emailed it through to me. The pair of them looked very cosy. If I'd realized they were having an affair I'd have got there before you did. I left the search of Booth's house to the local boys. Of course the picture didn't mean anything to them.'

Perez came in carrying a tray. A cafetiere, mugs and a packet of chocolate biscuits.

'You wouldn't have thought she had it in her, would you?' Taylor said, lowering his voice a little. 'She wasn't a big woman.' He sat up, stretched, took a mug from the tray.

'Strong, though. She still helped Kenny on the

croft, and she'd be used to lifting in the care centre. Booth wasn't expecting the attack. Once she had the wire round his neck he didn't struggle for long. Faking the suicide was easier.'

'She must have thought she'd got away with Lawrence's death. Even if the bones were found after all these years, no one would think of murder.'

'People thought Lawrence had disappeared because of a broken heart,' Perez said. 'He'd told Bella he was leaving. It suited her if everyone thought she was the reason he left. She's a proud woman. Kenny was on Fair Isle at the time, so there was no one here to follow it up, to check that Lawrence really did get on that ferry. By the time he got back the story was set in stone and he believed it: Lawrence had left because Bella refused to marry him.'

But there were people in Biddista who knew it hadn't happened like that, Perez thought. Suspected at least. A place like that, it was impossible to keep a relationship secret. They'd just kept their suspicions to themselves. It wasn't a conspiracy, because it had never been discussed. Lawrence disappeared and nobody asked any questions. They really didn't want to know. In Shetland sometimes it was the only way to survive. Perez thought Willy might have guessed what had happened, but he'd have wanted to protect Kenny. He'd given Booth a lift to the ferry the night after the murder.

'What brought Booth up here after all these years?' Taylor was still sitting on the floor, his legs stretched out in front of him.

'Greed,' Perez said. 'He'd just found his daughter again and he wanted to make up for lost time. Or give her a big present to make her love him. His business was limping along just as it had always done, but there was no spare cash. He was struggling just to survive. Then he saw the TV documentary, which apparently made Kenny and Edith out to be great landowners, and everything came together.'

'Why didn't he try blackmail at the time of Lawrence's death?'

'What would be the point? The Thomsons were struggling for money themselves. They've only become comfortable in the last few years. After the first time he was here Booth probably wanted to forget about the whole visit. Bella does a mean line in put-downs and he had a history of running away. Besides, I think Willy might have scared him off. He was a big man in those days and made sure he saw Booth on to the boat south.'

'But Booth came back and Edith decided she wasn't going to pay up.'

'She grew up without anything,' Perez said. 'She wasn't going to hand over cash she'd worked so hard for to a blackmailer. She was used to controlling events and keeping secrets. She thought she would get away with it.' He was sitting on the windowsill, looking out at the water.

'And the amnesia? What was all that about?'

'The scene at the party was Booth's idea of a prac-tical joke to spite Bella. He wasn't expecting to be taken to one side by a cop and I told him straight away what I did for a living. He certainly didn't want to explain why he was in Biddista. The amnesia was an excuse not to answer my questions.'

'Where did Wilding come into things?'

'He didn't. He was too wrapped up in his fairy stories and his new house to think about anything else. He talked to Willy, but about old Shetland folk tales. Material for his new series of books. Nothing more.'

Taylor stood up and set his mug back on the tray. He was frowning. 'You did it again,' he said. 'Got there before me.'

'It's my place,' Perez said. 'I wouldn't know where to start in Inverness.'

Taylor seemed about to speak again, but he only smiled.

Two days later Perez took Taylor to Sumburgh. Fran came along for the ride. She'd gone to buy coffee, leaving the two men standing in the lounge, when Taylor's flight was called. He picked up his bag and moved towards the queue, then turned back.

'I wasn't going to tell you,' he said suddenly. 'But I'm changing jobs. I've been head-hunted.' Taylor smiled his wolf-like grin. 'Imagine that, eh? I'm going back to Liverpool to head up their Major Crimes Unit. I wasn't going to take it. Too close to home, too many bad memories. But I never want to work in this place again. This weather, this light. Another case and I'd be as daft as the rest of you.'

He smiled again to show it was a joke, of a sort, then walked through the door. Through the long window they saw him cross the tarmac, but he didn't look back or wave.

'How do you fancy a bit of a walk?' They were in Perez's car on the way north. He'd been wondering how to ask her and the question sounded awkward, a bit abrupt.

'Sure.'

'I was thinking we could maybe call in to Biddista.'

'Why would you want to do that?' Fran said. 'It's over. Not your responsibility.'

'It feels that it is.'

'Do you really think they'll want to see you?'

'They'll have questions,' he said.

'It's a sort of arrogance, believing yourself indispensable.' But she said it kindly and he assumed that meant she would go with him. He was grateful. He wouldn't have wanted to do it alone.

They parked on the road by the Herring House and stood looking out on the beach for a while before going inside. There were no other customers in the café, but Martin and his mother sat at a table chatting quietly. Aggie saw them come in and stopped talking mid-sentence. Perez nodded to them.

'I'm sorry,' he said. 'The way it all turned out.'

For a moment they just stared. He wondered if this was how it would be in Biddista, that no one would speak to him again.

'I was just telling Martin,' Aggie said. 'I didn't know what had happened to Lawrence. Not for certain. You know what it's like here, Jimmy. Sometimes there are things you don't want to know. It doesn't stop me blaming myself for what's gone on since.'

There was a brief pause, then Martin got up to take their order. Suddenly things were ordinary again. Like a freeze-frame film running once more at normal speed. They could have been two tourists who'd dropped in for coffee.

391

'Ingirid and her man are going to move back into Skoles,' Aggie said. 'Keep Kenny company for a while. She's expecting a baby, due any time. It'll be good to have another child in Biddista.' Perez could tell she was thinking of her new grandchild too.

'Shame Willy won't be around to get them out in a boat.'

'Maybe,' she said. 'But those old times weren't so great.' She smiled at him. 'Get off home, Jimmy. A day like this, you'll have better things to do. We don't need you here.'

Fran slipped her arm into his. He felt the silky fabric of her sleeve against his bare skin. She turned and smiled at him.

'Yes, come on home, Jimmy,' she said. 'We've got much better things to do.'

CPSIA information can be obtained at www.ICGtesting.com
Printed in the USA
LVOW06s0807290714

396480LV00001B/1/P